RETHINKING ENVIRONMENTAL HISTORY

GLOBALIZATION AND THE ENVIRONMENT SERIES

SERIES EDITORS:
Richard Wilk
Department of Anthropology
130 Student Building, Indiana University
Bloomington, IN 47405 USA
wilkr@indiana.edu

Josiah Heyman
Department of Sociology and Anthropology
Old Main Building #109
University of Texas at El Paso
500 West University Avenue
El Paso, TX 79968 USA
jmheyman@utep.edu

Description
This AltaMira series publishes new books about the global spread of environmental problems. Key themes addressed are the effects of cultural and economic globalization on the environment; the global institutions that regulate and change human relations with the environment; and the global nature of environmental governance, movements, and activism. The series will include detailed case studies, innovative multisited research, and theoretical questioning of the concepts of globalization and the environment. At the center of the series is an exploration of the multiple linkages that connect people, problems, and solutions at scales beyond the local and regional. The editors welcome works that cross boundaries of disciplines, methods, and locales, and that span scholarly and practical approaches.

BOOKS IN THE SERIES:
The Power of the Machine: Global Inequalities of Economy, Technology, and Environment,
    by Alf Hornborg (2001)
Confronting Environments: Local Environmental Understanding in a Globalizing World,
    edited by James Carrier (2004)
Communities and Conservation: Histories and Politics of Community-Based Natural Resource
    Management, edited by J. Peter Brosius, Anna Lowenhaupt Tsing, and Charles Zerner
    (2005)
Globalization, Health, and the Environment: An Integrated Perspective, edited by
    Greg Guest (2005)
Globalization and the World Ocean, by Peter Jacques (2006)
Global Visions, Local Landscapes: A Political Ecology of Conservation, Conflict, and Control in
    Northern Madagascar, by Lisa L. Gezon (2006)
Cows, Kin, and Globalization: An Ethnography of Sustainability, by Susan A. Crate (2006)
Rethinking Environmental History: World-System History and Global Environmental Change,
    edited by Alf Hornborg, J. R. McNeill, and Joan Martinez-Alier
The World's Scavengers: Salvaging for Sustainable Consumption and Production, by Martin Medina

RETHINKING ENVIRONMENTAL HISTORY

World–System History and Global Environmental Change

EDITED BY
ALF HORNBORG, J. R. McNEILL,
AND JOAN MARTINEZ-ALIER

ALTAMIRA PRESS
A Division of Rowman & Littlefield Publishers, Inc.
Lanham • New York • Toronto • Plymouth, UK

ALTAMIRA PRESS
A Division of Rowman & Littlefield Publishers, Inc.
A wholly owned subsidiary of The Rowman & Littlefield Publishing Group, Inc.
4501 Forbes Boulevard, Suite 200
Lanham, MD 20706
www.altamirapress.com

Estover Road, Plymouth PL6 7PY, United Kingdom

British Library Cataloguing in Publication Information Available

Library of Congress Cataloging-in-Publication Data

Rethinking environmental history : world-system history and global environmental
    change / edited by Alf Hornborg, J. R. McNeill, and Joan Martinez-Alier.
        p.   cm. – (Globalization and the environment series)
    Includes bibliographical references and index.
    ISBN-13: 978-0-7591-1027-4 (cloth : alk. paper)
    ISBN-10: 0-7591-1027-1 (cloth : alk. paper)
    ISBN-13: 978-0-7591-1028-1 (pbk. : alk. paper)
    ISBN-10: 0-7591-1028-X (pbk. : alk. paper)
    1. Global environmental change–History.   2. World history.   I. Hornborg, Alf.
II. McNeill, J. R., 1954–   III. Martinez-Alier, Joan.
GE149.R49 2006
333.7—dc22
                                                                                                2006021775

Printed in the United States of America

♾™ The paper used in this publication meets the minimum requirements of American
National Standard for Information Sciences—Permanence of Paper for Printed Library
Materials, ANSI/NISO Z39.48-1992.

This book is dedicated to the memory of
Stephen G. Bunker (1944–2005)

CONTENTS

Acknowledgments

This book is one of two volumes emerging from the conference on *World-System History and Global Environmental Change*, arranged by the Human Ecology Division of Lund University, Lund, Sweden, on September 19–22, 2003. I gratefully acknowledge generous funding from the Bank of Sweden Tercentenary Foundation, which covered the bulk of our expenses, as well as additional funding from the Swedish International Development Cooperation Agency, the Swedish Research Council, the Swedish Environmental Protection Agency, and the Swedish Research Council for Environment, Agriculture, and Spatial Planning. I also want to thank Christian Isendahl for efficiently handling the practical details of conference organization, and my two coeditors, J. R. McNeill and Joan Martinez-Alier, for competently commenting on several chapters that particularly required the expertise of a historian or an economist. Finally, I thank Rosalie Robertson, Alden Perkins, Bess Vanrenen, and Sylvia Cannizzaro for helping me turn a pile of papers into a book.

Alf Hornborg

Introduction: Environmental History as Political Ecology

ALF HORNBORG

HERE ARE DIFFERENT WAYS of writing the history of environmental problems. The dominant mode has been to assume a common human history, a global "we" experiencing the arrow of time through cumulative changes such as population growth, technological development, and new patterns of resource use. Ecological degradation, seen from this perspective, is the collective concern of a generalized humanity prompted to exploit new territories, harness new energy sources, and develop new transport technologies. Environmental problems, although alarming, are presented as the inevitable side effects of "our" global success story.

The purpose of this book is to explore another way of writing environmental history. Rather than focus on the abstract accretion of landscape changes or technological inventions as a collective human experience over time, it seeks to highlight how such changes are distributed in space. It acknowledges that humanity is not a single "we" but deeply divided in terms of reaping the benefits versus carrying the burdens of development. The authors were asked to reflect on this *distributed* aspect of environmental problems by approaching ecological changes from a world-system perspective, viewing the world as a social system much more inclusive than individual nations (Wallerstein 1974–1989). If the world-system for a long time has built on unequal power relations between rich "core" areas and impoverished "peripheries," this inequality can also be expected to show in how environmental burdens have been distributed.

The authors were invited to illuminate this issue through either empirical or analytical contributions. As the field of environmental history is a concern of several disciplines, the contributors have offered a variety of approaches from archaeology, history, geography, anthropology, sociology, and economics. For this reason, it seemed appropriate to have an editorial team comprising an anthropologist, a historian, and an economist. Some of the contributors have explicitly adopted the world-system terminology, others have not. It soon became evident that authors were more prone to develop new analytical or methodological approaches to environmental inequalities the more recent their empirical material. This pattern is reflected in the division of this book into two parts. The chapters in Part I thus generally stay closer to empirical case studies of environmental transformations over the past centuries or even millennia, while those in Part II provide abstract ways of understanding environmental inequalities in the modern world. In this introductory chapter, I hope to show how the theoretical discussions in Part II might also be used to illuminate socioenvironmental processes in the past. In other words, this book seeks to suggest ways of applying modern concerns with unequal ecological exchange and "political ecology" to the study of environmental history. Bringing together fields, disciplines, and discourses that are as separate as these inevitably invites conceptual and methodological confusion, but I am convinced that such transdisciplinary communication is important and worthwhile.

The notion of exchange being unequal in an ecological sense can only be explored through transdisciplinary approaches. Conventional studies of exchange, for example in economics, are not concerned with the physical properties of the commodities that are traded or with the material consequences of their production, transport, and consumption. Economics is a science concerned with money, not with flows of matter and energy, waste disposal, or loss of biodiversity. The chapters in Part II all try to show how an understanding of the world-system in terms of such material parameters provides a completely different picture of economic growth and development than mainstream understandings based merely on monetary measures.

This book thus adopts a "materialist" perspective on environmental history, if taking the physical facts of ecology seriously means being "materialist." On the other hand, the chapters in Part I all show the great extent to which human patterns of consumption and production are shaped by cultural ideas about what is to be regarded as good food, a comfortable home, prestigious ornaments, a beautiful landscape, and so on. Such cultural ideals show great variation in time and space, illustrating how symbolically "constructed" they are. All symbolic constructs are in a sense arbitrary products of a specific time and place, and it is not surprising that many historians and anthropologists have found the material aspects of human societies as irrelevant as have mainstream economists. Some historians have even conceived of the field of environmental history as an exclusive concern with the succession of human *ideas* about the environment. The challenge for environmental history and environmental anthropology, however, is to take proper account of both these levels of reality: the idiosyncrasies of human meanings in particular contexts, and the material repercussions of such cultural systems. "Materialism" should not mean believing that cultural patterns of consumption and production are determined by the physical environment, only that cultural behavior takes place within a material world whose properties constrain what is possible and determine the environmental consequences of that behavior. We need to be able to acknowledge both the specificity of cultural motivation and the generality of material laws.

Political Ecology

Over the past few decades, the concept of "political ecology" has become a useful shorthand for the growing recognition, in several disciplines, of the extent to which environmental changes and societal processes are intertwined. The many proponents of this approach, for instance in anthropology (Paulson and Gezon 2005), geography (Bryant and Bailey 1997), and the philosophy of environmental justice (Low and Gleeson 1998), focus on what Martinez-Alier (2002:70) calls "ecological distribution conflicts" in modern, often Third World, settings. In integrating cultural, political, economic, and ecological perspectives on conflicts of interest between different social groups, political ecology requires transdisciplinary analyses that are able to handle the great variety of factors that enter into any such socioenvironmental conflict. Generally driven by a more or less activist concern with the predicament of marginalized local people in today's world, it has made great progress in understanding the political economy of contemporary environmental change. Although it is reasonable to assume that processes of environmental change were no less politicized in the past, studies of environmental history are much less frequently couched in such a political framework. The reasons for this are not hard to imagine. For one thing, environmental injustices seem less worthy of attention, and more difficult to document, when the victims are long gone. Nevertheless, there are many good reasons to apply the insights of political ecology to environmental history. Foremost, I would argue, is the importance of writing a politically valid environmental history of human civilizations, from the earliest agrarian empires to the present industrial world order. The political ecology of human civilizations would no doubt present a completely different picture of "our" global success story than mainstream historiography. In acknowledging the power inequalities and distribution conflicts framing the development of industrial civilization, it would ultimately provide a more realistic view of future prospects for "sustainable" development at the global level.

It is important here to emphasize that what I am suggesting is not merely an environmental history that acknowledges ecological degradation as the flip side of economic progress. This would be very far from a new idea. In chapter 11, Joan Martinez-Alier traces the modern history of "ecological economics," emphasizing how human economies are ultimately constrained by ecological conditions, to the mid-nineteenth century, and some of its roots to the eighteenth-century Physiocrats. As J. Donald Hughes shows in chapter 1, such connections were obvious even in ancient Rome. Awareness of environmental limitations has no doubt always been a part of human experience, whether hunter-gatherers' concern over game stocks or horticulturalists' concern over soil fertility. Much recent work in environmental history in fact remains analytically confined to such Malthusian worries about a fundamental contradiction between human society and the natural environment. Irrespective of their discipline of origin—whether geography, archaeology, or history—most authors of classical works on global environmental history, even when addressing European imperialism, thus tend to couch their concerns in the generalized "we" mode mentioned above (e.g. Thomas 1956; Turner et al. 1990; Simmons 1993; Redman 1999; Diamond 2005). Rather than subject the internal structures of societal systems to critical scrutiny, such studies seem to assume a simple dualism of society versus nature and to account for environmental problems in terms of the inexorable progression of technology or demography.

Rarer are historical studies that explicitly investigate contradictions *within* global human society *over* the natural environment. These studies are generally concerned with European strategies of environmental load displacement during the sixteenth to nineteenth centuries and sometimes make explicit use of the world-system terminology (Wilkinson 1973; Wolf 1982; Mintz 1985; Worster 1988; Ponting 1991; Pomeranz 2000; Richards 2003). They demonstrate a more profound understanding of the societal dynamics responsible for unevenly distributed environmental degradation and often present direct continuities with studies of twentieth-century political ecology (cf. Bunker 1985; Goldfrank et al. 1999; Bunker and Ciccantell 2005). Yet, I am convinced that our understanding of how societal and ecological systems are intertwined can progress even further than this, not only by politicizing the environment, but also by ecologizing the world-system. I shall begin by briefly summarizing the chapters in Part II, in order to be able to use concepts and findings from these studies to address the issues raised by the historical case studies in Part I. Although the chapters in this book are generally ordered in a chronological sequence, stretching from ancient Rome and China to modern Mexico and Brazil, I will review parts I and II in reverse order. This is justified by my attempts to project backward in time some of the analytical relevance of theories and methods developed to understand unequal ecological exchange in the modern world.

Unequal Ecological Exchange

A fundamental theoretical question, for any attempt to merge ecology and world-system analysis, is whether the global distribution of environmental deterioration is somehow structurally determined. If the answer is yes, does this structural determination hinge on the physical properties of the traded commodities? Are economic sectors specialized in the extraction of natural resources systematically disadvantaged—economically and/or ecologically—vis-à-vis sectors specialized in the production of industrial goods? The chapters in part II generally tend toward such a critical perspective on global social metabolism. Economic historian Joan Martinez-Alier (chapter 11) and sociologist Stephen G. Bunker (chapter 12) provide a theoretical framework for such a position, and the following four chapters (Hornborg; Jorgenson and Rice; Weisz; and Muradian and Giljum) present methodologies and empirical evidence that seem to support it.

Martinez-Alier traces the early dialogue between Marxism and natural sciences such as physics and agricultural chemistry on the material dimensions of economic productivity, illustrating the difficulties that continue to plague communication between the social and natural sciences on economic matters. Although Marx was keenly interested in the metabolic flows between urban and rural areas, he did not think of these flows as inherently exploitative or as a constraint on progress, as did Malthus, but was optimistic about new technological remedies such as chemical fertilizers. If Marx and Engels had paid more attention to Serhii Podolinsky's argument for an integration of thermodynamics and their notions of surplus exploitation, early Marxist theory might have incorporated the kind of sociometabolic perspectives that today provide a foundation for discussions on unequal ecological exchange. Martinez-Alier posits a tendency, over the past few centuries, for a shift in the character of ecologically unequal exchange between cores and peripheries of the world-system. Prior to modern transport technologies, as Wallerstein and so many other scholars have observed, long-distance transfers were largely restricted to "preciosities" (high-value, low-bulk commodities) like silver, spices, and ivory, the extraction of which has considerable ecological consequences in the periphery but slight significance for the metabolism of the core. By the mid-nineteenth century, however, the unequal, long-distance exchange of bulk commodities (e.g. sugar, guano, saltpeter) had become crucial to the metabolism of some importing countries in Europe. Whether such sociometabolic connections between world-system cores and peripheries can be traced farther back in history than this is a central issue for several of the chapters in part I.

In the next chapter, Bunker reiterates and expands the argument with which he pioneered the integration of ecology and world-system analysis (Bunker 1985). He posits a structural asymmetry between extractive economies in the periphery and "productive" economies in the core, which has been exacerbated with the increasing spatial separation of extraction and production. The structural polarizations of production versus extraction and of core versus periphery are in fact one and the same. One of his key points is that the dynamics of scale have inverse consequences for productive versus extractive sectors, yielding falling unit costs of production in the former but rising costs in the latter. Furthermore, as resources are depleted or technologies and market demand transformed, extractive economies are unable to sustain the continuous, cumulative development of labor and infrastructure that, by and large, have characterized productive core areas over the past two centuries. To account for such uneven development under capitalism, Bunker chooses to complement the Marxian labor theory of value with a notion of "natural values," which, like labor, are systematically underpaid and realized by the industrial core areas to which they are transferred.

In chapter 13, I present a similar understanding of the asymmetric relation between centers of industrial development and their extractive peripheries. The argument is based on previous theoretical work on the thermodynamic conditions of an industrial world order (Hornborg 2001), but focuses on the appropriation of land and labor "embodied" in the raw materials imported to Britain in the mid-nineteenth century. Using historical statistics on the inputs of land and labor in cotton and wool production, I estimate the amount of British land and labor that were saved by displacing fiber production to North America. By comparing inputs of land and labor in the textile exports of England with those in some commodities imported from its periphery, and juxtaposing these data with exchange rates, I also estimate the unequal exchange of (natural) space and (human) time underlying the Industrial Revolution. Using such methods, it is possible to bring together the Marxist concern with unequal exchanges of labor time, on one hand, with the more recent concern with ecological footprints (i.e. the land requirements of a given level of resource consumption), on the other. Rather than use the contested notion of underpaid "values," however, I am content to show that the earliest stages of industrial capitalism relied on an objectively measurable, unequal exchange of embodied land and labor. Another way of saying this is that technologies for locally saving time and space often tend to draw on investments of time and space (labor and land) in other parts of the world-system.

In the following chapter, sociologists Andrew Jorgenson and James Rice empirically investigate the proposition that developed core countries tend to externalize the environmental requirements of their consumption patterns by exploiting resources in the periphery. To resolve this issue, they offer a new methodological approach to examining the structure of international trade. This approach is based on weighted export flows, that is, quantifying the relative extent to which exports from a given country are sent to more developed countries with higher levels of consumption, measured as ecological footprints per capita. Their hypothesis is that countries with greater quantities of exports sent to more developed countries will exhibit lower domestic levels of resource consumption. Using data from the year 2000, they have found evidence supporting this hypothesis. Their study highlights the need for social scientists to investigate how more affluent nations use international trade to be able to reinforce their high levels of resource consumption, while continuing to externalize their environmental loads at the expense of the ecology and well-being of populations in less developed countries.

In chapter 15, biologist and ecological economist Helga Weisz explores an alternative method for defining and empirically measuring ecologically unequal exchange. Using Bunker's distinction between extractive and productive economies as a point of departure, she suggests that the combined use of a physical trade balance approach and input-output analysis can illuminate ecologically unequal trade between national economies or world regions. A physical trade balance is a variant of material flow analysis showing a nation's exports and imports measured in weight rather than money. Input-output analysis can be used to calculate, in economists' words, the "intensities" of traded commodities in terms of, for example, the amount of raw materials, carbon dioxide emissions, energy, or waste involved in their production. By multiplying such intensities with total quantities of imports and exports, it is possible to establish "ecological trade balances" of nations. In quantifying total imports, domestic extraction, the flows of goods between a nation's different production sectors, domestic consumption, and exports, an input-output model using such data can be employed to calculate the *indirect* environmental requirements of a given quantity of commodities beyond its mere physical volume. Applied to the economy of Denmark in 1990, this method shows that the conventional physical trade balance approach significantly underestimates the degree to which domestic consumption relies on material resources from other countries. In other words, although several sociometabolic calculations of physical trade balances have already clearly demonstrated that industrial core nations tend to appropriate net flows of natural resources from more peripheral nations, Weisz shows that a more refined methodology will yield even more unequivocal conclusions to the same effect. Her chapter illustrates some of the difficulties involved in trying to translate economic statistics, generally based on national territories as units of analysis, into ecological realities. In particular, her conclusions regarding Norway and even Britain as "extractive economies" remind us that Bunker's (1985) dichotomy of extractive versus productive economies was not primarily designed to classify entire nations but regions or sectors within nations. The dichotomy refers to a structural relationship that is only imperfectly reflected in the relations between complete nations.

In chapter 16, ecological economists Roldan Muradian and Stefan Giljum also apply the concepts and methods of material flow analysis to investigate how environmental burdens are distributed between nations. Their first finding is that so-called polluting sectors have generally increased their physical volume of export production in absolute terms over the past few decades, irrespective of world region. Second, they find that, in the period between 1978 and 1996, the proportion of total exports that derive from polluting sectors, measured in monetary value, has increased in South America and Africa while decreasing in Europe, the United States, and Japan. Third, they note that the European Union has remained a net importer of products from polluting sectors during the whole period analyzed. These findings are highly relevant for assessing the economists' notion of "dematerialization"—that is, the proposition that economies will become less of a burden on the environment the more developed they are—and the sobering counterproposition known as the "pollution haven" hypothesis—that is, that polluting industries tend to migrate toward poorer countries with weaker environmental standards. Much as economist Lawrence Summers infamously suggested in 1991, there is an impeccable economic logic in advocating a migration of "dirty" (i.e. polluting) industries to less developed countries. The chapters by Jorgenson and Rice, Weisz, and Muradian and Giljum all remind us that, although the appearance of a cleaner, seemingly dematerialized economy in affluent nations may suggest that economic growth is good for the environment, such a view may be the product of an illusion. An alternative interpretation is that economic growth makes it possible to shift a nation's environmental burden to other, less affluent countries. Moreover, we have reasons to be skeptical of indices of sustainability that measure environmental burdens *relative to* gross national product (GNP), suggesting that it does not matter if environmental loads increase in absolute terms, as long as GNP increases faster. The illusion of dematerialization thus simultaneously highlights the two main obstacles to understanding socioenvironmental metabolism using the kinds of data conventionally available to economists: the fact that statistics on trade generally use the *nation* as unit of analysis, and the fact that these statistics generally use *monetary value* as the only significant metric.

The significance of the nation-state in organizing socioenvironmental metabolism is indisputable, but in different ways than economists and historians have generally recognized. In the age of globalization, it should no longer be possible to imagine that a nation's geographical extent, its economic activities, and its environmental impacts coincide. Yet, to correlate national statistics on GNP and environmental quality in order to draw conclusions on the relation between economic growth and environmental performance is precisely to make such an unreasonable assumption. From a world-system perspective, on the contrary, it is only to be expected that one nation's environmental problems may be the flip side of another nation's affluence. Such connections are evident even where there are no indications of coercion or imperial ambitions. What, then, is the role of national boundaries in organizing the distribution of environmental resources and risks? They are obviously instruments of political agency, even when there are no attempts to expand them, simply by defining arenas within which power can be asserted in direct and uncontroversial ways. They may also define fields of responsibility and a minimum of social solidarity, prompting governments—to the extent that they are able and willing—to redistribute resources so as to cushion marginalized groups within their jurisdiction against the worst ravages of the polarizing tendencies of accumulative processes. Rural populations engaged in extractive activities within affluent nations can thus be financially subsidized by successful industrial sectors of the same nations, making it possible for them to enjoy high standards of living, healthy environments, and security, whereas their counterparts in poorer nations may be left virtually unprotected. The nation-state is thus the basic social unit capable of politically intervening in the socioenvironmental, metabolic processes generated by the logic of capital accumulation. Not only can it decide to alleviate the impoverishment of its internal, national periphery; states explicitly also struggle to promote—as national interests—activities that serve to make their external positions within world-systems as advantageous as possible. For centuries, the more powerful nation-states have used trade policies backed up by military force to secure vital flows of resources from the outside. As several of the chapters in part I remind us, not so long ago nation-states regularly struggled to expand their boundaries to achieve such goals. As trade has replaced conquest and tribute, national boundaries have begun to appear more stable over time, but the use of military force to secure resource flows is far from obsolete. Increasingly, states have also made it a national interest to export environmental risks.

As anthropologist Josiah Heyman shows in chapter 17, this gate-keeping function of nation-states, struggling to import resources and export risks, is most obvious on their borders. Focusing on the border between the United States and Mexico, he explores the many subtle ways in which this boundary zone serves to maintain the *difference* between citizens belonging to the two adjacent polities. This serves to remind us that the formation of nation-states involves a partly arbitrary construction of territorialized identity, but also that territorializations of sociometabolic relationships have very tangible consequences for people who happen to be living on either side of the border. The polarizing structures of world-systemic processes of capital accumulation are not necessarily organized in spatial terms to begin with, but the medium of nation-states has historically projected such structures onto geographical territories. It remains to be seen how far the current surge of globalization can go in challenging our attachment to the nation-state as a source of identity and a category for understanding the structure of world society. Heyman's contribution illustrates the very real material processes that continue to undergird the existence of nation-states precisely by asserting their boundaries. The environmental dimension of this particular boundary is epitomized by the maquiladoras, highly polluting industries concentrated along the Mexican side of the border, where wages can be kept low and environmental considerations ignored, but the profits from which often wind up among owners and executives residing north of the border. It is difficult to think of a more straightforward verification of the "pollution haven" hypothesis. Borders between countries with very different levels of affluence, such as Mexico and the United States, suggest sudden transformation points that make dramatically visible what is usually perceived as polarized core-periphery gradients in economic value. The chapter adds an important dimension to the discussion of how environmental problems are distributed by showing how such sociopolitical allocations are simultaneously also cultural: the concerns of people living on the U.S. side are often expressed in terms of keeping the "dirt" on the right (i.e. south) side of the border.

In chapter 18, anthropologist William Fisher takes us further south into Latin America, to the vast fields of soybeans industrially cultivated on the former savannas of Mato Grosso, Brazil. What locally is experienced as modernization and economic progress appears, in the light of social and environmental concerns as well as world-system analysis, as a highly dubious development. The transformation of the partly forested savanna landscape into treeless soybean monocultures has drastically reduced the unique biodiversity of the *cerrado* and turned impoverished and eroding soils into a medium for the conversion of imported fertilizers, pesticides, and other industrial inputs into exported crops. As much of the soybean exports are destined for livestock fodder in industrialized countries such as the Netherlands or Japan, these vast expanses of extractive surfaces clearly represent the ecological footprints—the displaced environmental loads—of distant and more affluent economies. Even locally, soybean cultivation has increased economic inequalities. Great numbers of small farmers have been forced to give up their land, only a minority have found low-wage jobs on the soybean plantations, and decreasing food security has brought an increase in rural hunger. This chapter provides a close-up view of the human agents who are compelled to fulfill the designs of world-systemic processes, even though they may regret their social and environmental consequences.

Tracing Socioenvironmental Processes through History

With this spectrum of approaches to ecological inequalities in the modern world, we are now prepared to reconsider the various historical case studies of socioenvironmental transformations presented in part I. We begin with historian J. Donald Hughes's account of the environmental impacts of the Roman economy during the first three centuries AD. Like other agricultural empires before and after it, ancient Rome used military power to expand the area of land under its control. By the second century AD, it was able to exploit the natural resources of an area of 7,800,000 square kilometers. Agricultural production was largely focused on grain, wine, and olive oil, which were widely traded throughout the Mediterranean area. Maritime trade in bulk goods such as timber and cereals had been established by the Greeks several centuries earlier, and contemporary sources claim that annual wheat imports to Rome from North Africa and Egypt in the first century AD could be over 400,000 tons, or about 6,000 shiploads (Debeir et al. 1991:29, 35). Long-distance exchange with India also brought elite preciosities such as spices, jewels, fine woods, birds, and delicate textiles in exchange for Roman gold, silver, art, wine, pottery, and slaves. Like ancient Greece, the Roman economy was to a very large extent based on slave labor, as obvious from the fact that slaves made up over 35 percent of the population of Italy during the time of Augustus. Hughes suggests that a slave economy is intrinsically detrimental to the environment, in part because slaves are not in a position to feel responsibility for the land. Also, the massive use of slave labor required a constant supply of energy in the form of food. Emperors such as Augustus struggled to increase grain imports from provinces like Egypt in order to feed the slaves and the urban poor. Deforestation and agricultural intensification brought erosion, siltation, salinization, soil exhaustion, and loss of biodiversity over much of the Mediterranean area. Mining and smelting required great quantities of firewood and charcoal, contributing to deforestation. Industrial pollution and urban sewage disposal also became serious problems. Hughes (1994:194) does not hesitate to suggest that environmental problems contributed to the decline of Greek and Roman civilization.

Hughes specifically mentions, as an index of biodiversity loss, records of the disappearance of various species such as lions, tigers, elephants, and rhinos from different parts of the Roman Empire. In chapter 2, historian Robert Marks focuses on similar records of the occurrence or disappearance of tigers as an index of environmental change over two thousand years in Lingnan, southern China. Records of tiger attacks, he notes, are indicators of human encroachment into tiger habitats. As in Rome, deforestation and agricultural intensification are the most tangible effects of human activity. Yet, the civilizations of Rome and China are sometimes contrasted as diametrically opposed in terms of strategies for dealing with environmental constraints (Debeir et al. 1991; Pomeranz 2000). Slavery was negligible in China, where slaves made up at most 1 percent of the population (Debeir et al. 1991:60), which means that the social appropriation of energy never took the form of a large-scale trade in slaves or in cereals to feed them. Rather than importing food, China was able to intensify rice production and under the Sung dynasty (AD 960–1279) exported parts of its harvests even to Southeast Asia (Debeir et al. 1991:45). From 1550 on, Marks observes, the commercialization of agriculture brought major changes in land use to satisfy the rising market demand for rice, carp, silk, and sugar. By 1600, European merchants bought silk, porcelain, and other preciosities in exchange for silver. The annual inflow into southern China of hundreds of tons of silver, largely derived from American mines, stimulated further intensification, including an expansion of mulberry tree plantations for silk production. The early-seventeenth-century scribe Deng Bi'nan, in suggesting that the extinction of tigers in southern China was the result of anthropogenic landscape change, was thus reflecting on socioenvironmental processes that implicated not only Chinese population growth but the entire world-system.

The Chinese landscape is one of the most obvious examples of "landesque capital"—that is, human investments in land—in the world. In chapter 3, geographer Mats Widgren discusses the definition and global distribution of landesque capital from several perspectives. Land improved for purposes of agricultural production is the main form of capital accumulation in preindustrial societies on all continents, and simultaneously one of the most tangible ways in which humans for millennia have changed their natural environments. There are many varieties—irrigation or drainage canals, terraces, raised fields, forest clearance, stone clearance, soil improvement—but only one common incentive: to increase agricultural yield per unit of land. It is thus closely connected with sedentary settlement and often the object of violent competition or even military conquest. Although there are examples of landesque capital precipitating environmental degradation (e.g. salinization, or erosion following abandonment), Widgren points out that it has often permanently improved the conditions for sustainable land use. He also notes that the concept is in conflict with the notion of "carrying capacity" as an immutable feature of a given environment. Although often attributed to central planning and hierarchical social organization, as in Wittfogel's classic discussion of "Oriental despotism" and "hydraulic" civilizations, Widgren observes that landesque capital can also be accumulated through the long-term labor investments of local communities, particularly under political, economic, and social conditions where investments in land are experienced as secure. The concept of landesque capital provides us with a foil against which to better understand what Amartya Sen has called "laboresque" capital, that is, machinery: while the latter saves labor, the former saves land. It also reminds us that land and labor are not as distinct factors of production as they are sometimes visualized, for landesque capital is so by virtue of representing embodied labor. The great variation in the quality and productivity of land presents a great challenge for any method of natural resource accounting based on units of land, for example, that of ecological footprints.

Landesque capital, it seems, was precisely what spurred the seventeenth-century military expansion of what economic historian Janken Myrdal in chapter 4 calls the Swedish Empire. As for Rome, the primary target was grain-producing areas around an inland sea, accessible via maritime transport. In the century between 1560 and 1660, Sweden (which then included Finland) briefly conquered most of the coasts around the southern Baltic, including significant portions of Estonia, Latvia, Poland, Germany, and Denmark. Myrdal discusses four different explanations of this expansion, the prevalent one being that Sweden sought to gain control over the maritime trade between Russia and western Europe. Although the different theories need not exclude each other, Myrdal argues that the main incentive was the pursuit of grain to alleviate an emerging food crisis and to maintain the imperial project. Rather than continue to export grain westward, as it had done in the sixteenth century, Sweden in the seventeenth century began to divert grain flows, from the newly conquered Baltic provinces, that had previously been directed to the Netherlands. The food crisis was partly a consequence of the massive diversion of labor from agricultural tasks to industry and warfare. The main industrial exports at this time were iron, copper, potash, and tar, but the Swedish arms industry also absorbed much labor. A peculiar but sociometabolically relevant observation is that the production of gunpowder from saltpeter deprived agriculture of great amounts of stable refuse previously used as manure, contributing to soil exhaustion. Iron production had also seriously impoverished the forests over large areas. This chapter illustrates the kind of situation in which several European nations found themselves in the sixteenth century, struggling to cope with agricultural stagnation and overexploitation of domestic resources. Even if the seventeenth-century Swedish strategy for coping with the situation soon proved unsuccessful, those of other nations were less so, and the remainder of world history can only be understood against this background.

The problem of deforestation recurs in most case studies in environmental history, and certainly plagued ancient Rome, China, and sixteenth-century Europe. In chapter 5, geographer Michael Williams provides us with a global overview of this pervasive mode of landscape change. He suggests that wood and wood products were one of four major categories of commodity frontiers (along with minerals, agricultural produce, and wild animal products) that can be understood through the lenses of Wallerstein's world-system perspective and Marx's analysis of capitalism. Of all land-cover changes in world history, forest clearing has affected a greater area than any other. This is partly because timber is the only commodity frontier where depletion actually creates a valuable resource in the form of agricultural or pastoral land (landesque capital, if you will). The many essential uses of wood itself, including construction materials for shelters and ships as well as fuel for heating and metallurgy, have given it a strategic importance second only to food. It has thus frequently defied von Thünen's and Wallerstein's generalizations to the effect that bulky, low-value commodities were not traded over long distances in precapitalist times. Roman writers mention ships' timbers imported from the Black Sea coasts, Turkey, Syria, and what is now Algeria. The Muslim-dominated Mediterranean world of the seventh to thirteenth centuries traded pine from Portugal and teak from India. Beginning in the same period, the Hansa league traded timber from the Baltic hinterlands to western Europe. By the sixteenth century, almost all Portuguese ships were built in India or Brazil, while Spain imported quality timber from Poland in order to build the Armada, and England imported timber from Scandinavia and Russia (Ponting 1991:278–279). Already in the late seventeenth century, British warships were being built in North America. By the early eighteenth century, wind- and water-driven sawmills with multiple blades had reached the far eastern end of the Baltic, and sawn timber was transported by ships. Journeys of up to 3,000 kilometers were commonly undertaken to transport bulky, low-value timber between different parts of Europe. With the European colonization of the New World, deforestation accelerated, often to give way to plantations of cash crops such as sugar cane, coffee, tobacco, and cotton. The global history of deforestation (Williams 2003) provides a very graphic account of the expansion of sociometabolic requirements (i.e. the displacement of environmental loads) of core areas of the world-system.

Deforestation plays an important role also in chapter 6, where geographer Jason Moore applies Wallerstein's perspective to the sixteenth-century relocation of silver mining from central Europe to Potosí in present-day Bolivia. For Wallerstein and Moore, the early modern expansion of Europe expressed a new kind of specifically *capitalist* socioecological relations predicated on the endless accumulation of capital and the export of environmental problems (cf. Moore 2003). In the mid-fifteenth century, the mining of silver, iron, lead, copper, zinc, and tin in central Europe had maintained the Roman legacy by seriously degrading the environment through air and water pollution, destruction of fisheries and wildlife, widespread deforestation, and soil erosion. The relocation of silver extraction to the New World offered not only richer ore deposits and cheaper labor power, but also displacement of a highly polluting industry. When ore quality and silver output at Potosí declined, the Spaniards devised a new technology for extracting silver from the ore as well as a system of forced labor drafts to keep the reluctant Andean miners working. The intensive mining activities brought severe deforestation, soil erosion, and floods. Moore suggests that the dual strategy of intensifying technological inputs and securing cheaper labor power represents a recurrent pattern of temporarily checking rising costs that is characteristic of early modern commodity frontiers, for example also the sugar frontier (Moore 2000). The degradation of the landscape and of human bodies was symptomatic of the same capitalist logic. The situation in the colonial New World illustrates most dramatically how the globalization of capital extended what Marx had referred to as the "metabolic rift" between town and country, so as to apply generally to the polarization of production and extraction, or core and periphery. Whether such polarizing tendencies are indeed uniquely "capitalist" in a Wallersteinian, post-fifteenth-century sense is a contested topic within world-systems discourse, but few would deny that the sixteenth-century expansion of Europe represented some kind of discontinuity in the socioenvironmental history of our planet.

In chapter 7, anthropologist Thomas Håkansson takes us to the savannas of East Africa to explore the impact of the ivory trade on local ecology and land use patterns, using historical data from the nineteenth century. Like silver, ivory is a typical preciosity or "prestige good" with high value-to-volume ratio and negligible metabolic significance for importing societies. Yet, its extraction, like that of silver, has had important ecological consequences for the exporting regions (cf. Håkansson 2004). Having been exported from East Africa as a material for prestigious ornaments at least since Roman times (first century AD), with a marked expansion between AD 1000 and 1500, ivory by the nineteenth century was used in Europe and the United States for items such as combs, piano keys, and billiard balls. Håkansson suggests that the ivory trade brought a reduction in elephant populations that may have caused an expansion of woodland and scrub at the expense of grass, which in turn would have attracted tsetse flies and bovine sleeping sickness, restricting opportunities for grazing in some areas. More significantly, the access to coastal goods and currencies stimulated an intensification of agriculture, pastoralism, and craft production along the trade routes in the interior, which in turn affected settlement patterns, food security, soils, vegetation, and faunal biodiversity. Even if the socioenvironmental changes in the nineteenth century were particularly accentuated, such linkages between world-systemic and ecological processes can probably be projected many centuries backward in time. Håkansson has thus posited a general connection over time between the intensity of specialized pastoralism and the economic trends of the ivory trade. Another form of export production in East Africa with considerable environmental consequences, which deserve to be analyzed in the same manner, is iron production. In addition to the direct ecological effects of extraction of commodities for the world market, he concludes, world-system analyses should reckon with a number of indirect environmental changes resulting from the circulation of foreign goods that stimulate political processes leading to new patterns of land use.

Similar conclusions emerge from chapter 8, in which archaeologist Rafael Gassón takes us back to South America, more specifically the moist savannas (*Llanos*) of Venezuela. Like Håkansson, he suggests that even pre-colonial patterns of land use were geared to long-distance exchange. Agricultural intensification in the form of raised fields on the pre-Columbian *Llanos* may reflect political developments stimulated by the long-distance exchange of prestige goods such as polished stone beads and pendants. The raw materials in these items can be traced to distant sources such as Ecuador and the Caribbean. The incorporation of the *Llanos* into the colonial world-system triggered a sequence of major socioenvironmental transformations. The impact of epidemic diseases, raids, and slavery struck sedentary farmers much harder than mobile hunter-gatherers, leaving agricultural lands open to European exploitation. The sixteenth-century introduction of cattle from Hispaniola eclipsed the indigenous fauna as the favored game species of Amerindian hunters in the area. Cattle ranching and the cultivation of tobacco and cotton further transformed the ecology of the *Llanos*. During the early decades of the nineteenth century, however, war and economic crisis destroyed this agrarian economy, and significant parts of the *Llanos* began to revert to tropical forests, which suggests that the original, open landscape encountered by the Europeans may in part have been anthropogenic. With the recovery of the forest came animal species such as herons, the feathers of which between the 1880s and 1920s were in great demand as ornaments for ladies' hats in Paris and New York. Most of the local labor force abandoned the ranches and fields to hunt herons, and the bird was almost driven to extinction. This case study, like the previous chapter, illustrates how cultural idiosyncrasies in core areas of the world-system—like the appetite for ivory or heron feathers—can be of decisive significance for socioenvironmental trajectories in the periphery.

Cultural idiosyncrasies of appetite are literally the topic of chapter 9, in which anthropologist Richard Wilk explores the origins of the eighteenth- and nineteenth-century global food system, which provided a standard set of foods to the armies of extractive workers all over the world. Dishes based on these rations—such as salted meats, wheat flour, pulses, and sugar—were eventually localized, and in many cases became the "traditional" foods of the twentieth century. This ration system was initially developed to support large military organizations and sailing fleets, but was gradually extended to include a global workforce engaged in extractive industries such as mining, logging, and fishing, as well as railroad construction. The production of foodstuffs to feed these workers transformed the economies and ecologies of North America, and many parts of Europe and South America. Like later periods of globalization, the eighteenth- and nineteenth-century wave of globalization brought serious environmental impacts that are heterogeneous and dispersed, and have thus rarely been linked to each other because of the complexity of commodity chains and trade relationships. The chapter illustrates how opaque are the global connections, even in the eighteenth century, between contexts of extraction, production, and consumption (cf. Appadurai 1986), and how this very opacity obstructs experiences of environmental responsibility. Several factors combine to make "extractivists" notoriously unconcerned with conservation of resources. Aside from showing the intricately specific connections between cultural, economic, and ecological systems, Wilk's study reminds us that the organization of extractive activities in the global periphery was modeled after, and often associated with, the organization of military conquest. The analogy suggests a war on nature.

If military conquests leave culturally specific imprints on ecosystems, ecosystems can also impinge on the fortunes of military conquest. In chapter 10, historian J. R. McNeill reveals how the interaction of landscape changes and human epidemiology from the seventeenth to the nineteenth century influenced the course of geopolitical history in the lowland tropics of the New World. The chapter illustrates the *recursive* relation between world-systems and ecosystems, viewed through the lens of yellow fever and its mosquito vectors. The establishment of sugar plantations in the largely depopulated American tropics in the seventeenth century, to satisfy European appetites, relied on slave labor imported from West Africa. The slave ships also brought the West African mosquito *Aedes aegypti*, vector of yellow fever, a disease to which the Africans, but not Europeans raised in temperate climates, were often immune. The conversion of tropical American landscapes into sugar plantations in several ways favored the breeding of *A. aegypti* and the transmission of yellow fever. French and British armies, composed of men raised in Europe, suffered disastrous losses from yellow fever as they vainly tried to wrest the Caribbean from Latin control. After the 1770s, the differential immunity to yellow fever was of similar importance in preventing Spain from holding on to its Caribbean colonies struggling for independence. McNeill aptly concludes that European empires, through the socioenvironmental changes they had inflicted on tropical America, had sown the seeds of their own destruction. His study clearly illustrates how sociopolitical and ecological systems are recursively intertwined in world-system history.

Conclusion

The chapters in part I provide us with a rich platform from which to reflect on the extent to which the arguments of political ecology and notions of ecologically unequal exchange can be projected backward onto the environmental history of the past two millennia. Even if the lack of comparable data prevents us from applying the same methodological tools as the authors in part II have applied to modern statistics, similar analytical perspectives can be shared by both approaches. The metabolic rift between economic cores and their extractive peripheries can be identified from ancient Rome to nineteenth-century England, and the tendency to displace environmental burdens ever farther from core areas is pervasive, irrespective of whether it implies extending or transgressing political boundaries. The ecological impacts of long-distance trade in the ancient world can be exemplified by the Roman appropriation of timber, grain, and metals from vast areas of Europe, Africa, and Asia. From the sixteenth century on, such impacts are all the more obvious, for example, in the extraction of timber and grain from eastern Europe, silver from the Andes, ivory from East Africa, and sugar from the Caribbean. The uncalculated, indirect environmental impacts (i.e. "ecological rucksacks") of the extraction of for example silver, ivory, or sugar are important aspects of the "ecological trade balances" of colonial Spain and Britain. The modern displacement of the most polluting industries from the E.U. to Latin America thus has antecedents in sixteenth-century silver mining. Loss of biodiversity in the periphery is a theme that can be traced from Roman North Africa to the savannas of modern Brazil (cf. Ponting 1991:161–193; Richards 2003:463–616). Another pivotal factor in human-environmental relations throughout the millennia is the accumulation, maintenance, and eventual abandonment of landesque capital, designed to produce for example grain, wine, olive oil, rice, silk, beef, sugar, cotton, or soybeans as commodities for impersonal, monetized markets. Equally ubiquitous is the lack of environmental foresight that characterizes most market-oriented extractive activities, whether conducted by Roman slaves or nineteenth-century loggers. Finally, it is striking how these trajectories of political economy tend to be determined by the seemingly arbitrary specifics of ecological and cultural systems in recursive interaction, for example the food preferences of mosquitoes and men. When Immanuel Wallerstein, in the final chapter, asks what is rational, the question can be extended beyond a critique of the logic of capitalism to a reflection on the general relation between social and ecological systems throughout the course of human history.

It is obvious that many of the imports to core areas, from ancient Rome to nineteenth-century Europe, were of negligible direct significance for the social metabolism of these areas. If we were to restrict our perspective to this observation, we might well agree with economic historian Paul Bairoch's (1993:97) remarkable conclusion that "the West did not need the Third World." But in looking at early-twentieth-century statistics to draw the conclusion that the dependence of the West on raw materials from the Third World prior to 1955 is a "complete myth" (Bairoch 1993:70), Bairoch seriously distorts our view of the dynamics of economic development and industrialization. Let us look closer at Bairoch's position as a foil against which to consolidate the argument in this book.

First, as Bairoch (1993:88–97) himself concedes, the consequences of incorporation as a world-system periphery can be destructive enough, even if the sociometabolic significance of the exports for importing core countries seems insignificant. To use a modern expression, the "ecological rucksacks" of such exports (e.g. spices, jewels, silver, gold, silk, ivory, feathers, sugar, tobacco, coffee, tea) were generally formidable, and this is but one of the ways in which the periphery was—and continues to be—forced to pay a high price for the economic development of the core.

Second, Bairoch's conclusion that the role of colonialism was unimportant in the birth of the British Industrial Revolution (Bairoch 1993:80) underestimates the recursive relation between mercantile and financial profits, on one hand, and investments in mechanization, on the other (cf. Wolf 1982:267–295). His mechanistic, linear notion that "during the eighteenth and nineteenth centuries colonization was primarily a result of industrial development and not vice versa" (Bairoch 1993:82) fails to appreciate the complex ways in which these two phenomena were mutually reinforcing aspects of the same process.

Third, his use of the category "the West" as a static economic and/or political entity extending indefinitely backward in time beyond 1955 is extremely misleading. Economic core-periphery relations are dynamic and multiscaled and frequently shift over the course of history, not to mention the variously constructed political boundaries asserted by different governments so as to maximize advantages and minimize risks in particular historical contexts. The imperial projects of Rome, Spain, Britain, and even Sweden are obvious examples. A sociometabolic perspective on the accumulation of industrial infrastructure must avoid being straitjacketed into the fetishized nation-state categories that organize economic statistics. We do not need to go very far back in time to find large parts of Europe peripheral to the industrial and commercial developments in Britain and the Netherlands. Nor should we forget how recently North America was a source of cheap (largely slave) labor and land serving as a vast extractive zone particularly for Britain. If Bairoch (1993:59–71) finds that, just prior to the First World War, the "developed West" was basically self-sufficient in minerals and other raw materials, it certainly does not mean that the accumulation of industrial infrastructure within its present-day political boundaries has not historically been characterized by ecologically unequal relations of exchange between core regions and *what were then* their peripheries.

The fundamental structural relationship, if we are to understand the social metabolism underlying economic development, is the exchange between geographical spaces experiencing an accumulation of physical capital (cores), on one hand, and extractive areas suffering net exports of natural resources (peripheries), on the other. Political boundaries and national statistics frequently—if not systematically—distort and mystify this relationship. At certain times and places an industrial core region in a given country will find its domestic, national periphery more or less sufficient for its metabolic requirements, at other times not. Although national statistics would make them seem comparable entities, Canada and Singapore obviously have very different capacities in this respect. Although the basic structural imbalance, which Marx identified as the "metabolic rift" between town and countryside, is as old and pervasive as urbanization itself (cf. McNeill 2000:281–295), the past few centuries of globalization have seen an increasing ambition—and capacity—of nation-states to displace such imbalances beyond their own borders to the international arena.

Finally, our review of the historical evidence from the past two millennia shows that developments in core areas, thus defined, have in fact systematically relied on imports of bulk commodities the significance of which, although they were much less voluminous per capita than today, was very far from negligible for their metabolism: foodstuffs, timber, metals, fuels, and fibers are only the most obvious examples. Even if the mid-twentieth century to Bairoch suggests a discontinuity in the sense that extraction of such resources for the "developed West" (Europe and North America) was increasingly externalized beyond its modern political boundaries, there are clear historical continuities in the fundamental structures of unequal ecological exchange. Not only was the "developed West" a rather recently constituted geographical and political category at that time, but, over the centuries, structures of unequal ecological exchange have frequently unfolded with little regard to political boundaries. As long as it is confined to statistics on the flows of exchange values crossing national borders, the discourse on development and underdevelopment will thus be severely constrained.

This indeterminate relationship between economic marginality and political inclusion is well illustrated in chapter 19, where anthropologist Joseph Tainter compares the shifting historical fortunes of two marginal areas, Epirus in present-day Greece and New Mexico in the present-day United States. Both areas have experienced the redrawing of political boundaries resulting in transfers from less to more affluent nation-states, from Turkey to Greece and from Mexico to the United States, respectively. Their parallel developments illustrate a trajectory shared by many rural areas within affluent nations today, suggesting a completely different kind of marginality than that of impoverished extractive zones. In these margins of the "developed" world, government subsidies have made extractive and subsistence activities obsolete, leaving landesque capital abandoned and overgrown, while communities have become increasingly dependent on distant centers and local cohesion is deteriorating. The landscape has been redefined and commodified as a repository of natural beauty and stereotyped cultural traditions marketed to urban tourists. Tainter suggests that a problem shared by local people in Epirus and New Mexico—like people everywhere—is that they do not have access to the global-scale information flows that increasingly affect them and make them vulnerable. Local communities lose political and economic autonomy but not their propensity to think locally. Tainter proposes, by way of remedy, that world-system perspectives incorporated into educational curricula within a generation or two might make thinking about the connections between the global and the local the normal state of affairs. I would add that this is no doubt already under way, not least with the aid of media such as television and the Internet, but that access to new information technologies, like other technologies, is in itself also a matter of unequal global distribution. Even more apparent are the inequalities in terms of capacity to act on such information. In these respects, the Epirotes and New Mexicans probably have less to worry about than local communities in the hinterlands of Bolivia, Zaire, or Pakistan. The significance of thinking globally, however, will certainly remain crucial as long as globalized capital flows continue to determine the fortunes of local communities. Tainter's chapter shows how the social, cultural, and environmental aspects of dependency and marginalization are intertwined.

The final word goes to Immanuel Wallerstein, originator of the world-system concept, who in chapter 20 discusses problems of global environmental change in terms of their intellectual, moral, and political implications.

He confirms what several of the other contributors have suggested, that the unequal distribution of environmental damage is not accidental but has been an intrinsic part of the capitalist system from the start. Turning our gaze around toward the future, he suggests that this capitalist world-system is presently undergoing a terminal structural crisis, and that the transition to a different kind of system will be completed within fifty years. The nature of the new system that shall replace it will be decided by all of us, he believes, through our political activity over these next few decades. The choice, it seems, can be symbolized by what Wallerstein calls the camp of Porto Alegre versus the camp of Davos. Although he is relentlessly pessimistic about the possibilities of sustainable development under capitalism, this very pessimism paradoxically permits him to end on an optimistic note. Another world is possible.

References

Appadurai, A., ed. 1986. *The social life of things: Commodities in cultural perspective.* Cambridge, U.K.: Cambridge University Press.

Bairoch, P. 1993. *Economics and world history: Myths and paradoxes.* Chicago: University of Chicago Press.

Bryant, R. L., and S. Bailey. 1997. *Third world political ecology.* New York: Routledge.

Bunker, S. G. 1985. *Underdeveloping the Amazon: Extraction, unequal exchange, and the failure of the modern state.* Chicago: University of Chicago Press.

Bunker, S. G., and P. S. Ciccantell. 2005. *Globalization and the race for resources.* Baltimore, Md.: Johns Hopkins University Press.

Debeir, J.-C., J.-P. Deléage, and D. Hémery. 1991. *In the servitude of power: Energy and civilization through the ages.* London and New Jersey: Zed Books.

Diamond, J. 2005. *Collapse: How societies choose to fail or succeed.* New York: Viking.

Goldfrank, W. L., D. Goodman, and A. Szasz, eds. 1999. *Ecology and the world-system.* Westport, Conn.: Greenwood.

Håkansson, N. T. 2004. The human ecology of world systems in East Africa: The impact of the ivory trade. *Human Ecology* 32 (5): 561–591.

Hornborg, A. 2001. *The power of the machine: Global inequalities of economy, technology, and environment.* Lanham, Md.: AltaMira.

Hughes, J. D. 1994. *Pan's travail: Environmental problems of the ancient Greeks and Romans.* Baltimore, Md.: Johns Hopkins University Press.

Low, N., and B. Gleeson. 1998. *Justice, society and nature: An exploration of political ecology.* New York: Routledge.

Martinez-Alier, J. 2002. *The environmentalism of the poor: A study of ecological conflicts and valuation.* Cheltenham and Northampton: Edward Elgar.

McNeill, J. R. 2000. *Something new under the sun: An environmental history of the twentieth-century world.* New York: Norton.

Mintz, S. 1985. *Sweetness and power: The place of sugar in modern history.* New York: Penguin.

Moore, J. W. 2000. Sugar and the expansion of the early modern world-economy. *Review* 23 (3): 409–433.

———. 2003. "The modern world-system" as environmental history? Ecology and the rise of capitalism. *Theory and Society* 32 (3): 307–377.

Paulson, S., and L. L. Gezon, eds. 2005. *Political ecology across spaces, scales, and social groups.* New Brunswick, N.J., and London: Rutgers University Press.

Pomeranz, K. 2000. *The great divergence: China, Europe, and the making of the modern world economy.* Princeton, N.J.: Princeton University Press.

Ponting, C. 1991. *A green history of the world: The environment and the collapse of great civilizations.* New York: Penguin.

Redman, C. L. 1999. *Human impact on ancient environments.* Tucson: University of Arizona Press.

Richards, J. F. 2003. *The unending frontier: An environmental history of the early modern world.* Berkeley and Los Angeles: University of California Press.

Simmons, I. G. 1993. *Environmental history: A concise introduction.* Malden, Mass.: Blackwell.

Thomas, W. L., Jr., ed. 1956. *Man's role in changing the face of the earth.* Chicago: University of Chicago Press.

Turner, B. L., II, W. C. Clark, R. W. Kates, J. F. Richards, J. T. Mathews, and W. B. Meyer, eds. 1990. *The earth as transformed by human action: Global and regional changes in the biosphere over the past 300 years.* Cambridge, U.K.: Cambridge University Press.

Wallerstein, I. 1974–1989. *The modern world-system.* 3 vols. San Diego: Academic.

Wilkinson, R. G. 1973. *Poverty and progress: An ecological perspective on economic development.* London: Methuen.

Williams, M. 2003. *Deforesting the earth: From prehistory to global crisis.* Chicago: University of Chicago Press.

Wolf, E. R. 1982. *Europe and the people without history.* Berkeley, Los Angeles, and London: University of California Press.

Worster, D., ed. 1988. *The ends of the earth: Perspectives on modern environmental history.* Cambridge, U.K.: Cambridge University Press.

THE ENVIRONMENT IN WORLD-SYSTEM HISTORY: TRACING SOCIAL PROCESSES IN NATURE

I

Environmental Impacts of the Roman Economy and Social Structure: Augustus to Diocletian

1

J. DONALD HUGHES

D URING THE THREE hundred years after its founding by Augustus Caesar (27 BC–AD 14), the Roman Empire first reached a peak of economic growth and prosperity, and then suffered a severe crisis and decline (Hughes 2005:196–213), so that by the end of this period the emperor Diocletian (284–305), a responsible ruler, believed it necessary to enact a coordinated series of measures designed to rescue the economy. This historical process took place within a context of environmental deterioration and resource depletion. Roman economic activity produced profound and long-lasting impacts on the landscape of the empire. Exploitation of forests, hunting and fishing, mining and metallurgy, pastoralism and agriculture, all meant the transformation of major segments of the ancient environment. Roman trade extended outside the empire, and had its effects on landscapes there also.

The Social Structure of the Roman Empire

The economy of the Roman Empire was organized primarily to benefit the upper strata of society: the landlords rather than the peasantry, the rich rather than the poor, the masters and certainly not the slaves. Above all, power and economic benefit were concentrated in the office of the emperor and in his household. The emperor controlled a separate treasury and his edicts had the force of law. The emperor could affect the economic structure and thus environmental impact, although it must be noted that Roman understanding of economic policy was limited, and that nothing like environmental policy existed.

A word about the social standing of women is appropriate at the outset. The Roman tradition was extremely patriarchal in the sense that a woman's status was determined by that of the man to whom she was primarily related: her father before her marriage, her husband during marriage, her son during widowhood, and a related male guardian if none of the previously named relationships obtained. She would be a member of the class to which the man belonged, but could not exercise direct political or legal participation. A woman might be of citizen class, but she was not a citizen. For example, there were no female senators or magistrates. There was often an empress (*Augusta*), but only in relationship to a male emperor. At the same time, upper-class women could wield considerable political and economic power through or on behalf of their husbands or other related men. Their influence in terms of environmental impact was, therefore, considerable. Whenever the masculine pronoun is encountered in what follows, therefore, this fact should be remembered.

The Upper Classes

The Roman class structure began in the single city-state of Rome and had spread across an empire that surrounded the Mediterranean Sea during the centuries before Augustus. The upper classes (*honestiores*) were designated both in terms of family and wealth. The three upper classes were the senators, equites, and decurions.

Highest among these were the senators, originally the descendants of patrician families, but augmented by worthy and wealthy plebeians and, by imperial times, powerful colonial and provincial leaders. Qualification as a senator required property in the form of landed estate. The influence of this class in terms of environmental impacts was paramount, since its members owned a major fraction of the land and along with the emperor had a determining role in legislation. Many of them owned extensive ranches (*latifundia*) where cattle, sheep, pigs, and various agricultural goods were produced including oil, wine, grains, and cloth. They might invest in various enterprises, but social and sometimes legal barriers kept them from direct involvement in trade and commerce.

The second class consisted of equites (equestrians), who were required to be freeborn (the emperor Tiberius added the qualification of two generations of free birth) and to have property. This class included an aristocratic Roman core, leading men from the colonies, and businessmen (*negotiatores*). Its members held important public offices including the prefectures in charge of supplying the cities with food and other necessities. The principal tax collectors (publicans) were equites. This class was the leading force in trade and commerce, organizing markets, investing in shipping, and controlling trade in such products as grain, wine, and oil. Crucial to the treatment of the environment, equites formed consortia (*societates*) to control the exploitation of important state-owned natural resources such as mines, quarries, and forests (Rostovtzeff 1971:110).

The third class, the decurions, consisted of members of municipal councils in the empire. Like the first two classes, they were expected to share high birth, wealth, and good reputation. They also performed public duties including local administration, finances, and tax collection. Environmental decisions on the local level, such as land questions or the creation of infrastructure, often fell to them. These three classes had an advantageous status under law. Together they constituted less than two percent of the population of the Roman Empire, but they controlled the vast preponderance of its economy.

There was a steady concentration of land ownership into the hands of the wealthy, because over time the small farmers had gone into debt to the large landowners, placing their land in security, and had not been able to pay back the loans (Simkhovitch 1921:104). "For neither knowledge nor effort can be of any use to any person whatsoever, without those expenses which the operations require" (Columella, *De Re Rustica* 1.1). The landowners controlled huge estates (*latifundia*), where tenant sharecroppers and contingents of cattle-herding slaves directed by bailiffs performed the labor. Large consortia of wealthy families contracted with the government to exploit mines, forests, and other resources. There were also many smaller enterprises run by citizens of lesser rank, including freedmen, and these often depended on funding from the more affluent. Trade was usually conducted by the dependent enterprises, since commercial occupations were considered demeaning to those of the upper classes, although nothing prevented the latter from profiting through the labor of the former. They therefore provided the construction funds and other venture capital for merchant fleets that crisscrossed the Mediterranean and other nearby seas including the near Atlantic Ocean, the Black Sea, and the avenue through the Red Sea to the Indian Ocean. The more direct route to India had been opened by a Greek sailor named Hippalus using the monsoon winds not long before the rule of Augustus. Pliny the Elder (first century) complained that Rome spent a hundred million sesterces every year in trade with India, and this money was exchanged not for bulky resources that might have benefited the common people, but for more easily transported luxuries such as spices, jewels, fine woods, birds, and delicate textiles to satisfy the tastes of the elite (Frank and

Gills 1993, 170). A statuette of the Indian goddess Lakshmi was found in Pompeii, providing one bit of evidence of this trade (Charlesworth 1951). Roman exports in exchange included gold, silver and silverware, works of art, wine, pottery, and slaves.

The Lower Classes

The lower classes (*humiliores*) were also divided into three recognized groups, the freeborn poor, freedmen, and slaves. The freeborn poor were those who had never been slaves and had no slave ancestry. The majority worked on the land, making up the preponderance of the population of the Roman Empire, but some were self-employed tradesmen, others were skilled or unskilled workers who sold their labor, and a large group made up a portion of the urban unemployed. Although it is not well represented in historical sources, the effect of this class on environmental change must have been major, taking place in a multitude of everyday decisions and activities throughout the empire.

Freedmen were emancipated slaves and those descended from them. They were eligible for Roman citizenship, but that citizenship might carry certain disabilities, and like the freeborn poor they might be dependent on patrons from among the *honestiores*. Some became rich, powerful, and envied, like the bureaucrats appointed by the emperor Claudius (41–54) or the millionaire Trimalchio, who although fictitious undoubtedly represented a class that existed. According to Petronius's *Satyricon* (first century), Trimalchio was considering the purchase of the entire island of Sicily to add to his landholdings, an obvious exaggeration but one with an edge of truth. Most of the freedmen were not rich, but people economically akin to the freeborn poor.

The vast majority of the Roman population was rural, lived at a subsistence level, and led precarious economic lives (Garnsey and Saller 1982:28). Most of them, probably 80 percent, labored on the land. Small farmers managed only a slight surplus margin of production, if any, and that was quickly commandeered by the landlords and by imperial taxes, which weighed heavily on the agricultural sector throughout the period with which we are concerned. The government's basic concern, above all, was to finance the imperial court, the bureaucracy, and the military, and to construct public buildings and infrastructure such as roads and sewers. The danger of famine in the countryside, and consequent political unrest, was recognized by the progressive emperors Nerva (96–98) and Trajan (98–117), whose edicts required landowners receiving government grants to make subsistence payments to poor children in rural districts. The practice of such government handouts did not genuinely ameliorate the socioeconomic structure that was in effect designed to benefit the social elite. The distributions may have been directed toward preventing unrest among the poor, and possibly also toward increasing the population.

Slavery

No picture of the effect of the Roman economy on the natural environment can be complete without an investigation of the role of slavery. As Aldo Schiavone (2002:122–23) recently explained it,

> The use of slaves became the ideal functional means of agricultural exploitation, slave labor the basis of all manufacturing, and the owner of land and slaves the ultimate protagonists of every organization of production.... [I]t is impossible to separate the society of Rome—its material foundations, obviously, but also its ideas, convictions, mentality, ethics, and even its anthropology—from the context of slavery.

The status of a slave was equivocal; the law treated a slave as a "speaking tool" (*instrumentum vocale*). It might perhaps be better to say that slaves were humans reduced to the state of sources of energy: for example, machines such as cranes used to raise masses of stone for construction were powered by men inside wheel cages using their weight to make the cages revolve. But gradually through Roman history, especially during the second century, a degree of personhood was recognized. A freed slave could become a Roman citizen, although of lower class. Slaves made up at least 35 percent of the population of Roman Italy during the time of Augustus, and were similarly numerous elsewhere in the Roman Empire. Slave owners among the higher classes were known to possess hundreds or thousands. In AD 61, for example, Lucius Pedanius Secundus had four hundred house slaves, while field slaves and mine slaves were much more numerous. Many agricultural slaves worked on latifundia where they would watch grazing animals and take them to mountain pastures in summer, but Columella (*De Re Rustica* 3.3.8) tells of specialized slaves skilled in viticulture, and there were slaves who managed business for their owners. But slaves could not be expected to exhibit initiative in improving agricultural methods or assuring sustained yields of renewable resources because they were obliged to obey the commands of their owners to do mechanical and repetitive work, had little time at their own disposal, and if they produced agricultural surplus or other income, it went to their masters. They lacked even the marginal incentives that tenant sharecroppers had in planning for personal and family rewards. A slave economy cannot as a rule benefit the environment: slave labor enabled exploiters to do more damage, and a slave class whose members were liable to be sold anywhere could not establish a relationship of responsibility with the land. Slaves performed most of the actual work in forestry, such as felling trees (Aubert 2001:101). In addition, as Pliny the Elder expressed it, the fact that "agricultural operations are performed by slaves with fettered ankles and by the hands of malefactors with branded faces" (*Natural History* 18.4.21), increased the tendency of Roman citizens to think of farming not as care of the earth, but as degrading work. The Roman system of slave labor was not only corrupting of human values, but environmentally destructive as well.

Roman Economic History and the Natural Environment

Augustus to Marcus Aurelius

Augustus inaugurated a period of peace within the Roman Empire, although wars of conquest and defense continued on the frontiers. The *Pax* Romana, which lasted with few interruptions until the early third century, enabled an expansion both of population and of the economy. Piracy at sea and banditry on land were suppressed, opening golden opportunities for commerce (Finley 1999:156). Expansion of the economy, however, meant that the richer orders of Roman society, which constituted a tiny minority, became richer. Augustus consolidated Rome's domination of the landscape of the entire Mediterranean world and beyond it in western Europe, Claudius added Britain in the first century, and Trajan conquered Dacia (Romania) in the second (Hughes 2001:73) and conducted a campaign (ultimately unsuccessful) in Mesopotamia (Iraq). This territorial control enabled Roman officials to enrich themselves at the expense of provincials, and Roman entrepreneurs to exploit natural resources over an area of some 7,800,000 square kilometers. The demand for timber in construction of large buildings and ships caused deforestation over large tracts of land. The once-flourishing forests of Lebanon, for instance, were so depleted that the emperor Hadrian (117–138) reserved them, prohibiting the cutting of cedars and three other species except by imperial permission. Today the famous cedars are represented by a few small groves.

Economic output increased due to an increase in scale rather than in efficiency. In agriculture, new areas were cleared and brought into production, and labor-intensive methods increased food production, a necessity during this period of rising population, especially because a larger proportion of people was living in cities. Rome, the capital, grew in population and area, spreading over the surrounding countryside and blurring the distinction between city and suburbs (Morley 1996:85). The imperial government continued to make every possible effort to provide a subsidized grain import to feed the urban poor, and under Augustus 80,000 tons of grain were distributed annually free to 200,000 people (Schiavone 2002:96). Augustus treated Egypt, one of the major sources of wheat imports, as his own personal property, thus securing the role of the emperor in providing the food supply. The emperor also took interest in an organized business that provided a continuous supply of gladiators and animals for entertainment in the amphitheater. These two enterprises constituted the famous "bread and circuses" (*panis et circenses*), intended to keep the mob happy and prevent revolution. They were also notorious engines of environmental depletion: the grain dole drained the agricultural production of the provinces, and the arena contributed to the extirpation of large species of wildlife everywhere. Lions disappeared from Europe, tigers from Hyrcania (Iran) and Armenia, and elephants, rhinoceroses, and zebras from North Africa, to mention a few.

The Crisis of the Third Century

Depletion of natural resources and wasteful methods of exploitation were underlying causes of the crisis of the third century, which manifested itself in the form of shortages and ruinous inflation. There were no important advances in agricultural or industrial technology except possibly the use of the vertical undershot waterwheel to grind grain. A population decline probably began with the great plague of 166–182 under the emperor Marcus Aurelius (161–180), after which violence, food shortages, and returns of the plague kept recovery at bay. Some emperors attempted state control of resources, raising taxes including those collected in kind, and assuming direct control over some aspects of trade. Archaeological deposits of amphorae, for instance, reveal that the imperial bureaucracy took charge of supplying oil and wine from Spain to Rome during the reign of Septimius Severus (193–211), but he was the only emperor of the first half of the third century to exercise consistent control of such matters (MacMullen 1988:14). The emperor Caracalla (211–217) enlarged the Roman citizen body and the tax rolls by an edict granting Roman citizenship to all free men in the empire in 212.

The size of the army, and its consumption of finances and resources, increased by leaps and bounds. Commanders in the provinces sought to seize power, plunging the empire into fifty years of sporadic warfare. The battlefields were in the settled regions of the central empire, and destruction was visited on houses, barns, orchards, and the rural population. The average period of rule of the emperors between 235 and 284 was two years, hardly enough time to establish policy, and all of the emperors were military men, few of whom had any understanding of principles of economy. Prices rose astronomically; the price of wheat in Egypt, for example, was 8 drachmas per artaba in the second century, 24 drachmas in the mid-third century, and 220–300 drachmas in the late third century (Duncan-Jones 1990:147). Emperors facing financial emergency increased the minting of coinage, thus exposing it to debasement. Due to the inflation of the value of precious metals, the cost of the metal in coins rose above their face value, forcing the issuing of coins in less valuable materials such as bronze or lead (perhaps with an easily eroded wash of silver). Silver could be used for coins of higher denominations, in a never-ending inflationary process, but the tax base of the empire, which depended on agricultural productivity, was shrinking. There were further onslaughts of plague in 251–266 and afterward, and emperors made up a deficit of manpower by allowing groups of barbarians to settle within the empire.

The Reforms of Diocletian

Population decline continued to be a problem in later antiquity, meaning fewer farm workers, so that reductions in population and agricultural production tended to be synergistic. This exacerbated what was happening at the end of the third century: although constant warfare and periodic plagues were also to blame, there was a chronic agricultural decline deriving from the environmental damage the Romans had caused. Food was becoming scarcer, prices were rising, and there was a general shortage of labor. Diocletian attacked these problems vigorously, if not entirely successfully. His edicts on occupations required civil and military officials, decurions, landowners, and shipowners to provide heirs for their positions, namely their own natural or adopted sons. This was intended to counteract the drop in population by encouraging those in essential jobs to produce children. It also turned these professions into hereditary castes. The same principle was later applied to others on whom the food supply depended: bakers, butchers, and food merchants, and then craftsmen, postal employees, workers in state factories, and ordinary soldiers. It was no surprise, then, when agricultural workers were included. Laws helped landlords tie peasants to the soil, restricting their freedom of movement and requiring them to remain permanently attached to the latifundia, thus beginning a process that led toward eventual serfdom in a later period. The flight from the land was largely stopped, but at the price of individual freedom.

Diocletian enacted edicts against inflation, while restructuring the empire to guarantee central control and restrict local autonomy. The Edict on Prices, issued in 301, set maximum allowable charges for various commodities, services, and wages. It lists approximately one thousand specific items in an attempt to control profiteering. The categories listed include food, raw materials such as timber, clothing, transportation, service charges, and wages. The exhaustive catalog reveals some of the environmental impacts of the Romans at the time; for example, prices are given for wild game such as gazelles, pheasants, and sea urchins, and for furs including badger, leopard, and sealskin. The prices overall appear to be fair, although perhaps a small percentage under the rates actually prevailing at the time. If Diocletian's wages and prices had become the actual practice, ordinary people would have had a supportable standard of living (Williams 1985:131). The edict did not succeed, however, because it failed to take account of such economic principles as wholesale and retail, supply and demand, and the availability of natural resources. When the price set by the edict for a commodity was considerably below what the market demanded, the item disappeared from the shelves in stores; as Lactantius said, "Men were afraid to display anything for sale, and the scarcity became more grievous and excessive than ever" (*Death of the Persecutors* 7). Of course a black market, with inflated prices, appeared under the noses of the authorities. The environmental base of the Roman world continued to deteriorate, and the system Diocletian envisioned collapsed along with the unity of the empire.

The Environmental Effects of the Roman Social and Economic System

The fact of environmental degradation as a result of the Roman economy and social structure is quite clear. Shortages of food and rising prices were among the debilitating effects. The landscape deteriorated: for example, abandoned olive presses of Roman date exist in the North African desert where today there are no trees at all, much less olives, in sight.

Deforestation in the mountains left the slopes vulnerable to torrential winter rains, as did the destruction of brush and grasses by grazing of domestic animals. Erosion swept away useful soil, so that trees could not grow again in areas that had been forested before. The sediments of this erosion still exist and can be studied in lowlands not far from Rome, and along some coastlines around the Mediterranean Sea, where they formed marshlands that became the haunt of malarial mosquitoes, which forced villages to relocate themselves to the hills wherever possible (Hughes 1994:82–86).

A related problem affecting agricultural productivity is salinization. Water used for irrigation has salt content, and this originates from contact with salt-bearing strata over which it flows. The amount of mineral content, including salt, is greater when the strata are exposed by erosion. As evaporation takes place in the fields, the salt is concentrated in the soil, making it more saline. This problem is particularly noticeable in poorly drained areas with warm, dry climates where irrigation is practiced, which were common in Iberia and the southern and eastern portions of the Roman Empire. In some limited areas it became so severe that food crops could not grow.

Roman farmers knew agricultural remedies for problems like siltation, salinization, and soil exhaustion through the leaching of essential minerals, but could not always apply them due to political and military pressures. The tax system bore most heavily on the agricultural sector of the economy, whether the levies were collected in coin or in kind. Farmers were often pressed into the army, so manpower available to care for the land declined. Then the theater of war was often the countryside; farm families were killed, their property requisitioned by the troops, their crops, buildings, and terraces destroyed. Sometimes damage could be repaired, but often ecosystems were not given the time to recover, making them vulnerable to insects and diseases.

The extinction of species of animals and plants was noted above. This has a negative effect on the total organic system of the environment. Generally speaking, a complex ecosystem is more resilient than a simple one. This is because an ecosystem with many species has more ways of resisting depletion if it is subjected to stress. As one species after another is removed, the total complex becomes more liable to disaster. Thus by killing off many animals, the Romans were unwittingly undermining the ecosystems that supported the economy. This was true even when the species seemed harmful. Wolves, foxes, wildcats, and other predators were hunted out because they sometimes raided domestic animals, but the ordinary diets of predators included rodents that were even more damaging to crops, thus keeping their numbers down. Ancient writers recorded disastrous plagues of mice, for example, that consumed crops and stored grain, and that the reduced numbers of predators were unable to control, although none of these writers saw the connection.

Several factors noted above affected agricultural productivity in the Roman Mediterranean, where the economy was based on the agrarian sector. The inevitable result of the human failure to support nature was that nature could support fewer human beings. Industry, although not as large a part of the total economy as agriculture, had important effects. The scars left by Roman mines are still visible today. Mining and smelting operations did more than lay waste to local areas, however. The fuel needs of a large operation like the iron center at Populonia could consume annually the growth of wood provided by an average forest of a million acres. There were many such centers, and one has to add to their fuel demands the great amounts of wood and charcoal required by the pottery industry.

Pollution was produced by Roman industry. Its extent and importance is a matter of controversy. That dangerous smoke was produced by some operations is a matter of record; Strabo (*Geography* 3.2.8) observed that silver-smelting furnaces in Iberia were built with high chimneys to carry the deadly smoke away from the workers. Lead is the predominant metal in silver ore: it and other poisonous elements like mercury and arsenic were present in industrial processes such as the working of other metallic ores, pottery, leather, and textiles. Workers in these materials were notably subject to poisoning. It is less clear how much the general population was exposed to toxic substances, but it is a public health factor of possibly major proportions. Lead, or silver with high lead content, was used in utensils, dishes, and cooking pots. Sweeteners, jam, and fish sauces contained a high concentration of lead compounds. It was of course the upper classes that used silver service and consumed these delicacies. Water was often conducted through lead pipes or aqueducts sealed with lead, and acidic water can be contaminated by lead. Studies of the Greenland ice cap have shown that lead in the atmosphere due to the smelting industry increased dramatically during Roman times. Bones from Roman burials exhibit a variable, but often very high, lead content. The effects of lead poisoning include interference with reproduction, physical weakness, and dulling of the intellectual faculties, and these are cumulative, slow to develop, long-lasting, and not easily seen to be connected with the cause. In addition, mercury was commonly used in gold refining, and arsenic appeared in pigments and medicines. It is likely that large numbers of people in the Roman Empire suffered from varying degrees of environmental poisoning produced by industrial processes.

The poor quality of the urban environment is a subject of frequent comment, particularly by Roman poets of the early empire. Noise pollution and smoke receive the most notice. Air pollution from smoke and dust was bad in the larger cities, judging from contemporary ancient comment. Food was cooked, and rooms were commonly heated, by open wood or charcoal fires. Cities in the Roman Empire had huge public baths whose furnaces and hypocausts were heated with prodigious amounts of fuel. Smoky lamps and torches provided light. The air was so polluted in Rome that those who could afford it tried to find relief by frequent trips out of the city, and some commented that people coming back from the countryside would lose their tan in smoggy Rome within a few days. Juvenal, in his *Third Satire*, expanded the list of urban ills, complaining of traffic congestion, fires, public works projects that destroyed natural beauty, chamber pots emptied out of upper-story windows, and ever-increasing crime and vandalism.

Garbage and sewage disposal presented a serious health problem in ancient cities. The larger cities had sewers like Rome's *cloaca maxima*, which emptied into the river Tiber, an efficient arrangement except when the not uncommon floods, exacerbated by the deforestation of the Tiber watershed, backed the effluents up into the city. It was said that at these times, the drain in the floor of the Pantheon looked like a fountain. The materials collected in latrines were sometimes used in tanneries. Many cities had carts to carry the worst of the garbage outside the walls, but much of it collected in the streets. Pompeii installed "stepping stones" so that pedestrians could cross the muck-filled avenues. The debris of living is, of course, one reason that ancient cities gradually rose above their surroundings on elevations of human origin. The effects on the health of urban populations, with water pollution, vermin, and diseases, are evident, and the sanitary conditions must have favored the spread of the plagues that swept across the Mediterranean world from time to time.

Conclusion

The conclusion that must be drawn is that the structure of the society and economy of the Romans caused environmental changes that depleted their natural resources and were of critical importance in hampering their ability to feed the population, to maintain health, and to prosper. These changes therefore weakened society, depleting its human resources.[1] Their effects were felt early, but were cumulative, reaching a devastating level by the middle of the third century. The problems, modified but not solved by the reforms of Diocletian, would continue to plague the empire in the following centuries.

Note

1. In mentioning probable declines in the population of the Roman Empire, as well as the various estimates of population percentages included earlier in this chapter, it must be admitted that these are qualitative estimates based on ancient literary

sources, inscriptions, and archaeological evidence. There are no dependable quantitative records or generally accepted proxies for them. The Roman government took censuses including the biblical one (Luke 2.1–5), and numbers exist, but they are of certain categories only and are not controlled geographically. Boak (1955:3–21) gave the widely varying estimates then available, which clustered around a population of from 50 to 65 million at the height of prosperity in the second century AD, with a drop to about 40 million in the ensuing period of plague and military crisis. Boak did not commit himself to a numerical estimate of his own, but indicated that he conservatively favored lower rather than higher figures. The situation has not improved much since then, with many scholars avoiding the subject entirely. A search for "population" or "census" in indices in recent studies is enlightening only in showing the lack of such entries. MacMullen (1988:1–57) made an impressive survey of quantitative evidence of many kinds, but scrupulously avoided any attempt to estimate population. Figures at this time cannot be regarded as definitive.

References

Aubert, J.-J. 2001. The fourth factor: Managing non-agricultural production in the Roman world. In *Economies beyond agriculture in the classical world*, ed. D. J. Mattingly and J. Salmon, 90–112. London and New York: Routledge.

Boak, A. E. R. 1955. *Manpower shortage and the fall of the Roman Empire in the west.* Ann Arbor: University of Michigan Press.

Charlesworth, M. P. 1951. Roman trade with India: A resurvey. In *Studies in Roman economic and social history*, ed. P. R. Coleman-Norton, 131–143. Princeton, N.J.: Princeton University Press.

Duncan-Jones, R. 1990. *Structure and scale in the Roman economy*. Cambridge, U.K.: Cambridge University Press.

Finley, M. I. 1999. *The ancient economy*. Berkeley and Los Angeles: University of California Press.

Frank, A. G., and B. K. Gills, eds. 1993. *The world system: Five hundred years or five thousand?* London and New York: Routledge.

Garnsey, P., and R. Saller. 1982. *The early principate: Augustus to Trajan.* Oxford: Clarendon Press.

Hughes, J. D. 1994. *Pan's travail: Environmental problems of the ancient Greeks and Romans.* Baltimore: Johns Hopkins University Press.

———. 2001. *Environmental history of the world: Humankind's changing role in the community of life.* London and New York: Routledge.

———. 2005. *The Mediterranean: An environmental history.* Santa Barbara, Calif.: ABC-CLIO.

MacMullen, R. 1988. *Corruption and the decline of Rome.* New Haven, Conn.: Yale University Press.

Morley, N. 1996. *Metropolis and hinterland: The city of Rome and the Italian economy, 200 B.C.–A.D. 200.* Cambridge, U.K.: Cambridge University Press.

Rostovtzeff, M. 1971. *The social and economic history of the Roman Empire.* 2nd ed. 2 vols. Oxford: Clarendon Press.

Schiavone, A. 2002. *The end of the past: Ancient Rome and the modern west.* Cambridge, Mass.: Harvard University Press.

Simkhovitch, V. G. 1921. Rome's fall reconsidered. In *Toward the understanding of Jesus and other historical studies,* 84–139. New York: Macmillan.

Williams, S. 1985. *Diocletian and the Roman recovery.* New York: Methuen.

"People Said Extinction Was Not Possible": Two Thousand Years of Environmental Change in South China

2

ROBERT B. MARKS

T HE IDEA OF SPECIES extinction emerged early in the nineteenth century, not only in Europe, but in China as well. In France, Georges Cuvier studied the anatomy of fossil remains, and, concluding that some species had indeed become extinct, in 1812 published his findings in *Discours sur les révolutions de la surface du globe*. Rejecting J. B. Lamarck's theory of "transmutation," which purported to explain fossil remains as old forms of existing species, Cuvier argued that great geological catastrophes accounted for extinctions (Bowler 1993:216–217).

In China, one year before the publication of Cuvier's book, an official by the name of Deng Bi'nan also wrote about extinctions. While posted in Leizhou prefecture in the South China province of Guangdong, Deng wrote in the "local products" section of the prefectural gazetteer:

> Northerners record that Leizhou produced teeth and ivory from black elephants, and noted that in Xuwen there were *bao niu* (a kind of buffalo). *The Records of Jiaozhou* [a fourth-century text] say that Xuwen had the giant centipede.... [An earlier] provincial gazetteer records that in the wilds of Leizhou deer were plentiful, and that the "fragrant navel of the civet" could substitute for musk-deer.... Today these do not exist [*wu zhe*]. (*Leizhou fuzhi* 1811:juan 2, 67a–b)[1]

Although both Cuvier and Deng had come to understand that entire species could vanish, they had come to that understanding in rather different ways, and they had quite different explanations for extinctions too. Like other European naturalists, Cuvier had been examining the stratifications in fossil records, in his case, from areas around Paris, and was seeking explanations for the observed changes. His "catastrophic" explanation soon gave way, via Charles Lyell in England, to a more gradualist explanation that located the processes of species extinction as "part of the normal operation of Nature" (Bowler 1993:283). Although Lyell did not posit a mechanism by which species became extinct, in 1859 Charles Darwin did with the publication of *On the Origin of Species*: evolution as a product of natural selection brought about by competition and the struggle for existence. Influenced by Malthus's *Essay on Population*, Darwin arrived at "a theory of evolution by ecological replacement. As he put it, he had arrived at 'the absolute knowledge that species die and others replace them" (Worster 1994:159).

Despite the differences among nineteenth-century European scientists, they all assigned "natural" causes to the extinction of species (Worster 1994:142). Not so Deng Bi'nan. Deng articulated a relationship of living things to "the land:"

> Because local products come from the land [and because there are changes in the land], the local products too change over time. Of the common ones mentioned in the ancient texts, just 80–90% exist today; of the rare ones, just 20–30% survive. [Today], there is no land that has not changed, so the times are no longer the same either. (*Leizhou fuzhi* 1811:juan 2, 67a–b)

The various plants and animals in Leizhou, Deng was saying, are connected with "the land," and as there were changes in the land, Deng reasoned, so too were there changes in the plant and animal community, sometimes leading to extinction.

The question, of course, is what caused those "changes in the land"? Deng did not have to state it explicitly, for the world in which he was living provided ample evidence for the cause of the changes: human activity. What this chapter will explore is the two-thousand-year history of human changes to South China, revealing a history in which virtually every inch of the landscape had been worked and reworked by human hands, a history that was palpable to Deng Bi'nan: "Today, there is no land that has not changed." Significantly, Deng's evidence for extinctions came from the written record, not the fossil record. Unlike Europeans, whose connection with their past was discontinuous and marred by the "dark ages," literate Chinese of the Qing dynasty (1644–1911) were connected to their three-millennia past via written records. And it was Deng's reading of these written records regarding the area of his posting that led him to conclude, contrary to what others believed, that anthropogenic changes in the land had led to extinctions.

The Land

This chapter deals with environmental changes in that part of China known historically as Lingnan. Lingnan is the region of South China stretching from Hainan Island in the south to the Nanling mountain range in the north; Lingnan means "south of the mountain range," which it is. Roughly speaking it is the area within a two-hundred-mile radius of Hong Kong, and is nearly coterminous with Guangdong and Guangxi provinces, an area about the size of France (Marks 1998:ch.1).

Given the virtual absence by the twentieth century of any natural forest, reconstructing what kind of forests originally (i.e. some two thousand years ago, before human populations dramatically altered the environment) might have covered Lingnan is not easy, requiring botanists to examine climatic conditions, compare conditions in Lingnan with regions elsewhere in the world, investigate the few, inaccessible mountain areas where forest still stands, consult historical records, and conduct field experiments. While much uncertainty remains, to date the most extensive considerations of the issue have been conducted by Wang Chi-wu (Wang 1961) and by Chinese scientists whose synthesized findings were published in 1982 (*Zhongguo ziran dili* 1982). According to these studies, the original forests of Lingnan included three main types: (1) an evergreen broad-leafed forest composed mainly of evergreen oaks (and associated trees like the laurel), which grew on the inland hills of northern Guangdong and throughout much of Guangxi; (2) a tropical rain forest, growing in the lower elevations (below 100 m) in the southern parts of Guangdong and Guangxi, and on Hainan Island, composed of many species of straight-trunked trees forming a high canopy above the forest floor; and (3) a littoral forest on the coast, including mangrove swamps submerged in brackish water. Lingnan two thousand years ago, in short, was covered by tropical and semitropical rainforests.

The People

The Original Inhabitants

Lingnan was inhabited first not by Chinese but by other peoples. To be sure, Chinese had settled in Lingnan as early as the Qin dynasty (ca. 221 BCE), albeit in small numbers, but even then the Chinese were invading territory inhabited for millennia by various non-Chinese groups. In the lowlands of the river valleys and along the coast were various Tai peoples, the largest group now called the Zhuang, with a smaller group called the Li in the littoral belt on the Leizhou peninsula and the coastal strip on Hainan Island (Csete 1995).

Others called Yao migrated in at various times, but with the lowlands already occupied, they settled in the hills and practiced slash-and-burn, shifting agriculture. In contrast, the lowland Tai peoples grew wet rice, cast bronze, wove silk, and by about 300 BCE had organized themselves into a state called Yue. With a state system and knowledge of sericulture and metallurgy, the Tai were the only people whom the Chinese did not consider barbarians (*man*). But that did not prevent the Qin from conquering them, which they did over a period of years (234–222 BCE). The Tai ruling elite fled south to organize another state in Thailand, leaving behind the Tai agriculturists in the lowlands.

Predating (or concurrent with, in the case of the Yao) Chinese settlement of Lingnan, then, a half million or so non-Chinese peoples had developed two different agricultural regimes, one for the lowlands and one for the uplands (Moseley 1973:12). In the lowlands, the Tai planted wet rice, maybe in paddies and maybe in the same plot year after year, while in the uplands the Yao slashed and burned their way through the hills, probably waiting twenty to twenty-five years before burning them once more, and on the coastal littoral and Hainan Island, Li peoples pursued a more desultory approach to growing food.

Chinese Migrants

Chinese migration into Lingnan came in three principal waves, the first a small one following the Qin subjugation of the Yue kingdom around 225 BCE, when some hundred thousand or so troops occupied Lingnan and then intermarried with local Tai women. The second wave came in the early fourth century CE, when nomadic tribesmen invaded north China and sacked the Chinese imperial capital at Loyang, bringing on the "Yongjia Panic," when inhabitants of North China fled south. The third wave began similarly in the twelfth century when Central Asians—this time the Jin armies (predecesors of the Mongols)—in 1126 CE took the Song capital in Kaifeng, forcing the Song to relocate their capital south of the Yangzi River in Hangzhou; this third wave continued in the 1270s, when the Mongols began their push to conquer all of China (Li et al. 1993:171–205). As many historians have noted, when northern nomadic invaders pressed south of the Great Wall, they set off a chain reaction wave of Chinese migration south (Gumilev 1987:23). Many of those fleeing the war and disorder in the north found their way through the Nanling passes and into Lingnan.

By 1850 the population of Lingnan had gone through three great waves. In the first, beginning from the time of the first recorded human settlement

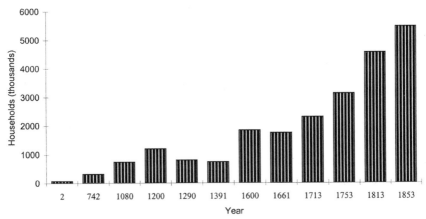

Figure 2.1.   Estimated population of Lingnan, 2–1853 CE. *Source:* Robert B. Marks, *Tigers, Rice, Silk and Silt: Environment and Economy in Late Imperial South China* (New York: Cambridge University Press, 1998), 278

in Lingnan in 2 CE, population increased to a peak around 1200 in the Southern Song, after which the Mongol invasions sent population declining until about 1400, when peace returned to China under the Ming dynasty. Relative to the population peak in the Southern Song, Lingnan in 1400 had become relatively depopulated, and had reached a low point from which population increased slowly but steadily for another 250 years. The second wave thus corresponds mostly to the Ming dynasty (1368–1644), with population declining by a quarter to a third in the mid-seventeenth century because of the wars, epidemics, and famines attending the transition to the Qing dynasty. The third wave began in the late seventeenth century, when peace once again returned and the population started growing, by 1700 surpassing previous levels and never declining to pre-1600 levels again. Indeed, the third wave is not yet complete, with population increasing still, and probably continuing until well into the twenty-first century.

The Farms

The most densely populated part of late imperial Lingnan (ca. 1400–1800)—the Pearl River delta—became the most agriculturally rich region in Lingnan, and hence the most densely populated. Formed of alluvial soils that had been captured from the silt flowing down from the major rivers, these "sand flats" (*shatan*), as the Chinese called them, were worked and re-worked, until they became very productive rice paddies producing, by the sixteenth century, two crops of rice and one of vegetables or wheat annually

(Braudel 1981:151). While peasant farmers produced much of the food the family consumed, agriculture in Lingnan could not be called "subsistence" farming, for many nonfood commercial crops were grown and exchanged in markets that dotted the countryside. Besides rice, peasant farmers in the Pearl River delta grew sugar cane, hemp, cotton, and mulberries for silk worms; the most important cycle of exchange involved rice for textiles (or the raw materials to make them, hemp and cotton), and vice versa. Indigo, tea, and fruits also were important crops.

But while commerce and market exchanges were an important part of the rural economy, even in the most remote parts of Lingnan, until about 1550 it is unwarranted to think of the rural economy as being commercialized. To be sure, as the population grew from 1400 to 1550, the gross amount of crops marketed and the number of rural markets increased, but they did so at the same rate as the growth of population. Indeed, the proportion of agricultural land devoted to commercial crops in 1550 was about what it had been in 1400. But from 1550 on, the agricultural economy of Lingnan became highly commercialized, by which I mean that markets and marketing activity expanded at a rate faster than that of the population.

The most immediate stimulus for the commercialization of the economy was the expansion of export possibilities for numerous goods produced in and around South China, especially silk, sugar, and porcelain, among other items that Chinese merchants capitalized on, spurring further expansion of agricultural and industrial productive capacity. Most of the trade in the early sixteenth century was with Japan and Southeast Asia, and later with Portuguese and Dutch traders as well. As is now well known, huge amounts of silver flowed into China, not necessarily in payment for Chinese exports, but because of the demand in China for silver expressed in high silver prices relative to gold and copper (von Glahn 1996:126–142; Flynn and Giraldez 1995:201–222; Frank 1998:111–116). After 1571, trade through Manila also brought silver into the South China economy. Chinese merchants from Guangdong and Fujian provinces sailed to Manila with their goods, which the Spanish exchanged for silver from the American mines; from there the silver flowed back to China, and the Chinese commodities found their way to Europe. By 1600, this trade resulted in an annual inflow of perhaps 200,000 kilograms of silver into the coastal economies of south and southeast China, from Ningpo south to Guangzhou (Atwell 1977, 1982).

The increased exports of silk precipitated significant changes in land-use patterns. In the Pearl River delta, the silk industry developed on a base that had been created first by the "sand flat" fields, and then a particular combination of fish ponds with fruit trees. In the fifteenth century, peasant farmers in the Pearl River delta began replacing some of their "sand flat" rice fields with fish ponds, probably in response to increased demand from the city of Guangzhou. The mud and the muck raked up into embankments above the flood plain protected the ponds from flooding, while the high water table filled the hole with water, and the pond was stocked with various kinds of carp fry netted from local waters. On the embankments, peasant farmers in the early Ming planted mostly fruit trees (*long-yan*, litchi, etc.), giving rise to the "fruit tree and fish pond" (*guo ji yu tang*) combination. The carp fed on organic matter that either dropped or was thrown into the pond, while the muck scooped up from the pond fertilized the fruit trees and the rice fields, and added height to the embankments and more protection for the fish ponds.

The "fruit tree and fish pond" culture provided a ready-made base for expansion of the silk industry when increased demand warranted. As the demand for silk increased, peasant farmers replaced the fruit trees with mulberry trees, giving rise to the "mulberry tree and fish pond" system, and then began digging up even more rice paddies. By 1581, in the Longshan area of Shunde county, 18 percent of the productive "land" was fish ponds, and when combined with the mulberry trees on the embankments, accounted for about 30 percent of the cultivated land area (Ye and Tan 1985:22).[2]

Commercialization of Rice

As peasant farmers dug up the rice fields for the "mulberry tree and fish pond" system, they turned to the market to purchase their food, and markets grew both in size and in number. To meet the food demands in the Pearl River delta, peasant farmers elsewhere in Lingnan began producing rice for export. Throughout the East, West, and North River drainage basins, local markets gathered rice from their hinterlands for export downriver to the delta. As far up the East River as Heyuan, the market exported rice downriver, and even the market in Yong'an, perhaps one of the most remote and least accessible counties in all of Lingnan, exported rice to Heyuan. In Guangxi, two of the three largest rice export markets were on the West River, one in Wuzhou and the other upriver at Xunzhou; a third collected rice from Liuzhou prefecture. Rice merchants from Guangzhou and Foshan established offices (*hui guan*) at all of the third-level markets, and were quite active in purchasing rice for the Guangdong market. Indeed, the most important commercial crop throughout the vast Lingnan hinterland drained by these major rivers was rice. So great was market demand for rice by the nineteenth century that peasants in Fengchuan county (up the West River near the border with Guangxi) "ate yams and sweet potatoes in order to sell rice for cash," and in Cangwu and Cenxi counties peasants without immediate access to water transportation carried sacks of rice on their backs to market (Luo 1987:8–15). By the middle of the eighteenth century, the trade in rice knit all of Lingnan together into a single market, sending rice from low-priced surplus areas to the place where demand and prices were the highest, in the Pearl River delta. Food flowed throughout the system, amounting to as much of 25 percent of all rice grown in Lingnan.

From the late Ming through the nineteenth century (and into the twentieth, for that matter), the commercialization of agriculture thus had precipitated changes in cropping and land-use patterns, transforming rice paddies into fish ponds and mulberry fields in the Pearl River delta, and into sugar cane fields all along the coast, down to and including the Leizhou peninsula. A landscape in Guangdong province that had been covered with rice fields thus was reworked under the demands of commerce into a new landscape, one that said "trade" rather than "food." But if these changes in the land were restricted to fields that already supported agriculture, in the eighteenth century pressures were building to clear more forested land for agriculture, transforming wooded hills and plains into human artifice.

Over the century from 1753 to 1851, official state figures for Lingnan register just a 10 percent increase in the amount of cultivated land, an amount more or less in line with the amount of land reported as reclaimed and added to the tax rolls. These official figures, though, are notoriously inaccurate, not just because the Qing state never conducted a land survey to begin with, but also because of underreporting of new lands brought into cultivation (and hence kept off the tax rolls).

In my estimation, between 1693 and 1853, an additional 20 million *mu* (one *mu* = approximately one-sixth of an acre) was brought into production in each of the Guangdong and Guangxi provinces, doubling to 80 million *mu* the cultivated land acreage in Lingnan from anything experienced before. In terms of the percentage of the total Lingnan land area under cultivation, the amount increased from about 14 percent around 1713 to 24 percent in 1853, representing some 10,000 square kilometers of land. And because of the way in which land reclamation unfolded, most of those 10,000 square kilometers were marginal fields in the hills. After 1853, little additional land was brought under the plow, indicating that the limits of cultivable land in Guangdong province had been reached by the middle of the nineteenth century.

The Tiger

The obverse of the story of land clearance is the story of deforestation, but since eighteenth- and even nineteenth-century sources do not speak directly to the issue, that story can only be pieced together using later and indirect evidence. By the early twentieth century, though, the results were plain to those who began to look. In the hills of northern Guangdong, the forestry expert G. Fenzel observed "vast stretches of flat, barren hills, [with] wild grass growth" (Fenzel 1929:81). If evidence both from earlier periods and from the twentieth century can be used to illuminate the eighteenth-century land clearance, fire had been used to remove the forest cover and to ready the hillside for planting (Fenzel 1929:92–93).

Land clearance for agriculture was not, of course, the only cause of deforestation: logging provided raw materials for the furniture, building, and shipping industries. Wood from forests also had been the major source of fuel for cooking and heating. How much this demand for energy contributed to deforestation is anybody's guess, but there is clear evidence from the early nineteenth century that wood was no longer available for use as a fuel, at least in some parts of Lingnan. According to Captain J. Ross, who traveled overland from Hainan Island to Guangzhou in 1819 following the wreck of his ship, "this part of China is badly supplied with firewood, and the people are obliged to substitute straw, hay, and cow-dung." It was not that there were no trees, but that there were so few: "the country . . . was well cultivated, though hilly, with a few groves of small pines." The reason for the scarcity of forest, of course, is that peasant farmers had cleared and planted the land, which Ross described as "hilly and poorly cultivated, producing chiefly sweet potatoes, with a sprinkling of other vegetables" (*The Chinese Repository* 1849:247).

The vast, treeless grasslands observed in the early twentieth century thus had emerged as a result of a historical process of burning off the forest, planting a crop for two or three years, and then moving on to another location without replanting trees. By the twentieth century, the Yao tribesmen whom Fenzel observed had taken to replanting trees after they moved on; but Chinese did not do so then, and probably had not in earlier times either. After abandoning a cleared hillside, "the land is often invaded so seriously by weeds that further cropping is impossible," according to Robert Pendleton, a botanist who had studied similar processes in the Philippines (Pendleton 1933:555). After five or ten years, scrub brush might grow, and the soil regain some fertility, making it possible to burn it off again. "If, however, the weeds and the brush growing up in the abandoned clearings are removed by annual burning, tree growth has little chance to develop" (Pendleton 1933:556).

And in Lingnan, at least in the twentieth century, peasants habitually burned off the hills every year or two, not only rendering the hills unfit for replanting, but also preventing trees from growing. In Guangxi, Steward observed that the peasant farmers "habitually fire most of the burnable slopes in the vicinity of the homes during the dry season each year. The continuation of this practice tends to destroy the majority of the species of woody plants and change the aspect of a once richly forested country to that of a hilly or mountainous grassland" (Steward 1934:1). In Guangdong too, according to Fenzel, Chinese farmers "annually burn down the grass covering the mountains" (Fenzel 1929:42).

In the twentieth century, peasant farmers gave several reasons why they burned off the hills. One was that "after burning off hills the grass ashes wash down the slopes serving as a source of fertilizing material for the lower agricultural land." Pendleton thought this unlikely, since "there are frequently dug contour ditches which carry away the water and eroded material from the hills to prevent flooding of the rice of other low lands" (Pendleton 1933:557). When Fenzel asked "the farmer why he annually burns down the grass covering the mountains . . . [the farmer] stereotypically replies that it is to deprive the robbers, tigers, and snakes of their dens" (Fenzel 1929:43).

Tiger Attacks

Along with notations on natural disasters, rebellions, and dragon sightings, the chronicles of local gazetteers are filled with reports of tiger attacks on villages. In 1680, for example, "In Xin'an county, many tigers injured people; [the tigers] were extremely numerous; the attacks stopped by the end of the year" (*Guangzhou fuzhi* 1879, juan 80–81, entry for KX19). Three years earlier, "hundreds of people" had been injured by tiger attacks in Lianping county (*Huizhou fuzhi* 1877, juan 17–18, entry for KX16). In the southwest littoral, tigers in 1723 attacked so many people and animals in Maoming that thirty-seven people died (*Gaoqing fuzhi*, juan 49, entry for YZ1). In Guangxi province too, tigers entered villages and attacked people and animals, as in Huaiji county in 1752, or in Liucheng county in 1696 (*Wuzhou fuzhi* 1769, entry for QL17; *Liuzhou fuzhi* 1764, entry for KX35). Villagers thus had reason to fear tigers, and tigers may well have been more numerous and threatening to peasant farmers than bandits.

The relevant and interesting thing about tigers, though, is their habitat: they live in forests, favoring in particular lowland riverine forests. Unlike lions, who prefer grasslands or savanna, tigers stalk their prey from the cover and the shadows provided by forests. The relationship is pretty simple: no forests, no tigers. The converse also held: where there were tigers, there were forests in Lingnan. And the forest had to have been quite large: a single adult tiger requires between 20 and 100 square kilometers of forested habitat to sustain itself, depending on the availability of large game. The tiger thus is a "star species," emblematic of an entire ecosystem and the rich biodiversity required to sustain it (Wilson 1992:259).

If Chinese peasant farmers and literate chroniclers paid no attention to forests and failed to comment on the deforestation of the hills, thereby leaving us with no written records from which to reconstruct the story of deforestation, they did note tigers, especially tigers who attacked villages. Since tigers are indicators of forests, reports of tiger attacks in the chronicles of Chinese gazetteers can serve as proxies for forests. Charting the time and place of the tiger attacks thus should produce a picture, however fuzzy, of where the forests were, and where they were not. For from the point of view of the Chinese agriculturists, land reclamation, the clearance of hills, and the annual burning over of the grasslands may have been existential activities assuring the human population its food supply, but from the point of view of the tiger, the same actions constituted the destruction of their habitat. The destruction of tiger habitat by burning off the forest cover reduced the tigers' food supply, and contributed both to tiger willingness to enter villages searching for food, and to their willingness to attack and eat people.

Tiger attacks thus are meaningful indicators simultaneously of forests and of the encroachment of humans into tiger habitat. What does the historical record for Lingnan show? Let us begin by working backward. Today, just a few tigers survive in the mountains on the border of northern Guangdong and Guangxi, not surprising in light of the extensive deforestation clearly documentable by the twentieth century (Lu 1987:71–74). In earlier centuries, the distribution of tigers was more general throughout Lingnan. Around 1700, according to Qu Dajun, "there are many tigers in Gaozhou, Leizhou, and Lianzhoufu. Merchants encounter them." Qu also noted that "in the wilds of Leizhou, there are many deer" (Qu 1974:531–532). For the rest of Lingnan we lack the sweeping generalizations provided by Qu Dajun, but the record of tiger attacks can tell the story. In densely populated Guangzhou prefecture, most of the tiger attack records are before 1700. Of interest in the Qing records are those from the 1660s, when the coastal population was relocated inland. When the people abandoned their fields, the land apparently rapidly reverted to scrub if not actually forest, and with the return of forest cover came the tigers: "Because of the relocation, grass and trees have grown in profusion [in the abandoned areas], and tigers have become bold" (*Huizhou fuzhi* 1877, juan 18, entry for KX6).

Significantly, in Guangzhou prefecture the last tiger attack on record is for 1690. After that, the record of tiger attacks ends, presumably coincident with the destruction of tiger habitat there. A similar story can be told about Chaozhou prefecture, where the last recorded tiger attack was in 1708. The last tiger attack in Gaozhou prefecture (which was second only to Guangzhou in population density in 1820) was recorded in 1723. To the east in Huizhou, though, the records of tiger attacks continue through the eighteenth century, and in peripheral Shaozhou and Nanxiong prefectures, the last records are in 1813 and 1815 respectively. Records are sparse in Guangxi, but in Wuzhou and Xunzhou, the last attacks were scattered from 1752 to 1777.

The records of tiger attacks in Lingnan are anything but complete—some prefectural gazetteers, such as Lianzhoufu and Leizhou, do not include annual chronicles, and certainly some tiger attacks escaped official notice. Furthermore, tigers lived in areas that did not record any attacks, such as Conghua county, which Qu Dajun said "has many tigers in the hills" (Qu 1974:531). Nonetheless, I think the story that the record of tiger attacks in Lingnan tells is clear enough. During the mid-seventeenth-century crisis when the human population decreased substantially and forest returned to much of Lingnan, the range of the tigers expanded, even into relatively densely populated areas like Guangzhou prefecture in the Pearl River delta. As population there (and elsewhere) began to recover and forests were cleared for agriculture, tigers and people came into contact. By 1700, tiger habitat probably had been destroyed in and around Guangzhou, while the hills in Guangdong and Guangxi remained forested, as was much of the southwestern littoral. As people moved into the hills and burned off forests, tiger attacks spread outward, ending in the early nineteenth century in northernmost Guangdong. The record of tiger attacks followed the destruction of their habitat, and the end of tiger attacks in the early nineteenth century dates the nearly complete destruction of tiger habitat in Lingnan by then.

The accumulated evidence thus suggests the rapid deforestation of Lingnan in the eighteenth century, coincident both with the population and cultivated land areas surpassing previous peaks in the Song and Ming, and with the periodic—if not annual—burning of grass off the hills. If, as Ling Daxie has estimated, forests in 1700 had covered about half of the land area of Lingnan, decreasing to 5–10 percent by 1937 (Ling 1983:25–35), then most of that deforestation and loss of habitat occurred during the eighteenth century.

The End

By 1800 the landscapes of Lingnan had been made and remade, and the Chinese had left evidence of their transformations of the land not just in the landscape, but in written records as well. Deng Bi'nan, the official we met at the beginning of this chapter writing in the "local products" section of the 1811 local gazetteer for Leizhou prefecture, thus was living at a time when the pace of environmental change was noticeable. If land clearance destroyed the habitat of the tiger, pushing it to the edge of extinction, the same fate awaited other wildlife too, as Deng reported. We can imagine Deng, an observant, curious, and scholarly man, turning to written records to find that they confirmed his feeling that species had been disappearing. With his observations confirmed by the written record, Deng then lamented both the passing of various species, and his fate at having recognized what was happening:

> The reason these extinctions were not recorded before is that people then said that extinction was not possible. . . . Today it is my task to record for posterity these extinctions in the appendix [to the local products section of the Leizhou gazetteer], [in the hope that my records will be of use] for later research. (*Leizhou fuzhi* 1811: juan 2, 67a–b)

Deng was not living in a scholarly vacuum in Qing China, for there was a long tradition of research with which he was no doubt familiar and which conditioned his views of the extent and causes of environmental change. Following the ancient Confucian injunction from *The Great Learning*—"the extension of knowledge lies in the investigation of things"—Chinese naturalists long had compiled treatises on plants and animals. One of the more recent (to Deng) would have been the early-eighteenth-century work by Chen Yuanlong, the *Perspective of Scientific and Technological Origins*, a work that included a wealth of information from rare and now lost books on plants and animals (Needham 1986:214). Whether Deng actually consulted that specific work or not, and who else in his time he might have discussed his ideas with, is not known. But the point is that Deng understood that he was writing in a specific scholarly tradition, and that his findings would be useful "for later research" of that particular scholarly community.

Indeed, the seventeenth and eighteenth centuries had seen the flourishing of a new school of scholarship, the *kaozheng*, or evidential scholarship. Deriving from a central concern for the reconstruction of antiquity based on rigorous study and critique of Han-era texts, *kaozheng* scholarship expanded in the eighteenth century to encompass most branches of knowledge as understood by the Chinese, including natural studies and historical geography. *Kaozheng* scholars kept notebooks for recording pertinent information as they read, and to note the sources of their information. Scholarly findings were passed via private meetings and letters among the scholarly elite (Elman 1984:174–77).

What Deng could not anticipate, of course, is how rapidly the world within which he lived, the one defined by the dynamics of the Chinese trade-tributary empire and the concerns of Confucian statecraft, soon would become enmeshed in the new world of competing, warring nation states emanating from western Europe, bringing an end to his other-ordered world. His work thus was not useful for "later research" as he understood it, but rather to an American historian at the end of the twentieth century.

Deng Bi'nan's lament, while providing evidence of extinction, also points to the significant question of causation of environmental change. For Deng, the world he lived in provided ample evidence of the anthropogenic origins of extinctions. Everywhere throughout Lingnan there were reminders of the power of the Chinese people to remake the landscape. Near Guilin was the Lingqu Canal, built by orders of the first emperor of Qin to link Lingnan's river systems with the Yangzi River; in northern Guangdong was the Meiling Pass, "chiseled" in 716 to facilitate trade from Guangzhou; in a prefecture neighboring Leizhou, a magistrate had redirected the flow of a river to increase irrigation to agriculture; and in Leizhou itself, seawalls some 25,000 *zhang* long (about 50 miles) constructed in the Song (ca. 1100) created over 10,000 *qing* (1 *qing* = 100 *mu*, or about 17 acres) of land (*Guangdong tongzhi* 1822: 2085–86). Additionally, the human population had increased so much in Deng's time that people pressed everywhere in Lingnan, eliminating the frontier; with the encouragement of their emperors, they cleared and terraced mountains to plant food; to meet foreign demand for their products, they tore up and replaced rice paddies with cane fields or fish ponds and mulberry trees; and to feed the urban population, they moved grain huge distances from where it was produced to where it was consumed. In short, there was ample evidence everywhere Deng looked of both changes in the land and of the causes of those changes: people.

That insight, of course, has a particularly contemporary ring, for it is quite different from the natural causes of extinction identified by nineteenth-century European scientists, including Darwin. So, which nineteenth-century body of thought is "true?" Deng's views—his scientific views—were grounded in his cultural, social, economic, and historic milieu. Does that make them "particular," "traditional," or "Oriental," as opposed to the universal, modern truths of Western science? Fortunately, social historians in the United States and Europe recently have dethroned the "heroic" model of science that arose in the culture wars of the Enlightenment (Appleby, Hunt, and Jacob 1994), insisting instead that "the ideas of science are open to much the same kind of treatment as other ideas. . . . Like all of man's [*sic*] intellectual life, scientific ideas grow out of specific cultural conditions and are validated by personal as well as social needs" (Worster 1994:x–xi).

Thus Darwin's ideas, as Donald Worster has shown, drew upon both Adam Smith's conceptualization of economic competition (reinforced by Darwin's encounters with the reality of industrialization in early-nineteenth-century London) and Malthus's "gloomy" explanation for the struggle for existence, thereby gaining acceptance in the Victorian world of raw capitalism and emergent imperialism: "The emphasis Darwin gave to competitive scrambling for place could not have been so credible to people living

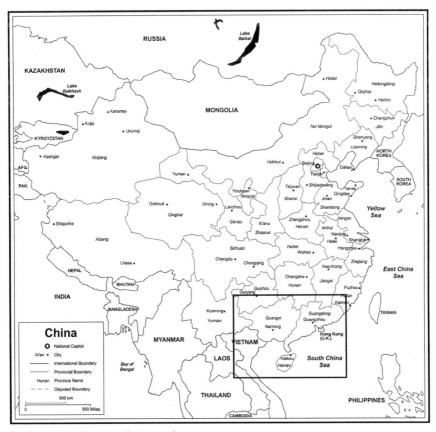

Map 2.1.   The location of Lingnan (box)

Map 2.2.   Lingnan ca. 1820

in another place and time" (Worster 1994:169). Moreover, while Herbert Spencer usually is blamed for extending Darwin's ideas into "social Darwinism," providing a rationale for both ignoring the poor at home and conquering others (barbarians) abroad, the fact of the matter is that Darwin himself harbored those ideas, especially the latter. Toward the end of his life, in 1881, Darwin opined that "the Caucasian races have beaten the Turkish hollow in the struggle for existence" and that "'an endless number of races' had to be wiped out by 'the higher civilized races'" for progress to occur (Worster 1994:165). In brief, since nature was an efficient economy, capitalism thus was natural, and Western dominance of the globe was inevitable. To most of the world's regret, we have lived with those equivalencies ever since. How different might the world have been had Deng Bi'nan's views instead spread to the West?

However congenial it might be for early-twenty-first-century environmental historians to consider, Deng Bi'nan's view of the anthropogenic causes of environmental change was not precocious, in the sense of an early flowering, for it came toward the end of two thousand years of China's imperial history, not at the beginning of the modern world. Hence his view of the anthropogenic, rather than natural, causes of extinction should be characterized more like Marx (famously paraphrasing Hegel) did the owl of Minerva, spreading its wings only as darkness began to fall (Hegel 1952:9).

Notes

1. The modern concept of "species extinction" was not available to Deng, so he used what was available to him in Chinese: the term *wu zhe*. *Wu* used alone means "without, apart from, none," but its antonym is *you*, meaning "to have, to exist." As the opposite of "to exist," *wu* thus meant "to not exist." And by adding the suffix *zhe* to *wu*, forming *wu zhe*, Deng created the term "those that do not exist." Whether Deng also had available to him a Chinese taxonomical concept of "species" is an open question.

2. The "mulberry (or fruit) tree and fish pond" system often is cited an example of a sustainable, premodern agricultural ecosystem. In any sustainable ecosystem, natural or otherwise, the mineral and energy resources necessary for life are recycled, and the losses from the system are so small that they can be easily replaced (such as by the weathering of rock or the fixation of nitrogen by bacteria). That, in essence, is what the fish pond system accomplished. Silk worm excrement, leaves from the trees, and other organic material were gathered and thrown into the fish pond, providing food for the carp; the fish were harvested annually, with the muck formed from the fish waste and other decomposed organic matter then scooped out and used to fertilize the mulberry trees and rice fields. In the words of a modern ecologist, "there is a closed nutrient recycling loop via decomposition and mineralization in orchards, fields, and ponds. Nutrient export across the system boundaries takes place only with stream runoff, and with sales of plant or animal products" (Bruenig et al. 1986).

References

Appleby, J., L. Hunt, and M. Jacob. 1994. *Telling the truth about history*. New York and London: Norton.

Atwell, W. S. 1977. Notes on silver, foreign trade, and the Late Ming economy. *Ch'ing Shih Wen-t'i* 3 (8): 1–33.

———. 1982. International bullion flows and the Chinese economy circa 1530–1650. *Past and Present* 95:68–90.

Bowler, P. J. 1993. *The Norton history of the environmental sciences*. New York and London: Norton.

Braudel, F. 1981. *Civilization and capitalism 15th–18th century*. Vol.1, *The structures of everyday life*, trans. Siân Reynolds. New York: Harper and Row.

Bruenig, E. F., et al. 1986. *Ecological-socioeconomic system analysis and simulation: A guide for application of system analysis to the conservation, utilization, and development of tropical and subtropical land resources in China*. Bonn: Deutsches Nationalkomitee für das UNESCO Programm "Der Mensch und die Biosphäre."

Csete, A. 1995. A frontier minority in the Chinese world: The Li people of Hainan Island from the Han through the high Qing. PhD diss., State University of New York at Buffalo.

Elman, B. A. 1984. *From philosophy to philology: Intellectual and social aspects of change in late imperial China*. Cambridge, Mass.: Harvard University Council on East Asian Studies.

Fenzel, G. 1929. On the natural conditions affecting the introduction of forestry as a branch of rural economy in the province of Kwangtung, especially in north Kwangtung. *Lingnan Science Journal* 7.

Flynn, D. O., and A. Giraldez. 1995. Born with a "silver spoon": The origin of world trade. *Journal of World History* 6 (2): 201–222.

Frank, A. G. 1998. *ReOrient: Global trade in the Asian age*. Berkeley and Los Angeles: University of California Press.

Gaoqing fuzhi. Qing era.

Guangdong tongzhi. 1822.

Guangzhou fuzhi. 1879.

Gumilev, L. N. 1987. *Searches for the imaginary kingdom of Prester John*, trans. R. E. F. Smith. New York: Cambridge University Press.

Hegel, G. W. F. 1952. Preface to *The Philosophy of Right*, trans. T. M. Knox. Chicago, London, and Toronto: Encyclopaedia Britannica.

Huizhou fuzhi. 1877.

Leizhou fuzhi. 1811.

Li, Z., et al., eds. 1993. *Lingnan wenhua*. Shaoguan: Guangdong renmin chuban she.

Ling, D. 1983. Wo guo senlin ziyuan de bianqian. *Zhongguo Nongshi* 2:25–35.

Liuzhou fuzhi. 1764.

Lu, H. 1987. Habitat availability and prospects for tigers in China. In *Tigers of the world: The biology, biopolitics, management, and conservation of an endangered species*, ed. R. L. Tilson and U. S. Seal. Park Ridge, N.J.: Noyes Publications.

Luo, Y. 1987. Shi lun Qing dai qian zhong qi Lingnan shichang zhongxin de fenbu tedian. Paper presented at the Fourth International Conference on Qing Social and Economic History, Shenzhen.

Marks, R. B. 1998. *Tigers, rice, silk, and silt: Environment and economy in late imperial south China*. New York: Cambridge University Press.

Moseley, G. 1973. *The consolidation of the south China frontier*. Berkeley and Los Angeles: University of California Press.

Needham, J. 1986. *Science and civilization in China*. Vol. 6, *Biology and biological technology*, pt. 1, *Botany*. Cambridge, U.K., and New York: Cambridge University Press.

Pendleton, R. 1933. Cogonals and reforestation with *Leucaena glauca*. *Lingnan Science Journal*.

Qu, D., ed. 1974 (1700 text). *Guangdong xinyu*. Hong Kong: Zhonghua Shuju.

Steward, R. 1934. The burning of vegetation on mountain land, and slope cultivation in Ling Yuin Hsien, Kwangsi province, China. *Lingnan Science Journal*.

The Chinese Repository. 1849. vol. 18.

Von Glahn, R. 1996. *Fountain of fortune.* Berkeley and Los Angeles: University of California Press.

Wang, C. 1961. *The forests of China.* Cambridge, Mass.: Harvard University Press.

Wilson, E. O. 1992. *The diversity of life.* Cambridge, Mass.: Belknap.

Worster, D. 1994. *Nature's economy.* 2nd ed. Cambridge, U.K., and New York: Cambridge University Press.

Wuzhou fuzhi. 1769.

Ye, X., and D. Tan. 1985. Lun Zhujiang sanjiaozhou de zu tian. In *Ming Qing Guangdong shehui jingji xingtai yanjiu.* Guangzhou: Guangdong renmin chuban she.

Zhongguo ziran dili. 1982. Vol. 10, *Lishi ziran dili.* Beijing: Kexue chuban she.

Precolonial Landesque Capital: A Global Perspective

3

MATS WIDGREN

T HIS CHAPTER ADDRESSES a phenomenon of wide significance for past and future agricultural potential—landesque capital. This is understood as investments made in land with an anticipated life beyond that of the present crop, or crop cycle. Irrigation canals and agricultural terraces are the most obvious forms of landesque capital, but the clearance of stones and the improvement of agricultural soils over the years are other, albeit less spectacular, examples. It is argued that, alongside the more obvious factors of climate and soil, the distribution of landesque capital—and hence the history of land use—is an important factor in understanding global differences in the productivity of agricultural lands. The occurrence of landesque capital has, over the years, been explained from a number of different perspectives: as a direct or indirect reflection of semiarid and arid lands, as the result of diffusion, as a consequence of historical "siege" situations, or as resulting from the accumulation strategies of chiefdoms and empires. It is argued that most of these general approaches to the explanation of landesque capital make the mistake of not fully taking into account the spatial aspect of landesque capital. They tend to reflect a historic and economic rather than a geographical understanding of investments. Unlike monetary capital, which is fluid in space but fixed in time, landesque capital is fixed in space but "fluid" in time. The chronological and social contexts of its use, managements, and further development can differ significantly from the contexts that once shaped it.

What Is Landesque Capital?

The term "landesque capital" came into wider use in the 1980s, when the Australian geographer Harold Brookfield (1984) used the term to characterize a type of innovation that "once created persists with the need only of maintenance." The term was later given a more strict definition as "any investment in land with an anticipated life well beyond that of the present crop, or crop cycle" (Blaikie and Brookfield 1987:9). In commenting on the origins of the term, Brookfield (2001b:55) recently clarified that the term "was developed within agricultural economics, and I cannot recall from where I borrowed it when I first used it in 1984. In the broad field of cultural ecology it is often attributed to me, but unfortunately I cannot claim that credit." The earliest documented use of the term that I have been able to find is in Amartya Sen's work on agricultural techniques (Sen 1968 [1960]). Brookfield's use of the term, however, does not (directly) relate to Sen's work and it was at least not directly from Sen that he borrowed the term (Brookfield, personal communication, February 2005). Sen made the distinction between two types of capital goods, "those which replace labour (e.g. tractors) and those which replace land (e.g. fertilisers). We may call them for the sake of brevity, 'labouresque' capital and 'landesque' capital respectively" (Sen 1968:82).

Sen exemplified landesque capital with fertilizers, irrigation, and pest control, all of which increase productivity per unit of land (laboresque capital, on the other hand, increases yield per unit of labor). Some of these landesque capital investments are not enduring in the sense implied by Brookfield's definition (the effect of the capital input does not necessarily extend beyond the actual cropping season, e.g. pest control). In one of his examples, Sen makes the assumption that both laboresque and landesque capital become exhausted on a yearly basis (Sen 1968:83). Other capital inputs exemplified by Sen (e.g. permanent structures for irrigation) do however correspond to Brookfield's definition of landesque capital. There is thus an important difference between Sen's definition and Brookfield's later one. It is of course important to note the difference in approaches adopted by these two scholars writing in different contexts: Sen's production-oriented approach from 1960, and Brookfield's approach to understanding land degradation and environmental problems from 1984.

If we are to search for antecedents to Brookfield's definition of landesque capital, it is in fact in Karl Marx's definition of "*la terre*-capital" or "land-capital" that more closely allied terms are to be found. With these terms, Marx meant that capital was "fixed in the land, incorporated in it" either in a transitory manner or on a more permanent basis (Marx 1959:618–619). Marx was well aware of the role that different kinds of land improvement could play, as well as the ways in which this capital could be devalued through improper use.

It seems that Brookfield's definition of landesque capital has gained more ground than Sen's. Indeed, I have only found a few articles that use Sen's conceptualization of landesque capital. Brookfield's usage, on the other hand, has become a widely used concept, especially within political ecology. There is thus no reason to argue further about the terms. In the following, I use Brookfield's "landesque capital" in a manner that approximates Marx's "land-capital," rather than the broader usage found in Sen's use of the term.

As such, the term "landesque capital" includes a wide variety of properties of land—from irrigation structures to anthropogenic soils and even tree vegetation (Brookfield 2001b:55). Brookfield provides several examples to demonstrate how the use of land has resulted in increased soil quality, and shows that these soils can retain their characteristics over long periods of time (Brookfield 2001b:97, 168).

The clearance cairn fields in southern Sweden provide a good example. In large parts of southern Sweden the forest soils are leached to a lesser extent than one would expect given the climatic conditions, the parent rock, and the time period since the retreat of the inland ice (Olsson and Troedsson 1990). These forest soils are hence more productive than would be expected had they been "naturally developed." This is to a large extent the effect of widespread cultivation and stone-clearance that began in the first millennium BC, and the subsequent periods of stone-clearance and cultivation on outlying lands especially during the first millennium AD and up until the early medieval period ca. 1400 (Widgren 2003; Lagerås and Bartholin 2003). The successive clearance of stones from peripheral lands has facilitated the reuse of such land for later cultivation—including forestry—and, furthermore, the tillage has served to delay the natural leaching process of the soils.[1]

An approach to the environment that considers landesque capital as central thus confronts stereotyped images of relations between humans and nature. First, it acknowledges the role of humankind in improving "natural" conditions. In many areas of the world, humans may have altered conditions for future sustainable use for the better, and not only for the worse, as is often the unproven assumption in much writing on environmental history. Another important implication of the concept of landesque capital is that it is hardly compatible with another widely used concept in environmental research—that of "carrying capacity." Since humans "can change the environment by adding fertility and building terraces" (Denevan 2001:301), it follows that similar natural environments have been developed differently and have received varying investments of landesque capital over time.[2] We can thus conceptualize landesque capital as a carpet of investments covering the surface of the earth. It can be argued that the distribution of landesque capital is as important a factor, in the understanding of global differences in the productivity of agricultural lands, as the more obvious factors of climate and naturally formed soils.

The Geographical Distribution of Landesque Capital

Landesque capital is unevenly spread at the global scale, a distribution that cannot be explained by differences in climate and soils. Furthermore, at the regional scale landesque capital often has a patchy distribution.[3] No easily accessible data currently exist to make it possible to map the intensity of landesque capital on a global scale. A crude estimation of the global distribution of precolonial landesque capital may be obtained from the classifications of the agricultural regions of the world that were made during the first half of the twentieth century (Whittlesey 1936). The areas on these maps that denote intensive subsistence agriculture roughly coincide with larger areas that other available sources document as having a long history of terracing and irrigation. They of course also show a concentration of intensive agriculture in eastern and southeastern Asia.

However, that map of course omits all the areas with abandoned terracing, field systems, irrigation systems or anthropogenic soils either within areas of modern commercial agriculture (as in North America) or in areas that were previously regarded as being "pristine," as in Amazonia (see below). Spencer and Hale published a rough sketch of abandoned and current terracing in the world. For the Americas, the overview by Denevan (1992, distribution map on p. 380) serves as an introduction.[4] Grove and Sutton (1989) have mapped precolonial terracing and irrigation in Africa. Farrington's seminal work, *Prehistoric intensive agriculture in the tropics* (1985), represents a broad approach on a global scale, while for arid lands Barker and Gilbertson (2000) provide a recent overview.

For one specific type of irrigation—*qanats* (subterranean aqueducts)—previously best known from Iran but now found in most parts of the Islamic world (Wulf 1968), the recent work by Lightfoot (1996a, 1996b, 1997, 2000) has given us a better picture of its distribution.

The most difficult estimation of distribution concerns anthropogenic soils. Brookfield has turned our attention to the "manufactured" soils in Europe (*plaggen*), in Papua New Guinea, in central Africa, in the ancient terraces of Peru, and in the Amazon (see references in Brookfield 2001a:185, and for *plaggen* Spek 2004:724–967).[5]

Compared to the information that was available some twenty years ago, we now have a much more detailed picture of the global distribution of precolonial landesque capital. North America and Africa do have rich occurrences of terraced agriculture and irrigation, as well as farming systems that have used different kinds of mounds, ridges, and so forth. However, compared to the situation in the Andes and in the southwestern fringe of North America, labor- and capital-intensive agriculture still seems to have been of less importance in eastern North America and in sub-Saharan Africa. At the global scale, the most pronounced difference is between Asia and the other continents. We can thus summarize the existing evidence in the form of a gradient: from intensively cultivated Asia, to the rich occurrences of irrigation and terraces in Mesoamerica and the Andes, to the more scattered occurrences of incipient intensification in North America, Amazonia, and sub-Saharan Africa.

Driving Forces behind Landesque Capital

The historiography of landesque capital runs partly parallel to the discussion concerning agricultural intensification in a long-term perspective (e.g. Boserup 1965; Morrison 1996). Landesque capital sometimes figures explicitly in these discussions, but aside from Brookfield's many contributions on the topic, few of these contributions take their starting point in the problem of landesque capital. A notable exception in this regard is Bayliss-Smith (1997). Even if it has not always been framed in terms of the concept of landesque capital, one can nevertheless say that landesque capital has its own historiography.

Diffusion

For the case of terracing, Spencer and Hale proposed that there had been a process of diffusion from centers in the "classical Near East" (Spencer and Hale 1961:32). The notion that terracing had diffused from a center seems, however, to fail on two grounds. First, their interpretation is too closely linked to the now abandoned models that contended that agriculture per se diffused from a single center in the Middle East. Second, it is doubtful whether basic practices such as the leveling of land or the construction of terraces were so original that their occurrence in one part of the world necessarily depended on information gained from another place—an aspect that is also discussed by the authors (Spencer and Hale 1961:36). In the case of *qanats*, which represent a rather elaborate form of underground technology, the diffusion thesis, as proposed by Lightfoot (2000:216), is more convincing.

Environmental Determinism

The idea that the distribution of irrigation has a simple environmental cause has a long history. It plays a central role in Wittfogel's influential work. According to his idea, large parts of Asia could only be farmed with irrigation, which in its turn provided the necessary conditions for the rise of hydraulic civilizations and Oriental despotism.[6]

It now seems clear that the origin of the idea of Oriental despotism and the Asian mode of production goes back to a (mis)understanding by Marx and Engels of the natural environments of Asia. Jim Blaut (1993) has demonstrated a close connection between Marx's and Engels's writing on irrigation and the way early-nineteenth-century geographers like Karl Ritter were describing one special type of geographical-cultural system. This system was associated with the civilizations of the river valleys of northeastern Africa and arid Asia, but the idea was later extended to also cover the river valleys in wetter parts of Asia. The connection between Ritter's "geographical-cultural" systems and Marx's understanding of the role of irrigation may go back to the fact that Ritter was Marx's teacher of geography in Berlin (Blaut 1993:82–84).

Whittlesey (1936), in his analysis of the distribution of intensive subsistence agriculture, turned this argument upside down when he commented that the agricultural regions of the world at the beginning of the twentieth century could *not* be understood on the basis of climate alone. He meant that the agriculture of east and south Asia "does not parallel counterpart climates in the other continents," and instead emphasized "Occidental versus Oriental society and progressive versus backward cultures" (Whittlesey 1936:209).[7]

Response to Siegelike Situations

The idea that terraced agriculture, and intensive agriculture in general, were caused by siegelike situations has had a strong standing, particularly in the African context. Within the broader context where hilltop settlement is understood as a reflection of periods of hostilities, terraced hillsides on marginal and rocky land have been associated with warlike situations. This idea figures in much writing on terracing and intensive agriculture in Africa (see references in Widgren 2004:13–14). The Belgian geographer Pierre Gourou developed this idea in the later editions of his book *The tropical world* (1961), and most recently in a book from 1991 (Gourou 1991). He saw intensive agriculture and terracing in much of Africa as the result of population pressure resulting from siegelike situations. This idea was one aspect of his work to develop an understanding of farming systems that went beyond simple environmental determinism. The case of the Iraqw intensive farming in Tanzania, which Gourou referred to as "a particularly clear example of intensive agricultural techniques developed by a people 'under siege' " (Gourou 1991:50),[8] has recently been empirically scrutinized by Börjeson (2004), who also criticizes the theoretical basis of the siege hypothesis.

The Political Economy of Landesque Capital

Archaeologists and anthropologists working from an explicit political economy approach often understand terracing and irrigation as elements of the accumulative strategies of elite groups. Control over both labor and the means of production are seen here as central in the development of landesque capital (see for example Earle 1997:67–104). In such political economy approaches to chiefdoms, investments in land represent but one factor in a longer chain of explanation.

In the same manner that Wittfogel identifies irrigation as only one link in his model, so too does Earle posit landesque capital as but one factor in a longer chain of explanation. Neither of these models (Wittfogel or Earle) is thus specifically aimed to advance a general explanation for investments in land. If we see them from the perspective of explaining investments in land, rather than from the perspective of understanding social stratification, the central point is that they both offer possible explanations for how labor demands for investments in land can be met.

The "political economy model," as developed by Håkansson (1989) in the context of African agricultural systems, has recently been scrutinized in an analysis of four examples of landesque capital in eastern Africa (Widgren and Sutton 2004). A central point concerning the formation of landesque capital is the character of the investments. As Doolittle has pointed out, the word "capital" might mislead us to think of inputs added over short periods of time as the result of socially coordinated efforts (Doolittle 1984:124). The construction and maintenance of capital in some of the cases investigated in eastern Africa do indeed require both a large number of people and a socially coordinated effort, but other cases are examples of incremental processes, where, to borrow Doolittle's words, cultivation and construction are "inextricably mixed activities" (Doolittle 1984:135; Börjeson 2004:91–94).

Concerning the mobilization of labor, we found both stratified (Watson 2004) and egalitarian cases (Östberg 2004). Landesque capital thus can take many forms, some of which can be understood as the result of incremental processes, whereas others rely on more substantial investments that are often concentrated to shorter periods of time. Most landesque-capital farming systems are by definition also labor-intensive. The forms of labor mobilization may vary, however. While there is a relation between landesque capital, labor mobilization, and social stratification—and Bayliss-Smith has also pointed to the marked inequality in gender roles (1997)—this relation is not absolute, since there are other ways of mobilizing the necessary labor, even for large construction works. A common theme in many of the accounts of landesque capital is the role of agricultural surplus—be it olive oil for the Roman Empire (Barker 2002:494), or fresh maize and food security for distant kinfolks in Tanzania (Loiske 2004:111). Such different kinds of geographical division of labor are important explanatory factors behind most landesque capital.

How Is Landesque Capital Used Up

If we consider landesque capital to be a type of fixed and immovable capital in the economic sense,[9] two interrelated problems require consideration. One problem concerns how this fixed and immovable capital can be used up. Closely connected to this is the question of whether landesque capital, which was built up hundreds or even thousands of years ago in different economical and technological contexts, can still be considered as capital today, or whether it has become devalued.

Some clear cases of devaluation can be identified. Cultivating manufactured soils without the continual reinvestment of nutrients and organic matter might exhaust them. Concerning terraces and irrigation systems, a decline in available labor power for their maintenance is usually the first step in their abandonment. Final abandonment often leads to increased erosion, and hence a successive degradation of the landesque capital (Brookfield 1986:180). While many local, capital-intensive, and sustainable systems were abandoned as a direct consequence of colonial expansion, the relative role of colonialism for the abandonment of landesque capital on a global scale is difficult to assess. The archaeological literature provides plenty of examples of irrigation and terrace systems that were abandoned or contracted considerably before the colonial encounter (Lightfoot 2000:219; Barker and Gilbertson 2000). In the case of the dry zone in Sri Lanka, the large irrigation systems declined and many were abandoned (already) in the thirteenth century. Recent studies by E. Myrdal indicate, however, that previous writers may have underestimated the survival of many small-scale village irrigation tanks well into the early nineteenth century. This opens for a deeper understanding of the relation between a first phase of precolonial decline of irrigation on Sri Lanka, and a second phase of decline directly connected to colonial warfare in the nineteenth century (Myrdal-Runebjer 1996; Myrdal 2003, 2004).

In the case of Africa, the historical context of abandonment is less evident. From the available evidence, however, one can conclude that two of the more spectacular and best-known examples of terracing and irrigation—Nyanga in Zimbabwe and Engaruka in Tanzania—were abandoned well before the period of colonialism (Soper 2002; Sutton 1998). In South Africa, however, it is possible that the extensive terracing in the Drakensberg around Lydenburg in Mpumalanga may have been abandoned as a direct result of contact between Boer expansion and local Pedi farmers (Tim Maggs, personal communication; see also Widgren 2004). In Tanganyika, Kjekshus saw the abandonment of sustainable intensive farming as a direct consequence of the arrival of colonialism (Kjekshus 1996:27ff.), but his conclusions have been much debated (for references to the discussion see Widgren 2004). Concerning the Pacific region, Tim Bayliss-Smith shows, in his comparison of three precolonial landesque-capital intensive systems, how old forms of landesque capital were either modified or their agricultural systems collapsed when the sociopolitical conditions changed during the colonial era (Bayliss-Smith 1997). In the case of Rusinga Island in Lake Victoria, for example, the intensive terraced agriculture declined during the 1900s as a result of a complex set of factors including competing economic activities, labor scarcity, low soil fertility, and pest infestations. On the neighboring but more isolated Mfangano Island, however, farmers continue with terracing, permanent cropping, and construction of an elaborate network of fencing that protects the crops from animal pests (Conelly 1994).

There is, however, no simple blueprint to explain the relationship between recent economic changes and the role of landesque capital. Labor shortages arising from migration can sometimes be countered by remittances and return migrations, which in some cases have been shown to lead to investments in agricultural improvement and the reestablishment of landesque capital.[10]

Landesque capital can also be devalued as a result of technological and economic change, which leads to new forms of capital investments in the land. The vine terraces in southern Europe are recent and obvious examples. Two phases of investments during the twentieth century can be documented.

In the first phase, mechanization left its mark in the landscape in the form of new forms of terraces. In the second phase, the modern type of sloping fields adjusted to mechanized farming came into existence (see Andresen and Curado 2003 for an example from Portugal).

Looking at the areas of the world that were influenced by colonial expansion we thus have to deal with three different chronological contexts where landesque capital has been abandoned. First, many large systems were abandoned well before European colonial expansion, as were also many capital-intensive systems in areas where colonial contact was not a factor. Second, in a certain number of instances, the direct connection between abandonment and colonial expansion can be proven. Third, recent developments, mainly in the form of rural-urban migration, can be seen as a factor behind much recent abandonment of capital and labor-intensive small-scale agriculture (cf. Denevan 2001:296).

Bringing Old Landesque Capital into Use

My argument above that old landesque capital is an important factor for understanding not only past but also future agricultural potential, rests, however, on the assumption that present-day technological complexes in farming do not differ much from those of the past. In large parts of the world, farming populations have not been drawn into heavily mechanized and commercial agriculture, but are mainly dependent on the land and their own labor for their immediate survival. Most of these farming societies are still nonmechanized. The choice is not between animal traction and mechanized farming. Tillage with hand implements is still important in large parts of the poor world. In these cases, inherited landesque capital is a capital asset in the true sense of the term.

Guyer and Lambin (1993) observe that the technological complexes associated with ancient terracing and irrigation may have a potential beyond subsistence farming. In the case of the urban hinterland of Ibadan in Nigeria, they show that fields cleared by hand rather than those cleared by tractor are "at the cutting edge of crop innovation" and that the "most rapidly expanding crops—tomatoes and peppers—are almost exclusively grown on hand-cleared plots" (Guyer and Lambin 1993:851). Recent success stories in sustainable smallholder farming, such as the case of Machakos, are also based on similar types of technology and terracing to those used in older examples (Tiffen et al. 1994). A volume by Reij et al. (1996) demonstrates the potential and current use of such methods for soil and water conservation in Africa.

There is, however, a big difference between systems that have continuity and those that today only remain as archaeological features. In the latter cases the knowledge and the social, cultural, and economic contexts have been lost. Prehistoric terraces and raised fields can also provide models and inspiration for small-scale, sustainable, labor-intensive agriculture. However, the documentation of successful attempts to bring abandoned landesque capital back into service is not overwhelming and mainly concerns initiatives made by development agencies (Brookfield 1996; Wessels and Hoogeveen n.d.; see also references in Denevan 2001:237). On the basis of these publications it is difficult to assess the wider possibilities for putting old landesque capital to use.

The most detailed studies of the role of ancient landesque capital in relation to new expansion of which I am aware are the ethnographical accounts of the recent cultivation of *terra preta* soils in the Amazon. For instance, German (2003) meticulously records crop repertoires, crop preferences for different soils, and the wider context of labor and political economy in which these old anthropogenic soils are used today. Through the identification of incentives and preconditions for their present cultivation, she also deepens our understanding of the intricate interplay between crops, social contexts, and surplus production that provides the framework within which these soils were once developed.

Conclusion

When landesque capital figures in broad syntheses of societies and their use of natural resources, it has thus been seen either as a cause of certain types of hierarchical political and social organization, as in the case of irrigation and "Oriental despotism" (Wittfogel 1957), or it has been seen as one of the *means* of accumulation in such a hierarchical organization (Earle 1997). As I have tried to show, neither of these approaches succeeds in fully explaining landesque capital. The main problem is that they both often make the mistake of underestimating the chronology involved by only connecting landesque capital to a certain phase of political and economic organization. This was a point made in Edmund Leach's criticism of Wittfogel, based on the chronology of the Sinhalese irrigation system:

> It all looks like a colossal and highly organised piece of bureaucratic planning, the work of one of Wittfogel's idealised Oriental Despots. But if so, the planning must have been done by a kind of Durkheimian group mind! The system took about 1,400 years to build . . . elaborations and modifications went on for at least another 600 years. (Leach 1959:13)

From the perspective of a historian, a certain type of agrarian landscape might be understood in terms of being connected with a specific period in the development of a chiefdom or empire. But in most cases, fields, terraces, and irrigation systems continue to play a role long after that period and they will usually also have antecedent phases. Anyone who has tried to investigate, for example, the chronology of canals in still-functioning irrigation systems, or of clearance cairn fields in the Swedish forests will be aware of the large chronological time span that is usually involved. Rather than being attributable to a specific social context at a specific time, landesque capital has a tendency to survive in different social contexts. Landesque capital is *incorporated* in the land and therefore its spatial character is much more evident than its chronology. Unlike monetary capital, which is fluid in space but fixed in time, landesque capital is better understood in terms of being fixed in space but "fluid" in time.

Furthermore, systems of capital-intensive land use are not only based on the physical structures involved. They are usually the expressions of continuous learning processes in the communities involved (Geertz 1968:34). The spatial fixity of landesque capital is thus not only a question of the physical structures. It also involves the locally developed knowledge systems of agriculture, irrigation, weather, crops, and so on, within a certain region, a complex best understood with the French term *terroir* (Lévy and Lussault 2003:919).

I am thus skeptical of too close associations between landesque capital and hierarchical political and economic structures. I do of course agree with those who say that ownership and control of landesque capital, under certain circumstances, can be crucial for the accumulation strategies of political entities, from chiefdoms to empires. But that is not the same as to say that the development of landesque capital is dependent on the existence of chiefdoms or empires, any more than it is an indicator of arid lands. The conditions of the political economy of societies that are conducive to the development and maintenance of investments in land must be sought along another gradient. Political instability, a lack of social control of labor, and rural insecurity are at the extreme negative end of this gradient (cf. Blaikie and Brookfield 1987:17; Butzer 1996:147). At the positive end are the political, economic, and social conditions where investments in land are likely to be seen as secure, and where individuals and communities can perceive the long-term returns. While the exchange of agricultural products was important in many of the cases discussed above, whether through informal exchange or formal trade, there is no simple correlation between the volume of exchange and investments in land. It is probable that the nature of exchange is more important than its volume for creating incentives to invest in the land.

Notes

1. See also Renberg et al. (1993) and, for similar field systems in Norway, Pedersen (1999).

2. According to Denevan, carrying capacity can "only be calculated at a given point in time for a specific piece of uniform land with a specific technology and a specific standard of living" (2001:301). Marx argues along similar lines when he writes that soil fertility "always implies an economic relation" (Marx 1959:651).

3. Africa: Widgren (2004:2–6), Amazonia: Glaser et al. (2001).

4. Detailed accounts are found in Butzer (1992); Denevan (2001); Whitmore and Turner (2001); and Doolittle (2000). See also the recent popular account by Mann (2005).

5. The understanding of prehistoric land use in Amazonia has turned many assumptions of virgin rainforests upside down (Denevan 2001:104–110, 123–124; Glaser et al. 2001; Lima et al. 2002; German 2003). Willis et al. (2004) have recently compared this to similar evidence in other parts of the world, including the Congo basin and the Indo-Malay region of southeast Asia. The question of whether prehistoric land use in these latter areas has also led to profound transformations of soils remains to be researched.

6. Wittfogel (1957:12) qualified the circumstances under which these relations might have operated:

> It is only above the level of an extractive subsistence economy, beyond the influence of strong centers of rainfall agriculture, and below the level of a property-based industrial civilisation that man, reacting specifically to the water deficient landscape moves towards a specific hydraulic order of life.

7. A more recent discussion of environmental determinism can be found in Morgan (1988), who compares Tamil Nadu and eastern Tanzania (see also Gunnel 1997).

8. My translation.

9. Cf. Harvey's (1982:232) discussion on the built environment and infrastructure.

10. See for example Tiffen et al. (1994) and, for the arguments relating to migration, Jokisch (2002).

References

Andresen, T., and M. J. Curado. 2003. Shaping the future of a cultural landscape: The Douro Valley wine region. In *Landscape interfaces: Cultural heritage in changing landscapes*, ed. H. Palang and G. Fry, 109–124. Dordrecht and London: Kluwer Academic.

Barker, G. 2002. A tale of two deserts: Contrasting desertification histories on Rome's desert frontiers. *World Archaeology* 33:488–507.

Barker, G., and D. Gilbertson, eds. 2000. *The archaeology of drylands.* London and New York: Routledge.

Bayliss-Smith, T. P. 1997. From taro garden to golf course? Alternative futures for agricultural capital in the Pacific Islands. In *Environment and development in the Pacific Islands*, ed. B. Burt and C. Clerk, 143–170. Port Moresby, PNG: Australian National University and University of Papua New Guinea Press.

Blaikie, P., and H. C. Brookfield. 1987. *Land degradation and society.* London and New York: Methuen.

Blaut, J. 1993. *The colonizer's model of the world: Geographical diffusionism and eurocentric history.* New York: Guilford.

Börjeson, L. 2004. *A history under siege: Intensive agriculture in the Mbulu highlands, Tanzania, 19th century to the present.* Stockholm: Almqvist and Wiksell International.

Boserup, E. 1965. *The conditions of agricultural growth.* Chicago: Aldine.

Brookfield, H. C. 1984. Intensification revisited. *Pacific Viewpoint* 25:15–44.

———. 1986. Intensification intensified. *Archaeology in Oceania* 31:177–180.

———. 1996. People, land management, and environmental change: The problems that a United Nations University programme is studying. In *Population, land management and environmental change*, ed. J. I. Uitto and A. Ono. Tokyo: UNU Press.

———. 2001a. Intensification, and alternative approaches to agricultural change. *Asia Pacific Viewpoint* 42:181–192.

———. 2001b. *Exploring agrodiversity.* New York: Columbia University Press.

Butzer, K. W., ed. 1992. The Americas before and after 1492: Current geographical research. *Annals of the Association of American Geographers*, vol. 82. Washington, D.C.: Association of American Geographers.

———. 1996. Ecology in the long view: Settlement histories, agrosystemic strategies, and ecological performance. *Journal of Field Archaeology* 23:141–150.

Conelly, W. T. 1994. Population pressure, labor availability, and agricultural disintensification: The decline of farming on Rusinga Island, Kenya. *Human Ecology* 22:145–170.

Denevan, W. M. 1992. The pristine myth: The landscape of the Americas in 1492. *Annals of the Association of American Geographers* 82:369–385.

———. 2001. *Cultivated landscapes of native Amazonia and the Andes.* Oxford: Oxford University Press.

Doolittle, W. E. 1984. Agricultural change as an incremental process. *Annals of the Association of American Geographers* 74:124–137.

———. 2000. *Cultivated landscapes of native North America.* Oxford: Oxford University Press.

Earle, T. 1997. *How chiefs come to power: The political economy in prehistory.* Stanford, Calif.: Stanford University Press.

Farrington, I. S., ed. 1985. Prehistoric intensive agriculture in the tropics. Oxford: British Archaeological Reports, vol. 232.

Geertz, C. 1968. *Agricultural involution: The process of ecological change in Indonesia.* Berkeley: University of California Press.

German, L. A. 2003. Historical contingencies in the coevolution of environment and livelihood: Contributions to the debate on Amazonian black earth. *Geoderma* 111:307–331.

Glaser, B., L. Haumaier, G. Guggenberger, and W. Zech. 2001. The "terra preta" phenomenon: A model for sustainable agriculture in the humid tropics. *Naturwissenschaften* 88:37–41.

Gourou, P. 1961. *The tropical world*. London: Longmans.

———. 1991. *L'Afrique tropical: Nain ou géant agricole?* Paris: Flammarion.

Grove, A. T., and J. E. G. Sutton. 1989. Agricultural terracing south of the Sahara. *Azania* 24:98–112.

Gunnel, Y. 1997. Comparative regional geography in India and West Africa: Soils, landforms and economic theory in agricultural development strategies. *Geographical Journal* 163:38–46.

Guyer, J. I., and E. F. Lambin. 1993. Land use in an urban hinterland: Ethnography and remote sensing in the study of African intensification. *American Anthropologist* 95 (4): 839–859.

Håkansson, N. T. 1989. Social and political aspects of intensive agriculture in East Africa: Some models from cultural anthropology. *Azania* 24:12–20.

Harvey, D. 1982. *The limits to capital*. Oxford: Blackwell.

Jokisch, B. D. 2002. Migration and agricultural change: The case of smallholder agriculture in highland Ecuador. *Human Ecology* 30 (4): 523–550.

Kjekshus, H. 1996 (1977). *Ecology control and economic development in East African history. The case of Tanganyika 1850–1950*. 2nd ed. London: Currey.

Lagerås, P., and T. Bartholin. 2003. Fire and stone clearance in Iron Age agriculture: New insights inferred from the analysis of terrestrial macroscopic charcoal in clearance cairns in Hamneda, southern Sweden. *Vegetation History and Archaeobotany* 12 (2): 83–92.

Leach, E. R. 1959. Hydraulic society in Ceylon. *Past and Present* 15:2–26.

Lévy, J., and M. Lussault, eds. 2003. Dictionnaire de la géographie et de l'espace des sociétés. Paris: Belin.

Lightfoot, D. R. 1996a. Moroccan khettara: Traditional irrigation and progressive desiccation *Geoforum* 27:261–273.

———. 1996b. Syrian *qanat* Romani: History, ecology, abandonment. *Journal of Arid Environments* 33:321–336.

———. 1997. Qanats in the Levant: Hydraulic technology at the periphery of early empires. *Technology and Culture* 38:432–451.

———. 2000. The origin and diffusion of *qanats* in Arabia: New evidence from the northern and southern Peninsula. *Geographical Journal* 166:215–226.

Lima, H. N., C. E. R. Schaefer, J. W. V. Mello, R. J. Gilkes, and J. C. Ker. 2002. Pedogenesis and pre-Colombian land use of "terra preta anthrosols" ("Indian black earth") of Western Amazonia. *Geoderma* 110:1–17.

Loiske, V. 2004. Institutionalized exchange as a driving force in intensive agriculture: An Iraqw case study. In *Islands of intensive agriculture in eastern Africa*, ed. M. Widgren and J. E. G. Sutton, 105–113. Oxford: Currey.

Maggs, T. 1995. From Marateng to Marakwet: Islands of agricultural intensification in eastern and southern Africa. *Abstracts for 10th Congress of the Pan African Association for Prehistory.* Harare: University of Zimbabwe and National Museums and Monuments of Zimbabwe.

Mann, C. 2005. *1491: New revelations of the Americas before Columbus.* New York: Knopf.

Marx, K. 1959. *Capital: A critique of political economy*, bk. 3, *The process of capitalist production as a whole.* London: Lawrence and Wishart.

Morgan, W. T. W. 1988. Tamil Nadu and eastern Tanzania: Comparative regional geography and the historical development process. *Geographical Journal* 154:69–86.

Morrison, K. D. 1996. Typological schemes and agricultural change: Beyond Boserup in precolonial South India. *Current Anthropology* 37:583–608.

Myrdal, E. 2003. Water harvesting and water management: A discussion of the implications of scale in artificial irrigation: A Sri Lankan example. *Current Swedish Archaeology* 11:65–96.

———. 2004. The archaeology of colonial warfare: Changing land-use patterns in Sri Lanka in its 19th century context. Abstract in *Structures of vulnerability: Mobilisation and resistance.* Interdisciplinary research conference, Stockholm University, January 12–14, 2005, 289. Stockholm.

Myrdal-Runebjer, E. 1996. *Rice and millet: An archaeological case study of a Sri Lankan transbasin irrigation system.* Göteborg: Department of Archaeology, University of Göteborg.

Olsson, M. and Troedsson, T. 1990. Soil forming factors and spodosol properties in Sweden. In *Proceedings from the fifth international soil correlation meeting: Characterization, classification and utilization of spodosols*, ed. J. M. Kimble and R. D. Yeck, 422–432. Lincoln, Neb.: U.S. Department of Agriculture—Soil Conservation Service.

Östberg, W. 2004. The expansion of Marakwet hill-furrow irrigation in the Kerio Valley of Kenya. In *Islands of intensive agriculture in Eastern Africa*, ed. M. Widgren and J. E. G. Sutton, 19–48. Oxford: Currey.

Pedersen, E A. 1999. Transformations to sedentary farming in eastern Norway: AD 1000 or 1000 BC. In *Settlement and landscape: Proceedings of a conference in Århus, Denmark, May 4–7 1998*, ed. C. Fabech and J. Ringtved. Højbjerg: Jutland Archaeological Society.

Reij, C., I. Scoones, and C. Toulmin, eds. 1996. Sustaining the soil: Traditional soil and water conservation in Africa. London: Earthscan.

Renberg, I., T. Korsman, and H. J. B. Birks. 1993. Prehistoric increases in the pH of acid-sensitive Swedish lakes caused by land-use changes. *Nature* 362:824–826.

Sen, A. K. 1968 (1960). *Choice of techniques: An aspect of theory of planned economic development.* 3rd ed. Oxford: Blackwell.

Soper, R. 2002. *Nyanga: Ancient fields, settlements and agricultural history in Zimbabwe.* London: British Institute in Eastern Africa.

Spek, T. 2004. *Het Drentse esdorpenlandschap: Een historisch-geografische studie.* Utrecht: Matrijs.

Spencer, J. E., and S. A. Hale. 1961. The origin, nature and distribution of agricultural terracing. *Pacific Viewpoint* 2:1–10.

Sutton, J. E. G. 1998. Engaruka: An irrigation agricultural community in northern Tanzania before the Maasai. *Azania* 33:1–38.

Tiffen, M., M. J. Mortimore, and F. Gichugi. 1994. *More people, less erosion: Environmental recovery in Kenya.* Chichester, U.K.: Wiley.

Watson, L. 2004. Agricultural intensification and social stratification: Konso in Ethiopia contrasted with Marakwet. In *Islands of intensive agriculture in eastern Africa*, ed. M. Widgren and J. E. G. Sutton, 49–67. Oxford: Currey.

Wessels, J., and R. J. A. Hoogeveen. (n.d.). Renovation of *qanats* in Syria. www.inweh.unu.edu/inweh/drylands/Publications/Wessels.pdf.

Whitmore, T. M., and B. L. Turner II. 2001. *Cultivated landscapes of Middle America on the eve of conquest.* Oxford: Oxford University Press.

Whittlesey, D. 1936. Major agricultural regions of the earth. *Annals of the Association of American Geographers* 26:199–240.

Widgren, M., ed. 2003. *Röjningsröseområden på sydsvenska höglandet: Arkeologiska, kulturgeografiska och vegetationshistoriska undersökningar.* Stockholm: Kulturgeografiska institutionen, Stockholms universitet.

———. 2004. Towards a historical geography of intensive farming in eastern Africa. In *Islands of intensive agriculture in eastern Africa*, ed. M. Widgren and J. E. G. Sutton, 1–18. Oxford: Currey.

Widgren, M., and J. E. G. Sutton, eds. 2004. *Islands of intensive agriculture in eastern Africa.* Oxford: Currey.

Willis, K. J., L. Gillson, and T. M. Brncic. 2004. How "virgin" is virgin rainforest? *Science* 304:402–403.

Wittfogel, K. A. 1957. *Oriental despotism: A comparative study of total power.* New Haven, Conn., and London: Yale University Press.

Wulf, H. E. 1968. The *qanats* of Iran. *Scientific American* 218:94–105.

Food, War, and Crisis: The Seventeenth Century Swedish Empire **4**

JANKEN MYRDAL

The Empire as an Option

It is an enigma that a small country in the north, with about one million inhabitants, for a time in the seventeenth century, could play a role as a great power in Europe. The explanation could point to the inherent strength of this particular state, but also to a period of crisis in Europe when the Swedish Empire was both a result and a cause of crisis.

The definition of "empire" used in this chapter is: an aggregate of separate states, where one politically sovereign state dominates over its dependencies. A large state consisting of equal parts is not an empire, but a relatively small core that controls a subjugated periphery can be considered an empire. The option to build "empires" thus appears to arise as soon as sovereign states have been formed.

The specific question approached in this chapter concerns why and how the Swedish Empire was built. At a more general level of abstraction I am also asking why empires are built. Discussions of this issue often focus on the largest and most famous empires known, but examining the history of a rather small "empire" can also make some contribution to a better understanding of the general question.

All nations do not struggle to build empires. Culture and economy can thrive in a context of political fragmentation, the long history of Europe being a prime example. Two mutually interacting and sovereign nations can create a win-win situation, while an empire can in fact constitute a lose-lose situation, that is, disadvantages for both the core and the periphery.

Throughout history a general tendency to form larger political entities prevails, but not in a linear and simple fashion. Certainly, Rein Taagepera

(1978, 1997) could prove that by measuring the area of territory under control, one could estimate the degree of political concentration.[1] Area is, however, an insufficient measure, principally because no differentiation is made between control over wastelands and control over regions with affluent economies and high population densities. In a later calculation of the proportions of global population concentrated in large states, Taagepera (1997:489) came to the conclusion that the concentration of power over populations had been "essentially stationary" over the last two thousand years.[2] If one considers the most populous state in the world (normally China), this state has accounted for about 20–30 percent of the world's population over the last two thousand years (McEvedy and Jones 1978:126–127). The second in order, in terms of population size, has seldom accounted for more than 15–20 percent of the world population, often less.[3] Peak periods for concentration of world population to the largest states were from the second century BC to the second century AD and again from the sixteenth century to the twentieth century.

During these long waves of history there has been an ongoing reshuffling of regions into different constellations. Many nations of today have previously had periods as a "Great Power," during which they have controlled surrounding regions. Nostalgia for those glorious days, "the zenith of the nation," may prove hazardous if allowed to affect politics (consider, for example, the case of the Balkans), which suggests a further reason to discuss the inner logic not only of the largest but also of the smaller empires.

A Baltic Empire

In the aftermath of the Black Death, a Scandinavian Union was formed, in which Norway and Sweden were in effect placed under Danish suzerainty, even if the union was formally between three sovereign states. Civil wars followed, in which the Swedish nobility fought together with a militarized peasantry, organized from below on the community level but led by the nobility. Foremost among the goals of these struggles were the lowering of taxes levied on the peasantry and the Swedish nobility's control over the state. Following a hundred years of struggle, an autonomous Swedish Kingdom reappeared in the early sixteenth century.

This Lutheran kingdom emerged as one of the best organized in Europe. The centralized state bureaucracy registered every single farm on an annual basis, and the kingdom could mobilize resources and manpower to an extent that few other nations could match at the time (Roberts 1968). The nobility in Sweden had been rather weak, and could thus easily be recruited as loyal state servants, which was one of the factors that facilitated the establishment of a strong state (Anderson 1974:173–185). Having been well organized during the civil wars, the peasantry could be molded into a state army based on conscription. The peasantry had political representation in the form of a recognized estate of peasants in the *riksdag* (the other estates being for the nobility, the clergy, and the bourgeoisie). The more influential and prosperous peasants thus took some responsibility for state policies regarding wars and taxes (Myers 1975:11, 88–90, 114–116). From its former suppressed position, Sweden was gradually transformed into an expansionist state, a metamorphosis not uncommon in history.

This formation of a strong state was connected with the expansion and economic transformation of Sweden. Not only agriculture but also internal trade in bulk products expanded in the sixteenth century. For example, state protection of the trade in oxen from southern Sweden to the mining districts in the north was a prerequisite for the rapid growth in exports of iron and copper. This geographical division of production in the country strengthened the state because it stimulated both political support and economic development. Relative to population, the size of the Swedish ox-trade, for instance, was comparable in size to the continental trade (Söderberg and Myrdal 2002; Dalhede 1999). An efficient state and a growing economy were the foundation for political expansion.

Using Taagepera's methodology, I have estimated the geographical expansion of Sweden in figure 4.1. The territory of Sweden-Finland grew from an original size of about 0.6 million square kilometers in the early sixteenth century to about 0.9 million square kilometers in the middle of the seventeenth century. This was followed by a decline in the early eighteenth century, and subsequently a collapse during the Napoleonic Wars, when Sweden lost Finland and contracted to its present borders, albeit for a time in union with Norway. The task of quantifying the area is not without problems, as the importance of different regions is ignored. However, maps can be used to show the course of events regarding the acquisition or loss of provinces (map 4.1).

Expansion started on a small scale with the takeover of northern Estonia in the 1560s, following the disintegration of the Teutonic Order. Sweden's expansion then continued eastward during a period of Russian weakness around 1600. Livonia (today southern Estonia and northern Latvia) was incorporated after successful wars with Poland. In the late 1620s, ports along the Prussian coast fell into Swedish control for a period of time.

The Thirty Years' War had been in progress for a decade when Sweden intervened in 1628. The Protestants had been close to defeat, but the

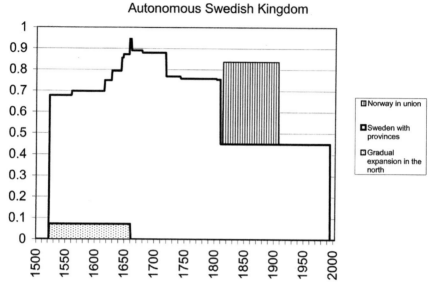

Figure 4.1.   The increase in area under control of the Swedish state. Diagram by P. Myrdal and J. Myrdal

Swedish armies changed the fortunes of war with their more mobile military system and more aggressive style of warfare (Parker 1996:23–24). "The Swedish period" turned into a demographic catastrophe in Germany. After years of brutal warfare, peace negotiations were initiated, and in 1648 Sweden gained control over Bremen and West Pomerania in northern Germany, two relatively small but important provinces.

In the 1640s Swedish armies attacked Denmark and forced it to relinquish some of its provinces. In 1655–1657 the Swedish armies under King Charles X Gustavus occupied large tracts of Poland, but were eventually expelled largely as a result of widespread popular resistance (Topolski 1986:96–99). This victory is, to this day, mentioned in the Polish national anthem. Denmark accordingly seized the opportunity to attack its old foe Sweden, but following their retreat from Poland the Swedish armies marched on Denmark and overran the country during the winter of 1657–1658. Denmark was again forced to cede provinces, and had by then lost one third of its total area. In a follow–up attack in 1658–1659 Swedish armies besieged the Danish capital of Copenhagen, threatening Denmark as a sovereign nation. However, the Dutch fleet was able to save the Danes from this fate. This marked the zenith of the period of Swedish expansion, which was followed by a prolonged period of decline. Sweden's career as an expansionist empire thus lasted about one century.

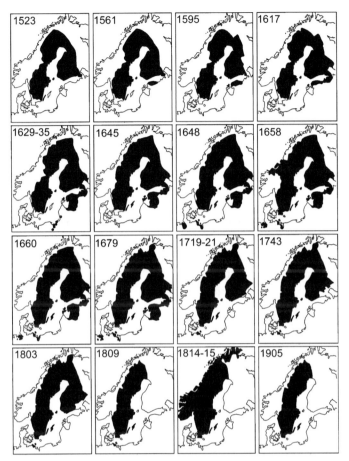

Map 4.1.   The extension of Sweden and dependent provinces. Maps by J. Myrdal and K. Hallgren

Interpretations

The aims of the Swedish expansion have been a topic for Swedish historiography for decades. The main theories are as follows:

First, the Thirty Years' War was fought for the sake of the Protestant faith (cf. Oredsson 1994). Sweden was threatened by the Catholic Habsburg emperor, whose armies had subjugated Denmark. King Gustavus Adolphus of Sweden struck first, before his country could be attacked. After he led his army south from northernmost Germany in 1630, the inner logic of the war unfolded. Swedish armies marched as far as south of the Danube. This is the traditional interpretation.

Second, the geopolitical position of Sweden provides an important explanation, and was mentioned in King Gustavus Adolphus's declaration of war as he became engaged in the Thirty Years' War. Potential enemies surrounded Sweden. The Danish king maintained a claim to Sweden long after 1520. Sweden and Poland were both ruled by the same royal family, the Vasa family. The Polish branch of the Vasa line was the oldest, and had a justified claim to the Swedish crown. Russia had been pressing westward since the late Middle Ages and had been in nearly constant conflict with Sweden-Finland. German princes and the Hanseatic towns had intervened in Sweden for centuries. The wars were mainly defensive. This explanation has often been combined with the above-mentioned interpretation based on religious motives.

Third, Sweden tried to gain control over the lucrative trade flowing across the Baltic from Russia into western Europe. After several attempts to gain control over all of the Baltic ports, Sweden even tried to lay hold of the Sound between Sealand and Scania by attacking Denmark. This is the modern interpretation of economic history, which has been prevalent since the 1940s (see maps in Attman 1944; Barraclough 1978:188–189).

Fourth, the basic energy source needed to fuel an empire was food, and the aim of the expansion was to conquer regions with a surplus production of grain. This is the explanation favored in this chapter. Before turning to the fourth explanation, I will comment on the first three.

The religious factor is important. In contemporary propaganda King Gustavus Adolphus of Sweden was presented as the lion from the north who sought to protect the true faith. When Sweden entered the religious war her main allies were the Protestant German princes. But the religious interpretation has some deficiencies. One is the repeated conflicts with Protestant Denmark; another is that Catholic France was Sweden's ally already in 1631, and in fact her main ally from 1638.

A theory presented by Randall Collins seems to support the geopolitical explanation. In his general "Geopolitical Theory," resources are considered as the primary factor. A second factor concerns the "marchland" position. A state on the geographical periphery often has the advantage of having its back free, an advantage that is lost during expansion (Collins 1999:39–42).[4] This theory relates fairly well to the Swedish period of expansion, when real and potential enemies tended to grow with every war—the Polish adventure being a prime example.

Trade over the Baltic had been a cornerstone for the Hanseatic League during the Middle Ages. The sixteenth century saw a rapid increase in the volume of trade. Dutch and to some extent also English merchants took over more of the trade. From Russia and the Baltic countries came flax, linen, hemp, furs, hides, tallow, and wax through ports such as Reval and Riga. Poland and the Baltic countries exported grain from these ports and from ports along the southern coast of the Baltic Sea, especially Danzig. The Swedish government imposed heavy duties on trade, and in the late 1620s a considerable part of the state budget was financed with revenues collected from toll stations.

A problem with this interpretation is that the trade goal could only partly be achieved through conquest, as Swedish decision-makers must have realized. For example, when Sweden attacked Poland in the 1650s, Dutch trade interests rightly feared the imposition of heavy Swedish tolls on the Russian trade and intervened (Roberts 1967:149).

Population and Food Production

In general textbooks on seventeenth-century Sweden, the country is often described as a dynamic exception to the situation in most of Europe, where economic depression reigned.[5] This positive rendition of Sweden is, however, only partly correct. Sweden was hit by the general crisis, but reacted in a specific way.

In the sixteenth century, populations were growing throughout Europe. In Sweden, the household growth rate was about 0.6–0.7 percent per annum, which corresponded to growth rates in other European countries. In the seventeenth century, most of Europe experienced population stagnation or even regression. In Sweden, however, the number of inhabitants continued to increase, albeit at a slower pace (Myrdal 1999b:222; Palm 2000:49). The population in the area corresponding to contemporary Sweden increased from about half a million inhabitants in 1500 to 1.5 million in 1700. Woodland and mining districts were regions of expansion, but the plains followed the European pattern of stagnation. In the decades around 1700, the size of the population in Sweden-Finland experienced a brief downturn as a combined result of famine, war, and plague, but the population soon recovered and began to expand again.

Agrarian production, however, did not follow the population figures. While the sixteenth century had been characterized by colonization and some technological innovation, as in much of Europe, this was not the case for agriculture in the seventeenth century, either in Sweden or in much of Europe (Myrdal and Söderberg 1991; Myrdal 1999b; Söderberg and Myrdal 2002). Measuring total production is a complicated task, and several sources have to be combined, each one with its specific information.

The main sources for estimating overall food production are: (1) tithe registers; (2) land registers; (3) manorial accounts concerning production and consumption; (4) registers over import and export of grain; and (5) grain prices.

Tithe registers from Sweden are among the best that exist for early modern Europe, both in terms of quality and quantity. From around 1540, all farms were registered on an annual basis, and the tithe for each farm was normally given in the different varieties of grain (rye, barley, wheat, or oats). Most of these accounts have been preserved. Lately this enormous quantity of material has been researched using source-critical perspectives, and a national diagram of tithes in Sweden has been constructed for the period 1540–1680 (Leijonhufvud 2001). Increase of the tithe in grain production in the woodland areas and the stagnation on the plains corresponds to the overall population change. The tithe also confirms what we know from other sources about famine and food shortage for specific years.

The main question is, however, whether this material provides an accurate assessment of grain production in a long-term perspective and at the national scale. The collection of a tax will often be undermined by the taxpayers' tendency to cheat, and an old tax is often less properly paid than a newly introduced tax because people have learned how to take advantage of the system. Notwithstanding these shortcomings, the tithe is a form of taxation that was common for all of Europe and can thus be used for international comparisons.

The total amount of tithe collection in Sweden increased slightly in the sixteenth century, but was followed by a slight decrease in the seventeenth century. Similar rather flat curves have been constructed for France, Belgium, and other countries.[6] A conclusion is that Sweden's trend in agrarian production was similar to that prevailing in other countries (even if the curve probably underestimates the increase in the sixteenth century).

Land registers are abundant in Swedish state archives. Most of the sixteenth century was characterized by an expansion of acreage, with clearances and the establishment of new cottages and farms. From the seventeenth century, the rate of expansion began to diminish. Large-scale village maps represent one specific type of land register. In an ambitious project, the state planned to draw up a map for every village in the country. This project was launched in the 1630s and continued until the 1690s. Most villages and hamlets were in fact covered—several of them more than once (Tollin 1991:11–15). The increase in acreage in production during the seventeenth century was limited, and in reality many fields were left deserted, the most common reason being unpaid taxes (Myrdal 1999b:371).

In the manorial accounts, the yield is assessed in terms of the size of the harvest in relation to seed. Yields did increase somewhat in the sixteenth century, but in many regions there was a decrease in the second half of the seventeenth century (Leijonhufvud 2001).

Food Crisis and Political Aggression

Manorial accounts document information about food consumed by the staff, including ordinary farm workers. A comparison between the sixteenth and the seventeenth century shows a significant decrease in the amount of calories available to an ordinary farmhand or dairywoman. Even if we consider the sources critically, the difference is so large that it must have reflected a real change (see Morell 1989). The quality of food also decreased, with relatively less meat and butter being given to the staff. It is important to add, however, that the Swedish population was comparatively well fed in the sixteenth century, and the decrease started from a high level.

Bones from archaeological excavations of cemeteries provide further information. Male stature had been rather stable during the Middle Ages and into the early modern period, with a mean height for males of approximately 172–173 cm throughout the Middle Ages. The osteological evidence from later periods is scanty, but excavations from one cemetery with sufficient material from the Middle Ages to the mid-seventeenth century show that male stature began to decline in the seventeenth century. The stature of military recruits as documented in soldier enlistment rolls from the early eighteenth century completes the picture. These sources indicate that the mean stature for males at this time had decreased to around 165 cm (Werdelin, Sten, and Myrdal 2000). The connection between height and nutrition is not straightforward, but this change adds to the general picture of a declining standard of living in Sweden during the seventeenth century.

Grain prices are determined by market organization, the efficiency of transportation, and not least by levels of demand. During the sixteenth century the grain prices in Sweden, as in the rest of Europe, rose in relation to other commodities. In most of Europe this trend continued until about 1630, but then grain prices started to fall in Germany, France, England, and other countries. Demographic stagnation caused a slump in demand and this trend was to continue until the early eighteenth century. In Sweden, however, grain prices continued to increase in relation to other commodities throughout the seventeenth century (Fischer 1996; Söderberg and Jansson 1988; Palm 1991). The cumulative evidence suggests that Sweden struggled with a stagnating domestic food production and was facing an emerging food crisis in the seventeenth century, as population continued to increase while agricultural production declined.

Trade represented one potential solution to the problem, but Sweden was not a rich country. Bulk trade had been growing in the sixteenth century and most of the grain from the Baltic was shipped to the Netherlands, the industrialized economic center of western Europe. Indeed, even Sweden was exporting grain to the Netherlands in the sixteenth century, principally in the form of wheat from the plains in eastern Sweden.

This situation had totally changed by the mid-seventeenth century. Sweden not only ceased to export grain, but had instead begun to import, or rather commandeer, grain from its new provinces. From about 1630, tens of thousands of barrels were imported every year from Estonia and Livonia. The Baltic provinces that had been conquered in the early seventeenth century had been contributors of grain to the Netherlands. Approximately one hundred thousand barrels of grain, mostly rye, were exported westward in the 1620s. In the 1630s, these grain exports were increasingly channeled to Sweden, and after about 1650 all grain from the Baltic provinces was directed to Sweden. During years of famine, which were common in the late seventeenth and early eighteenth centuries in Sweden, several hundred thousand barrels of grain were more or less forcibly exported from the provinces on the eastern shore of the Baltic and shipped to Sweden (Åmark 1915; Heckscher 1935–1936; Soom 1961; Hegardt 1975; Sandström 1990).

Scania (then eastern Denmark, now southern Sweden) was conquered by Sweden in the 1650s. Before the Swedish occupation about one hundred thousand barrels, mostly barley, were exported to Germany every year from this province. Immediately after the Swedish conquest, all of this export was directed to Sweden proper, and farmers in Scania were prohibited from sending any grain abroad (Bjurling 1945, 1956; Ersgård 1977; Tomner 1977; Johannesson 1969).

Parts of northern Germany were annexed to Sweden in the peace negotiations that marked the end of the Thirty Years' War. These provinces had been devastated by the war, but already in the mid-1680s Pomerania sent more than ten thousand barrels of grain to Sweden. Later, in the eighteenth century, Pomerania was one of the main exporters of grain to Sweden (Boëthius and Heckscher 1938; Peters 1966; Högberg 1969). The Swedish attack on Poland can also be understood as an attempt to gain control over the richest granary in northeastern Europe. The immediate result of the war was a sharp decrease in grain exports from Poland to the Netherlands.

Estimating the proportion of total grain consumption in Sweden that was covered by imports from the provinces is problematic. An informed guess is that this proportion rose to about one-tenth of the total production in the old provinces of Sweden, and more in years of scarcity. King Gustavus Adolphus and his successor King Charles X Gustavus both declared that their goal was to conquer rich provinces, by which they meant those with fertile soils capable of generating reliable agricultural surpluses. Accordingly, when Sweden faced the loss of its main provinces along the Baltic coast in the early eighteenth century, Fabian Wrede, an elderly Swedish statesman, wrote in a memorandum: "It is so with Sweden that it cannot support itself with grain: the Baltic provinces are our granary" (Myrdal 1999b:244).

Efforts to seize food-producing provinces were not unique to the Swedish case, nor the self-defeating character of expansion. However, comparisons with other historical cases must consider their specific circumstances and settings. The Roman Empire is no doubt the most famous parallel, but it endured for many centuries, through both expansion and decline. It also covered a vastly larger land mass. Nevertheless, there is a similarity with the small Swedish empire of the seventeenth century, as Rome similarly conquered one grain-producing region after the other and directed exports to the imperial center. Sicily was the first granary of Rome, then came northern Africa, and last and most important, Egypt. The rest of the empire was also similarly organized to support the center.[7] Another similar case is the Ottoman expansion into southeastern Europe, which annexed one food-producing province at a time.[8]

The Inner Logic of a War Economy

An important explanatory factor for the agricultural stagnation in the seventeenth century was the Little Ice Age. It struck hardest in marginal climatic regions, which applies to most of Sweden. A second factor was that the sixteenth-century expansion had reached its maximum extent, in relation to ecology and available technology. After the crisis of the late Middle Ages many fields could be recultivated. This, together with a more intense cultivation, caused an initial rise in levels of productivity. However, without further technological change, this increase had finally, in the early seventeenth century, to come to an end.

A third factor may have been that the dynamic nonagrarian sector absorbed great amounts of labor previously employed in agriculture, and the expansion of this sector was itself a part of the war economy. An "economic-military structure" was established. The army and the fleet needed resources created in Sweden, even if plundering often financed the actual warfare. Resources were raised in the home country through ever-increasing levels of taxation and conscription.

The Swedish armies consisted to a comparatively large extent of conscripts from Sweden and Finland. About one-third of every generation of young men who had reached the age of twenty went to war, most of them never to return (Lindegren 1992; Myrdal 1999b). The losses were at their highest during the period from the 1620s to the 1650s, in the 1670s, and again in the early eighteenth century. Young men from other peripheral regions in Europe, such as Scotland and Switzerland, also went to war, but in Sweden they did not go voluntarily.

A sustained population increase could thus actually be seen as one of the factors that allowed the Swedish state to build an empire. Even if not clearly stated in contemporary sources, population growth may also have tempted the Swedish government into war as a solution to the potential problems created by villages overflowing with young men who had poor prospects in life: better they should fight in foreign wars than rise in rebellion at home.

During the most intensive periods of warfare there were 1.3 women to every man in the Swedish home provinces (Myrdal 1999b:230). The women on the farms often had to take over male duties such as ploughing and heavy transports.

Sweden had exported iron and copper since the Middle Ages. In the sixteenth century there was an increase in production, at least partly facilitated by technological innovation. Exports of iron grew about threefold from the late Middle Ages, and reached 4,000 metric tonnes per year by the middle of the sixteenth century. Exports subsequently increased at an even faster rate and by the late seventeenth century 30,000 metric tonnes of iron were exported on an annual basis, much of it to England. Sweden was then one of the main exporters of iron in Europe. About 80 percent of the labor needed to produce iron was supplied by the peasants; they cut wood, produced the charcoal, transported the coal and the iron, and so on. An estimation of the amount of labor provided by peasants for iron production in the middle of the seventeenth century is 3–4 million workdays per annum (Sundberg et al. 1995; Myrdal 1999b).

Copper exports grew from less than 100 metric tonnes per year in the mid-sixteenth century, to 2,000 metric tonnes annually in the mid-seventeenth century. Sweden then dominated European copper export. Other products based on utilizing forest resources and peasant labor were potash and tar, and Sweden-Finland became the leading exporter in Europe of both products. Exports of tar, for example, increased from around 400,000 liters in the mid-sixteenth century to 12–15 million liters in the mid-seventeenth century. In large areas of Sweden-Finland, men and women had to devote months of labor each year to nonagricultural tasks (Heckscher

1935–1936; Karlsson 1990; Åhman 1983; Liljewall 1996), workdays taken from agriculture and enforced mainly by fiscal pressure. Peasants had to pay their taxes largely in money or iron and were thus forced to work in these nonsubsistence sectors.

Furthermore, a military industry was established, and Sweden produced not only all of the cannons, muskets, rapiers, and other weapons that were needed to satisfy the country's military requirements, but even exported to countries such as Denmark. In the eighteenth century, this proto-industry was redirected to nonmilitary production (scythes, shares, etc.) and became an important generator of economic progress.

A peculiar result of the war economy in the seventeenth century was that the state demanded that all stable refuse be collected so that the saltpeter could be used in the production of gunpowder. Accordingly, a nation-wide organization comprising one thousand saltpeter collectors was instituted. This was harmful in that it deprived the agricultural sector of nutrients that could have been used as valuable manure (Myrdal 1999b:302–304).

A well-organized state apparatus mobilized resources: young men, forest products, iron, copper, small industry, and so on. The economic-military structure acquired provinces that could sustain the core of the empire with grain. The center of the empire was the fast-growing capital of Stockholm, the population of which had increased from around eight thousand in the mid-sixteenth century to sixty thousand in the late seventeenth century. The capital had to be fed, and most of the grain imports arrived at the port of Stockholm itself.

At the end of the seventeenth century the Swedish armies were defeated, and internal social conflicts grew. Soldiers deserted the army, copper production declined as a result of overexploitation, and years of famine plagued the country. Ideological legitimacy for the war economy diminished. The peasants protested, the bourgeoisie protested, the clergy protested, and even the lesser nobility protested, as their wages were not being paid as a result of impending federal bankruptcy.[9] The end of the seventeenth century witnessed a political revolution, and the former basis of the war economy—that is, high taxation and the conscription of young men into the army—was brought to an end. Sweden's time as an empire was over.

However, Sweden was to emerge from its war economy with a more developed infrastructure for nonagrarian production. Swords could literally be turned into ploughshares. The country continued to import grain from Estonia and Livonia even after these provinces had been lost to Russia, but now by paying for these imports.

A Dysfunctional Empire in a European Crisis

Monocausal explanations for historical phenomena should generally be avoided. Religion, geopolitics, and the Swedish attempt to control the Baltic trade were all important factors in the imperial expansion of Sweden. The first two factors were essential for mobilizing popular support in the home country, a support that gradually declined as the burdens increased.

However, a fourth factor in understanding the Swedish Empire as an economic-military structure was the goal of conquering rich provinces so that these could be used to finance further expansion.[10] This, of course, was not something peculiar to Sweden in this period. Rather, it was a part of a general military revolution in Europe and the rest of the world, which heralded an enlarged scale of warfare. Armies now engaged hundreds of thousands of soldiers, fortresses covered huge areas, and investments in artillery and ships raised state expenditure to new levels (Roberts 1967; Parker 1996; McNeill and McNeill 2003:189–191).

Immanuel Wallerstein (1974) has emphasized that a European-wide (and worldwide) division of labor in basic production and bulk trade represented a fundamental change at this time in history. This was also a decisive factor for the Swedish endeavors—otherwise there would have been no markets for the products generated by mobilizing resources in Sweden. Sweden produced bulk products for the wartimes of the seventeenth century. The first breakthrough for bulk trade had been based on textile and food products in the late Middle Ages and the sixteenth century, but the prolonged wars in the following century harmed large-scale trade with agricultural products, such as the ox-trade from Denmark and eastern Europe, and the grain exports from Poland.

The general European crisis in this period has been a topic of fierce discussion over the years. Nearly all countries experienced stagnation, but with pronounced regional differences. In Spain and Italy the stagnation began in the late sixteenth century, and much of France also experienced a stagnating economy at that time. Germany was hit in the early seventeenth century, while England and Holland experienced stagnation in the late seventeenth century.[11]

The Malthusian doctrine suggests a basic explanation for this stagnation, and because change in agricultural techniques ceased there was stagnation in the overall production of food (Le Roy Ladurie 1974; Overton 1996). The Swedish reaction to this crisis in agricultural production was, as we have seen, political expansion. This can actually be seen as the general reaction in Europe at a time when the continent engaged in all-embracing warfare.

Many scholars have stressed the importance of wars as a central component in the ensuing vicious circle (Hobsbawm 1967:15; Trevor-Roper 1967:85; Elliot 1967:112; Steensgaard 1978:39).

The Swedish Empire can thus be seen as both a consequence and a cause of crisis. War zones along its advancing front were ravaged by massive destruction. In Lithuania the wars in the 1620s caused a steep decrease in population, and many villages were deserted and "overgrown with brushwood and their former position was unknown even to local peasants" (Liitoja-Tarkiainen 2000:240). Estonia and much of the Baltic region experienced a series of wars, and between the late sixteenth and the late seventeenth centuries the population fell to half (or even a third) of what it had been (Turpeinen 1997:408; Bardet 1997:574). In Poland, population decreased by 25–40 percent in the 1650s as a result of "the Swedish deluge," but other disasters including plague and wars with Russia also contributed to the Polish decline (Topolski 1986:99–100; Gieysztor 1997:569; Kriedte 1983:102). In Germany there was an overall population decrease of 40 percent during the Thirty Years' War—and in large areas in northern Germany and southwestern Germany the population decrease was over 66 percent (Pfister 1994:14; *Atlas zur Geschichte* 1973:59; Moore 1981:47).

The "Swedish wars" in Denmark from 1643 to 1660 caused depopulation, especially at the end of the period. In the area covered by contemporary Denmark, that is Jutland and the isles, the total population was about 555,000 in 1650 and fell to about 430,000 in 1660. In the early 1650s the country was ravaged by the plague, but an even worse decimator was the war of 1657–1660. In southern Jutland about sixty thousand succumbed, and in some parishes two-thirds of the population died. Farms were left abandoned for decades, and their fields were covered by heather (Lassen 1958, 1965:11; Johansen 2002:21–23).[12] In Scania the population remained stagnant between 1620 and 1690, and the region experienced a slump in the intervening decades.

In this huge, devastated area of Europe, fields and farms were left deserted, much as they had been during the late medieval crisis following the plague. A difference compared to the late medieval crisis, however, was that depopulation in the seventeenth century had a more patchy pattern, reflecting the routes of the armies. The Swedish armies were not the only ones to blame—the Habsburgs, the French, the Russians, and others also conducted ruthless warfare, leaving plague and famine in their wake.

At the core of the Swedish Empire we instead find a situation with considerable pressure on resources, especially on the woodlands. Iron production, for example, had to be spread over half of Sweden because of the shortage of timber in the mining districts.[13]

The Swedish Empire can thus be understood as part of a dysfunctional societal reaction to a growing European crisis. Michael Roberts provides an excellent account of the events in his classical essay on the military revolution. The medieval concept of war as an extension of feud had included a legal right to loot and to take booty. But when the scale of warfare expanded, Europe endured a period of wars where the "ordinary conduct was of exceptional savagery" (Roberts 1967:214–215). Enormous armies lived off the countryside, stripping it bare, or sometimes simply destroyed it to make it useless for the enemy armies. A new international agreement had to be reached in order to restrict the looting, and a new national policy had to be established, where the protection of a country and defense of its borders became even more important. From chaos came order.

Empires can be perceived as the result of expanding economies. The Swedish Empire, however, clearly resulted from a crisis, if seen at the European level. A stagnating economy spawned a more intense competition over resources, typical for all complex societies (Tainter 1988:121–122). This struggle took the form of ruthless wars between nations, a societal reaction that placed further burdens on economy, population, and ecology.

Notes

1. Taagepera's estimates have often been used, but seldom been studied from a source-critical perspective, which is especially relevant for earlier periods.

2. The reliability of estimations decreases as one goes back in time.

3. Table in Myrdal (2003). The state that controlled northern India was normally second largest in terms of population (cf. Livi-Bacci 1992:31).

4. Collins remarks that states in the middle of a geographical region tend to break up into smaller units, which would be an appropriate description of Germany in the seventeenth century.

5. For quite the opposite picture, of an underdeveloped Sweden, see Wallerstein (1974:312).

6. For a wider discussion of the tithe as a source, see Le Roy Ladurie and Goy (1982). On France: see Neveux, Jacquart, and Le Roy Ladurie (1975:17, 244); on Belgium: Daelemans (1978); Jansen (1978); on The Netherlands: Priester (1998). For a critique of the tithe as a source, see e.g. Hoffman (2000).

7. The classical economic history of the Roman Empire is Rostovtzeff (1957[1926]). For modern archaeological research, from an economic-historical perspective, see Greene (1986). Concerning the Roman Empire as a self-organizing

system, with several examples e.g. from southern France, see Van der Leeuw and de Vries (2002).

8. I thank John McNeill for pointing out this example to me.

9. The lesser nobility often owned little or no land at all, but were employed as state servants such as officers and clerks.

10. Wallerstein (1974:312–313) gives a similar account. He argues that the expansion of grain production in Sweden was hindered by climatic downturn. The Swedish nobility hence needed conquest and thus a strong state, which in the seventeenth and eighteenth centuries used mercantilism as a lever for industrial advancement.

11. On this debate, see Aston (1967) and Parker and Smith (1978). Cipolla (1981:248–249) has emphasized regional differences, with a relative expansion of the North Sea regions. For summaries, see Kriedte (1983:62–69); de Vries (1994:13–14); and Fischer (1996:72–96, 468–472).

12. The Swedish army had plundered for two years, but was driven out from Jutland by Denmark's allied forces from Poland, Brandenburg, and the Habsburg emperor's Austrian armies. Economic collapse followed with typhus and famine.

13. See Sundberg et al. (1995) for an "emergy analysis," inspired and coauthored by H. T. Odum, of the use of Swedish woodlands at this time.

References

Åhman, S. 1983. *Pottaskebränning i Sverige och Danmark under 1600-talet*. Växjö: Växjö högskola.

Åmark, K. 1915. *Spannmålspolitik och spannmålshandel i Sverige 1719–1830*. Stockholm: Stockholms högskola.

Anderson, P. 1974. *Lineages of the absolutist state*. London: NLB.

Aston, T., ed. 1967. *Crisis in Europe 1560–1660*. New York: Anchor.

Atlas zur Geschichte. 1973. Vol. 1, ed. L. Berthold. Leipzig: Zentralinstitut für Geschichte der Akademie der Wissenschaften der DDR.

Attman, A. 1944. *Den ryska marknaden i 1500-talets baltiska politik 1558–1595*. Lund: Lunds universitet.

Bardet, J.-P. 1997. Le pays Baltes. In *Histoire des populations de l'Europe*, vol. 1, ed. J.-P. Bardet and J. Dupâquier, 573–576. Paris: Fayard.

Barraclough, G., ed. 1978. *The Times atlas of world history*. London: Times Books.

Bengtsson, T., and J. Oeppen. 1993. *A reconstruction of the population of Scania 1650–1760*. Lund: Lunds universitet.

Bjurling, O. 1945. *Skånes utrikessjöfart 1667–1720*. Lund: Gleerup.

———. 1956. 1658–1792. In *Ystads historia*, vol. 1, 175–514. Ystad: Ystad stad.

Boëthius, B., and E. F. Heckscher. 1938. *Svensk handelsstatistik 1637–1737* [Swedish foreign trade statistics, 1637–1737]. Stockholm: Thule.

Cipolla, C. 1981. *Before the industrial revolution: European society and economy 1000–1700*. 2nd ed. London: Methuen.

Collins, R. 1999. *Macrohistory: Essays in sociology of the long run.* Stanford, Calif.: Stanford University Press.

Daelemans, F. 1978. Tithe revenues in rural south-west Brabant. In *Productivity of land and agricultural innovation in the Low countries (1250–1800),* ed. H. van der Wee and E. van Cauwenberghe. Louvain: Leuven University Press.

Dalhede, C. 1999. The European ox trade in early modern time: Southern Germany, the southern Netherlands and western Sweden. In *Agrarian systems in early modern Europe,* 57–95. Stockholm: Nordiska museet.

De Vries, J. 1994. Population. In *Handbook of European history 1400–1600,* ed. T. A. Brady, H. A. Oberman, and J. D. Tracy, 1–50. Leiden: Brill.

Elliott, J. H. 1967. The decline of Spain. In *Crisis in Europe 1560–1660,* ed. T. Aston, 107–205. New York: Anchor.

Ersgård, H. 1977. Stadens historia 1658–1718. In *Malmö stads historia,* vol. 2, 189–348. Malmö: Allhem.

Fischer, D. H. 1996. *The great wave: Price revolutions and the rhythm of history.* Oxford: Oxford University Press.

Gieysztor, I. 1997. La Pologne. In *Histoire des populations de l'Europe,* vol. 1, ed. J.-P. Bardet and J. Dupâquier. Paris: Fayard.

Greene, K. 1986. *The archaeology of the Roman economy.* London: Batsford.

Hegardt, A. 1975. *Akademiens spannmål: Uppbörd, handel och priser vid Uppsala universitet 1635–1719.* Uppsala: Uppsala universitet.

Heckscher, E. 1935–1936. *Sveriges ekonomiska historia.* Vols. 1–2. Stockholm: Bonniers.

Hoffman, P. 2000 (1996). *Growth in traditional society: The French countryside 1450–1815.* Princeton, N.J.: Princeton University Press.

Hobsbawm, E. J. 1967. The crisis of the seventeenth century. in *Crisis in Europe 1560–1660,* ed. T. Aston, 5–62. New York: Anchor.

Högberg, S. 1969. *Utrikeshandel och sjöfart på 1700-talet: Stapelvaror i svensk export och import 1738–1808.* Stockholm: Bonniers.

Jansen, C. G. M. 1978. Tithe and the productivity of land in the south of Limburg 1348–1790. In *Productivity of land and agricultural innovation in the Low countries (1250–1800),* ed. H. van der Wee and E. van Cauwenberghe, 77–84. Louvain: Leuven University Press.

Johannesson, G. 1969. Näringslivet. In *Hälsingborgs historia,* vol. 3, 15–321. Hälsingborg: Hälsingborgs stad.

Johansen, H. C. 2002. *Danish population history 1600–1939.* Odense: University Press of Southern Denmark.

Karlsson, P.-A. 1990. *Järnbruken och ståndssamhället.* Stockholm: Jernkontoret.

Kriedte, P. 1983. *Peasants, landlords and merchant capitalists: Europe and the world economy 1500–1800.* Oxford: Berg.

Lassen, A. 1958. *Skaebneåret 1659: Hungersnød og pest over Sydvestdanmark.* Aarhus: Jysk selskab for historie, sprog og literatur.

———. 1965. *Fald og fremgang: Træk af befolkningsudviklingen i Danmark 1645–1660.* Aarhus: Jysk selskab for historie, sprog og literatur.

Le Roy Ladurie, E. 1974. *The peasants of Languedoc.* Urbana: University of Illinois Press.

Le Roy Ladurie, E., and J. Goy. 1982. *Tithe and agrarian history from the fourteenth to the nineteenth centuries.* Cambridge, U.K.: Cambridge University Press.

Leijonhufvud, L. 2001. *Grain tithes and manorial yields in early modern Sweden: Trends and patterns of production and productivity c 1540–1680.* Uppsala: Sveriges lantbruksuniversitet.

Lindegren, J. 1992. *Maktstatens resurser.* Manuscript. Department of History, University of Uppsala.

Liitoja-Tarkiainen, Ü. 2000. *Hajatalud ja külad Põhja-Liivimaal: 17 sajandil.* Tartu: Kirjastus Eesti Ajalooarhiiv.

Liljewall, B., ed. 1996. *Tjära, barkbröd och vildhonung: Utmarkens människor och mångsidiga resurser.* Stockholm: Nordiska museet.

Livi-Bacci, M. 1992. *A concise history of world population.* Cambridge, U.K.: Blackwell.

McEvedy, C., and R. Jones. 1978. *Atlas of world population history.* Harmondsworth, U.K.: Penguin.

McNeill, J. R., and W. H. McNeill. 2003. *The human web: A bird's-eye view of world history.* New York: Norton.

Moore, R. I., ed. 1981. *The Hamlyn historical atlas.* London: Hamlyn.

Morell, M. 1989. *Studier i den svenska livsmedelskonsumtionens historia: Hospitalhjonens livsmedelskonsumtion 1621–1872.* Uppsala: Uppsala universitet.

Myers, A. R. 1975. *Parliaments and estates in Europe to 1789.* London: Thames and Hudson.

Myrdal, J., and J. Söderberg. 1991. *Kontinuitetens dynamik: Agrar ekonomi i 1500-talets Sverige.* Stockholm: Stockholms universitet.

Myrdal, J. 1999a. The agrarian revolution restrained: Swedish agrarian technology in the 16th century in a European perspective. In *Agrarian systems in early modern Europe,* 96–145. Stockholm: Nordiska museet.

———. 1999b. *Jordbruket under feodalismen.* Det svenska jordbrukets historia 2. Stockholm: LT:s förlag.

———. 2003. Syntesens roll och världshistorien: Samhällelig komplexitet och imperiernas historia. In *Historisk tidskrift,* 259–284. Stockholm.

Neveux, H., J. Jacquart, and E. Le Roy Ladurie. 1975. L'âge classique de 1340 à 1789. In *Histoire de la France rurale,* vol. 2. Paris: Seuil.

Oredsson, S. 1994. *Geschichtsschreibung und Kult: Gustav Adolf, Schweden und der Deissigjährige Krieg.* Berlin: Duncker und Humbolt.

Overton, M. 1996. *Agricultural revolution in England: The transformation of the agrarian economy 1500–1850.* Cambridge, U.K.: Cambridge University Press.

Palm, L. A. 1991. Priser i Västsverige. In *Dagligt bröd i onda tider: Priser och löner i Stockholm och Västsverige 1500–1700,* 88–192. Göteborg: Institutet för lokalhistorisk forskning.

———. 2000. *Folkmängden i Sveriges socknar och kommuner 1571–1997.* Göteborg: Göteborgs universitet.

Parker, G. 1996. *The military revolution: Military innovation and the rise of the West 1500–1800*. 2nd ed. Cambridge, U.K.: Cambridge University Press.

Parker, G., and L. Smith, eds. 1978. *The general crisis of the seventeenth century*. London: Routledge and Kegan Paul.

Peters, J. 1966. Unter den schwedischen Krone. In *Zeitschrift für Geschichtswissenschaft*, 33–51. Berlin.

Pfister, C. 1994. *Bevölkerungsgeschichte und historisches Demographie 1500–1800*. Munich: Oldenbourg.

Priester, P. 1998. *Geschiedenis van de Zeeuwse landbouw circa 1600–1910*. Wageningen: Landbouwuniversiteit Wageningen.

Roberts, M. 1967. *Essays in Swedish history*. London: Weidenfeld and Nicolson.

———. 1968. *The early Vasas*. Cambridge, U.K.: Cambridge University Press.

Rostovtzeff, M. 1957 (1926). *The social and economic history of the Roman empire*. 2nd ed. Oxford: Clarendon.

Sandström, Å. 1990. *Mellan Torneå och Amsterdam: En undersökning av Stockholms roll som förmedlare av varor i regional- och utrikeshandel 1600–1650*. Stockholm: Stockholm stad.

Söderberg, J., and A. Jansson. 1988. Corn-price rises and equalisation: Real wages in Stockholm 1650–1719. *Scandinavian Economic History Review* 36: 42–67.

Söderberg, J., and J. Myrdal. 2002. *The agrarian economy of sixteenth-century Sweden*. Stockholm: Stockholms universitet.

Soom, A. 1961. *Der baltische Getreidehandeln im 17. Jahrhundert*. Stockholm: Kungl. Vitterhets Historie och Antikvitetsakademien.

Sundberg, U., J. Lindegren, H. Odum, S. Dohtery, and H. Steinlin. 1995. *Skogens användning och roll under det svenska stormaktsväldet: Perspektiv på energi och makt*. Stockholm: Kunglig Skogs- och Lantbruksakademien.

Steensgaard, N. 1978. The seventeenth-century crisis. In *The general crisis of the seventeenth century*, ed. G. Parker and L. Smith, 26–56. London: Routledge and Kegan Paul.

Taagepera, R. 1978. Size and duration of empires: Systematics of size. *Social Science Research* 7:108–127.

———. 1997. Expansion and contraction patterns of large polities: Context for Russia. *International Studies Quarterly* 41:475–504.

Tainter, J. A. 1988. *The collapse of complex societies*.Cambridge, U.K.: Cambridge University Press.

Tollin, C. 1991. *Ättebackar och ödegärden: De äldre lantmäterikartorna i kulturmiljövården*. Stockholm: Riksantikvarieämbetet.

Tomner, L. 1977. Stadens historia 1500–1658. In *Malmö stads historia*, vol. 2, 9–188. Malmö: Allhem.

Topolski, J. 1986. *An outline history of Poland*. Warsaw: Interpress.

Trevor-Roper, H. R. 1967. The general crisis of the seventeenth century. In *Crisis in Europe 1560–1660*, ed. T. Aston, 63–102. New York: Anchor.

Turpeinen, O. 1997. La Suède et la Finlande de 1300 à 1720. In *Histoire des populations de l'Europe*, vol. 1, ed. J.-P. Bardet and J. Dupâquier, 399–402. Paris: Fayard.

Van der Leeuw, S., and B. de Vries. 2002. Empire: The Romans in the Mediterranean. In *Mappae Mundi: Humans and their habitats in a long-term socio-ecological perspective*, ed. B. de Vries and J. Goudsblom, 209–256. Amsterdam: Amsterdam University Press.

Wallerstein, I. 1974. *The modern world system.* Vol. 1, *Capitalist agriculture and the origins of the European world-economy in the sixteenth century.* New York: Academic Press.

Werdelin, L., S. Sten, and J. Myrdal. 2000. Patterns of stature variation in medieval Sweden. *Hikuin* 27:293–306.

The Role of Deforestation in Earth and   **5**
World-System Integration

MICHAEL WILLIAMS

T HE TASK OF COMBINING world-system history and global environmental change (the Earth system) is an important and intellectually
complex challenge. However, the union is not easy, has rarely been
attempted, and barely been successful. Most historians of environmental
change remain steadfastly empirically historical (e.g. Hughes 2001; McNeill
2000; Richards 2003), ignoring the theoretical contributions of those like
Braudel (1984), Wallerstein (1974, 1980, 1989), Foster (1999), and Marx
(Berman 1981).[1] They "don't know quite what to do with social theory,"
Jason Moore has written recently, "and the environmentally-orientated social scientists don't quite know how to translate their perspectives into historical research" (Moore 2003:307). Of course the division is not quite so
stark; there have already been some interesting exercises in cross-fertilization.
For example, Terlouw's (1988, 1992) attempts to integrate world regional
geography with the world-system, Hans-Jürgen Nitz's (1993:1–25) attempt
to give historical specificity to the theoretical concerns at a variety of scales,
and Dodgshon's (1993) critique of the inner social dynamics of the world-
system.

For Moore, the way forward to achieve this synthesis between the two
systems has been to look at the details of silver mining and sugar plantations as
exemplars of the major global commodity frontiers. He investigates how the
geographical entities of core, periphery, semiperiphery, and external arena
interacted, as feudalism went through crisis and capitalism rose triumphant.
The analysis of these commodity frontiers is seen through the lenses of
Wallerstein's socioecological insights and Marx's ecological critique of capitalism. Each enables one to analyze the "emergence of far-flung divisions

of labour and the consolidation of a capitalist world economy predicated on the endless accumulation of capital" (Moore 2003:309). The environmental transformations that accompanied these commodity frontiers were both the result and the cause of further expansion and transformation of the world-system, sending out recurrent waves of exploitation to the farthest corners of the globe.

Silver and sugar were by no means the only commodity frontiers. An extended list could well include other minerals (gold, iron, phosphates) and more especially and importantly many different foods (tea, coffee, cocoa, wheat, rice) and organic consumer goods (cotton, tobacco), and of course, animal products like whale meat and oil, fish protein, and furs, feathers, and skins—what Richards (2003:463–616) calls the products of "The World Hunt." These are all reminiscent of Walter Prescott Webb's (1952) early, but curiously neglected, work on the post-Columbian exploitation by the European world of what he called "The Great Frontier" of fish, furs, metals, wheat, and meat. In addition to mineral, food, and animal products there was a fourth major category of commodity frontier. That was wood and wood products, which next to food was "the other great basic need" in the early modern economy and a "continuing 'growth' crop" (Wallerstein 1974:44–45, 1980:161–162).

This chapter looks at timber and timber products in an attempt to integrate studies of the "Earth system" with studies of the "world-system," focusing on the role of long-distance trade and export production in transforming the natural environment (Lund Symposium 2003). In order to do that the chapter is divided into four main sections:

1. The nature of deforestation and wood procurement and trade as a manifestation of the Earth system is examined.
2. Some of the main characteristics of the Wallersteinian/Braudelian world-system will be discussed, against which the historical specificity of the early modern European situation will be placed.
3. Both the Earth system and world-system are then brought together in an examination of case studies of the long-distance timber trade.
4. Finally, the very special nature of timber depletion is emphasized: it is about the only commodity frontier where the depletion of the main product—timber—frequently creates a new and valuable resource in the form of changed land-covers of agricultural and pastoral land.

Although the exact order in which these four themes are examined may be questioned, taken together they may, among other things, lend greater understanding to the political and distributional aspects of environmental deterioration and change, and global inequalities.

The Earth System: The Nature of Deforestation

There can be no better way of achieving the complex and interrelated aims of synthesizing the world-system with the Earth system than by concentrating on the processes that have transformed the land-cover of the globe. Humans have cleared the forests to create cropland, converted grasslands to create grain lands, drained wetlands to create dry land, and irrigated arid land to create productive land. Of these processes, forest clearing has affected a greater land area than the others. At least 7.01×10^6 km^2 of dense forest and 3.13×10^6 km^2 of open forest have been eliminated by humans since postglacial times, the bulk of it before 1950 (Williams 2003).

Deforestation is as old as the human occupation of the Earth, and is part of the age-old quest of humanity for shelter, warmth, and food. Consequently, the attraction of forested environments is not difficult to appreciate. Trees provide wood for construction, for shelter, and for making a multitude of implements. Wood provides the fuel to keep warm, to cook food and make it palatable, and even to smelt metal and make ceramics. The nuts and fruits of the trees are useful for human foods, medicines, and dyes, and the roots, young shoots, and branches provide food for animals. Very simply, the forest has provided essential materials for human survival, second only to food.

But wood has a multiple importance. Because it is an energy source in metal-making it has been crucial in the manufacture of armaments, and until the mid-nineteenth century was the basic material for constructing ships, the very means of long-distance trade and capitalism's exploitation of the commodity frontiers of the world. Consequently, until recently, wood occupied a strategic position in most parts of the world akin to that of petroleum today, or what steel was before. So important was the supply of timber and naval stores for maintaining a navy that they were worth going to war over in order to ensure supplies; witness the British efforts to keep the Baltic Straits out of hostile hands during the Napoleonic Wars.

But timber is even more multifaceted than that; it was more than a positive, useful, and essential commodity, because its clearing (i.e. deforestation) provided the land for growing crops—land, moreover, often covered by a deep humus accumulation and initially rich in nutrients. Thus, as we will see in the fourth and final section of this chapter, deforestation was the prelude to the emergence of many other commodity frontiers, especially those of the food and vegetable crops of the tropical world, like coffee, sugar, tobacco, and rubber. In short, deforestation is subsumed in the global emergence of most food crops, with the notable exception of grain crops in the world's grasslands, which flourished after the invention of the steel-tipped plough in the mid-1830s.

In contrast to draining and irrigating, clearing requires no sophisticated technology or cooperative effort. In prehistory individual humans with stone or flint axes needed only boundless energy to fell trees. The addition of fire and browsing animals completed what the axe did not accomplish. The substitution of metal for stone axes around 3,500 years ago, and then saws in the medieval period, eased the back-breaking task of clearing and accelerated the rate of change, but neither altered the basic process of destruction and land-use transformation. In contrast, since the mid-twentieth century, power saws have made a major and accelerating impact. Nevertheless, taking the long view, tropical forest destruction since 1950 is a mere continuation of an ever-upwardly sloping curve. Admittedly, compared to previous deforestation episodes it is more rapid and detrimental to global biodiversity, and it is occurring in more sensitive and irreversibly damaged environments.

So, in summary, wood has been an essential raw material for energy and construction throughout most of human history, it has had strategic importance for shipbuilding and metal-making, its clearing was the means of making new land, and felling is a reasonably easy resource conversion technique.

Wood Procurement

The procurement of wood presents a paradox. It is a bulky, low-cost commodity that in theory should not travel far. The classical position is laid out in what was probably the first-ever theoretical statement on commodity exploitation by Johann Heinrich von Thünen (1826), a wheat farmer from the Mecklenburg district of northern Germany. He postulated that there would be a roughly concentric zonation of land use around the marketplace, dependent on the transport costs, which rose with increasing distance from the center. In that zonation timber (unlike grain, for example) would be located close to the marketplace because of its bulky, low-cost nature. While the zonation of grain seemed to happen at a local scale on the preindustrial northern European plain, the essential nature of timber produced a more complicated picture. Constant demand meant that it was soon chopped out on nearby locations, and deficiencies in the region were made up for by imports from further afield. Similar movements happened on a world scale.

It was not as if lumber was a high-value product. Perhaps the nearest comparable commodity moved in bulk was wheat, and that was anything between four to six times more valuable than sawn lumber and ten to twelve times more valuable than logs per unit weight—and even wheat was said not to be worth moving if the price was low (Rector 1953:28–29). That lumber continued to be moved around the world irrespective of its bulkiness and low per-unit value was a measure of its essential nature. We have become accustomed to the idea that strategic wooden products like masts for sailing ships were moved vast distances, but it is salutary to think that prosaic English drawing rooms built during the early seventeenth century were often paneled with oak that came from Silesia or Galicia, and occasionally with "Riga wainscot," oak that came from Kazan on the Russian forest-steppe edge. Timber had turned the trade of the world upside down, propelled land-cover change over vast areas, and pushed the commodity frontier into new far-flung regions.

World Trade System: The Wallersteinian Model

Let us now shift our focus from the changing Earth system (as exemplified by deforestation and the timber trade) to the role of timber and land-use change in the emerging world-system. The von Thünen land-use model does not explain or capture the complexities of the spatial structure of the early modern European world-system. However, the model devised by Wallerstein (and Braudel before him) has greater utility.

Wallerstein developed the concepts "core," "periphery," and "external arena," which have pronounced geographical expression and historical continuity. The economic system is conceived of as being centered around the "core" with its trade metropolis, which controls the world economy. The core controls world trade by setting prices for goods both at the point of production and at the point of consumption. It is a coerced and unequal exchange based on exploitation. The second domain is the "peripheral" zone, which is dependent on the core. It supplies the core with raw materials, which are the "lower-ranking goods" (that is, goods whose labor is less well rewarded), but which are an integral part of the overall system of the division of labor, because commodities involved are essential for daily use. The third domain is the "external arena," defined as those other world-systems with which a given world economy has some kind of trade relationship, based primarily on the exchange of preciosities, or what was sometimes called "the rich trades" (Wallerstein 1974:302).

In both Wallerstein's and Braudel's models there is a fourth structural zone located between the core and the periphery, Wallerstein's "semi-periphery" and Braudel's "intermediate zone." This characteristic of indeterminacy refers to its intermediate geographical position, intermediate wealth, and intermediate economic diversification. It is more diverse than the periphery and has many intermediate trade centers that deal directly with the metropolitan core area. They are what Braudel calls "relay cities."

This theoretical model lends understanding to the historical situation. Before the sixteenth century, Europe was a peripheral appendage of the civilized world—a mere "peninsula of peninsulas" in the words of H. C. Darby (1961:20). That world consisted of the land-based empires of Ming China, the Ottoman Middle East (soon to spread to North Africa), and the precursors of Safavid Persia and Mughal north India, soon to become (1508 and 1526 respectively) the mighty polities that they eventually were. In these empires contacts by sea were relatively unimportant (figure 5.1).[2] The continents were isolated from one another, except for a few overland trading routes that linked Europe with India and Africa for the movement of high-cost goods, such as tea, porcelain, indigo, spices, and pearls, that is, what Wallerstein called "preciosities." With the application by the European trading nations of improved technology for ships' rigging, ocean maps, and navigational aids, it was Europe that leaped ahead. It broke out of its land-based territory, and by making use of its access to the Atlantic, Baltic, and North Seas, turned the continents inside out and in effect reoriented them to face the sea, and established sea contacts between them.

By 1700 it was a very different picture from that of the late fifteenth century. From being on the periphery, Europe now moved to being at the center or core of innovation, trade, and change, to become the most dynamic region in the world. Peripheries and external arenas of raw materials were created around it. Western Europe's periphery stretched from Scandinavia (fish, wood, and metals), through the Baltic rimlands region (grain, wood, flax, naval stores), to the Black Sea and Hungary (livestock). In the south it encompassed the Italian and Iberian peninsulas (sheep, wool, wine) and extended across the Atlantic to the Caribbean islands and fringing lands, which provided tropical products. Of course, it was not a stable arrangement. As the commodity frontiers and their environmental transformations changed, so did the "zones." In the process, "the external arenas of one country often became the periphery of the next" and even "core states became semi-peripheral, or semi-peripheral areas peripheral" (Wallerstein 1974:350). It was a highly dynamic arrangement.

c. 1500

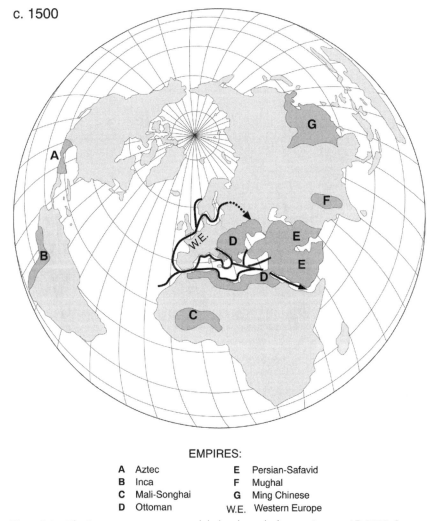

EMPIRES:

A	Aztec	**E**	Persian-Safavid
B	Inca	**F**	Mughal
C	Mali-Songhai	**G**	Ming Chinese
D	Ottoman	W.E.	Western Europe

Figure 5.1.   The European economy on a global scale, and other empires, ca. AD 1500. *Sources*: After F. Braudel, *Civilization and Capitalism, 15th–18th Century*, vol. 1, *The Structures of Everyday Life: The Limits of the Possible* (New York: Harper and Row, 1981), 26; and G. Barraclough, ed., *The Times Atlas of World History* (London: Times, 1978), 154–155

Despite the seeming simplicity of the Wallerstein/Braudel geoeconomic megastructures, it is difficult to give the constituent domains geographical specificity, as they are dynamic and shift through time (Taylor 1988; Terlouw 1992; Wallace 1990). Nevertheless, an attempt has been made in figures 5.1 and 5.2 to give a generalized view of the global arrangement. The situation

c. 1775

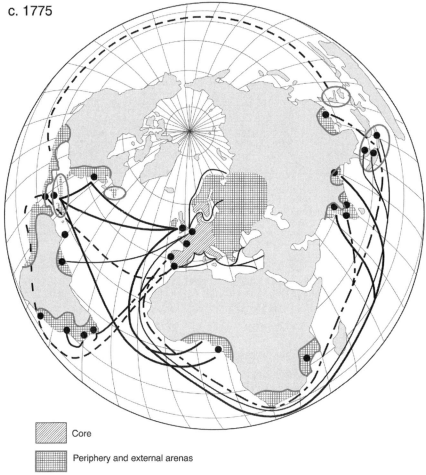

Core

Periphery and external arenas

Figure 5.2.   The European economy on a global scale, and the emergence of a core and periphery/external arena, ca. 1775. *Sources*: After F. Braudel, *Civilization and Capitalism, 15th–18th Century*, vol. 1, *The Structures of Everyday Life: The Limits of the Possible* (New York: Harper and Row, 1981), 27; and G. Barraclough, ed., *The Times Atlas of World History* (London: Times, 1978), 198–199

around 1500 is relatively simple to reconstruct, as it incorporates actual or potential political entities and their predecessors, but the late-eighteenth-century pattern cannot be defined by nation states, and can only be sketched broadly, especially at the scale at which we are working. In reality, the parts of the structure are vague, especially as Wallerstein initially considers nation-states as the elementary units of the system and then later asserts that market forces ignore national boundaries. Because of the scale and the uncertainty, the periphery and external arena are combined—in theory, the external arenas become incorporated into the periphery—and the relay cities are indicated schematically, while the intermediate areas are sketched in broadly. Despite its imperfections and limitations, however, it is offered as a visual guide to what is basically a geographical concept.

Ever since the breakdown of feudalism in the late fourteenth century, Europe had been moving toward a more entrepreneurial, commercial, merchant, money- and credit-driven, profit-oriented market system—capitalism, no less. This transition is best described as the advent of modernity. It was first clearly discernible in the late sixteenth century, when truly capitalist states engaged in a new sort of international exchange economy were in evidence first in northern Italy, then by 1650 in the Low Countries and then Britain (Williams 2003:155–159). The concomitant rise of Amsterdam and London as international trading, financial, and information-exchanging centers was important. "Everywhere," said the Dutch historian Herman Van der Wee, "money was on the march" (Van der Wee 1970:290).

A driving force that stimulated consumption was the increase in Europe's population from about 82 million in 1500 to about 105 million in 1600, and then 140 million in 1750. But rising numbers alone were of less significance than the increasing purchasing power of the population, a power aided by the influx of gold and silver bullion from the New World. For the rich of western Europe, all aspects of life improved considerably, as they did for the expanding urban commercial and professional classes. The intermediate group of skilled artisans and small farmers were also marginally better off, and the "fairly ordinary man as consumer was beginning to emerge as a person of importance in the demand picture" (Minchinton 1977:168).

As Europe shifted from being periphery to being core, the economic system and means of production interacted with each other in an upwardly ascending spiral of consumption and production. The link between the two was overseas trade, and the ship its symbol. That archetypal discoverer, entrepreneur, colonizer, and adventurer, Sir Walter Raleigh, was convinced of the preeminence of those "ascendant at sea" when he coined the dictum, "Hee that commaunds the sea, commaunds the trade, and hee that is Lord of the Trade is Lord of the wealth of the worlde" (Lefranc 1980:600). It was an awesome prediction of what was going to happen. The traditional relationships between people and their environment in the peripheral parts of the world were shattered as Europe extracted the potential of the land and its vegetation, commodifying nature for its own use.

In summary, the increase in demand for all goods put increased pressures on land resources. In particular there was a shift from the medieval preoccupation with land-based trade in small quantities of high-value luxury goods—Wallerstein's "preciosities"—from the largely unaffected external arenas of contact in Africa and most of Asia, to the movement of lower-ranking goods in bulk from the periphery of the Americas and the East Indies. The very names of these goods indicate their origin and have passed into everyday usage. For example, "muslin" for high quality, lightweight fabric from Mosul, "calico" for thicker cotton fabric from Calicut, and "china" for tableware. All these and many more were destined in large quantities for an increasingly widening segment of affluent people who consumed a disproportionate amount of the world's resources.

Linking Earth and World Systems

Now let us bring together the first two strands of this argument, the paradox of the low value but long distance traveled in the procurement of wood and wood products, and the early modern European place in the world-system. These are joined in the examination of (1) the long-distance trade of timber, and (2) the very special characteristics of deforestation, namely the substitution of food and fiber crops for trees. These were crops that grew mainly in the tropical world and eventually entered into world trade.

Long-Distance Timber Trade: Antecedents

The most common and most bulky commodity traded was timber. Its long-distance trade had many antecedents that went back into antiquity.[3]

THE ROMAN AND MUSLIM MEDITERRANEAN. Reasonably well documented are the movements that focused on Rome, which grew to be one of the largest cities in the world until modern times. It had nearly half a million inhabitants in 86 BC, 1 million in 5 BC, and between 1.2 and 1.4 million in the fourth century AD. Not only were there more buildings that demanded large constructional timbers but also bigger buildings, as well as the demands for heating, baths, and cement-, plaster-, and glass-making. Consumption far outstripped local supplies, and wood was garnered from a radius of about 100 km. Larger timbers were floated down the west-flowing peninsular rivers up to 500 km to the north and then coastwise to the Tiber and upstream to Rome.

When it came to the strategic interest of ships' timbers, the local trade changed to a more regional one that spanned the whole Mediterranean and Black seas (map 5.1). Theophrastus and other writers give clear details of the sources of supply. Timbers came from the Pontus and Bithynian provinces

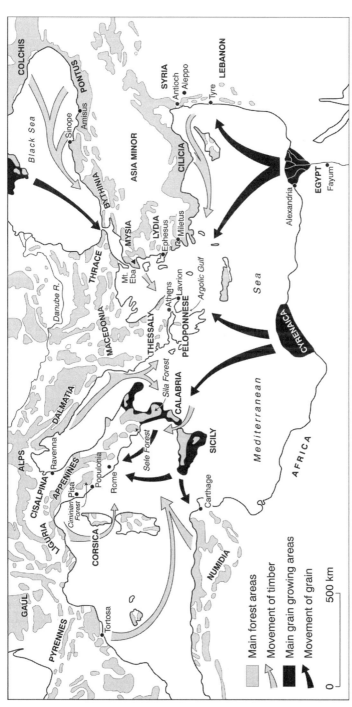

Map 5.1.   Major timber- and grain-growing areas and trade routes in the Mediterranean basin, fourth to first century BC. *Sources:* After M. M. Lombard, "Une carte du bois dans la Méditerranée musulmane (VIIe–XIe siècle)," *Annales, Economies, Sociétés, Civilizations* 14 (1959): 23–54; and A. G. Sherratt and S. Sherratt, "The Growth of the Mediterranean Economy in the Early First Millennium BC," *World Archaeology* 24 (1993): 361–378

on the southern coast of the Black Sea, Colchis on the far western shore, where the Bolshay Kavkaz mountains rise and run to the Caspian Sea, Cilicia on what is the Toros Daglar (Taurus) mountains of southern Turkey, the Syrian mountains, the Dalmatian coast, Liguria, and Catalonia. Some even came from Numidia on the north African coast in what is now Algeria. It is impossible to know the quantities moved but they must have been considerable.

The timber supply lines of the Muslim seventh- to thirteenth-century world were not that dissimilar, focusing particularly on the pine of Catalonia and Dalmatian timber (when the Venetians were not being vigilant). Supplies, which were gathered within the Mediterranean, were supplemented by even longer-distance trading of pine from the Atlantic coast of Portugal and teak from the Malabar coast of India (map 5.2). Timber for shipbuilding was the prime attraction of these long-distance routes, but timber for construction and fuel for metal-smelting, ceramics, and domestic heating also loomed large.

THE BALTIC TRADE. The Baltic trade was vast and of long standing, and was the first global manifestation of low-value goods being moved in bulk. From the Middle Ages the Hanseatic League had organized trade in naval stores (masts, wood, pitch tar, turpentine, flax) and general timber, potash, and wheat, upstream from the settlements on the river edges to the towns established at their mouths by the Teutonic Knights. The Baltic hinterland was what Wallerstein (1974) called one of Europe's "Internal Americas," and a notable exception to the pre-1500 trade in preciosities. A wave of colonization in Poland and Lithuania in the fifteenth and sixteenth centuries stimulated further clearing for more extensive agricultural and urban needs, as well as exports. Danzig, with its many water-driven saw mills, emerged as the dominant shipbuilding center and hub of the export trade, with lesser centers at Konigsberg and Riga.

So profitable was this trade that the landowning nobility on the Polish, southern shores pressured the peasantry into grain-growing during the summer and into logging during the winter, and the German princes in Prussia and Lithuania claimed the forest as a state monopoly. Thus lumbering became an adjunct to the feudal system, and the "lopsided development of agriculture and forestry under massive pressure of western demand" took place in Poland and adjacent territories at the expense of local crafts and industries (Glamman 1974:459; Malowist 1959, 1960a, 1960b).

With their labor supply secure, the landowners contracted out their exploitation to Dutch, German, and increasingly British large-scale

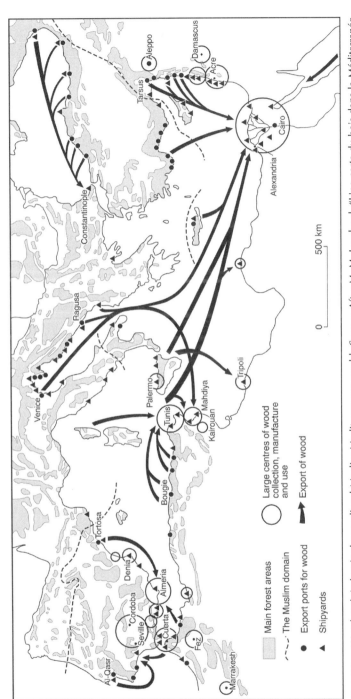

Map 5.2. Wood and timber in the medieval Muslim Mediterranean world. *Source*: After M. M. Lombard, "Une carte du bois dans la Méditerranée musulmane (VIIe–XIe siècle)," *Annales, Economies, Sociétés, Civilizations* 14 (1959): 23–54

entrepreneurs. A contract would be drawn up in, say Deptford, Amsterdam, or La Rochelle, and credit advanced to a Baltic merchant house, which would engage middlemen to negotiate with forest-owners to produce the required amount of timber, and sometimes to transport the trunks to port, paying so much per tree.

Resource exploitation was aided by local topographical and climatic conditions. Gradients were gentle, and felling could be done in the winter months when the sap was low, and the huge spars and trunks hauled out of the forest easily on horse- and ox-drawn sleds on the snow cover to the edge of the many substantial rivers that flow across the north European plain. Then, with the spring thaw, individual logs were thrown into the smaller streams to be collected at some strategic point and assembled into great rafts of over a thousand logs that could be navigated downstream, and these "rafts" were piled high with smaller sawn lumber, fuel wood, grain, and also potash.

At the Baltic ports, the rafts were floated into mast ponds, broken up, the choicest "sticks" reserved for the highly strategic masts, and the rest sawn into whatever lengths and widths the market demanded—balks, planks, deals, or battens. Lumber was originally sawn laboriously by hand, but productivity was stepped up manyfold with Dutch- and German-designed wind- and water-driven mills with up to 10 blades per frame. As these had already diffused east into the Finnish/Russian towns of Narva, Nyen, and Vyborg by 1700, and Fredrikshamn and Helsingfors by 1710, they must have been adopted in the main south Baltic milling centers well before that date. The timber was loaded into comparatively small ships of 250–400 tons which had shallow drafts, and were preferred because of the many offshore spits and bars in the shallow and sandy Baltic ports (Åström 1975; Albion 1926; Soom 1961).

Each river had a major trans-shipment port at its estuary, and each tapped specific supplies in its hinterland (map 5.3). The Stettin trade along the Oder and Warta was almost exclusively in oak from central Germany and even Silesia, but fragmented political control upstream hindered development, and it was both easier and less costly for Prussia to transport lumber from Mazovia and Lithuania. The Danzig trade along the Vistula reached into Galicia and even to the Carpathian edge, from where both oak and fir were obtained. Riga on the Dina specialized in masts from Livonia, and later as far east as Vitebsk, and with connecting canals it could draw on the fir and oak from as far south as Volhynia, and along the Dnieper beyond Kiev in the Ukraine, from where the famed "Riga Wainscot" came. Memel on the Neman was developed in the eighteenth century to exploit the areas of oak

Map 5.3.   The Baltic and Scandinavian timber trade in the seventeenth and eighteenth centuries. It is impossible to show political boundaries with any certainty over this long period because of the frequent and substantial changes of states. For example, Sweden extended around the eastern Baltic and included Livonia until 1658; the two parts of Prussia were joined after 1720; and Poland did not exist as a separate state entity but was variously partitioned between neighbors until 1810

and fir not reached from either the Vistula or Duna. St. Petersburg traded almost exclusively in fir; what little oak existed was used by the Russian navy (Malowist 1960b; Albion 1926:140–142).

So essential were the rivers as the means of cheap transportation in this trade that this was one place where von Thünen's rule held sway. As distance increased from the river edge so overland transport costs rose, and that affected the type of land use and production, resulting in commodities of higher value replacing those of lesser value per unit of weight. Thus fuel was produced in the zone nearest the river, beams, masts, and planks further inland, and labor-intensive high-value products like tar, pitch, turpentine, and potash in more distant locations. Further away still, in the most remote zone, glass- and iron-making based on charcoal and finished wooden products dominated. An associated feature of this production regime was the temporary summer lumber camps that replaced permanent settlement, the huts being moved on as the supplies were cut out (Åström 1988).

For over three hundred years these forests were repeatedly cut over and culled for large mast timbers so that by the sixteenth and seventeenth centuries, when the huge demands of the Dutch, English, French, and even Spanish navies came into being, the wave of exploitation was forced eastward into the less disturbed forests of the Russian borderland, and especially of Finland. The oak forests of east Prussia were exhausted (Mager 1960), and exploitation moved far into the headwaters of the Rhine, Weser, Main, and other rivers to tap timber resources in the remote Thuringian and Black Forests.

It is difficult to capture the total complexity of this trade because of the many different products, different measures, and discontinuities of the record. Of the many geographies of trade just one must suffice. Map 5.4 shows the export and import of deals (wide planking) in 1784, the unit of measurement being the "long hundred," or 120 pieces of up to 20 feet long (Åström 1970). Europe was clearly divided into "timber-rich" and "timber-deficient" areas, and one-way journeys of up to 3,000 kilometers were commonplace for this low-value product. Timber transcended the commonsense rules of production and trade.

NORTH AMERICA: MASS MOVEMENT OF TIMBER. All the lessons learned in the Baltic trade were multiplied many hundredfold in the trade within North America in later centuries, where industrial logging reached its apogee. Now mechanization and steam power for mills and railroads were allied to bulk transport along rivers. Loggers realized that half of the cost of getting a log from the stump to the mill involved transport. Therefore they explored every means possible of moving the bulky logs en masse in astronomical quantities. Allied to this mass movement was the monopolization of the business. Owners attempted, and often succeeded in, owning vast tracts of timber land for their exclusive use, cutting off all available timber and rarely being concerned with the regeneration of the forest. In the nineteenth century there always seemed to be new and more forest to cut out and the mill could move on, though by the early years of the twentieth century timber exhaustion tempered this exploitative attitude, mills became fixed, and replanting took place.

The details of this trade would on its own fill a paper. Suffice it to say, distances of 1,000 to 2,000 miles by river and then by rail were not uncommon

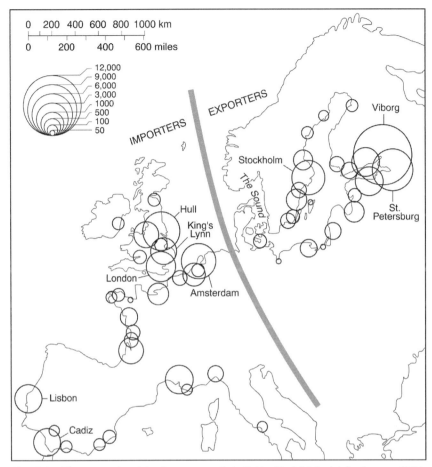

Map 5.4.   The geography of the European trade in Baltic "deals" (planks) for the year 1784. The map shows shipments originating in the Baltic and customs-cleared through the Baltic Sound (Straits). The unit of measure is the long hundred, or 120 pieces, up to 20 feet long. *Source*: Based on S.-E. Åström, "English Timber Imports from Northern Europe in the Eighteenth Century," *Scandinavian Economic History Review* 18 (1970): 31–32

as supplies in the American west and south reached the consuming core in the industrial northeast seaboard, which was fast running out of large timber. The point is that timber was so essential for construction and fuel that its procurement transcended all economic considerations and was achieved at any cost. In the process over 153 million acres (around 62 million ha) were deforested by lumber companies alone, and this says nothing of the 304 million acres (122 million ha) that were cleared for agriculture (Williams 2003:301–324, 1989:193–330).[4]

Affluence, Deforestation, and Changed Land-Cover

While timber procurement was a resource-destroyer, destructive of the original vegetation, it could be a resource-creator as well. In the Wallersteinian world-system model the "external arenas" provided the preciosities, while the "peripheral zone" supplied the raw materials and the "lower-ranking goods" produced by labor, which, although poorly rewarded, were integral to the global division of labor, because the goods were essential for the daily use of the core. However, this is where the spatial divisions become blurred. Initially these goods were regarded as preciosities—expensive, exotic products or luxuries that only the wealthy could afford. Yet, from the mid-seventeenth century onward, rising affluence for many, better global transport, and the consequent cheapening of commodities meant that their consumption filtered down through the various layers of society until they became staples or commonplace "necessities of everyday life," as Fernand Braudel (1984a) called them. Preciosities were now produced in bulk and in that process the external arenas took on more of the characteristics of the classical periphery, but now at a global scale.

Tea, coffee, chocolate, and sugar were not essential but they certainly varied diet, and rapidly became part of what Marshall Sahlins (1988:40–45) has called the West's "soft drug culture." Some goods like silks and tobacco were more purely optional. Cotton answered to basic needs for cheap and hygienic over- and underclothing. These tropical staples were thus added to the traditional staples of wheat, wood, wine, and dyes.

Many of these "lower-ranking" goods were tropical products, the growing of which led directly to tropical forest clearing and changes in land-cover. Sugar is the classic example of this global shift. Geographically its growth was "a means of both financing colonial endeavours as well as a motive for the occupation of yet more territory" (Galloway 1989:48). Socially it fostered habits of consumption, changed dietary habits, and was a source of wealth and power; economically its production in the plantation system altered the global distribution of population through slavery and emigration (Moore 2003:347–357).

When that transition in consumption got underway, the impact on the biomes of the world really began, as sugar cane, tea bushes, coffee bushes, and numerous other crops replaced wild tropical vegetation, and global land-cover was irrevocably altered. Peasant proprietors shifted imperceptibly from predominantly subsistence agriculture to an agricultural regime with a considerable cash crop element in it. The development and refinement of the plantation, with its cowed and subjugated indigenous labor or imported slave labor left an indelible mark on huge expanses of the world. Said one eighteenth-century observer:

> Whether coffee and sugar are really necessary to the happiness of Europe, is more than I can say, but I can affirm that these two vegetables have brought wretchedness and misery upon America and Africa. The former has been depopulated, that Europeans may have land to plant them in; and the latter is stripped of its inhabitants, for hands to cultivate them. (de Saint-Pierre 1775:105)

In a word, both the societies and the landscapes of the tropical world changed forever. Forests were cleared and converted to the profitable production of crops, many of them not even indigenous to the region. From Java to Jamaica, Fiji to Malaya, Brazil to the Congo, tropical regions were utterly transformed by the drive toward managed tropical agriculture (Walvin 1997).

When the purposeful movement of "settler societies" to the temperate lands of North America, Argentina, Australia, New Zealand, southern Africa, and southern Brazil got under way in later years, the impact on the global forests was devastating. Through timber procurement and timber elimination, the world-system irrevocably enmeshed the Earth system within its workings, always reacting reciprocally as both cause and effect in an ever-upwardly ratcheting cycle of change, and the modern global economy was under way.

Notes

1. It is difficult to cite Marx's many publications but a good summary of his "environmental" writing can be found in Berman (1981).

2. How great this trade was is difficult to discern, though it might have been considerable. However, it was only with European expansion that there was the *mass movement* of bulky commodities and raw materials (Abu-Lughod 1989; Chaudhuri 1985).

3. The following paragraphs are based on Williams (2003:85–95, 128–130).

4. The American story is dealt with in Williams (2003:301–324), and even more fully in Williams (1989:193–330).

References

Abu-Lughod, J. L. 1989. *Before European hegemony: The world system, AD 1250–1350*. New York: Oxford University Press.

Albion, R.G. 1926. *Forests and sea power: The timber problem of the Royal Navy, 1652–1862.* Cambridge, Mass.: Harvard University Press.

Åström, S.-E. 1970. English timber imports from northern Europe in the eighteenth century. *Scandinavian Economic History Review* 18:12–32.

———. 1975. Technology and timber exports from the Gulf of Finland, 1661–1740. *Scandinavian Economic History Review* 23:4–14.

———. 1988. *From tar to timber: Studies in northeast European forest exploitation and foreign trade, 1660–1860.* Commentationes Humanarum Litterarum, no. 89. Helsinki: Societas Scientiarum Fennica.

Berman, M. 1981. *All that is solid melts into air: The experience of modernity.* London: Verso.

Braudel, F. 1973. *Capitalism and material life, 15th to 18th Century.* Vol. 1, *1400–1800,* trans. Miriam Kochan. New York: Harper and Row.

———. 1984a. *Civilization and capitalism, 15th–18th century.* Vol. 2, *The structures of everyday life: The limits of the possible,* trans. Siân Reynolds. New York: Harper and Row.

———. 1984b. *Civilization and capitalism, 15th–18th century.* Vol. 3, *The perspective of the world,* trans. Siân Reynolds. New York: Harper and Row.

Chaudhuri, K. N. 1985. *Trade and civilization in the Indian Ocean: An economic history from the rise of Islam to 1750.* Cambridge, U.K.: Cambridge University Press.

Darby, H. C. 1961. The face of Europe on the eve of the great discoveries. In *The new Cambridge modern history.* Vol. 1, *The Renaissance, 1493–1520,* ed. G. R. Potter. Cambridge, U.K.: Cambridge University Press.

Dodgshon, R. A. 1993. The early modern world system: A critique of its inner dynamics. In *The early modern world-system in geographical perspective,* ed. Hans-Jürgen Nitz, 26–41. Erkundliches Wissen, Heft 110. Stuttgart: Franz Steiner Verlag.

De Saint-Pierre, J. H. B. 1775. *Voyage to the Isle de France, the Isle of Bourbaon, the Cape of Good Hope, etc, with observations and reflections on nature and mankind by an officer of the king.* 2 vols. London: Griffin.

Foster, J. B. 1999. Marx's theory of metabolic rift: Classical foundations for environmental sociology. *American Journal of Sociology* 105:366–405.

Galloway, J. H. 1989. *The sugar cane industry: An historical geography from its origins to 1914.* Cambridge, U.K.: Cambridge University Press.

Glamman, K. 1974. European trade, 1500–1700. In *The Fontana economic history of Europe.* Vol. 2, *The sixteenth and seventeenth centuries,* ed. C. M. Cipolla, 427–526. Brighton: Harvester Press.

Hughes, J. D. 2001. *An environmental history of the world: Humankind's role in the community of life.* New York: Routledge.

Lefranc, P. 1980. *Sir Walter Ralegh: Érivain: L'oeuvre et les idées.* Paris: Armand.

Lund Symposium. 2003. Aims and themes. www.humecol.lu.se/woshglec/.

Mager, Friedrich. 1960. *Der wald in altpreussen als wirtschaftsraum.* Cologne and Graz: Böhlau.

Malowist, M. 1959. The economic and social development of the Baltic countries from the fifteenth to the seventeenth centuries. *Economic History Review* 12:177–189.

————. 1960a. L'approvisionnement des ports de la baltique en produits forestiers pour les constructions navales aux xve et xvie siècles. In *Le navire et l'économie maritime du nord de l'Europe du moyen-âge au xviiie siècle,* ed. M. Mollat, 25–44. Paris: S.E.V.P.E.N.

————. 1960b. "Les produits des pays de la baltique dans le commerce international au xvie siècle." *Revue Nord* 42:175–206.

McNeill, J. R. 2000. *Something new under the sun: An environmental history of the twentieth-century world.* London: Penguin.

Minchinton, W. 1977. Patterns and structure of demand, 1500–1700. In *The Fontana economic history of europe.* Vol. 2, *The sixteenth and seventeenth centuries,* ed. C. M. Cipolla, 83–176. Brighton: Harvester Press.

Moore, J. 2000. Environmental crises and the metabolic rift in world-historical perspectives. *Organization and Environment* 13:123–158.

————. 2003. The modern world-system as environmental history? Ecology and the rise of capitalism. *Theory and Society* 32:307–377.

Nitz, H.-J., ed. 1993. *The early modern world-system in geographical perspective.* Erkundliches Wissen, Heft 110. Stuttgart: Steiner.

Rector, W. G. 1953. *Log transportation in the lake states lumber industry, 1840–1918: The movement of logs and its relationship to land settlement, waterway development, railroad construction, lumber production and prices.* American Waterways Series, no. 4. Glendale, Calif.: Clark.

Richards, J. R. 2003. *The unending frontier: An environmental history of the early modern world.* Berkeley and Los Angeles: University of California Press.

Sahlins, M. 1988. Cosmologies of capitalism: The trans-Pacific sector of the "world-system." *Proceedings of the British Academy* 74:1–51.

Soom, A. 1961. Der ostbaltische Holzhandel und die Holzindustrie im 17. Jahrhundret. *Hansisch Geschichtblätter* 16:17–49.

Taylor, P. J. 1988. World-systems analysis and regional geography. *Professional Geographer* 4:259–265.

Terlouw, C. P. 1988. De ecumene als wereldsysteem: Een overzicht van de wereldsysteemtheorie van Wallerstein. *De Aardrijkskunde* 4:321–334.

————. 1992. The regional geography of the world system: External arena, periphery, semiperiphery, core. *Nederlanse Geografische Studies* 144. Utrecht.

Van der Wee, H. 1970. Monetary, credit, and banking systems. In *The Cambridge economic history of Europe.* Vol. 5, *The economic organization of early modern Europe,* ed. E. E. Rich and C. H. Wilson, 290–393. Cambridge, U.K.: Cambridge University Press.

Von Thünen, J. H. 1826. *Der isolierte staat in Beziehung auf landwirtscchaft und nationalökonomie.* Berlin. Translated into English by C. M. Wartenberg as *Von Thünen's isolated state.* Oxford: Pergamon, 1966.

Wallace, I. 1990. *The global economic system*. London: Routledge.

Wallerstein, I. M. 1974. *The modern world system*. Vol. 1, *Capitalist agriculture and the origins of the European world-economy in the sixteenth century*. London: Academic Press.

———. 1980. *The modern world system*. Vol. 2, *Mercantilism and the consolidation of the European world-economy, 1650–1750*. London: Academic Press.

———. 1989. *The modern world system*. Vol. 3, *The second era of great expansion and the capitalist world-economy, 1730–1840s*. New York: Academic Press.

Walvin, J. 1997. *Fruits of empire: Exotic produce and British taste, 1600–1800*. Basingstoke, U.K.: Macmillan.

Webb, W. P. 1952. *The great frontier*. Boston: Houghton Mifflin.

Williams, M. 1989. *Americans and their forests: An historical geography*. New York: Cambridge University Press.

———. 2003. *Deforesting the earth: From prehistory to global crisis*. Chicago: University of Chicago Press.

Silver, Ecology, and the Origins of the Modern World, 1450–1640

6

JASON W. MOORE

T HE DEBATE OVER THE "RISE OF THE WEST" has sharpened in recent years, particularly with the New World History's critique of Eurocentric historiography (Frank 1998; Pomeranz 2000). In the process, however, the specificity of Europe's overseas expansion has often been eclipsed (e.g. Richards 2003). This is unfortunate, because Europe's early modern expansion—while not the talisman of technological or economic superiority once assumed—expressed a new and destabilizing crystallization of socioecological power and process, one predicated on the endless accumulation of capital. But far from a narrowly social logic, endless accumulation embodied a globalizing mode of producing nature that presumed the endless export of ecological problems. This was something new. For ecological degradation was not simply a consequence of European expansion, but constitutive of capitalism's very essence—its (presumably) limitless drive to accumulate capital.

Early modern silver mining sheds light on the ways that environmental transformations were at once cause and consequence of the rise of capitalism. Clustered geographically in a central European zone encompassing parts of present-day southern Germany and southern Poland, Hungary, and the Czech Republic, Europe's mining and metallurgical sectors at the end of the long medieval crisis expressed a remarkably prefigurative form of capitalist production. From the 1450s, central Europe's booming mining regions were sites of huge capital investment, large-scale industrial production, and aggressive monetization. "In no other branch of the economy did early forms of capitalism develop so fast or entrench themselves so firmly as in the mining industry" (Kellenbenz 1976:80). The extraction of ore and production of metal was closely and strategically articulated with leading agencies of capital accumulation, foremost among them the Augsburg-based Fuggers (Nef 1964; Lynch 2002). Out of this peculiar set of local-global antagonisms emerged a specifically capitalist configuration of nature-society relations predicated on the endlessly globalizing conquest of nature.

Silver loomed especially large in this movement of endless conquest. The modern world's first extractive efflorescence predated American silver, nourishing the arteries of accumulation in a European economy "desperately" short of "sound money" at the dawn of modernity (Yun 1996:119). This infusion of sound money at the scale of accumulation was articulated in the closest fashion with transformations in the division of labor. Foremost among these latter were the rapid extension and deepening of commodity relations in the central European countryside, propelled at once by silver mining's profitability and the environmental degradation that consistently threatened to undermine such profitability. These interlinked transformations at multiple scales—not simply local and global, to be sure[1]—fueled a significant accumulation of monetary wealth in the hands of (so-called) "merchant" capitalists such as the Fuggers, who were directly involved in extractive enterprises from Castile to Sweden to Hungary. By itself such newfound monetary wealth would have achieved little that was new. What gave this accumulation its revolutionary character was the world-historical alchemy of transforming "wealth" into "capital." For the era's metallurgical sectors were producing not only wealth qua "sound money" and resources, abstractly conceived. They were implicated in the production of a new set of socioecological relations—significantly, the formation of large-scale industrial capital and a quite prefigurative metallurgical proletariat (Kellenbenz 1976:80–81)—that compelled and presupposed infinite growth. It was this very presupposition that underpinned the metallurgical sector's significant contribution to world accumulation and compelled and enabled a subsequent geographical shift in silver mining—and a renewed wave of global capitalist expansion—by the mid-sixteenth century.

This chapter tells the environmental history of this global shift through the optic of the commodity frontier and the relocation of silver mining from central Europe to Potosí in the 1540s. The socioecological contradictions set in motion by the silver commodity frontier in late-sixteenth-century Peru (including present-day Bolivia), by the 1640s would in turn give way to another round of geographical expansion, as silver mining's center of gravity shifted to New Spain (Mexico). In this the silver frontier expressed a broader pattern—including tobacco, fisheries, wheat, timber, indigo, and dyewood, but sugar and silver above all—namely, capitalism's tendency toward an unusually rapacious and globally expansionary form of what Gadgil and Guha call "sequential overexploitation" (1992). In one region after another, ecological sustainability was increasingly subordinated to the imperatives of profit-maximization and empire-building: a strategy whose short-run gains were realized through rising ecological problems (and costs) over the middle run. Typically within fifty to seventy-five years, these contradictions undermined regional profitability and compelled a shift in the frontier's center of gravity.

Capitalism did not invent large-scale mining. But if mining and its monstrous record of environmental devastation dates back to antiquity (Hughes 2001:63–66), its revival in the 1450s embodied and enabled broader changes in Europe's political economy. Metallurgical production of all sorts rose dramatically, particularly war-driven copper and iron output. The annual output of central Europe's silver mines expanded fivefold between 1460 and 1530, an astounding production figure not reached again until the nineteenth century (Nef 1964:42). While Europe's fifteenth-century silver boom resembled premodern extractive cycles in certain respects, its articulation with European expansion made a crucial difference. The rapid geographical expansion effected by Europe's overseas empires meant that mining's socioecological contradictions could now be attenuated—and extended—through global expansion.

These contradictions were evident from the 1450s. Even at this early date, central Europe's gigantic ironworks "filled [the air] with such a stench and smoke as to trouble travelers as well as inhabitants" (Nef 1964: 44). Even contemporary boosters were forced to concede that "the strongest argument of [mining's] detractors" was environmental degradation—the poisoning of streams and the ensuing destruction of fisheries, widespread deforestation, the "extermination" of wildlife, and soil erosion (Agricola 1556:8). A significant share of this pollution derived from the confluence of the economic expansion with a new smelting process involving a gigantic volume of lead—on the order of 50 kilograms of lead for every kilogram of silver extracted (Lynch 2002; Novak et al. 2003:439).[2] Much as mercury would do in the sixteenth century, most of this lead found its way into rivers and streams, effectively enclosing the riparian commons as a dumping ground for metallurgical capitalism. It would do much the same to workers' bodies, who suffered not only predictable forms of silicosis but also—in the great Joachmistal mining town especially—from lethal exposure to uranium ores (Mould 2001; Agricola 1556:6).

Of much more direct concern to the world-historical trajectory of central Europe's mining boom was the enclosure of the forests. Everything turned on wood, it seemed. And it was not just the volume but the speed at which the new demands were made, for construction and above all for fuel. For no silver or iron could be produced without wood fuel, and lots of it. The metallurgical commodity zone expanded into the forests at a ferocious pace. A pound of pig iron—which except for cast-iron products typically required further processing—consumed approximately 15–20 lbs. of charcoal, reduced from about 75–100 lbs. of wood (Smil 1994:150, 156). While central Europe boasted enormous forest resources, what counted was proximity; charcoal's fragility limited transport to about five miles, less if the terrain was treacherous (Hammersley 1973:606). This attenuated but did not eliminate a generalized condition of sharply rising demand on the region's forests after 1450, stemming from the broad-based upsurge in multiple extractive activities, comprising lead, copper, and zinc in addition to iron and silver. Of special importance was iron. After 1450 central Europe emerged not only as the leading silver producer but also its leading iron manufacturer, accounting for half of Europe's output by 1500 (Cameron 1993:118).

Producing some 30,000 tons of iron annually, a figure rising fast through the first half of the sixteenth century, demanded access to forests on a massive scale. Looking at England in the early seventeenth century, Hammersley proposes that one ton of pig iron could be produced on a sustainable basis from the "natural increment" of 8–10 acres. Factoring in additional fuel consumption for wrought- or bar-iron manufacture, on this basis we might estimate conservatively the sector's consumption at 400,000 acres (give or take), not a large figure relative to regional forest cover. But except under very unusual circumstances sustainability was not the rule; especially in boom years (and there were many in the century after 1450), early modern smelters would have been under enormous pressure to expand production beyond the "natural increment." This increased profitability and cut costs over the short run but undermined the ecological basis for it over the middle run of a quarter-century or so. Even if we assume a modest rate of relative deforestation, say 5 percent annually of the forests engaged by iron smelters,[3] we would have a fairly consistent pattern of "original" forest clearance, somewhere on the order of 15–20,000 acres each year, or somewhere on the order of 1.1–1.5 million acres for the period between 1450 and 1525.

Is this an overestimate? Probably quite the opposite. Kellenbenz (1974:256) cites a 1564 forestry report on the Neusohl copper smelters that puts annual consumption at twenty-four thousand loads of charcoal; surely an exaggeration, but if true this would have required the "natural increment" of 580,000 acres.[4] Moreover, smelters, especially iron smelters, relocated frequently as local forest stocks dwindled. This relocation, in turn, favored a transition from hardwood forests such as oak to softwoods like pine and fir. These latter assumed a virtually monocultural presence in mining regions such as the Upper Palatinate by the end of the sixteenth century; forests outside the sustained grasp of the metallurgical sectors retained their diversity for several centuries (Westermann 1996:938). Although the softwoods grew faster than hardwoods, they were poor substitutes in charcoal manufacture, which meant consuming even greater numbers of trees.

This metallurgical revolution devoured central Europe's forests with unprecedented velocity. By the sixteenth century there was "a general deforestation in Europe, which surpassed that of the thirteenth" (Appuhn 2000:865; for Germany, see Blickle 1981:37–39, 73–74; Westermann 1996; Williams 2003). What took some six centuries for feudal Europe to effect (Darby 1956), the emergent capitalist order achieved in just over a century. The new scale of metallurgical production surely played a crucial role in this, even if we recognize with Michael Williams (2003) that the demographic recovery of the peasantry was statistically predominant in aggregate forest clearance. Two points here deserve special attention. First, in mining-intensive regions such as the Upper Palatinate the direct metallurgical activities of extraction and smelting constituted about half of peasant consumption; a similar figure holds for the great mining center of Joachmistal in the early sixteenth century (Westermann 1996:934–35, 937). Second, the demographic expansion can in no way be considered autonomous—although not mechanically derivative—from the transition to capitalism. While the old seigneurial-agrarian demographic order retained some vigor (Seccombe 1992), the remarkable expansion of "proto-industrial" activities was taking its toll on Braudel's allegedly stable "biological *ancien régime*" (1981). Mining and metallurgical production loomed especially large in this destabilization, their expansion constituting favored "secondary occupations" for peasant households (Kellenbenz 1974:263). To the extent that such semiproletarianization proceeded—central Europe's metallurgical sector alone was reported to have employed upward of one hundred thousand workers in 1525 (Nef 1964:43)—sociobiological reproduction was correspondingly unhinged from access to land and the conditions established for rapid population growth (Seccombe 1992).

It was, then, less population expansion qua independent variable (pace Williams 2003) than the demographic transformations—not to mention the social tensions (Scott 2002)—associated with the penetration of commodity production and exchange into peasant society. The social organization of human nature and the social organization of extra-human nature together worked new pressures on central Europe's forests. From this standpoint it is scarcely surprising that fuel costs moved sharply upward from the last quarter of the fifteenth century. "From 1470 onward, in all of central Europe, the price of wood was rising, slowly at first, *then rapidly*" (Cipolla 1976:229). Charcoal was by far the largest item in the budget of any smelter, sometimes as high as 70 percent of operating costs (Kellenbenz 1974:257). Already by the 1460s, fuel scarcity had compelled Nuremberg—not coincidentally the first site of modern "forest sowing" (Powers 1999:265)—to relocate its copper smelters some two hundred kilometers northward following the industry's virtual shutdown; that is, at the very moment when the extractive boom was commencing, and therefore precisely at the time when demands on the forest were escalating most rapidly (Wellmer and Becker-Platen 2002:725). Fuel demands intensified still further with declining ore quality. The rich veins tapped, tin yields declined by nearly half and silver yields by more than 90 percent over the course of the fifteenth century (Blanchard 1978:88). The ensuing escalation of the fuel/ore ratio entrained rapid forest exploitation, by 1500 bringing some metallurgical complexes to the brink of "economic collapse" (Powers 1999:264). The following half-century would bear witness to a cascading series of such socioecological crunches, of which rising fuel costs were only the tip of the iceberg (Kellenbenz 1974:256–257; Cameron 1993:118).

Ecological politics entered into this situation in three important ways. First, by the later fifteenth century, territorial states began to actively regulate forest access for their own revenue-maximizing interests, above all favoring fuel-intensive commodity sectors (Kellenbenz 1974:257; Waring 1987:239). These measures "regulated" forest access typically by seeking to limit peasant access (Westermann 1996), which predictably generated a kind of Polanyian countermovement of the "self-protecting society" (1957). Forest enclosures intensified the contradictions of the peasant demographic regime and set in motion increasingly serious resistance. This took the form of a series of agrarian revolts beginning in earnest by 1476, culminating in the German Peasants' War of 1525 (Brady and Middlefort 1981). Access to forest commons loomed large in the revolt's famed "Twelve Articles" (Blickle 1981:198–199). The timing is important, for it coincided with the very apex of the central European mining boom. The contrast with the situation a century earlier was sharp indeed. In 1450, "there were still extensive forests, so there were few conflicts between peasants and forest overlords. ...By 1525 the situation was *entirely changed*" (Blickle 1981:73, emphasis added). Not forest scarcity in the abstract but forest enclosures were central to the concerns of the movement. The radical cleric Thomas Munzer in 1524 decried these enclosures through which "every creature should be transformed into property—the fishes in the water, the birds of the air, the plants of the earth: the creatures too should become free" (quoted in Marx 1972 [1843]:49). Finally, mining and working-class formation were, then as now, closely interwoven. Worker unrest intensified after 1500, and wages rose accordingly, inducing a further squeeze on profitability (Blickle 1981:120–122; Kriedte 1983:39; Lynch 2002:34–35; Nef 1964:49; Waring 1987).

By the 1540s these contradictions had reached a boiling point. Braudel (1982:325) puts this well:

> Europe, because of her very expansion, was acting as if she had decided to delegate the trouble of handling of the mining and metallurgy industries to dependent regions on her periphery. In the heart of Europe, not only were falling yields limiting profits, but the 'fiery furnaces' were destroying forestland, and the price of wood and coal was becoming prohibitive, so that the blast furnaces could only operate part of the time, thus immobilizing fixed capital to no purpose. Meanwhile wages were going up. Small wonder then that the European economy as a whole applied to Sweden for iron and copper; to Norway for copper; before long to distant Russia for iron; to America for gold and silver.

Braudel's perceptive observation reveals the dialectical connection between the rise of capitalism and the global extension of extractive industries. Ecological contradictions were interwoven with those of market, state, and class in central Europe's decline. This may well be a useful means of conceptualizing ecological crisis, positing environmental determinations as opposed to a narrow environmental determinism. As we have seen, central Europe's metallurgical-led ecological revolution crystallized an unstable cocktail of rapid commodification with the largely "premodern" structure of peasant society. The competitive dynamics of the silver commodity complex—articulated closely with financial capital on a continental scale—gave rise to new large-scale mining enterprises that devoured forests with unprecedented speed, while the resilience of peasant society limited the possibilities for fundamental internal restructuring. Within fifty to seventy-five years, these reached a crescendo that signified the demise of central Europe's extractive regime as central to world accumulation. Large-scale mining did not disappear; the region's centrality was however displaced through global expansion. It was the inability of regional socioecological formations—such as central Europe's extractive regime—to regain the competitive edge (once lost) that expressed early capitalism's profound geographical restlessness. Thus did central Europe's silver regime give way to Potosí in the mid-sixteenth century.[5]

The relocation of silver mining to the New World offered a near-perfect combination of relatively favorable ecological and social conditions: fabulously rich ore deposits and accessible sources of cheap labor power. If Europe's mining complex faced formidable obstacles at home, in the New World it could play a crucial role in reshaping the hemisphere's socioecological order. Among other things, while the peasantries of western and central Europe remained formidable political actors, the Andean peasantry had been politically disarmed by virtue of epidemiological assault and brute force following Pizarro's 1532 invasion. By 1600, Europe produced only one-tenth of the American bullion arriving in Seville, and this was only a portion (albeit a large one) of New World bullion exports (Brading and Cross 1972:545).

City-building was the lynchpin of Spain's colonial strategy. This approach, "the direct opposite of the British gradualistic model, permitted Spain to conquer and control an entire continent in a few years with a very small occupying force" (Portes 1977:61). In Peru, this urban-imperial logic was carried to an extreme. At once dominant and dominated, mining boomtowns ruled over their hinterlands, even as they were subordinated to broader imperial and economic structures. They were the organizing centers not only of underdevelopment in the economic sense, but of a profoundly unequal ecological exchange between American peripheries and European cores, enabled by a new, multilayered and globalizing town-country antagonism. The mining frontier thereby created an increasingly serious rift in the metabolism between the country and the city—a "metabolic rift"—within Latin American regions and at the scale of the world-economy (Foster 1999). Ecological wealth flowed from country to city in the New World, and thence from urban centers in the periphery to the core. Such wealth could take the form of agricultural and pastoral commodities as final products, or constitute crucial industrial inputs for extractive centers. Mineral wealth above all represented an astonishing crystallization of organic energy. Among the chief consequences of this globalizing metabolic rift was a pattern of "sequential overexploitation" (Gadgil and Guha 1992:121), whereby the exhaustion of local ecological wealth (including local sources of labor power) necessitated the geographical expansion of commodity relations, either through the progressive extension of city-hinterland relations within regions or the outright relocation of production.

Nowhere did the socioecological contradictions of the extractive-driven metabolic rift appear more starkly than in Potosí, located in the viceroyalty of Peru (present-day Bolivia). The New World accounted for 74 percent of the world's silver production in the sixteenth century (Barrett 1990:225). Potosí's output dwarfed its closest competitor, Zacatecas (Mexico), by a factor of seven (Garner 1988:911). Almost overnight, Potosí emerged as one of the capitalist world-economy's largest cities; with 100,000 residents in the 1590s and 160,000 by 1611, it was in the same league as London, Seville, and Amsterdam (Larson 1988:89; Hanke 1956:54; Mols 1974:42). Together with the mercury mines of nearby Huancavelica, Potosí's silver complex pioneered a rapid expansion of commodity production throughout the viceroyalty of Peru, with profound implications for the health of land and labor alike.

Potosí's dramatic ascent owed as much to Europe's expansionary political economy as it did to geology. In the quarter-century following the discovery of silver in 1545, the path from rock to pure silver was circuitous indeed. In this era, mining remained largely under Indian control. Indians mined silver ore, much of which found its way into Spanish hands as tribute. These tributary payments were then sold back to the Indians, who smelted the ore in thousands of dispersed *guayras*, small wind-ovens specially designed for the high altitude. Subsequently, the Spaniards acquired the pure silver through the market, where their purchasing power was augmented by their control of the highly lucrative coca leaf trade (Stern 1988:850–851). Coca, it seems, was the opium of the sixteenth century.

This system worked as long as ores remained rich. As ore quality declined, more and more fuel was necessary to extract less and less silver. By the 1560s smelting was no longer an effective—that is to say profitable—means of extracting silver (Cobb 1947:124). Fuel costs began to rise, and silver output fell two-thirds between 1546 and 1571 (Bakewell 1987:239). Mine work became correspondingly more arduous and less remunerative for Indian workers, who increasingly decided that the game was not worth the candle. By 1561, there were 20,000 Indians living in Potosí but just 300 working the mines, 94 percent fewer than a decade earlier (Cole 1985:4). "In short, the pillage/conquest economy established after 1532 had reached its limit" (Andrien 2001:49).

Potosí's socioecological crisis did not go unnoticed from above. Spain's imperial ambitions fed on American silver (McNeill 1982:109). The contraction of silver production was a very serious matter indeed, all the more so as it was followed by: (1) "an enormous increase" in military expenditures after 1566; and (2) an increasingly severe fiscal crisis within Castile, where Philip II tripled taxes and thrice declared "bankruptcy"—in reality converting short-term into long-term debt—between 1557 and 1577

(Parker 1974:561–569). As if to go from bad to worse, Philip's financial woes were underpinned by an impending agroecological crisis that would only deepen in the closing decades of the sixteenth century (Phillips 1987). It was in this context that the Crown convened a "special junta" in 1568 to address the emerging crisis, empowering a new viceroy—Francisco de Toledo—to implement a sweeping reorganization of the Peruvian mining frontier (Assadourian 1992: 56–58).

Toledo's challenge? Find a cost-effective solution to the problem of declining silver output. Potosí's revival depended on two decisive innovations: (1) the replacement of smelting with an amalgamation process that used mercury to extract silver from the ore; and (2) the large-scale replacement of voluntary with forced labor through a system of rotating forced labor drafts, called the *mita*.[6] The first presupposed the second. The perfection of an amalgamation process adapted to Andean conditions preceded by just a year Toledo's proclamation of a geographically expansive *mita* in 1572. Mercury amalgamation made possible the profitable extraction of silver from low-grade ores, but it demanded a huge and tractable labor supply. Thus amalgamation and the *mita* were at the core of a series of socioecological transformations that were profoundly implicated in the commodification of land and labor throughout the region and its deepening articulation with a globalizing capitalist system.

This era of accelerated social and environmental transformation unfolded at multiple geographical scales. At the point of production, control passed from Indian to European hands, replaying on an extended scale the earlier transition from small-scale artisanal mining to large-scale industrial extraction in central Europe a century earlier (Waring 1987; Cole 1985:18). Gone were the small wind-ovens used by Indian miners. In their place were huge stone tanks, capable of holding 5,000 lbs. of crushed ore (Bakewell 1987:214). The ore itself was crushed in stamping mills (*ingenios*) powered by hydraulic infrastructures that outstripped by a considerable margin their European predecessors (Lynch 2002). Some thirty dams stored water accumulated during the brief and torrential wet season, driving 140 *ingenios* (Craig 1993:218). Silver production skyrocketed nearly 600 percent between 1575 and 1590 (Bakewell 1987:242). In equal measure, the ambitious reshaping of the region's waterscapes generated ecological contradictions that would ultimately seal Potosí's fate. "Potosí was [consistently] plagued by disastrous floods," likely intensified by widespread deforestation (Brown and Craig 1994:305). The collapse of the principal reservoir dam in 1626 killed several hundred and destroyed many *ingenios*, adding to Potosí's cumulative woes on the eve of the seventeenth-century crisis. From this disaster, "the *ingenios* of Potosí never fully recovered" (Craig 1993:145).

Relative to smelting, mercury amalgamation was a "cold" rather than "hot" technology. Yet, because it enabled such a large increase in output over so short a time, the consequence was more, not less, deforestation. Mercury extraction itself demanded a considerable volume of charcoal, resulting in deforestation around the mercury mines at Almaden (Spain) and Huancavelica (Peru) (Parsons 1962; Brown 2000). Moreover, the mercury-silver amalgam required further heating to get at the pure silver. A 1603 source reports 2,000 Indians bringing wood and firewood to Potosí, with another thousand transporting and making charcoal; this compared to 4,600 working directly in the mines (Cole 1985:29). The surrounding area was quickly stripped of trees, and timber for stamp mills was trucked in from as far as 200 miles away (Bakewell 1984:24). By 1600, rising fuel costs led refiners to stop heating the stone tanks containing crushed ore and mercury (Bakewell 1987:214).

Deforestation weighed particularly heavily on highly vulnerable mountain ecosystems, which suffer from high rates of soil erosion and enjoy only a "fragile stability, easily upset by unintentional human action" (McNeill 1992:352). By the mid-seventeenth century, one contemporary would observe that there "is no sign" that the mountains surrounding Potosí "ever had a forest," although

> when it was first discovered it was fully covered of trees. . . . Today, not even weeds grow on the mt., not even in the most fertile soils where trees could have grown. The barrenness is most alarming because the mt. is now merely a conglomerate of loose gravel with little or no fertile land, pockmarked with sterile mineralized outcroppings. (quote from Burke 2000)

Ecological contradictions degraded bodies much as they denuded the landscape. The course of events in Potosí captures what seems to be the basic socioecological pattern of early modern commodity frontiers.[7] In the early stages, high yields translate into high wages and decent working conditions. But sooner or later yield declines. When this happens, profitability begins to hinge on (1) rising capital intensity, manifest not only in surface infrastructures but also in deeper mines; and (2) securing cheap labor power. While technological and social innovations could temporarily check rising costs, they could not do so indefinitely *within the region*.

Drawing workers either from outside the commodity economy, or only loosely articulated with it, mineowners found themselves in a favorable position not only to enjoy the fruits of cheap labor but to exploit them with little regard to their workers' health (Tandeter 1981:104). In itself, the death and bodily damage suffered by Indian mineworkers posed no serious threat to profitability over the short run. In contrast to African slavery, however, the exploitation of the *mitayo* "did not place any investment at risk. . . . Immediate profitability was the overriding consideration of the entrepreneur in his relation with the forced laborers" (Tandeter 1981:104). To this extent, the *mitayo* regime may have been even more lethal than slavery. This problem was reinforced further as the practice of hiring out *mitayos* increased in the later sixteenth century. As we shall see, such overexploitation represented not only a monstrous legacy of early European expansion, but also favored the reconstitution of the region's division of labor in a strongly capitalist direction.

Potosí's renaissance was driven initially by the exploitation of tailings, ore that resisted the smelters. But these were exhausted by the end of the 1570s. The solution? Dig deeper. A rising proportion of *mitayos* was put to work in the increasingly deeper, and as a consequence increasingly dangerous, mines. Work-related fatalities and disease escalated sharply. Mineowners increasingly disregarded colonial prohibitions and imposed fixed quotas, dramatically extending the working day. In the 1570s, for instance, the colonial state prohibited more than two trips a day for *apiris*, workers who carried the ore from the mine depths to the surface. By the 1580s they were carrying as many as two dozen loads of 25 kilograms upward some 300 meters. Mine shafts often flooded, forcing *mitayos* to work "knee-deep in water," rendering them susceptible to all manner of respiratory diseases, especially pneumonia. Rest periods—originally two weeks for each one worked—were increasingly disregarded (Cole 1985:23–25; Cobb 1947:86–89). By 1600, "the proprietors decided they were losing time changing shifts, so they started keeping the workmen underground continuously from Monday evening to Saturday" (Rowe 1957:174). The mines, said mineowner Luis Capoche, had become a "harsh executioner of Indians, for each day it consumes and destroys them, and their lives are made misery by the fear of death" (quote in Bakewell 1984:145). Notwithstanding this increasingly brutal labor regime, ecology proved stubbornly resistant. Yields continued to decline. By the mid-1580s, "workers were taking out only half the amount formerly produced" (Cobb 1947:77).

The contradictions that flowed from the point of production were enabled by the imperial refashioning of Latin American political ecology. The late-sixteenth-century silver boom presupposed a radical recomposition of Peru's ecological wealth and its sociospatial division of labor in ways that favored the maximization of commodity production in Potosí, and the progressive commodification of internal and external nature (labor and land) throughout the region. All of Peru was to be at the service of Potosí.

Our attention goes first to labor recruitment. Needless to say, the Indians were not in a hurry to work for the Spaniards. The solution was found in the *mita*, a rotating annual labor draft. Imposed in 1572, the *mita* conscripted one in seven adult males for work in the mines, textile workshops, "and any other task . . . deemed worthy of the state's patrimony" (Stern 1982:82). The Potosí *mita* was by far the largest and most geographically expansive. In the 1570s, the annual draft mobilized some 13,500 workers, drawn from a region that stretched some 800 miles north to south and as much as 250 miles east to west (Bakewell 1987:222).

This large-scale mobilization of bodies was predicated on the large-scale reorganization of space. The *mita*'s immediate precondition was the empire's reorganization of village life throughout the Andes. Beginning in 1567, the colonial state initiated the "wholesale resettlement of the native population"—perhaps as many as 1.5 million people, roughly the population of contemporary Portugal—into "Spanish-style towns" (Rowe 1957:156). These nucleated villages (*reducciones*) effected three major socioecological transformations, reinforcing their obvious advantages for tax collection and political control (Gade 1992). In the first instance, the concentration of Indians into more densely populated encampments provided fertile epidemiological terrain for Eurasian diseases (Andrien 2001:57). Second, large-scale resettlement often entailed the removal of Indians from lands prized by Spanish colonials (Ramirez 1996:71–72). Third, the *reducciones* undermined pre-conquest political ecology based on "verticality," the core strategy of which involved "working as many different microenvironments as possible" so as to minimize ecological vulnerability (Stern 1982:5). Throughout the Andes, the close proximity of distinct regional environments—"the coast, the piedmont, the altiplano highlands, and the tundra steppe (puna)"—encouraged highly interdependent agropastoral linkages. Potato cultivation in the highlands, for instance, was supported by fertilizer (guano) supplied by coastal communities, which in turn consumed highland foodstuffs. Throughout the Andes, there had evolved a "synchronized [pattern of] ecological relationships between coast, piedmont, highland, and puna," constituting "a finely calibrated system of food transfers" (Wolf 1982:59, 134–135).

The *reducciones* insisted on a new agroecological order corresponding to the labor demands of the silver frontier. At its center was common-field agriculture, a cultivation system that emphasizes agropastoral linkages, access to commons, and community regulation of landholding (Thirsk 1964). Where verticality presumed exchanges across ecological zones, such that farming and herding were geographically discrete, common-field agriculture sundered such exchanges by stressing agro-pastoral integration. From the standpoint of the colonial state, the great advantage of the common-field system was its geographically expansive character, emphasizing land as a means of maximizing the productivity of scarce labor in place of older, intensive land-use practices. The new system minimized the labor formerly allocated to supervising and guarding herds and fields, and maintained soil fertility by substituting European livestock for vertical guano transfers (Godoy 1991). Its adoption was accelerated by viceroy Toledo's 1575 "edict mandating a plow and oxen for each Indian agglomeration" (Gade 1992:469). This technological innovation promised an important change in Andean socioecology, shifting from a labor-intensive to a land-extensive approach—one also linked to the sharp reduction of agricultural diversity that preconquest peasants deployed to safeguard against crop failure (Wolf 1959:198–199; Zimmerer 1996:44–55).

The livestock-plow system was complemented and indeed made possible by a second moment of "ecological imperialism": the invasion of Europeans' favored crops, wheat above all. Commercial production dates from the late 1530s. "In some locales [Indians] were growing it as . . . a food staple by the late 16th century" (Gade 1992:465). If the common-field system reduced necessary labor by cutting supervision costs, and the livestock-plow system effectively substituted land and animal power for human labor, wheat offered a further labor-saving (but land-consuming) bonus. Relative to indigenous crops, wheat demanded little labor and enabled plow agriculture by tolerating the new animals' grazing patterns (Godoy 1991:407). In contemporary Europe, the chief ecological trade-off was its tendency toward low yields and soil exhaustion: wheat "devours the soil and forces it to rest regularly" (Braudel 1977:11). It was the colonizers' great fortune, however, that the New World's fertile soils attenuated this tendency. Initially, wheat cultivation in Peru supported seed/yield ratios three to six times higher than Europe's average, liberating still more labor from the demands of subsistence production (Slicher van Bath 1963:330; Super 1988:20–22). American soil favored the transfer of a European agronomic complex that created a relative surplus population in the face of demographic contraction, and provided a crucial subsidy for the mining economy.

The increasing frequency of famines and the generalization of malnutrition that ensued (Cook 1981) expressed the dietary moment of what we might call "disarticulated primitive accumulation" in the Americas. An ecological surplus was extracted from the bodies and fields of the indigenous peasantry in a way that paralleled the extraction of surplus labor, in both instances for the benefit of accumulation centers abroad rather than the creation of a home market.[8] This was the "disarticulated"—and therefore intrinsically globalizing—nature of the New World's metabolic rift in the transition to capitalism. Silver was central to an epochal reworking of nature-society relations in the long sixteenth century, a reworking that was cause no less than consequence of the rise of capitalism. The large-scale transformation of nature was not new. But its global and theoretically endless transformation certainly was. The sociotechnological capacities that enabled overseas expansion also, crucially, enabled (and indeed necessitated) capitalist and territorialist agencies to "jump scale" when the going got rough in any particular locale—this is the story of the silver commodity frontier, and not the silver frontier only.

The globalization of capital that was part and parcel of the rise of capitalism created everywhere, but in the Americas most dramatically, a globalizing rift in the metabolism of town and country. The silver mining frontier not only ensnared whole regions in its commodity-producing web but ensured that ecological wealth would flow from countryside to (mining) town, and from colonial city to imperial metropole. At each step nutrient cycling was disrupted as local ecologies were harnessed to Europe's territorial and capitalist ambitions. In classic Polanyian fashion (1957), the ensuing "fictitious" commodification of labor and land undermined the socioecological bases for regional accumulation regimes, setting the stage in these instances not just for the eventual resurgence of the "self-protecting society" but also for a new round of global expansion. Hence the recurrent waves of global conquest, from central Europe to Peru to New Spain. By the sixteenth century, it seems, Europe's ruling strata had discovered not just America, but a new and radically transformative political ecology of civilizational expansion.

Notes

Special thanks to Alf Hornborg, J. R. McNeill, and Diana C. Gildea for comments on an earlier draft of this chapter.

1. See White's important—and largely unheeded—essay (1999) on environmental history and geographical scale.

2. Silver ore was found in combination with a heavy concentration of either copper or lead in central Europe's mining regions, and this naturally affected the volume of lead imported for smelting purposes.

3. Westermann (1996:938) believes the rate of deforestation was higher—around seven percent annually for iron producing Upper Palatinate in the sixteenth century. This figure, he stresses, must be taken as a "minimal estimate" that does not account for unusual periods of high demand.

4. Calculated from Smil (1994) and Hammersley (1973).

5. This is not to deny the significance of Japan's silver production for the history of east Asia during this period (Frank 1998). From the standpoint of the rise of capitalism, however, Japanese silver was not decisive, quite aside from the quantitative predominance of American silver production (Flynn and Giraldez 2002). The real distinction rests in the distinctive historical geographies of the Japanese and American complexes. In stark contrast to the former, the Potosí-centered silver frontier was a *commodity* frontier. In this respect, it expressed and contributed to a movement of endless global expansion whose success or failure turned on the generalization of commodity production and exchange. Japan's silver frontier did not.

6. The Incas deployed a broadly similar system of labor drafts, also called the *mita*. Stern (1982) distinguished the two systems by calling the Inca institution the *mit'a* and the Spanish, the *mita*.

7. The resemblance to the sugar frontier is striking (Moore 2000b).

8. The European peasantry too was subjected to a similar logic of dietary immiseration, albeit with less gruesome consequences (Moore 2003b).

References

Agricola, G. 1556 (1950). *De re metallica*. New York: Dover.

Andrien, K. J. 2001. *Andean worlds*. Albuquerque: University of New Mexico Press.

Appuhn, K. 2000. Inventing nature: Forests, forestry, and state power in renaissance Venice. *Journal of Modern History* 72:861–889.

Assadourian, C. S. 1992. The colonial economy: The transfer of the European system of production to New Spain and Peru. *Journal of Latin American Studies* 24 (Supplement): 52–68.

Bakewell, P. J. 1984. *Miners of the red mountain: Indian labor in Potosi, 1545–1650*. Albuquerque: University of New Mexico Press.

———. 1987. Mining. In *Colonial Spanish America*, ed. L. Bethell, 203–249. Cambridge, U.K.: Cambridge University Press.

Barber, R. K. 1932. *Indian labor in the Spanish colonies*. Albuquerque: University of New Mexico Press.

Barrett, W. 1990. World bullion flows, 1450–1800. In *The rise of merchant empires*, ed. J. D. Tracy. Cambridge, U.K.: Cambridge University Press.

Blanchard, I. 1978. Resource depletion in European mining and metallurgical industries, 1400–1800. In *Natural resources in European history*, ed. W. N. Parker and A. Maczak. Washington, D.C.: Resources for the Future.

Blickle, P. 1981. *The revolution of 1525*. Baltimore: Johns Hopkins University Press.

Brading, D. A., and H. E. Cross. 1972. Colonial silver mining. *Hispanic American Historical Review* 52 (4): 545–579.

Brady, T. A., and H. C. E. Middlefort. 1981. Translators' introduction. In *The revolution of 1525*, by P. Blickle, xi–xxvi. Baltimore: Johns Hopkins University Press.

Braudel, F. 1977. *Afterthoughts on material civilization and capitalism*. Baltimore: Johns Hopkins University Press.

———. 1981. *The structures of everyday life*. New York: Harper and Row.

———. 1982. *The wheels of commerce*. New York: Harper and Row.

Brown, K. W. 2000. Workers' health and colonial mercury mining at Huancavelica, Peru. *The Americas* 57(4): 467–496.

Brown, K. W., and A. K. Craig. 1994. Silver mining at Huantajaya, viceroyalty of Peru. In *In quest of mineral wealth*, ed. A. K. Craig and R. C. West. Baton Rouge: Louisiana State University Press.

Burke, E., III. 2000. Environment and world history, 1500–2000. Unpublished paper. Department of History, University of California, Santa Cruz.

Cameron, R. 1993. *A concise economic history of the world: From paleolithic times to the present*. 2nd ed. Oxford: Oxford University Press.

Charney, P. 2001. *Indian society in the valley of Lima, Peru, 1532–1824*. Lanham, Md.: University Press of America.

Cipolla, C. M. 1976. *Before the industrial revolution*. New York: Norton.

Cobb, G. 1947. *Potosi and Huancavelica: Economic bases of Peru, 1545–1640*. PhD diss. University of California, Berkeley.

———. 1949. Supply and transportation for the Potosi mines, 1545–1640. *Hispanic American Historical Review* 29:25–45.

Cole, J. A. 1985. *The Potosi mita, 1573–1700*. Stanford, Calif.: Stanford University Press.

Cook, N. D. 1981. *Demographic collapse: Indian Peru, 1520–1620*. Cambridge, U.K.: Cambridge University Press.

Craig, A. K. 1993. The ingenious *ingenios*: Spanish colonial water mills at Potosi. In *Culture, form, and place*, ed. K. Mathewson. Baton Rouge: Louisiana State University Press.

Cronon, W. 1983. *Changes in the land*. New York: Hill and Wang.

———. 1991. *Nature's metropolis*. New York: Norton.

Crosby, A. W. 1972. *The Columbian exchange*. Westport, Conn.: Greenwood.

Darby, H. C. 1956. The clearing of woodland in Europe. In *Man's role in changing the face of the earth*, ed. W. L. Thomas Jr., 183–216. Chicago: University of Illinois Press.

Flynn, D. O., and A. Giraldez. 2002. Cycles of silver: Global economic unity through the mid-eighteenth century. *Journal of World History* 13 (2): 391–427.

Foster, J. B. 1999. Marx's theory of metabolic rift. *American Journal of Sociology* 105 (2): 366–405.

Frank, A. G. 1998. *ReOrient*. Berkeley: University of California Press.

Gade, D. W. 1992. Landscape, system, and identity in the post-conquest Andes. *Annals of the Association of American Geographers* 82 (3): 460–477.

———. 1999. *Nature and culture in the Andes*. Madison: University of Wisconsin Press.

Gadgil, M., and R. Guha. 1992. *This fissured land: An ecological history of India.* Berkeley: University of California Press.

Garner, R. L. 1988. Long-term silver mining trends in Spanish America. *American Historical Review* 93 (4): 898–935.

Geertz, C. 1963. *Agricultural involution.* Berkeley: University of California Press.

Godoy, R. 1991. The evolution of common-field agriculture in the Andes. *Comparative Studies in Society and History* 33:395–414.

Hammersley, G. 1973. The charcoal iron industry and its fuel, 1540–1750. *Economic History Review* 26 (4): 593–613.

Hanke, L. 1956. *The imperial city of Potosi.* The Hague: Nijhoff.

Hughes, J. D. 2001. *An environmental history of the world.* New York: Routledge.

Kellenbenz, H. 1974. Technology in the age of the scientific revolution 1500–1700. In *The Fontana economic history of Europe*, vol. 2, ed. C. M. Cipolla. London: Fontana.

———. 1976. *The rise of the European economy.* London: Weidenfeld and Nicolson.

Kriedte, P. 1983. *Peasants, landlords and merchant capitalists.* Cambridge, U.K.: Cambridge University Press.

Larson, B. 1988. *Colonialism and agrarian transformation in Bolivia: Cochabamba, 1500–1900.* Princeton, N.J.: Princeton University Press.

Lovell, W. G. 1992. "Heavy shadows and black night": Disease and depopulation in colonial Spanish America. *Annals of the Association of American Geographers* 82 (3): 426–443.

Lynch, M. 2002. *Mining in world history.* London: Reaktion.

Marx, K. 1972 (1843). *On the Jewish question.* In *The Marx-Engels reader*, ed. R. C. Tucker, 24–51. New York: Norton.

———. 1977 (1867). *Capital.* New York: Vintage.

McNeill, J. R. 1992. *The mountains of the Mediterranean world.* Cambridge, U.K.: Cambridge University Press.

McNeill, W. H. 1982. *The pursuit of power.* Chicago: University of Chicago Press.

Mols, R. 1974. Population in Europe 1500–1700. In *The Fontana economic history of Europe*, vol. 2, ed. C. M. Cipolla, 15–82. London: Fontana.

Moore, J. W. 2000a. Environmental crises and the metabolic rift in world-historical perspective. *Organization and Environment* 13 (2): 123–158.

———. 2000b. Sugar and the expansion of the early modern world-economy. *Review* 23 (3): 409–433.

———. 2003a. Nature and the transition from feudalism to capitalism. *Review* 26 (2): 97–172.

———. 2003b. The modern world-system as environmental history? Ecology and the rise of capitalism. *Theory and Society* 32 (3): 307–377.

Mould, R. F. 2001. Depleted uranium and radiation-induced lung cancer and leukemia. *British Journal of Radiology* 74:677–683.

Nef, J. U. 1964. *The conquest of the material world.* New York: Meridian.

Newson, L. A. 1985. Indian population patterns in colonial Spanish America. *Latin American Research Review* 20 (3): 41–74.

Novak, M., et al. 2003. Origin of lead in eight central European peat bogs. *Environmental Science and Technology* 37 (3): 437–445.

Parker, G. 1974. The emergence of modern finance in Europe, 1500–1730. In *The Fontana economic history of Europe*, vol. 2, *The sixteenth and seventeenth centuries*, ed. C. M. Cipolla, 527–595. London: Fontana.

Parsons, J. J. 1962. The cork oak forests and the evolution of the cork industry in southern Spain and Portugal. *Economic Geography* 38:195–214.

Phillips, C. R. 1987. Time and duration: A model for the economy of early modern Spain. *American Historical Review* 92:531–562.

Polanyi, K. 1957. *The great transformation*. Boston: Beacon.

Pomeranz, K. 2000. *The great divergence*. Princeton, N.J.: Princeton University Press.

Portes, A. 1977. Urban Latin America. In *Urbanization in the Third World*, ed. Janet Abu-Lughod and Richard Hay Jr., 59–70. Chicago: Maaroufa.

Powers, R. F. 1999. On the sustainable productivity of planted forests. *New Forests* 17:263–306.

Ramirez, S. E. 1987. The "*dueno de indios*": Thoughts on the consequences of the shifting bases of power of the "*curaca de los viejos antiguos*" under the Spanish in sixteenth-century Peru. *Hispanic American Historical Review* 67 (4): 575–610.

———. 1996. *The world turned upside down: Cross-cultural contact and conflict in sixteenth-century Peru*. Stanford, Calif.: Stanford University Press.

Richards, J. F. 2003. *The unending frontier*. Berkeley: University of California Press.

Rowe, J. H. 1957. The Incas under Spanish colonial institutions. *Hispanic American Historical Review* 37 (2): 155–199.

Scott, T. 2002. The German peasants' war and "crisis of feudalism." *Journal of Early Modern History* 6 (3): 265–295.

Seccombe, W. 1992. *A millennium of family change*. London: Verso.

Slicher van Bath, B. H. 1963. *The agrarian history of western Europe, 500–1850 A.D.* New York: St. Martin's.

Smil, V. 1994. *Energy in world history*. Boulder, Colo.: Westview.

Smith, C. T. 1970. Depopulation of the central Andes in the 16th century. *Current Anthropology* 11:453–463.

Spalding, K. 1975. Hacienda-village relations in Andean society to 1830. *Latin American Perspectives* 2 (1): 107–121.

Stavig, W. 2000. Ambiguous visions: Nature, law, and culture in indigenous-Spanish land relations in colonial Peru. *Hispanic American Historical Review* 80 (1): 77–111.

Stern, S. J. 1982. *Peru's Indian peoples and the challenge of Spanish conquest*. Madison: University of Wisconsin Press.

———. 1988. Feudalism, capitalism, and the world-system in the perspective of Latin America and the Caribbean. *American Historical Review* 93:829–873.

Super, J. C. 1988. *Food, conquest, and colonization in sixteenth-century Spanish America.* Albuquerque: University of New Mexico Press.

Tandeter, E. 1981. Forced and free labor in late colonial Potosi. *Past and Present* 93:98–136.

Thirsk, J. 1964. The common fields. *Past and Present* 29:3–25.

Waman Puma, F. [Guaman Poma de Ayala]. 1613 (1980). *El primer nueva cronica y buen gobierno*, trans. and ed. J. Murra, et al. Mexico City: Siglo XXI.

Waring, G. H. 1987. The silver miners of the Erzebirge and the Peasants' War of 1525 in the light of recent research. *Sixteenth Century Journal* 18 (2): 231–247.

Webb, W. P. 1964. *The great frontier.* Austin: University of Texas Press.

Wellmer, F.-W., and J. D. Becker-Platen. 2002. Sustainable development and the exploitation of mineral and energy resources. *International Journal of Earth Sciences* 91:723–745.

Westermann, E. 1996. Central European forestry and mining industries in the early modern period. In *L'uomo e la foresta: Secc. XIII–XVIII*, ed. S. Cavaiocchi, 927–953. Florence: Le Monnier.

Westoby, J. 1989. *Introduction to world forestry.* Oxford: Blackwell.

White, R. 1999. The nationalization of nature. *Journal of American History* 86 (3): 976–986.

Williams, M. 2003. *Deforesting the earth.* Chicago: University of Chicago Press.

Wolf, E. R. 1959. *Sons of the shaking earth.* Chicago: University of Chicago Press.

———. 1982. *Europe and the people without history.* Berkeley: University of California Press.

Yun, B. 1996. Economic cycles and structural changes. In *Handbook of European history, 1400–1600*, vol. 1: *Late middle ages, renaissance, and reformation: Structures and assertions*, ed. T. A. Brady Jr., H. A. Oberman, and J. D. Tracy, 113–146. Grand Rapids, Mich.: Eerdmans.

Zimmerer, K. S. 1996. *Changing fortunes: Biodiversity and peasant livelihood in the Peruvian Andes.* Berkeley: University of California Press.

Trade, "Trinkets," and Environmental Change at the Edge of World-Systems: Political Ecology and the East African Ivory Trade

7

N. THOMAS HÅKANSSON

URING THE LAST two thousand years the capitalist world-system and its predecessors have flooded the unincorporated areas of the world with vast amounts of glass beads, cowries, pieces of cloth, brass, copper, and iron, guns, tools, and utensils (Guyer 1995; Einzig 1949). Such trade occurred in the absence of political domination or alienation of producers' access both to the means of production and to raw material extraction. Unfortunately, with respect to this type of trade there is very little theoretical guidance to understand the linkages between regional historical developments and world-systemic processes. Because the populations are not forced to participate through political means, Chase-Dunn and Hall (1997:63) suggest that such areas should be regarded as being only weakly incorporated into world-systems. Accordingly, I call this type of economic interaction "unincorporated trade." The ivory trade of precolonial eastern Africa is an example of economic relationships that have been common for millennia between world-system centers and areas not directly under their political and economic control.

During the nineteenth century, the ivory trade system in East Africa underwent two related transformations that are salient to my analysis. First, there was a change from a decentralized system of trade without any clearly defined exchange nodes to a pattern of well-defined trade routes and nodal points of commerce. Second, the decentralized trade was controlled by the communities of the coastal hinterland while in the later development trade was conducted and controlled by coastal merchants and international capital. This historical change enables me to examine the effects of changes in the spatial and organizational parameters of long-distance trade on land use in the context of trade between the interior of Kenya and the coast.[1]

Although most work in political ecology tends to focus on the impact of capitalism on labor and the commoditization of resources, the distribution of power and labor control are factors that apply to kin-ordered societies as well (cf. Robbins 2004:79–80). In any society the ability of those who wield power to mobilize the labor of others and to constrain their management of land has effects on land-use patterns (Blaikie and Brookfield 1987:74; Franke 1987). I argue here that long-distance trade affects local social relations of production and power, which, in turn, structure the incentives of households in using the natural environment. The particular character of environmental exploitation depends both on indigenous political and economic structures and processes, and the character of the wider exchange system. Thus, the analysis of the political ecology of unincorporated trade must be more open-ended than that of incorporated areas, where local production is affected and coordinated by political and military power deriving from outside centers and interests. The political ecology of unincorporated trade should include analyses of how local societies convert trade goods into social labor through kinship, marriage, and various forms of clientage, rather than through systemic center-periphery hierarchies (cf. Chase-Dunn and Mann 1998; Hornborg 2001:81).

The Ivory Trade and the World-System

At the end of the eighteenth century, the coastal towns of Lamu, Mombasa, and Tanga/Pangani were the principal nodes that linked the northern East African interior to the Indian Ocean trade. Scattered in between were also a number of smaller ports and settlements that acted as outlets for interior products. The island of Zanzibar, under Omani rule, was beginning to overtake these towns as the major entrepot for the overseas trade with the interior. The East African coast came under the political and economic domination of Oman, whose new commercial orientation and relationship to the British led to a program of political conquest of the coast. In the beginning of the 1800s, the capital of Oman was moved to Zanzibar and soon took over Lamu, and then Mombasa in 1837. The Omani administration tried to centralize all trade through Zanzibar, made money on customs, and invited local Indian financiers to take over the ivory trade. The Omani governors had little interest in fostering political alliances with the hinterland traders but encouraged the unfettered expansion of caravans and profit seeking (Sheriff 1987).

At this time the trade was still organized according to a pattern that can be traced back at least to the beginning of the second millennium. Prior to the 1800s, the demand for ivory emanated primarily from India, the Middle East, and China. Trade was embedded in multiplex social networks, political alliances, and intermarriage. The relationships between the towns and their mainland neighbors included military cooperation against common enemies, participation in town governments by interior people, mediations, hospitality and feasting, and gift giving (Willis 1993). Procurement of ivory and its transport and marketing was in the hands of the interior peoples. Seldom did the towns themselves organize any trading expeditions to the interior, and throughout the first half of the nineteenth century interior communities actively resisted any such attempts (Sinclair and Håkansson 2000).

As the demand for ivory in the Western world boomed in the mid-nineteenth century, the coastal towns became increasingly involved in organizing trade, financed by Indian trading firms. In addition, localized slave trade was emerging in parts of the region. Ethnic boundaries and confederacies collapsed as a result of the reorientation of trade from an interior initiative to large intrusive caravans originating from the coast. In response to this shift in trade structure, new forms of political mobilization emerged that were based on the control of nodes in the trade routes. This change was the result of several interdependent factors. The steep increase in demand for ivory could not be satisfied through the established trading organization, and the cost of ivory on the coast increased partly as a result of inflation in the value of cloth currency in the interior. The increase in capital accumulated on Zanzibar enabled the coastal merchants to mobilize and provision large armed caravans of thousands of people that could easily put down any resistance in the interior.[2]

The Trade System before 1850

A crucial aspect of the early trade system was that the main goods involved were difficult to control by any single group. Elephants were widespread and not possible to monopolize. Before the nineteenth century elephants probably inhabited all of eastern Africa and were found in most habitats, from dry steppe to the mountain rain forests (Kingdon 1979:40). During the first half of the nineteenth century, elephants were still common in many parts of the region (Håkansson 2004). The supply of coastal goods was likewise difficult to control by the societies in the interior. By 1800 a multitude of coastal towns and villages were reception points for ivory and the source of exotic goods. These towns provided the interfaces for exchange along the coast, but their inhabitants did not send caravans into the interior. Along the coast, and in the interior, a wide variety of products and services were exchanged through many different arrangements[3] such as periodic markets, individual trade partnerships, kinship, and marriage links.

In order to assess the impact of the ivory trade on political ecology we must distinguish the effects of the flow of coastal goods from regional exchange processes internal to eastern Africa. Until the nineteenth century, the interior of eastern Africa was divided into several regions of frequent economic and social interaction. Within these smaller systems, livestock, people, agricultural products (grains, root crops, and bananas), as well as iron, tools, decorations, copper, salt, medicines, religious/magical artifacts, and specialist services, circulated. The East African economies were integrated through a common value system based on cattle, which were everywhere in demand and exchangeable for other products as well as serving as the most valued prestige goods in social transactions. The social reproduction of families and kinship was dependent on a regional system of exchange in which cattle were ultimately used to build political power and to secure the growth and wealth of kin groups (Håkansson 1994, 1998; Schneider 1979; Waller 1985).

The coastal goods entered the regional systems as one further category of value that provided additional avenues for investment and transactions, and that affected social and economic relationships.[4] Cloth and beads were major articles of barter from at least the ninth century onward (Freeman-Grenville 1966:8, 21, 110). Burton and Speke (1858:215) observed that "Money is not current at Usambara. The small change is beads, the higher specie is American domestics [cotton cloth]." By exploiting the variations in exchange rates that followed a spatial continuum, traders could optimize returns in trade goods, which were in turn diverted into local social payments (Håkansson 2004).

Traders and Hunters: The Kamba

In his landmark study of the political economy of Zanzibar, the historian Abdul Sheriff (1987:169–170) states that when the coastal traders had taken over the ivory trade, the Kamba "were [an] exhausted shell, sucked dry of their economic vitality by international trade and thrown by the wayside." Although a colorful metaphor of capitalist exploitation, it is based on a misunderstanding of the nature of the Kamba trade, which cannot be understood as a form of unequal exchange.

The Kamba both hunted elephants and purchased ivory from others. The trade was organized through large enterprises that coordinated up to one thousand people in hunting, trading, and transporting as well as smaller kin-based groups of hunters and traders. At their peak the Kamba organized caravans numbering around five hundred persons, who traveled the 300-kilometer journey from Kitui to the coast several times per year (Jackson 1977:49). In addition to hunting, ivory was obtained from communities in central Kenya, where cloth and beads entered into the regional markets (Leakey 1977:442; Muriuki 1974:108). For example, Athi foragers supplied the Gikuyu with ivory that they traded to the Kamba, and also traded directly with Maasai and Kamba in exchange for goats (Muriuki 1974:101).

The Kamba of Kitui became the dominant ivory traders in the central part of the East African interior from the end of the 1700s, when they expanded their trading networks from Lake Turkana in the north to Kilimanjaro in the south (Lamphear 1970; CMS n.d.:Krapf, March 16, 1848). The highlands around Mount Kenya receive much rain, have fertile volcanic soils, and were covered with dense forests. As the land slopes toward the coast average annual rainfall decreases from 1,000–1,200 mm at an elevation of 1,000–1,400 meters to 600 mm at 650 meters in the plains below the fringes of the Kenya highlands. Soils become thinner, and the vegetation changes to a dry wooded grass savanna (map 7.1) that extends to the humid coastal strip (Morgan 1973:292–293). Except in the higher elevations, rainfall is extremely variable both temporally and spatially, and droughts are frequent. Highland Kitui receives enough precipitation for a successful harvest in seven out of ten years, and the plains only in one year out of three (O'Leary 1984:14).

According to oral traditions, the Kamba ancestors first settled in the seventeenth century at Ulu in the highlands east of Mount Kenya, in what is now known as Machakos, where they combined irrigated agriculture on terraced slopes and shifting cultivation with cattle husbandry (Jackson 1976:197–198; Lindblom 1920:502). Unlike the highlands, the plains country usually offered excellent pasturelands and hence a chance to accumulate wealth. The large-scale cattle owners were concentrated in dry open country in Ulu and Kitui (Ambler 1988:54). The basic social units of the Kamba were patrilineages of different size that agglomerated into neighborhoods with cross-cutting kinship and affinal ties. The clans were dispersed, and the localized lineages were the effective kinship units. Lineages from different clans formed neighborhoods that cooperated in everyday affairs (Forbes Munro 1975:14).

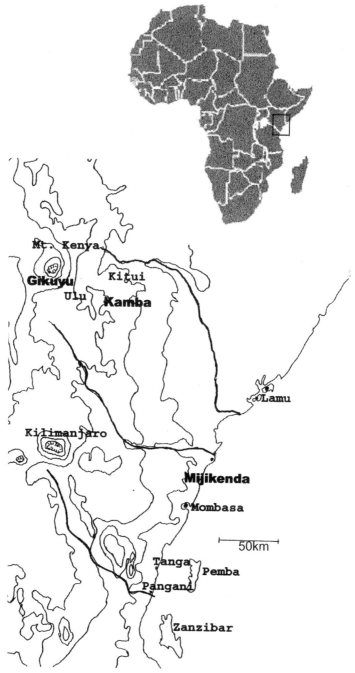

Map 7.1. The East African hinterland

The bulk of the ivory trade emanated from the pastoral communities in Kitui while the people of Ulu provided considerable support in the form of porters, hunters, and some financing in the form of livestock. Little is known about the political ecology of the Ulu communities at that time. In this area local leaders also built wealth in cattle and people, but pronounced inequalities seem to have been precluded by two factors. First, participation in the ivory trade as porters and hunters allowed families to gain access to coastal goods that they bartered for livestock and food. Second, while agricultural surplus was produced for exchange purposes, the accumulation of cattle led to a shift in residence from Ulu to Kitui rather than continuous expansion of cultivation (Ambler 1988:14).

During the late eighteenth and first half of the nineteenth century the Kitui settlements grew in size as a response to their expanded engagement in the ivory trade. The expansion of trade led to the integration of coastal goods into the regional network and enabled further expansion east into Kitui (Jackson 1976:240). Many Kitui Kamba used the coastal goods both to enlarge their herds and to obtain foodstuffs, on an annual basis as well as during food shortages and droughts, from Ulu and the Gikuyu (Jackson 1976:218; Muriuki 1974:86).[5] Cloth from the Kitui provided the Ulu communities with the means to obtain food from the highland communities where bead and cloth currencies entered into the regional markets (Leakey 1977:442; Muriuki 1974:108). The amount of grain that was needed during a severe drought can be illustrated by the famine of 1898, when five thousand Kitui people traveled to the highlands, where they obtained about 150 metric tonnes of grain from the Gikuyu and other cultivators in exchange for livestock (KNA n.d.:57). Hence, access to currencies among the Kamba contributed to agricultural intensification outside their home areas.

From the perspective of world-system theory this trade did not appear to have entailed any clear exploitation of the interior by the coastal elites and the centers of the world-system. Agriculture was not the dominant economic activity in Kitui, where people invested trade gains in cattle. In addition, the labor demands of cultivation in Ulu and Kitui were seasonal and allowed men and women to engage in trade during the dry seasons. Furthermore, from a regional perspective there were increased productive diversification and perhaps more agricultural products available than if the Kitui had spent more time in trying to produce more crops on their own land. As several authors have argued with respect to East Africa and other regions in the world, the importation of currencies can reduce transaction costs and thereby stimulate trade and productive diversification and provide food security (Chase-Dunn and Mann 1998:143). Although the suppliers of food obtained cloth and beads with no use value, Kitui's access to these currencies actually freed labor for other activities that contributed to the economic diversity of the region as a whole. Especially Kamba women were active in regional trade and transported a variety of goods throughout the highlands and adjacent lowlands. Furthermore, the increased engagement in the ivory trade was also accompanied by a considerable degree of diversification in the local production of consumption goods, such as pottery, iron implements, poisons, medicines, and leather, that circulated in exchange for food, livestock, cloth, beads, and imported metals (Jackson 1976:216–218). There were even specialized craft villages (Jackson 1977). The goal of the households was to minimize cultivation and accumulate cattle. While the Kamba colonies near the coast had become completely pastoral (CMS n.d.:Krapf, September 1, 1845), those living in Kitui regarded cultivation as a necessary evil that they were forced to maintain as a supplement to other food sources in the form of milk and imported crops (Lindblom 1920:501; Krapf 1968 [1860]: 356; CMS n.d.:Krapf, November 30, 1849).

The Kamba conformed to Cohen's (1974:xvi–xvii) model of ethnicity as a form of political mobilization that facilitates the control and monopolization of trade. A supracommunity identity above the neighborhood and clan emerged among the Kamba during the nineteenth century. Indeed, the diaspora settlements maintained social and ethnic boundaries vis-à-vis their host communities by refusing intermarriage and by upholding their own particular customs (CMS n.d.:Krapf, January 30, 1845). These practices earned them reputations as aloof and arrogant (Lindblom 1920:572). Although trading families transformed coastal goods into cattle and social expansion, the organization of the trade required extensive redistribution of wealth, which precluded the development of pronounced inequalities (Jackson 1976:210).

Wealth and poverty of people in most East African societies were measured in terms of how many heads of livestock a person or family owned and how many dependents a person could count as subservient to him or her. How did the relative equality in livestock per family or household affect land use? First, the size of the family herds was constrained by the availability of labor. Second, the welfare of the herds was directly connected to the welfare of the family. Hence, herd owners dispersed their settlements to optimize sustainable land use and herd growth throughout the highlands in Kitui (Mutiso 1979; O'Leary 1984:26), and localized concentrations of cattle must have been avoided.

Intermediaries: Rabai and the Mijikenda

As the Kamba caravans approached the coast they were blocked by the Mijikenda communities that controlled all trade with Mombasa and other ports in their vicinity. Having traveled 300 kilometers through the dry and nearly unpopulated steppe, caravans entered the humid coastal region, which from Lamu to Pangani is characterized by a relatively high annual rainfall from 900 mm in Lamu to 1,200 mm in Tanga on the northern Tanzania coast. Rainfall permitting agriculture is restricted to a strip of land about 50 km wide in the north, extending to a width of 150 km in the south at the Pangani River. Beyond this, rainfall declines rapidly to less than 700 mm per year, and the lush coastal vegetation changes abruptly into dry scrubland and semidesert. South of the Sabaki River the coastal hinterland forms a band of relatively high agricultural potential and is populated by several communities of Bantu speakers that today are known as the Mijikenda, Giriama, Kauma, Chonyi, Jibana, Kambe, Ribe, Rabai, Duruma, and Digo to the south. Their ethnic and political loyalties centered on fortified sacred villages called Makaya (pl. Kaya).[6] Their total population in the mid-nineteenth century was estimated to be about fifty thousand, of which thirty thousand belonged to Digo south of Mombasa (Krapf 1968 [1860]:159; CMS n.d.: Rebmann, January 20–21, 1848).

These groups were mainly cultivators but also kept varying numbers of cattle, sheep, and goats. The traditional food crops were sorghum, millet, and finger millet, which were largely replaced by maize during the nineteenth century. In addition, beans, cassava, sweet potatoes, and yams were cultivated. Coconut palms were also grown, especially in Digoland and Rabai. The tree provided a strong drink made from fermented coconut milk, which was traded throughout the coastal ridge and coast itself (Spear 1978:3). Other goods such as metals, metal tools, ornaments, and salt were obtained from the Swahili (CMS n.d.:Krapf, January 1, 1845).

The social organization of the Mijikenda during this period is little known. The primary means of group identification was the fortified Kaya villages that served mainly as ritual centers. Kaya members constituted a political and ethnic community that conferred rights and obligations on its members. At the end of the nineteenth century most were patrilineal, but Rabai and Duruma practiced double descent, and the Digo were matrilineal.

However, it was the collective community institutions of Rabai and Giriama that enabled them to control and benefit from the ivory trade. Although both groups were organized according to descent, such allegiances were contained within a system of cross-cutting collective institutions of age-sets and -grades, and semisecret societies of elders that organized community rituals for healing and fertility (Burton 1872:89; Udvardy 1990; Spear 1978:59).

Most Kamba trade had to pass through Rabai, and those caravans who passed through the territory had to pay fees to the elders (CMS n.d.:Krapf, March 25, 1845; Spear 1978:88). The Rabai acted as intermediaries and brokers to the Kamba caravans and either bought ivory from the Kamba and resold it to the traders in Mombasa or extracted brokers' fees from both the former and the Swahili traders. The Kamba caravans usually went to Rabai, and frequented Giriama mainly during the annual trade fair at Emberria in western Giriamaland. The goods were either resold to coastal traders residing in the area or taken directly to Mombasa. This system of government ensured that the Rabai could act collectively to tap the proceeds of the ivory trade, and the redistribution of the proceeds among the homestead heads. Although the Kaya institutions gave elders as a group power over younger people, they also prevented significant accumulation of wealth and clients by individual families (Willis 1993:43). The ivory trade was controlled by the male council of elders through appointed Kaya agents (*mwanandia*), who were responsible for dealing with the Swahili. The coastal goods were monopolized by the old men (Spear 1978:106), who shared the goods among themselves (CMS n.d.: Krapf, February 17, 1845). As among the Kitui Kamba, trade made it possible for the Rabai and Giriama to minimize the use of land for food production.

By the second half of the nineteenth century, the Rabai were not self-sufficient in food but relied on their profits from the trade in palm wine to purchase crops and livestock. According to one historian, they became food importers and wine exporters as a result of their specialization in coconut farming (Herlehy 1985a:95). However, this deficit in subsistence production predates the dominance of the wine economy. Already in the beginning of the 1800s Rabai food production was so low that they had to obtain grain from Mombasa on a regular basis (Willis 1993:50). The earliest eyewitness account of Rabai and other Mijikenda is that of Lieutenant Emery, commander of the short-lived British protectorate in Mombasa 1824–1826. In his log he notes the frequent visits of "Whaneekas" (Rabai and other neighboring Mijikenda) to deliver ivory and copal but seldom any attempts to sell foodstuffs (PRO n.d.). Although reluctant to leave Mombasa he apparently made a short trip to what must have been southeastern Rabai territory (Emery 1833:282), which he describes as follows:

> Their lands are little cultivated; cassada [cassava] is the chief produce of their grounds, although the country is capable of producing any thing: it resembles a park with clusters of trees here and there, as if planted by art. Small pieces of water are also seen to which the natives drive their cattle always before sunset, previous to taking them to the pens.

Further east, about 15 km from Mombasa, a belt of semideciduous forest stretched northward along a limestone ridge and surrounded most of the Mijikenda Kaya villages. This forest was part of a distinct floristic region called the Zanzibar-Inhambane Regional Mosaic, characterized by widespread forest mixed with wooded grassland with a high number of endemic forest trees (Chapman and Chapman 1996). From the detailed accounts found in the diaries of the missionaries Krapf (CMS n.d.:February 17, 1845) and Rebmann (CMS n.d.:January 20–21, 1848), it is clear that, in the middle of the nineteenth century, this forest still formed a largely continuous band from the border of Rabai to Giriamaland (map 7.2). In Rabai, however, most of the forest had been removed and replaced by coconut plantations. Today only remnants surrounding the Makaya remain, the largest of which are only about one and a half square kilometers (Chapman and Chapman 1996).

Before discussing the reason for this expansion, it is necessary to briefly explain the cultural context of palm wine (*uchi* in Kirabai). All Mijikenda used *uchi* for important rituals, for drinking, for libations to the dead, and as part of bridewealth payments. Rabai grew palms for their own rituals as well as for export to other Mijikenda and to hinterland neighbors who consumed it purely for recreation. Palm wine symbolism is complex and combines ideas about both female and male fertility (Udvardy 1990:74). Although Rabai referred to the palm as mother (*ame*) and as a source of nourishment and sustenance, only men could own palms, which were also planted next to graves of deceased older men (Herlehy 1985a:77–78).

During the eighteenth century the ritual needs for *uchi* seem to have been supplied by Swahili plantations on the coast. As regional and coastal commerce grew in volume through the expansion of the ivory trade and the inclusion of new export products such as copal, Rabai and others on the coast had to strengthen their collective organization in order to capture more of the gains from that commerce. Although the male elders who resided in Kaya could, as a collective, extract resources from younger men and women in the forms of fees and fines, they could not exploit labor outside kinship and marriage relationships. Only kinship contained the long-term institutional

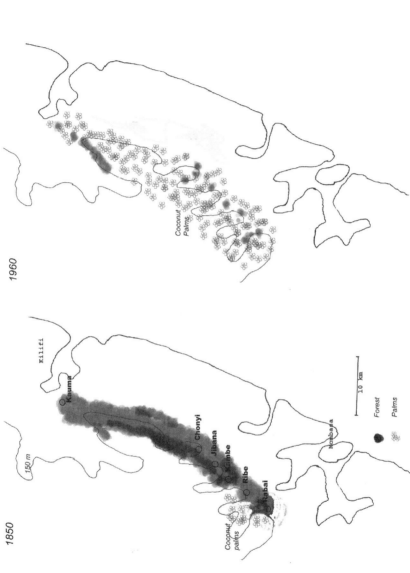

1960

1850

Kilifi

150 m

Kauma

Chonyi

Jibana

Kambe

Ribe

Rabai

Mombasa

Coconut
palms

Coconut
Palms

10 km

Forest

Palms

Map 7.2.   Approximate extents of Kenyan coastal ridge forest and coconut palms around 1850 (map 7.2a) and 1960 (map 7.2b). *Sources:* CMS: Krapf, February 17, 1845; Rebmann, January 20–21, 1848; *The Kenya Coast: Map and Guide* 1973; Spear 1978; Willis 1993

means of controlling social labor and maintaining access to resources over generations.

The redistribution of trade gains left families vulnerable to fluctuations in trade. Intermittent lack of trade goods led to food shortages that could only be alleviated by pawning children to the coastal Swahili in exchange for food (cf. Willis 1993:43). Hence, in order to avoid indebtedness, and to build social and economic power, family households attempted to accumulate wealth independently of the Kaya and to use it to attract clients and dependents that provided labor and political support. Family households transformed gains from local and coastal trade into livestock and also planted palm trees, which were considered family property.[7] Both provided long-term assets that families could draw on for survival and expansion. The intensified commerce in the area and population increase in the towns provided an expanded market for *uchi*. Already in the middle of the nineteenth century, palm trees had become a remunerative investment that led to the removal of indigenous forest.

Ironically, the very process of strengthening and maintaining collective political control contributed to demand. During the eighteenth century, *uchi* was used by Kaya elders only during important rituals such as initiation into age-sets and secret societies. During the nineteenth century, collective rituals and feasts increased in number (Herlehy 1985a:73–76). Although it is impossible to demonstrate a clear causal link, there is a relationship in time between the increase in coastal commerce and the proliferation of community events. As trade with the coast and the hinterland increased, so did the opportunities for elders to skim the gains as community leaders. At the same time, the trading activities in goods such as palm wine, livestock, copal, and foodstuffs created opportunities for individual accumulation, threatening both the political position of the elders (Spear 1978:116; Herlehy 1985a:287) and the control of the ivory trade. Hence, the increase in civic events that entailed the consumption of palm wine and livestock can be seen as a way to reinforce collective control by forcing individual households to share their potential wealth while at the same time stressing community values.[8] However, the very act of intensifying community rituals generated an increased demand for palm wine and thus the planting of more palms.[9]

The Political Ecology of the Caravan Trade

With the expansion of industrial capitalism in the United States and Europe the demand for ivory increased, as did the profits to be made on the East

African coast. The spatial structure and volume of trade changed radically from a diffuse pattern of flexible pathways to a more rigid network of trade routes and points for provisioning and for the purchase of ivory and slaves. The shift in the trade system simultaneously established exploitation of labor and environmental resources by local leaders and outside economic interests. In the late 1840s, coastal caravans from Pangani, Mtangata, and Tanga in Tanzania took control over much of the trade with the interior of Kenya and northern Tanzania (Sheriff 1987; Glassman 1995).[10]

The caravan trade from the coast represented a geographical shift in commerce from Kitui to Ulu, and a reorganization of Kamba participation from network-based collective enterprises to more individualized operations (Cummings 1985:201).[11] Caravans from Mombasa and Pangani destined for Lake Victoria and northern Kenya camped in Machakos primarily to obtain food supplies, and to hire Kamba men as porters, because this was the only major provisioning center for caravans going inland or to the coast across the dry steppe toward Mombasa (Forbes Munro 1975:25). The collective trading networks in Kitui began to disintegrate in the 1860s. The leadership that was once dependent on hunters and warriors no longer required their support. Individual big-men were now able to obtain capital or trade goods without reliance on extensive networks of supporting households (Cummings 1985).

The trade-induced transformation in the political economy of Ulu was accompanied by a change in the exploitation of the environment. The new leaders of Ulu did not base their political influence on large-scale redistribution (Jackson 1976:241). With the establishment of provisioning stations and the shift in the ivory trade to individual networks and contacts, it became possible to control the flow of goods and to concentrate wealth within the leaders' families and immediate kin groups. The path toward building large families and political power still went through cattle, but the coastal goods used to obtain them could be secured without large-scale organization and redistribution of wealth. The provisioning of food to the caravans became a new means to obtain wealth, either by using the trade goods in barter for livestock elsewhere or through the direct exchange of crops for livestock (Forbes Munro 1975:41). The inequalities in cattle holdings that resulted from the new trade pattern allowed the new elites to exploit the labor of less fortunate Kamba in exchange for food or livestock for bridewealth (Cummings 1985).

While successful cattle accumulation prior to the shift in the trade pattern had compelled households to migrate into Kitui, herds were now retained on the restricted grazing areas in Ulu, close to the trade routes. Such concentrations of cattle may have reduced the grass cover, in part because the declining frequency of fires allowed the tree cover to expand (Gichohi, Mwangi, and Gakahu 1996). Indeed, there are accounts from the late nineteenth century that describe former grazing areas of cattle accumulators as covered by thick bush and trees (Mutiso 1979). Furthermore, the emigrants from formerly prosperous but drought-ridden areas (Jackson 1976:241) increased the human population in Machakos, which together with the production for sale to caravans by petty traders led to an expansion of cultivation using client labor to expand food production. In the Kenya highlands numerous local traders and leaders competed to attract caravans to their settlements. Caravans went to the supplier who could promise the most reliable and abundant supply of agricultural products (Ambler 1988:102; Cummings 1985). The pressure to cultivate led to precarious agricultural activities such as planting on steep hills and along watercourses, which promoted erosion. The reduced fallow period depleted soil fertility, and the cutting of trees for fuel resulted in serious deforestation (Ambler 1988:118–119; Lindblom 1920:26).

On the coast, as a consequence of the diminishing number of caravans from Kitui, the Rabai lost their role as intermediaries. The other Mijikenda groups also suffered from this economic and political marginalization. The Giriama, who had been active traders, continued to sell ivory at the coast but in lower volumes, and the smaller Kaya groups that had indirectly profited from the trade by selling foodstuffs and crafts also found themselves faced with declining access to wealth. The only remunerative alternative source of wealth was palm trees. Consequently, from the end of the nineteenth century, the indigenous forest was cut at an increasing rate to provide space for coconut plantations. By 1900 all the Mijikenda were to some extent cultivating coconut palms (Herlehy 1985b). As the Rabai and other Mijikenda lost their control over the ivory trade they began to exploit their local resources in order to regain access to wealth. Deforestation was not a result of subsistence needs dictated by population growth but emerged from strategies to build individual and family power in a changed political economy.

Conclusion

Unincorporated trade was involved in political processes that acted on the environment through settlement patterns and land use. The pattern of land use was shaped by the access to valuables and investment in wealth-generating assets such as cattle and palms rather than direct subsistence needs (cf. Kelly 1985:241). Hence, a political ecology of unincorporated trade must include the way in which exotic goods were made commensurable with valuables and assets in the regional economy, and the way in which exotic goods were connected to prestige spheres.

The transformations in the exchange system marginalized the interior communities from the profits of the coastal trade. The effects of this exclusion on land use parallel the marginalization thesis in the political ecology of capitalist penetration in rural and disempowered areas (Robbins 2004:77), but with one important difference. While marginal populations that are incorporated into capitalist relations of production are transforming their environment to manage subsistence, the Kamba and Mijikenda were struggling to maintain access to wealth for social reproduction, not subsistence. Nevertheless, their changed position in the world-system similarly led to increased exploitation of local resources in order to access wealth.

World-system theories do not offer much guidance for understanding the relationship between exchange and environmental exploitation in the context of unincorporated trade. Before the onset of the coastal caravan trade it is difficult to detect any core-periphery processes of exploitation in the interior. Rather, there are indications that trade contributed to regional integration, productive specialization, and economic growth during the first half of the nineteenth century. Under conditions of internal control of the coastal trade, those communities that were part of the ethnic trading confederations practiced sustainable land use. They relied on access to trade goods to import food and used the trade to increase their holdings of long-term assets that yielded prestige goods. The highly redistributive nature of the collective political economy ensured widespread access to the means of social reproduction in the form of livestock. The result was a close reciprocal relationship between family households and the land they used. However, the reliance on coastal goods as currencies created a dependency on outside economic fluctuations.

Although exploitation in terms of labor time or economic value is difficult to ascertain, there is the intriguing possibility that the intensified killing of elephants for the ivory trade reduced ecological complexity and productive potential for human societies. Reduction in elephant herds would have led to an increased growth of scrubs and trees, transforming a species-rich savanna and pasturelands to a wooded expanse infested with tsetse flies and reduced biodiversity (Håkansson 2004). Thus, the ivory trade reduced the productive potential of the land, but it did so indirectly, rather than by draining the land of resources exported to Europe.

The caravan trade created the preconditions for increased agricultural exploitation not only by providing the opportunities for local elites to exploit labor but also by creating food shortages that forced people to enter into clientage. This led to population concentrations and, in some regions, exploitation of areas not suitable for intensive cultivation. The crucial variable involved, in conjunction with hierarchy and inequality, was competition between local leaders for access to trade goods (cf. Allen and Crittenden 1987). These elites had their own sources of subsistence and could manage agricultural production purely for exchange purposes, while dependent households lacked the power to independently regulate their own use of the land. This in turn led to environmental transformations that predated the incorporation of these areas into the capitalist world-system.

Notes

1. I would like to thank John McNeill and Monica Udvardy for critical comments on the manuscript and the Swedish Research Council for financial support. Archival research has been carried out in the Church Missionary Society archive and the Public Records Office in Kew, England. Seven months of field research in Rabai, Kenya, were conducted in 1985–1986.

2. Most of the slaves imported to Zanzibar and the East African coast came from south-central Africa: Malawi, southern Tanzania, and Mozambique. The slave raiding in northern Tanzania was relatively modest and short in duration.

3. Since, except for short distances, river transport was not feasible, much of the transport was human, and to some extent donkeys were used. Distance became a very important variable for positioning within the system.

4. The societies were thus not caught in a strong dependency on coastal goods for the realization of social relationships, and the original qualities of indigenous currencies may have had the capacity to mitigate instabilities introduced by the interface currencies (Guyer 1995:8).

5. Although Ulu (Machakos) big-men and -women were not directly involved in the ivory trade, the Kitui traders spent considerable time maintaining social relationships with them. These men and women were leaders of villages that supplied a large portion of porters and hunters (Jackson 1972:259–260).

6. Already in the first half of the nineteenth century, and possibly much earlier, several of these groups identified themselves in relation to their Kaya of origin (Willis 1993:28).

7. According to one informant: "Prior to the adoption of palms, the wealth of Rabai was cattle." Today the palm is of cultural importance to most Mijikenda. According to one of my informants, palms are necessary for life and income—they provide cash for education. Cattle never lost their importance as prestige goods but palms provided durable wealth that required less space and care.

8. During community civic and religious ceremonies all were expected to bring *uchi*. If anyone did not attend these events or did not bring *uchi* they were severely fined. These drinking feasts occurred with more regularity and by midcentury these festivals were so frequent that some European observers commented that the Rabai seemed to spend all their time drinking (Herlehy 1985a:76). Elders also received gifts

of *uchi* as guardians of Rabai society and economy. It was common to give at least one *kadzama* for advice and services in rendering judgment (Herlehy 1985a:81).

9. Finally, the graded system of collective power that culminated in the secret societies required high fees of cloth, money, livestock, palm wine, and food. The highest-ranking societies demanded considerable wealth to be distributed by the applicants to the members in the form of bulls, cloth, palm wine, and food (CMS n.d.: Krapf, September 11, 1852; Spear 1978:61). Only those who had access to social labor from a large household could enter the inner circles of collective power. To build a large following, an individual needed access to wealth such as palm trees and livestock that could be accumulated outside the redistributive system. Thus, the very collective institutions that worked to redistribute wealth contributed to the growth of household-based resources in the form of palm trees and livestock.

10. In contrast to their activities in Kenya, the caravans in Tanzania also searched for slaves. Often the traders extended capital and guns to local big-men or -women who emerged as local chieftains at certain points (Giblin 1992:55). The slave raids devastated production systems and contributed to population shifts to areas of trade and areas where protection and patronage could be obtained.

11. The reason for this decline has not been fully investigated. It is known that warfare among the pastoralist Maa-speakers in the region, together with incursions of the Orma pastoralists from the north, created difficulties for traders (Lamphear 1970).

References

Allen, B., and R. Crittenden. 1987. Degradation and a pre-capitalist political economy: The case of the New Guinea Highlands. In *Land degradation and society*, ed. P. Blaikie and H. Brookfield, 145–156. London: Methuen.

Ambler, C. 1988. *Kenyan communities in the age of imperialism*. New Haven, Conn.: Yale University Press.

Blaikie, P., and H. Brookfield. 1987. Defining and debating the problem. In *Land degradation and society*, ed. P. Blaikie and H. Brookfield, 1–26. London: Methuen.

Burton, R. 1872. *Zanzibar*. Vol. 2. London: Longmans.

Burton, R., and J. H. Speke. 1858. A coasting voyage from Mombasa to the Pangani River. *Journal of the Royal Geographical Society* 28:188–226.

Chapman, C. A., and L. J. Chapman. 1996. Mid-elevation forests: A history of disturbance and regeneration. In *East African ecosystems and their conservation*, eds. T. R. McClanahan and T. P. Young, 385–400. Oxford: Oxford University Press.

Chase-Dunn, C., and T. D. Hall. 1997. *Rise and demise*. Boulder, Colo.: Westview.

Chase-Dunn, C., and K. M. Mann. 1998. *The Wintu: A very small world-system in northern California*. Tucson: University of Arizona Press.

CMS. n.d. Church Missionary Society Archives Microfilms. Diaries of Ludwig Krapf and Johann Rebmann. Church Missionary Society Archive (CMS): CMS CA5/016. Center for Research Libraries, Chicago, Ill.

Cohen, A. 1974. Introduction: The lesson of ethnicity. In *Urban Ethnicity*, ed. A. Cohen, ix–xxiv. London: Tavistock.

Cummings, R. J. 1985. Wage labor in Kenya in the nineteenth century. In *The workers of African trade*, ed. C. Coquery-Vidrovitch and P. Lovejoy, 193–208. Beverly Hills, Calif.: Sage.

Einzig, P. 1949. *Primitive money in its ethnological, historical and economic aspects.* London: Eyre and Spottiswoode.

Emery, J. B. 1833. A short account of Mombas and the neighbouring coast of Africa. *Journal of the Royal Geographical Society* 3:280–283.

Franke, R. W. 1987. Power, class, and traditional knowledge in Sahel food production. In *Studies in power and class in Africa*, ed. I. L. Markovits, 257–285. Oxford: Oxford University Press.

Forbes Munro, J. 1975. *Colonial rule and the Kamba.* Oxford: Clarendon Press.

Freeman-Grenville, G. S. P. 1966. *The East African coast.* Oxford: Clarendon.

Giblin, J. L. 1992. *The politics of environmental control in northeastern Tanzania, 1840–1940.* Philadelphia: University of Pennsylvania Press.

Gichohi, H., E. Mwangi, and C. Gakahu. 1996. Savanna ecosystems. In *East African ecosystems and their conservation*, eds. T. R. McClanahan and T. P. Young, 273–298. Oxford: Oxford University Press.

Glassman, J. 1995. *Feasts and riot.* London: Currey.

Guyer, J. 1993. Wealth in people and self-realization in equatorial Africa. *Man*, n.s., 28:243–265.

———. 1995. Introduction: The currency interface and its dynamics. In *Money matters*, ed. J. L. Guyer, 1–34. London: Currey.

Håkansson, N. T. 1994. Grain, cattle, and power: The social process of intensive cultivation and exchange in precolonial western Kenya. *Journal of Anthropological Research* 50:249–276.

———. 1998. Rulers and rainmakers in precolonial South Pare, Tanzania: The role of exchange and ritual experts in political fragmentation. *Ethnology* 37:263–283.

———. 2004. The human ecology of world systems in East Africa: The impact of the ivory trade. *Human Ecology* 32:561–591.

Herlehy, T. 1985a. An economic history of the Kenya Coast: The Mijikenda coconut palm economy, ca 1800–1980. PhD diss., Boston University.

———. 1985b. Ties that bind: Palm wine and blood-brotherhood at the Kenya Coast during the 19th century. *International Journal of African History* 17:285–309.

Hornborg, A. 2001. *The power of the machine.* Walnut Creek, Calif.: Altamira.

Jackson, K. 1972. An ethnohistorical study of the oral traditions of the Akamba of Kenya. PhD diss., University of California, Los Angeles.

———. 1976. The dimensions of Kamba precolonial history. In *Kenya before 1900*, ed. B. A. Ogot, 174–261. Nairobi: East African Publishing House.

————. 1977. Ngotho (the ivory armlet): An emblem of upper-tier status among the 19th century Akamba of Kenya ca 1830–1880. *Kenya Historical Review* 5:35–68.

Kelly, R. C. 1985. *The nuer conquest.* Ann Arbor: Michigan University Press.

The Kenya coast: Map and guide. 1973. Nairobi: Survey of Kenya.

Kingdon, J. 1979. *East African mammals: An atlas of evolution in Africa.* Vol. 3, pt. B. Chicago: University of Chicago Press.

KNA. n.d. Kenya National Archives. Stanner, W. F. H. The Kitui Kamba. Kenya National Archives (KNA):DC KTI 6/2/2.

Krapf, J. L. 1968 (1860). *Travels, researches, and missionary labours during an eighteen years' residence in eastern Africa.* London: Frank Cass.

Lamphear, J. 1970. The Kamba and the northern Mrima coast. In *Pre-colonial African Trade*, ed. R. Gray and D. Birmingham, 75–102. London: Oxford University Press.

Leakey, L. B. S. 1977. *The southern Kikuyu before 1903.* Vol. 1. New York: Academic.

Lindblom, G. 1914. *Afrikanska strövtåg.* Stockholm: Bonniers.

————. 1920. *The Akamba.* Uppsala: J.-A. Lundell.

Morgan, W. T. W. 1973. *East Africa.* London: Longman.

Muriuki, G. 1974. *A history of the Kikuyu 1500–1900.* Nairobi: Oxford University Press.

Mutiso, G. C. M. 1979. Kitui ecosystem, integration and change. In *Ecology and history in East Africa*, ed. B. A. Ogot, 128–152. Nairobi: Kenya Literature Bureau.

O'Leary, M. 1984. *The Kitui Akamba.* Nairobi: Heinemann.

PRO. n.d. Public Record Office, Great Britain. Emery, Journal 1824–1826.

Robbins, P. 2004. *Political ecology.* Oxford: Blackwell.

Schneider, H. K. 1979. *Livestock and equality in East Africa.* Bloomington: Indiana University Press.

Sheriff, A. 1987. *Slaves, spices, and ivory in Zanzibar.* Athens: Ohio University Press.

Sinclair, P., and N. T. Håkansson. 2000. The Swahili city-state culture. In *A comparative study of thirty city-state cultures*, ed. M. H. Hansen, 462–483. Copenhagen: The Royal Academy of Sciences and Letters.

Spear, T. 1978. *The Kaya complex.* Nairobi: Kenya Literature Bureau.

Udvardy, M. L. 1990. Kifudu: A female fertility cult among the Giriama. In *The creative communion*, ed. A. Jacobson-Widding and W. V. Beek, 137–152. Uppsala Studies in Cultural Anthropology 14. Stockholm: Almqvist and Wiksell International.

Waller, R. 1985. Economic relations in the central Rift Valley: The Maa-speakers and their neighbors in the nineteenth century. In *Kenya in the nineteenth century*, ed. B. A Ogot, 83–151. Nairobi: Bookwise.

Willis, J. 1993. *Mombasa, the Swahili, and the making of the Mijikenda.* London: Oxford University Press.

Steps to an Environmental History of the Western *Llanos* of Venezuela: A World-System Perspective

8

RAFAEL A. GASSÓN

I T IS ESSENTIAL TO DEVELOP an environmental history that combines social and natural aspects of the landscape. However, many ecologists, geographers, anthropologists, and historians who work in the lowland savannas of western Venezuela, the *Llanos*, still prefer to deal with just one side of the nature/society interface. A brief review, from a world-system perspective, of four examples (agricultural intensification, cattle ranching and hunting, tobacco farming, and the trade in feathers) taken from different periods of the history of the *Llanos* prompts us to reconsider this view. A world-system perspective is important in studies related to environmental history and landscape use, because it provides a way to study both environmental and social changes within the same theoretical framework. In this chapter I discuss how the incorporation of local societies and productive landscapes into pre-Columbian, colonial, and capitalist economies transformed specific aspects of traditional technologies, relations of production, and productive landscapes. World-systems are defined as intersocietal networks where the interaction is an important condition of the internal structure of the composite units and generates changes in these local structures. World-systems refer not only to global or large-scale interaction networks, but also to the world in which these peoples lived and which was important to their lives (Chase-Dunn and Hall 1991:7, 34).

The western *Llanos* of Venezuela are located in a large, irregular area between the Oirá River valley, at the southwestern Colombian-Venezuelan border, and the Sarare River valley, a tributary of the Cojedes River, and from the eastern Andean piedmont to the left bank of the Apure River. Topographically, the region can be divided into the piedmont, characterized by low hills, alluvial fans and terraces, and the alluvial plains, with an extensive network of rivers and meandering seasonal streams (Vila 1960:109). In general, the *Llanos* have a continental, homogeneous, macrothermic and isotherm climate, with two "seasons." All living creatures of the area must adapt to this seasonal climatic regime, which alternates rainy and dry periods with marked changes in plant phenology, water and nutrient economy, fire, biomass, and so forth. These cycles show unpredictable variations over the medium and long term (Harris 1980; Moran 1993; Sarmiento 1984; Solbrig 1993). Soils are of Quaternary origin, with heavy texture and imperfect drainage, and are affected by seasonal water stress (Sarmiento 1990:17). The savanna's vegetation is characterized by high primary production and abundant phytomass, which exhibits marked seasonal fluctuations. The savanna/forest boundary has always been dynamic, which can be attributed to climate, soil types, microrelief, and human activities (Hills and Randall 1968:105; Corpooccidente 1982).

Prehispanic Agricultural Intensification and Long-Distance Exchange

The current consensus about prehispanic human adaptation and evolution in the western *Llanos* of Venezuela was summarized by Garson (1980:44) as follows: The *Llanos* (1) must be distinguished from highland savannas and tropical forests; (2) were the historic loci of diverse peoples including large-scale, complex cultures; (3) are favorable for agriculture and the provision of protein needs for large populations; (4) have a culture history that can be explained by ecological variables, directly affecting human demography; and (5) should no longer be viewed as peripheral areas but as centers of development in their own right. The available data indicate that in the western *Llanos* of Venezuela, a great diversity of ways of life and levels of social organization coexisted, which included diversified hunters-and-gatherers, specialized fishers, and food producers, organized in egalitarian as well as hierarchical societies. The ancient farmers of the piedmont and the lowland savannas used a variety of agricultural techniques, which included terracing, irrigation systems, and slash-and-burn in the piedmont, and kitchen gardens, clear gardens, slash-and-burn, and raised fields agriculture in the lowlands (Morey 1975; Zucchi 1984).

The prehispanic raised and drained fields of the lowlands of Venezuela have often been interpreted as examples of small and peripheral agrosystems, albeit important in view of their possible relation to evidence for demographic and sociopolitical phenomena (Sanoja 1981; Denevan 1982;

Matheny and Gurr 1983; Zucchi 1984; Spencer, Redmond, and Rinaldi 1994). Spencer and Redmond's studies have indicated that complex societies or "chiefdoms" appeared in the *Llanos* between AD 500 and 600. This conclusion is supported by the appearance of settlement hierarchies, the presence of monumental architecture and engineering works, a large increase of the regional population, social differentiation of housing and funerary structures, and the presence of complex social relations with other political units, which included long-distance exchange and war (Redmond and Spencer 1990; Spencer 1991; Spencer, Redmond, and Rinaldi 1994:138–139). Specialized techniques for intensive cultivation were already in use in the savannas of Barinas during the Late Gaván phase. The analyses suggest that the productive potential of site B27 (La Tigra), a 35-hectare drained-field facility located near the regional center, exceeded the needs of consumption of the associated local community. Since there is no evidence of population pressure, the authors propose that the agricultural surpluses were used as the economic base of chiefly activities such as long-distance exchange and warfare (Spencer, Redmond, and Rinaldi 1994:138–139).

Other investigations of the political economy and landscape organization of these complex societies are being conducted at El Cedral, dated between AD 680 ± 50 and 690 ± 50 (Gassón 1998; Redmond, Gassón, and Spencer 1999). In examining the possible reasons for agricultural intensification in this region, we similarly discovered that the productive potential of the drained fields system associated with the regional center at El Cedral was higher than the estimated needs of the regional population. Hence, we proposed that part of the agricultural production could have been devoted to other activities, including exchange, war, and ceremonial feasting. Ceramic evidence of public feasting at El Cedral indicates that this activity was one of the most important components of the political economy of this polity. In spite of the fact that the local population and food production were more centralized, the importance of ceremonial feasting suggests a pursuit of social consent and the need to secure allies and followers through the redistribution of goods (Gassón 2003:197).

Long-distance exchange has been documented in the *Llanos*. For instance, in the Gaván and Cedral regions, several types of polished stone artifacts such as beads and pendants indicate that raw material was imported from distant areas such as the Venezuelan Andes, the Maracaibo Lake Basin, and even Southern Colombia, Ecuador, and the Caribbean (Spencer and Redmond 1992:153–154). A green stone pendant from El Cedral representing a small frog or reptile belongs to the class of objects that Boomert considered as one of the main items traded in exchange networks between the tribes of the lowlands and coasts of northern South America (Boomert 1987:33–37). This does not mean that these systems of intensification appeared *because* of the incorporation of local polities into world-systems, but it can safely be assumed that long-distance exchange played a role in the development of these productive landscapes.

However, raised fields were apparently not in use during the posthispanic period. The available archaeological data indicate that the best-known systems were used only during prehispanic times, while the ethnohistoric data of the area indicate that the European explorers and conquerors only rarely came across intensive areas of cultivation in other areas than along the main riverbanks. The few references available refer to these techniques as something from the past, as if they were from another epoch or in disuse. The famous verse written by Juan de Castellanos reads, "*de labranzas, viejos camellones,*" that is, old raised fields (Castellanos 1955:539). The recently discovered chronicle of Galeotto Cey also refers to earthen structures like mounds and causeways that were made *in times of prosperity*, that is, in former times (Cey 1994:78).

Climatological and comparative archaeological evidence suggests that climatic change might have played an important role in the disappearance of intensive agricultural systems in northern South America before the arrival of the Europeans, at least for those systems that depended on rain water. A global climatic phenomenon called the Little Ice Age (a period from about 1430 to 1850, during which the climate in the northern hemisphere was cooler and drier) affected the climate of the Venezuelan Andes, and probably also modified the hydrological regime of the *Llanos* (Rull 1987:13; Rull and Schubert 1989:71).

The vegetational and climatic sequence revealed by the analysis of the palynological record from the Venezuelan Andes is strikingly similar to those obtained in Bolivia, Colombia, and other parts of South America. There are many indications that drier conditions were predominant in South America during the last centuries before European contact. In the Central Andes, data obtained from the Qelccayya ice cap indicate a significant decrease in precipitation that persisted until around AD 1400. These climatological changes have been suggested as the proximate cause for the collapse of the Tiwanaku state (Ortloff and Kolata 1993:205). Similar episodes have been recognized in the high Cordilleras of Colombia, the eastern *Llanos*, and the San Jorge River basin. In the low San Jorge River, a long sequence of sociocultural development and raised field construction ended around AD 1200–1300 as a consequence of a long dry period (Plazas et al. 1988:76). Bray concludes that: "The sequence of wetter and drier periods ... may, therefore, be valid for the whole of northern South America" (Bray 1995:104). More research is obviously needed on the differences between the agrarian landscapes of the first millennium AD and the time of the European invasion.

The Colonial Encounter

It is commonplace to state that the incorporation of the western *Llanos* into the global economy brought many changes to the Amerindian communities. However, a closer look at what happened to large agricultural communities in contrast to hunter-and-gatherer communities, and the consequences of the introduction of cattle ranching and large-scale tobacco cultivation, is useful in order to illustrate the fundamental changes that occurred in landscape organization.

Nancy and Robert Morey used the changes experienced by the Achagua and Guahibo to illustrate the fate of farmers and hunter-foragers of the *Llanos* after contact with colonial society. The Achagua were once one of the most complex groups in the area, with large and well-organized farming communities. The Guahibo, on the other hand, were hunters-and-gatherers organized in small and mobile bands. Traditionally, these two groups maintained economic relationships based on the exchange of agricultural staples for fish and meat (Morey and Morey 1973:229–228).

Unfortunately for the Achagua, their large and impressive towns also sealed their fate. Since the very beginning of colonization, the Achagua were brought to the Spanish settlements or *encomiendas* as regular laborers. The Catholic missions also contributed to the reduction of the population, by exposing the Indians to epidemic diseases such as measles and smallpox. There is no doubt that disease had a far-reaching impact on the aboriginal population (Morey 1979:96). In addition, armed raids or *entradas* in search of new souls for the missions and/or slavery frequently ended in the killing of many Amerindians. In contrast, hunters-and-gatherers like the Guahibo and Yaruro largely escaped these problems. Although there is no way to measure the impact of epidemic diseases, armed raids, and slavery on these people, their social organization and settlement pattern limited the extent of their destruction. By the end of the seventeenth century, the Guahibo began to play an active role in the slave trade, thus replacing the exchange relationship with the Achagua with predation (Morey and Morey 1973:237). As a result of these events, by the end of the nineteenth century, the majority of the sedentary farmers had disappeared, while others had been assimilated into the communities of hunter-and-gatherers.

The introduction of cattle into the western *Llanos* of Venezuela set the conditions for the appeareance of a new way of life, the *hatero* (from *hato*: cattle ranch), and of a new category of local inhabitants, the *llaneros*, the mixed-blood descendants of Indians and colonizers. Historical accounts indicate that cattle entered the region long before the colonizers, and immediately became one of the most important prey for Amerindian hunter-gatherers. Cattle hunting still constitutes an important activity for hunters-and-gatherers like the Guahibo and Yaruro, and it is one of the main reasons for conflict between Indians and local cattle ranchers (Montiel 1993:36–37). Among the Hiwi (Guahibo), Hurtado and Hill found that although they hunt at least six mammal species, cows are the main source of meat. They do not provide additional data on these activities, given their sensitive nature (Hurtado and Hill 1990:305, 342).

Although Crosby states that it took several generations for the bovine stock to adapt to the humid lowlands of Brazil, Colombia, and Venezuela (Crosby 1988:199), there are plenty of indications that cows and horses were well adapted to the *Llanos* environment before the establishment of European settlements in the area. Cattle were introduced on the mainland by the Germans between 1529 and 1538, when northwestern Venezuela for a short period of time was under their governorship, in lieu of payment of large sums of money owed by the emperor Charles V to the Welser bankers. The original herd, brought from the island of Hispaniola, was composed of about three hundred to five hundred animals, which were moved from Coro (Falcon state) to El Tocuyo (Lara state). Several historians have argued that some animals of the original herd might have escaped or been stolen by the Indians who handled them during the journey from El Tocuyo to Tunja, Colombia. Others believe that the Indians obtained some animals through trade, learning to handle them long before the colonizers introduced cattle ranching in the colonial economic structure (García and Rojas 1996:64). Although there are no factual data to support these arguments, it is clear that colonizers found an abundance of wild cattle in the *Llanos*: "To the East, on the *llanos* and the banks of the Casanare and Apure rivers, there are more than four hundred thousand head of feral cattle which are good only as prey for the tigers born in that land as well as other wild animals and poisonous snakes" (Simón 1992:129). It should be pointed out that the Spaniards thus appear to have come across an abundance which existed in situ, instead of having to create it themselves. As an example, in the Pedraza region (Barinas), great herds of wild cattle were discovered in 1607 (Santamaria 1968:21).

In spite of the early presence of wild cattle in the western *Llanos*, cattle ranching was only developed during the late seventeenth century, when the first ranching settlements were established in the region, and leather and candle grease became profitable exports (Briceño 1985:49). However, this early pastoral economy did not favor the peopling of the *Llanos*, since cattle ranches needed few laborers and only simple facilities. Later on, however, the development of a cattle ranching economy came into contradiction with the Indians and mestizos not settled in towns or *hatos*, because they began to appropriate the wild cattle that roamed the savannas. The *llaneros* did not consider them as private property, but as game. To stop this hunting, two strategies were adopted: a legislation against cattle hunters and branding of cattle (Pinto 1980:23–24). An example of this are the measures adopted in 1787 by the governor of Barinas to try to eradicate "cattle thieves and malefactors" (García 1996:29). The conflict between the cattle ranchers and the *llaneros* endured until after the War of Independence, being one of the main causes of the failure of the First Republic of Venezuela in 1814.

Tobacco cultivation also illustrates the changes that occurred in the organization and use of the landscape of the *Llanos*. Tobacco production by the *encomiendas* and missions, along with maize, cotton, beans, manioc, and livestock, was the basis of the agrarian economy of the western *Llanos* (Montiel 1987:19). During the early colonial period, the Dutch were the main consumers of tobacco from Barinas. This excellent tobacco, called *Varinium*, was exported in large quantities to Europe (Wagner 1991:36). During that time, the consumption of tobacco was more popular in England, Holland, and Germany than in Spain, and the farming and smuggling of tobacco became a problem for the Spanish crown, which tried to limit tobacco's cultivation and trade (Rivero 1972:42). The importance acquired by *Varinium* tobacco on the international market led to greater efforts to satisfy the demand, and this increased the exploitation of indigenous labor and further contributed to the reduction of the Indian population. Alonzo Vasquez de Cisneros reported that in 1593 there were 950 Indians in the local *encomiendas*, while at the time of his visit, in 1620, he counted only 233 Indians. The decline of the local indigenous population forced Vasquez de Cisneros to establish regulations on the recruitment, treatment, and payment of the Indians. Workers could not live more than two leagues away from the *haciendas*, and were to be paid two and a half *pesos* per month (Montiel 1987:15). In the end, Spain tried to stop tobacco cultivation on the mainland, which only led to the impoverishment of the Province of Venezuela, since many farmers left tobacco cultivation to the Indians and mestizos. Regarding this development, Simón stated that

> This town [Barinas] . . . is one of the most famous in the world because of its fine tobacco, particularly in foreign nations: England, France, Flanders, Germany, Hungary, and in many parts of Asia. . . . It has two hundred and fifty indians divided among eight encomenderos and the same number of neighbors, who make a living from the tobacco trade cultivated by negroes who produce each year more than three thousand loads. (Simón 1992: 128–129)

Around 1660, the scarcity of labor for tobacco cultivation and the numerous taxes led to economic stagnation in Barinas, aggravated by the new taxes imposed to cover military expenditures. The problem of tobacco smuggling became so acute that, in 1777, a royal decree known as the *Estanco del Tabaco* established a monopoly on the tobacco trade. This provided Spain with large amounts of money with which to cover increasing military expenses in America, due to competition with rival nations such as England, Holland, and Portugal (Arcila Farias 1977:9). The royal decree empowered the intendent to charge 24 silver *reales* from the local producers for each load of tobacco. The tobacco farmers were free to manage their businesses as long as they payed the tax but, if they failed to do so, the intendent was authorized to prohibit further cultivation. In addition to this, only the royal tobacco store was authorized to sell tobacco products.

Despite all of these problems, in the western *Llanos* the period between 1750 and 1810 was one of relative prosperity, with a dense population and significant production of tobacco, maize, cotton, meat, leather, and many other products. However, social and economic world processes such as the conflict between Spain and her colonies continued to have an impact on this corner of the world.

The Crisis of Colonial Society and the Feathers Trade

The crisis of colonial society destroyed the agrarian economy of the *Llanos*. As is well known, the Venezuelan War of Independence (1810–1821) was particularly violent, causing the loss of many human lives and also of great numbers of livestock (Lynch 1980:246). In 1811 the new Republic of Venezuela published the so-called *Ordenanzas de Llanos*, a legislation for the consolidation and protection of the incipient private property of the region. The new laws imposed a tax penalty and a hundred whiplashes on cattle hunters, unless they had been authorized by the landowners. The intention underlying this measure was to associate cattle with land ownership, to eliminate the communal, traditional ways of life, and to promote the extension of private property in the area, assigning rights to cattle only to the ranch owners. These new laws reduced the formerly free Indians and *llaneros* to a condition of semiservile workers, forcing them to carry an identity card and to accept the status of cattle ranch employees. Anyone encountered more than once without employment would be condemned to prison for a year, while cattle thieves were condemned to death. This was the main reason why, at the beginning of the war, the *llaneros* strongly opposed the wealthy *criollo* landowners (Izard 1986:128–132; Lynch 1980:232).

Several factors contributed to the destruction of the agrarian economy of the *Llanos*. The first was the drastic reduction of the population and livestock, and the abandonment of great expanses of land formerly dedicated to agriculture and cattle ranching. Brito Figueroa indicates that Venezuelan livestock (cows, horses, and mules) were reduced from 4,500,000 head in 1812 to 256,000 in 1823 (Brito Figueroa 1975:221). In addition, the traditional technology was very primitive in relation to the global economy, since agriculture was basically based on the slash-and-burn system inherited from the Indians. Between 1800 and 1930, the *hato* economy mainly focused on the production of leather, salted meat, and live cattle. Barinas cattle were exported through internal ports of the Apure and Orinoco rivers to Angostura, Colombia, or Maracaibo. However, there were few investments in infrastructure such as roads (García and Rojas 1996:77–78). Finally, conflict arose not only between the powerful and the powerless, but also between farmers and cattle ranchers. The diverging interests of cattle ranchers and farmers generated contradictions in the organization and use of the landscape, and in 1846 Codazzi wrote that

> the Barinas province has two guilds engaged in constant and reciprocal fighting . . . the farmers and the cattle ranchers. To the former, it is convenient to have many people concentrated in the farmlands. . . . The others need vast tracts of lands even if they are bad, and badly located. If some prefer to be in the crossroads traveled by many, the others search for lonely places, where no one passes. (Codazzi 1960:172–173)

The official end of the War of Independence did not end the crisis of the colonial society, which continued until 1870 with the so-called *Guerra Federal* (Carrera Damas 1984:67). To make things worse, the growing international market was not interested in an independent Venezuela, which only produced tropical luxury products such as tobacco, leather, and coffee.

Although the end of the Spanish monopoly brought free trade, the competition with other areas producing for the European markets revealed the low competitive capacity of the Venezuelan producers.

An unexpected consequence of the destruction of the agrarian economy was the recovery of the tropical forests that covered the western *Llanos*. Estimates made by Veillon (1976:105) show that, just before the War of Independence, only 21 percent of the western *Llanos* was covered by forests. With the exception of the dense forests of Ticoporo, San Camilo, and Caparo, these had a patchy distribution. As a result of the wars (1810 through 1870), urban centers of the *Llanos* were reduced to sparsely populated hamlets, and in many cases, towns simply disappeared. In addition, vast expanses of savanna were abandoned, and extensive secondary forests appeared. Thus, 125 years later (1950), up to 45 percent of the western *Llanos* was again covered with forests. With the recovery of the forest, many species of animals returned to the area. This brought another unexpected consequence: the hunting of birds for their feathers.

One of the strategies used by cattle ranchers to cope with the economic crisis was to exploit heron feathers, since the nuptial feathers of the white heron (*Casmerodius albus*) and the small white heron (*Leucophoyx thula*) were in great demand in the fashion markets of Paris and New York, where they were used as ornaments for ladies' hats. Depending on their quality, these feathers, called *aigrettes*, could fetch a price even higher than gold (Zerpa Mirabal 1998:199).

This short-lived industry began in the 1880s, and during the following years experienced a tremendous increase in demand that brought about an economic boom that lasted until 1913, when the First World War affected the fashion industry. In addition, conservationists in the consumer countries arranged campaigns against the use of feathers, which also reduced the demand. After the war the prices rose again, but the economic crisis of Venezuela and the changes of fashion in the 1920s led to the final fall of this industry (Zerpa Mirabal 1998:199).

During this short time period, the exploitation of *aigrettes* had a considerable impact on the economy of the *Llanos* region, stimulating capital accumulation that supplemented the cattle ranching economy. However, it also caused conflicts between the landowners and the heron hunters, since the former considered that the birds nesting on their land were private property. In order to solve these problems, special regulations were established for this activity. The demand for heron feathers was so great that it almost caused the bird's extinction, since the hunters not only gathered fallen feathers, but killed the birds to obtain more of them. To make things worse, the nests were left without protection, thus killing the brood (Mondolfi 1993:184). The exploitation affected not only the local fauna, but also agriculture and cattle ranching, since most of the labor force abandoned the ranches and agricultural fields to hunt birds and collect feathers, deepening the economic crisis of the area. In addition, the cattle ranchers and landowners who had become feather traders did not take advantage of their sudden wealth by investing it in their property. In spite of the efforts that were made in some cities (e.g. San Fernando de Apure) to improve the local infrastructure, this was not the norm, and the lack of foresight and change in fashion soon ended the feather boom. Finally, the 1922 oil boom brought a sudden end to the agrarian and pastoral economy that had characterized preindustrial Venezuela (Salas 1982:47).

Conclusion

The research carried out on prehispanic complex societies of the western *Llanos* of Venezuela suggests that an important part of the agricultural surplus was used to maintain regional exchange networks. With the Spanish arrival and the expansion of the world-system in the western *Llanos*, the regional networks gravitated toward the Orinoco River axis, which was dominated by Europeans in alliance with indigenous tribes. Through this process, the dense and sedentary food-producing societies were destroyed, favoring the development of small, semisedentary, and decentralized groups, which became the foundation of the *llanero* way of life, based on slash-and-burn agriculture and the exploitation of wild cattle. Cattle ranching and agriculture were the basis of colonial wealth until the crisis of colonial society and the subsequent periods of war. As in many other parts of the world, the application of a world-system perspective here reveals a series of economic patterns centered on the production or exploitation of sumptuary goods (primitive valuables, leather, tobacco, feathers) destined to satisfy the needs of an impersonal, international market beyond the reach and comprehension of local actors. These economic activities produced a series of changes in the *llanero* landscape, some of which are still observable today.

References

Arcila Farias, E. 1977. *Historia de un monopolio: El estanco del tabaco en Venezuela 1779–1833*. Caracas: Universidad Central de Venezuela.

Boomert, A. 1987. Gifts of the Amazons: "Green stone" pendants and beads as items of ceremonial exchange in Amazonia and the Caribbean. *Antropologica* 67:33–54.

Bray, W. 1995. Searching for environmental stress: Climatic and anthropogenic influences on the landscape of Colombia. In *Archaeology in the lowland American tropics*, ed. P. Stahl, 96–112. Cambridge, U.K.: Cambridge University Press.

Briceño, T. 1985. *La ganaderia en los Llanos centro-occidentales Venezolanos 1910–1935*. Biblioteca de la Academia Nacional de la Historia, no. 69. Caracas: Academia Nacional de la Historia.

Brito Figueroa, F. 1975. *Historia economica y social de Venezuela*. Vol. 1. Caracas: Universidad Central de Venezuela.

Carrera Damas, G. 1984. *Una nación llamada Venezuela*. Caracas: Monte Avila Editores.

Castellanos, J. de. 1955. *Elegías de varones ilustres de Indias*. Vol. 1. Bogotá: Editorial ABC.

Cey, G. 1994. *Viaje y descripción de las Indias 1539–1553*. Caracas: Fundación Banco Venezolano de Crédito.

Chase-Dunn, C., and T. D. Hall. 1991. Conceptualizing core/periphery hierarchies. In *Core/periphery relations in precapitalist worlds*, ed. C. Chase-Dunn and T. D. Hall, 5–44. Boulder, Colo.: Westview.

Codazzi, A. 1960. La gobernación de Barinas. In *Obras escogidas*, vol. 2, 157–341. Caracas: Ediciones del Ministerio de Educación.

Corpooccidente. 1982. *Corporacion de desarrollo de la region centro-occidental: Ordenamiento territorial de los estados Portuguesa y Barinas*. Vol. 1, *Marco General*. Barquisimeto: Departamento técnico de reproducción de FUDECO.

Crosby, A. 1988. *Imperialismo ecológico: La expansión biológica de Europa, 900–1900*. Barcelona: Crítica.

Denevan, W. 1970. The aboriginal population of western Amazonia in relation to habitat and subsistence. *Revista Geografica* 72:61–86.

———. 1982. Hydraulic agriculture in the American tropics: Forms, measures, and recent research. In *Maya subsistence: Studies in memory of Dennis Puleston*, ed. K. Flannery, 181–203. New York: Academic Press.

García, L. 1996. *La formación social barinesa: Estructuración económico-social*. Barinas: Ediciones de la Universidad Ezequiel Zamora.

García, L., and V. Rojas. 1996. *El hato Barinés en los llanos occidentales Venezolanos*. Barinas: Ediciones de la Universidad Ezequiel Zamora.

Garson, A. 1980. *Prehistory, settlement and food production in the savanna region of La Calzada de Paez, Venezuela*. PhD diss., Yale University.

Gassón, R. 1998. *Prehispanic intensive agriculture, settlement pattern and political economy in the western Venezuelan Llanos*. PhD diss., University of Pittsburgh.

———. 2003. Ceremonial feasting in the Colombian and Venezuelan *Llanos*: Some remarks on its sociopolitical and historical significance. In *Histories and historicities in Amazonia,* ed. N. Whitehead, 179–201. Lincoln and London: University of Nebraska Press.

Harris, D. 1980. Tropical savanna environments: Definition, distribution, diversity and development. In *Human ecology in savanna environments*, ed. D. Harris, 3–27. New York: Academic Press.

Hills, T. L., and R. L. Randall. 1968. *The ecology of the forest/savanna boundary*. Proceedings of the International Geographical Union Humid Tropics Commission Symposium, Venezuela, 1964. Montreal: McGill University, Department of Geography.

Hurtado, A. M., and K. Hill. 1990. Seasonality in a foraging society: Variation in diet, work effort, fertility, and sexual division of labor among the Hiwi of Venezuela. *Journal of Anthropological Research* 46 (3): 293–346.

Izard, M. 1986. *Tierra firme: Historia de Venezuela y Colombia*. Madrid: Alianza Editorial.

Lathrap, D. 1970. *The upper Amazon*. New York and Washington: Praeger.

Lynch, J. 1980. *Las revoluciones hispanoamericanas 1808–1826*. Barcelona: Editorial Ariel.

Matheny, R., and D. Gurr. 1983. Variation in prehistoric agricultural systems of the new world. *Annual Review of Anthropology* 12:79–103.

Mondolfi, E. 1993. Pasado, presente y futuro de la fauna en Venezuela. In *500 años de la América tropical*, coord. L. Aristeguieta, 177–202. Biblioteca de la Academia de Ciencias Físicas, Matemáticas y Naturales, vol. 28. Caracas: Academia de Ciencias Físicas, Matemáticas y Naturales.

Montiel, N. 1987. *Materiales para la comprensión de la historia económica de Barinas*. Barinas: Fundación Cultural Bum-Bum.

———. 1990. Notas sobre historia económica de Barinas. In *Evolución histórica de Barinas*, ed. V. Autores, 5–32. Barinas: Universidad Nacional Experimental de los Llanos Ezequiel Zamora.

———. 1993. *Etnohistoria del Llanero*. Barinas: Universidad Nacional Experimental de los Llanos Ezequiel Zamora.

Moran, E. 1993. *Through Amazonian eyes: The human ecology of Amazonian populations*. Iowa City: University of Iowa Press.

Morey, N. 1975. *Ethnohistory of the Colombian and Venezuelan Llanos*. PhD diss., University of Utah, Department of Anthropology.

———. 1976. Ethnohistorical evidence for cultural complexity in the western *Llanos* of Colombia and the eastern *Llanos* of Venezuela. *Antropologica* 45:41–69.

Morey, N., and R. Morey. 1973. Foragers and farmers: Differential consequences of Spanish contact. *Ethnohistory* 20 (3): 229–246.

Morey, R. 1979. A joyful harvest of souls: Disease and the destruction of the *Llanos* Indians. *Antropológica* 52:77–108.

Morey, R., and N. Morey. 1975. Relaciones comerciales en el pasado en los llanos de Colombia y Venezuela. *Montalban* 4:533–563.

Ortloff, C. R., and A. Kolata. 1993. Climate and collapse: Agro-ecological perspective on the decline of the Tiwanaku state. *Journal of Archaeological Science* 20:195–221.

Pinto, M. 1980. *Un censo ganadero en 1791.* Caracas: Ediciones de la Presidencia de la República.

Plazas, C., A. M. Falchetti, T. Van der Hammen, and P. Botero. 1988. Cambios ambientales y desarrollos culturales en el bajo rio San Jorge. *Boletín del Museo del Oro* 20:54–88.

Redmond, E., and C. Spencer. 1990. Investigaciones arqueologicas en el Piedemonte y los Llanos altos de Barinas, Venezuela. *Boletin de la Asociacion Venezolana de Arqueologia* 5:4–24.

Redmond, E., R. Gassón, and C. Spencer. 1999. A macroregional view of cycling chiefdoms in the western Venezuelan *Llanos.* In *Complex polities in the ancient tropical world,* ed. E. Bacus and L. Lucero, 109–129. Archaeological Papers of the American Anthropological Association, vol. 9. Arlington, Va.: American Anthropological Association.

Rivero, J. R. 1972. *Lozas y porcelanas en Venezuela.* Caracas: Ernesto Armitano.

Rull, V. 1987. Evidencias de una posible oscilación climatica en los Andes Venezolanos: La "Pequeña Edad de Hielo." *Boletín de la Asociación Venezolana de Arqueologia* 4:13–27.

Rull, V., and C. Schubert. 1989. The little ice age in the tropical Venezuelan Andes. *Acta Científica Venezolana* 40:71–73.

Salas, G. 1982. *Petróleo.* Caracas: Monte Avila.

Sanoja, M. 1981. *Los hombres de la yuca y el maiz.* Caracas: Monte Avila.

Santamaria, R. 1968. *Nuestra señora de Pedraza.* Barinas: Imprenta y Publicaciones del estado Barinas.

Sarmiento, G. 1984. *The ecology of neotropical savannas.* Cambridge, Mass.: Harvard University Press.

———. 1990. Ecologia comparada de ecosistemas de Sabanas en America del Sur. In *Las sabanas Americanas: Aspectos de su biogeografia, ecologia y utilizacion,* comp. G. Sarmiento, 15–56. Caracas: Fondo Editorial Acta Cientifica.

Simón, F. P. 1992. *Noticias historiales de Venezuela.* Biblioteca Ayacucho, vols. 173–174. Caracas: Biblioteca Ayacucho.

Solbrig, O. T. 1993. Ecological constraints to savanna land use. In *The world's savannas: Economic driving forces, ecological constraints and policy options for sustainable land use,* ed. M. D. Young and O. T. Solbrig, 21–47. UNESCO, Man and the Biosphere Series. London: Butler and Tanner Ltd.

Spencer, C. 1991. The coevolution and the development of Venezuelan chiefdoms. In *Profiles in cultural evolution: Papers from a conference in honor of Elman Service,* ed. A. T. Rambo and K. Gillogly, 137–165. Ann Arbor: University of Michigan Press.

Spencer, C., and E. Redmond. 1992. Prehispanic chiefdoms of the western Venezuelan Llanos. *World Archaeology* 24 (1): 134–157.

Spencer, C., E. Redmond, and M. Rinaldi. 1994. Drained fields at La Tigra, Venezuelan Llanos: A regional perspective. *Latin American Antiquity* 5 (2): 119–143.

Veillon, J. P. 1976. Las deforestaciones en los Llanos occidentales de Venezuela desde 1950 a 1975. In *Conservación de los bosques húmedos de Venezuela*, ed. L. S. Hamilton, J. Steyermark, J. P. Veillon, and E. Mondolfi, 97–110. Caracas: Sierra Club–Consejo de Bienestar Rural.

Vila, P. 1960. *Geografía de Venezuela*. Vols. 1 and 2. Caracas: Ministerio de Educación.

Wagner, E. 1991. *Mas de quinientos años de legado americano al mundo*. Caracas: Cuadernos Lagoven, Editorial Arte.

Zerpa Mirabal, A. J. 1998. *Explotación y comercio de plumas de Garza en Venezuela*. Caracas: Talleres Gráficos del Congreso de la República.

Zucchi, A. 1984. Alternative interpretations of pre-Columbian water management in the western Llanos of Venezuela. *Indiana* 9:309–327.

The Extractive Economy: An Early Phase of the Globalization of Diet, and Its Environmental Consequences

9

RICHARD WILK

T HE LITERATURE ON GLOBALIZATION is replete with millenarian and utopian ideas about the uniqueness of the present moment, constantly showing us that the intoxication of modernism has not really disappeared, at least from the world of professional visionaries. For those of us interested in the world food system, it is commonplace to hear that we have just entered an era of globalization and McDonaldization, and that until recently all food was local, traditional, seasonal, and diverse. The real history of the globalization of food systems is much deeper and more complex than I can even begin to describe here. Instead I want to pull out one part of an earlier global food system, to show that it had common qualities, a coherence that allows us to trace some common characteristics in many localities around the world.

Further, I want to demonstrate that this food system was not simply determined by costs and benefits, but that to understand it we need to incorporate culture and particularly gender at a fundamental analytical level. They cannot be added as an afterthought, or be treated as an epiphenomenon. The gendering of consumption is fundamental to understanding the environmental impact of this food system, as is the particular social organization and cultural expressions of the consuming groups.

Early modern European economic expansion involved very diverse ways of wresting resources and wealth from nature. Colonization, trade, and plantation agriculture have all been well studied, and each reflects innovation and rapid adaptation to local circumstances, culture, labor sources, and geography. Another form of extraction was simply an extension of methods that had long been used by Europeans for the direct appropriation of the products of nature through fishing, logging, mining, and intensive gathering. This involved the formation of mobile male work groups, armed with specialized tools and skills to spend long periods in distant and often hostile environments. This was a specialized extractive workforce that was progressively deployed over larger and more distant parts of the earth as the modern period progressed.

Most of the scholarship on extractive economies has focused on the direct effects of extraction; the destruction of forests through logging, the hunting of beaver, flamingos, and whales to the edge of extinction, and the despoiling of rivers from mining. Scholars have neglected the indirect effects of extraction; they are much harder to study because they are so diffuse in time and space. These indirect effects are directly mediated by social organizations and cultural practices that characterize the extractivist labor force.

The key distinguishing feature of the extractive economy that bears most directly on these indirect impacts is that the labor force was not responsible for its own reproduction. The extractivist worker was usually a male living in a homosocial group, apart from women most of his life, provisioned by other people. The gendering and isolation of the workforce was crucial to its particular relations with the natural world.

The Extractivist Economy

Extractive economies, by their mobile frontier nature, are poorly documented. My primary research has focused on the forestry economy in Belize, but comparative accounts from extractive economies in other parts of the world disclose striking parallels with the Belizean case, which shows that each one is a variation on a common theme. Extractive economies were heterogeneous and locally specific, each with its own unique characteristics. They varied widely in their relationships to colonial and plantation communities; in some cases they were seasonal, as with chicle gathering in Central America. Sometimes workers were only extractivists for a part of their lives, as with modern crab fishermen in Alaska. In other cases they were lifelong full-time specialists, like Belize loggers, Georgia pine tar tappers, and New England whalers. Sometimes, as with the North American fur trade, or the rubber tapping in South America, these industries appropriated and intensified indigenous foraging and hunting economies. Yet each shared a number of common characteristics and had a common pattern of effects on both local and far distant natural environments.

On the face of it, the only advantage of a specialist extractive workforce is its low cost and mobility. But how could it be cheaper to pay the full cost of provisioning a worker, when colonialists found it possible in many places to extract labor and commodities at far below the cost of reproduction (Meillassoux 1981)? To make extractive labor pay, a source of cheap food was required, so the foundation of the global extractive economy was a system for preserving and providing a low-cost reliable diet. The second advantage of a mobile extractive workforce, completely detached from the social support of a subsistence economy, was the high degree of specialization and work discipline. Most extractive work required arduous labor and high degrees of skill, gained through harsh training. In small spaces, as on board ship or in hard-rock mines, it was possible to create the necessary discipline through coercion and force. But in forests and frontiers, most extractivists worked in gangs organized by entrepreneurs, or acted as independent contractors, and discipline was enforced by a system of debt-servitude, usually based on advances against wages or payments. Sometimes the prospect of high rewards and instant wealth provided the incentive to accept privation and danger.

Another key aspect of the extractive economy was the danger and insecurity of the working conditions. Extractivists were constantly exposed to workplace injury and death, hostile indigenes, warfare, crime, and often to arbitrary authority and corporal punishment. Given the nature of the global markets for their products, extractivists were often subject to boom-and-bust cycles that left them unemployed and impoverished for lengthy periods, if not redundant for the rest of their lives. Industrial synthetic products gradually replaced many of the raw materials they produced; for example, the logwood that was extracted from the swamp forests of Belize in the eighteenth century was replaced by aniline dyes in the second half of the nineteenth century. Changes in metropolitan fashions for corsets or feathered hats could destroy the livelihood of an entire workforce halfway around the world, causing them to disperse and seek entry into other extractive work, or attempt to return to an agricultural or industrial economy. Different groups of extractivists often competed with one another in the same market, so the success of one led to the decline of another. New rich territories could open up, leading to gluts, price collapse, and the displacement or idling of workers. The Belize mahogany economy endured at least five boom-and-bust cycles between 1840 and 1950. New technologies like steam tractors or harpoon guns could suddenly make a lifetime of skill and experience useless and redundant.

The cyclic and insecure nature of the extractive economy, combined with its tendency to despoil the resources it depended on, led to constant exploration for new resources at the margins of the world economy, which meant that extractivists were often the first Europeans to penetrate territories that had not previously been part of the capitalist trading world. This was usually to the great detriment of the indigenous inhabitants. The cyclic and harsh nature of their work, the discipline and debt, gave extractivist workers little stake in legal systems or property rights. The transition from extractive worker to bandit, pirate, smuggler, or poacher was easy, and it was often possible to move quite freely back and forth between the legal and illegal economies, or to inhabit the gray areas in between.

The insecurity of their livelihood made any kind of long-term resource management implausible. As others have noted, most extractivists have little incentive to conserve or ensure for the future; their approach to any resource is more like mining than it is like any form of cultivation. The lack of legal regulation at the margins of the expanding European world economy meant that property rights were impossible to enforce, so with open entry, it made sense to exploit a common resource until it was gone. Some markets worked well enough to drive up prices when commodities were increasingly scarce, giving extractivists an incentive to press resources into extinction, as with sandalwood on Vanuatu.

The indirect, often geographically distant, effects of the subsistence system that supported extractivists vastly compounded these direct effects on resources. Beginning in the sixteenth century, Europe became the center of a vast global network that provisioned the highly diverse extractive communities with a surprisingly uniform ration, as well as a changing set of luxury products and drugs that were an incentive to maintain production.

The Extractivist Ration

Staples

The history of rations is long, extending back as far as the first establishment of standing armies, and the first long-distance mariners. Roman soldiers got about two or three pounds of grain, especially barley and wheat, per day, and variable amounts of wine, olive oil, fermented fish paste, and spices (Roth 1998). In later Europe the ration was based on grain, pulses, and preserved meat or fish. When the English Tudor ship *Mary Rose* sank in 1545, it took to the bottom samples of the sailor's daily ration of the time: hard biscuit made from wheat flour, salted meat, peas, and hard salted cheese (Nelson 2001). British naval rations remained remarkably stable through time; figure 9.1 reproduces the weekly diet of the common sailor aboard Horatio Nelson's flagship *Victory* in 1797. Beer, oatmeal, and cheese were provided only because the ship was close to port; on longer voyages biscuit and salt meat

TABLE OF THE DAILY PROPORTION OF PROVISIONS ALLOWED TO EVERY PERSON ON BOARD HIS MAJESTY'S SHIPS.

	SUN.	MON.	TUE.	WED.	THU.	FRI.	SAT.	TOT. PR. WK.
Bread, lbs.	1	1	1	1	1	1	1	7 lbs.
Beer galls.	1	1	1	1	1	1	1	7 galls.
Beef, lbs.			2				2	4 lbs.
Pork, lbs.	1				1			2 lbs.
Pease, pts.	½			½	½	½		2 pts.
Oatmeal, pt.		½		½		½		1½ pts.
Sugar, oz.		2		2		2		6 oz.
Butter, oz.		2		2		2		6 oz.
Cheese, oz.		4		4		4		12 oz.

Figure 9.1.

were served seven days a week, supplemented only with peas, and a higher rum ration substituted for beer. The ration was similar, though often less abundant, on merchant ships. The rations of other navies and armies were similar, though southern Europeans tended to substitute wine for beer, and included olive oil, salt fish, and more pulses.

Stimulants were just as essential to the ration as the carbohydrates and protein provided by bread and meat. Alcohol, coffee, and tobacco were ubiquitous, and by the nineteenth century sailors expected sugar as well. Even slaves expected a steady supply of tobacco. Those who consumed this ration were understandably a very large market for a wide variety of nostrums, potions, liniments, and patent medicines, which they usually had to buy for themselves. Alcohol, opium, coca, and other non-European drugs were common ingredients.

By the eighteenth century, most European countries had developed a semi-industrial infrastructure to provide the rations to support the navy, military, and merchant marine, often under direct government control. The large-scale processing of flour into ship's biscuits, for example, was a very early example of machine-aided mass production (Falconer 1815). There were several reasons why this ration became the basis for the support of extractive labor. First, the infrastructure for production, processing, trade, and transport of the victuals was already in place. Second, they were cheap and widely available. Third, extractivists were often recruited directly from the military and naval establishments; as Rediker (1987) points out, the trade economy of the seventeenth through nineteenth centuries was largely a maritime enterprise, built on the language and culture of sailors and ships. The ration was an accustomed diet for extractive laborers, one that stored and traveled well, and required minimal preparation. Only large boiling pots (called "coppers" on board ship) were needed to make the salt meat edible. The food was otherwise preprocessed.

The infrastructure built in Europe to provide this ration was formidable; it was one of the earliest industrial processes. National security in many countries depended on the steady provision of naval stores, and salt in particular became a vital resource. The preservation and preparation of rations required the combined and coordinated efforts of trades as diverse as butchers, coopers, salt makers, blacksmiths, bakers, brewers, millers, woodcutters, fishermen, and distillers. (These are in addition to the already formidable trade establishment required to make the most complex of all preindustrial artifacts, the sailing ship.) Farmers throughout Europe saw a growing demand for pork and beef, a market that became the cash cornerstone of otherwise self-sufficient peasant economies. The Baltic, North Sea, and Newfoundland fleets provided a steady stream of preserved fish. In the early stages, the demand for bulk commodities supported smallholders and artisanal fisheries throughout Europe, but as demand grew and markets became more centralized, large commercial enterprises dominated the trade, fueling an expansion that turned many independent small producers into poorly paid laborers.

This countertrade in foodstuffs was an essential element in the growth of the European, and later, North American economy, as was the import trade in agricultural and extractive commodities. In fact, some of the very commodities produced by extractivists, for example, sarsaparilla used in patent medicines, and salt from the Caribbean coast of South America, were imported to Europe, processed, and then reexported to be consumed by extractivists themselves. The tobacco, coffee, and sugar that formed such an essential part of the ration were also the products of colonial plantation agriculture that were exported to Europe and North America for elaborate processing, preservation, and packaging, before being reexported around the world to support extractive industries.

Initially, a majority of extractivist rations were drawn from longstanding European regional specialties and trade routes. Scottish and North Sea herring, Cheddar cheese, Brittany sardines, Yorkshire ham, Irish salt pork, and Dijon mustard, for example, were established local products in European markets which later became recognizable protobrands within the world market in preserved provisions. From at least the late seventeenth century, however, the British colonies in North America provided cheaper flour, meat, fish, and rum than was available elsewhere (Marx 1973:65). By the nineteenth century, North American staple products had driven most European goods out of the mass markets and back into specialty niches. Even Norwegian loggers ate American bacon.

Various studies of the growth of the North American colonies suggest that this export trade was crucial in capital formation (McCusker and Menard 1991). The earliest New England fortunes were founded on the export trade in dried cod. Pork proved a crucial export product for the colonies, for swine consumed waste products of other industries; they were also an advance guard along the expanding western forest frontiers.[1] They were fattened on mast in unclaimed forests, and with the products of swidden agriculture, then driven to rivers where they were slaughtered, salted, barreled, and sold. In 1859 a Kentucky writer reported seeing six acres of pork barrels piled three tiers high at the Louisville slaughterhouses (Simmonds 2001:84). Few countries could compete with the low price of North American wheat and salted meat, until improved preservation techniques (including canning, industrial drying, and chilling) allowed other low-cost producers, particularly in Australia and South America, entry into the market in the nineteenth century.[2]

Of course, low-cost basic rations were not only used to support gangs of men engaged in extractive industry. While slaves on some of the sugar producing islands of the Caribbean had time off to work their own "provision grounds," on many islands they received rations including salt fish, salted or dried meat, and flour. Aboriginal populations around the world developed tastes for particular products from this food system, or were dependent on it after being dislocated from their own subsistence systems. Groups as diverse as Western Desert Australian aborigines, Plains Indians, and Hawaiians depended on wheat flour in barrels, rum, sugar, tobacco, and coffee.

The industrial labor forces in Europe became dependent on some elements of the extractive ration, though local fresh and preserved products could sometimes compete with the cheap imports because of tariffs and other barriers to trade (Tannahill 1988). Nevertheless, salt beef, fish, and pork became the cheap protein sources for poor people in many parts of Europe and developed areas of North America. Today some of their descendants have transformed the same products into nostalgic luxury foods such as corned beef and bacalao.

The provision of these staples had enormous environmental conse-quences that are difficult to trace, because production was so widely dis-persed. These effects were further ramified, because the labor forces en-gaged in producing, processing, and transporting the rations of extractivists also had to eat.[3] Supporting a global extractive workforce entailed the de-pletion of fisheries in places as geographically distant from one another as the North and Baltic Seas, Newfoundland, and Monterey Bay. Swine production in North America exerted economic pressure that destroyed aboriginal subsistence, and altered and destroyed forest ecosystems. The im-pact of the extensive grazing of cattle, first on the island ecosystems of the Caribbean, and then on the mainlands of Mesoamerica and North Amer-ica, has been well documented (Crosby 1973; Sauer 1992). Sailors let goats, swine, cattle, and other domestic animals loose on island after island in the hope of returning to hunt, with drastic consequences for local flora and fauna.

Intensive fishing no doubt contributed to the disastrous failure of the North Sea herring fishery in the late nineteenth century, which devastated the coastal economy, despite a shift to alternative species (especially mack-erel). The effects of expanding cultivation of coffee, tobacco, and sugar on rainforest and riverine environments are equally well known. What is rarely appreciated is that many of these products were not just directly imported to Europe and other metropolitan centers for direct consump-tion, they also supported hordes and teams of extractive laborers who were further destroying and despoiling in order to produce still different commodities.

Luxuries

Any study of colonial imports discloses huge quantities of luxury products from Europe, including everything from fine millinery to musical instru-ments and fine wines. Figures 9.2, 9.3, and 9.4 reproduce advertisements from Belize City merchants from 1826 to 1882, listing cargos of merchandise that include both workers' rations and a long list of luxury products. Con-ventional colonial historians tend to view these imports as the perquisites of the local elite, for whom they were essential signifiers of gentility and metropolitan sophistication. They maintained the cultural superiority of lo-cal European elites. Close attention to the habits of the working classes as described by contemporary accounts show, however, that when money was available, laborers, often to the extreme discomfort of the local elite, con-sumed many of the same luxury products. Periodic binges were an essential

PUBLIC  SALE

NOTICE.

ON MONDAY, NEXT

The 17th. Inst. at 12 o'clock precisely, there will be exposed to

PUBLIC VENDUE,

At the Subscriber's Store, the following articles, imported in the Brig

HOPE, John Mourant, from Jersey,

Puncheons Best Holladns, & Cognac Brandy.
Barrels Prime Pork, & Boxes Soap.
Boxes Prunes, Sugar & Quatre Fruits.
Boxes Olive Oil, Mustard, Cornichons, & Olives.
Cases White Wine Vinegar, of 3 doz. each.
Cases Vespetro, Parfait Amour, Orange Creme, Imperial, Citronade, & Cassis Cordials of excellent quality.
Cases Old Frontignac, Teneriff, Marsalla & Palermo Wine.

And in order to close Sales the remainder of the cargoes per Brigs, WILLIAM PENN, & JANUS; and Schooner, ALICE & NANCY: from the United States of America.

ALSO,

Six Pipes P. Madeira Wine, from London,

Which will peremptorily be sold.

LIKEWISE, (JUST IMPORTED,)

Barrels Howard-Steet Flour (Superfine)
Half Barrels ditto., same quality.
Barrels Pork,. Beef, & Mackerel.
Boxes Cod Fish, & Kegs Butter.
Hogsheads & Bales Prime Virginia Tobacco.
Boxes Bloom Raisins, & Mould Candles.
Hogsheads American Bacon.
Bales Brown & Bleached Shirting & Sheeting, &c. &c. &c.

☞ PAYMENT FOR THE ABOVE WILL BE TAKEN IN MAHOGANY.

THOMAS FICKSTOCK.

Figure 9.2.

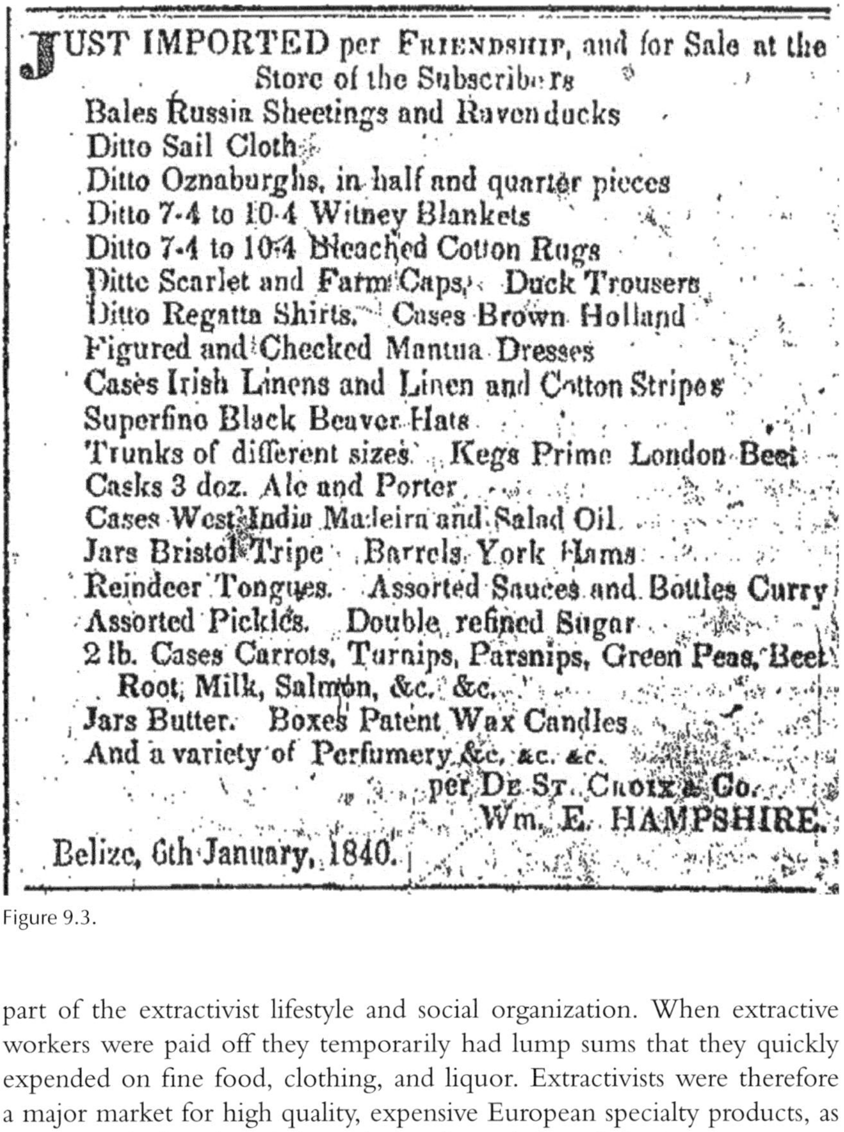

JUST IMPORTED per FRIENDSHIP, and for Sale at the
Store of the Subscribers
Bales Russia Sheetings and Ravenducks
Ditto Sail Cloth
Ditto Oznaburghs, in half and quarter pieces
Ditto 7-4 to 10-4 Witney Blankets
Ditto 7-4 to 10-4 Bleached Cotton Rugs
Ditto Scarlet and Farm Caps; Duck Trousers
Ditto Regatta Shirts. Cases Brown Holland
Figured and Checked Mantua Dresses
Cases Irish Linens and Linen and Cotton Stripes
Superfine Black Beaver Hats
Trunks of different sizes. Kegs Prime London Beef
Casks 3 doz. Ale and Porter
Cases West India Madeira and Salad Oil.
Jars Bristol Tripe Barrels York Hams
Reindeer Tongues. Assorted Sauces and Bottles Curry
Assorted Pickles. Double refined Sugar
2 lb. Cases Carrots, Turnips, Parsnips, Green Peas, Beet
Root; Milk, Salmon, &c. &c.
Jars Butter. Boxes Patent Wax Candles
And a variety of Perfumery &c. &c. &c.
per DE ST. CROIX & Co.
Wm. E. HAMPSHIRE.
Belize, 6th January, 1840.

Figure 9.3.

part of the extractivist lifestyle and social organization. When extractive workers were paid off they temporarily had lump sums that they quickly expended on fine food, clothing, and liquor. Extractivists were therefore a major market for high quality, expensive European specialty products, as well as the bulk unbranded goods that formed their daily diet.

From reading hundreds of these advertisements, it is clear that liquors of all kinds, particularly flavored liqueurs and wines from France and southern Europe, were imported in huge quantities. Pickles and dried fruits, traditional ship-board luxuries, were always well represented, and throughout the nineteenth century, fine hams, salmon, and tongues were the luxury counterparts of the everyday salted meats and fish. Fine biscuits and soda crackers

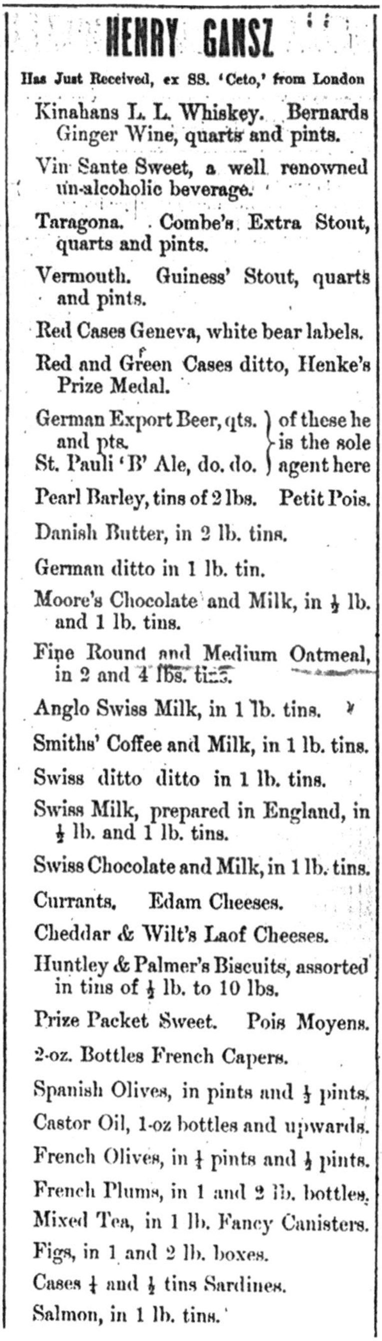

HENRY GANSZ

Has Just Received, ex SS. 'Ceto,' from London

Kinahans L. L. Whiskey. Bernards Ginger Wine, quarts and pints.

Vin Sante Sweet, a well renowned un-alcoholic beverage.

Taragona. Combe's Extra Stout, quarts and pints.

Vermouth. Guiness' Stout, quarts and pints.

Red Cases Geneva, white bear labels.

Red and Green Cases ditto, Henke's Prize Medal.

German Export Beer, qts.) of these he
and pts. } is the sole
St. Pauli 'B' Ale, do. do.) agent here

Pearl Barley, tins of 2 lbs.   Petit Pois.

Danish Butter, in 2 lb. tins.

German ditto in 1 lb. tin.

Moore's Chocolate and Milk, in ½ lb. and 1 lb. tins.

Fine Round and Medium Oatmeal, in 2 and 4 lbs. tins.

Anglo Swiss Milk, in 1 lb. tins.

Smiths' Coffee and Milk, in 1 lb. tins.

Swiss ditto ditto in 1 lb. tins.

Swiss Milk, prepared in England, in ½ lb. and 1 lb. tins.

Swiss Chocolate and Milk, in 1 lb. tins.

Currants.   Edam Cheeses.

Cheddar & Wilt's Laof Cheeses.

Huntley & Palmer's Biscuits, assorted in tins of ½ lb. to 10 lbs.

Prize Packet Sweet.   Pois Moyens.

2-oz. Bottles French Capers.

Spanish Olives, in pints and ½ pints.

Castor Oil, 1-oz bottles and upwards.

French Olives, in ¼ pints and ½ pints.

French Plums, in 1 and 2 lb. bottles.

Mixed Tea, in 1 lb. Fancy Canisters.

Figs, in 1 and 2 lb. boxes.

Cases ¼ and ½ tins Sardines.

Salmon, in 1 lb. tins.

Figure 9.4.

similarly mirrored ship's hardtack and daily flour "journey-cakes." In Belize, even the basic rations of slaves, and later waged workers, were of relatively high quality, compared to the daily fare of the European poor. The Belize mahogany worker's weekly ration of five pounds of pork, seven pounds of flour, a pound of sugar, and a half-gallon of rum would far exceed in both quality and quantity the diet of a contemporary English factory worker, or a French peasant farmer. Of course only men collected these rations, and only when they were working. Women had to fend for themselves and their children.

Another interesting trend over time is the transformation in the practice of branding. Quality was always a concern when buying bulk food commodities, and adulterated wheat, rotten salt pork, and sour wine were common problems. Branding was an attempt to provide a history for goods to serve as a mark of quality and reliability. Initially only the higher-priced luxury products carried the pedigree of a place of origin. In the earliest advertisements, towns and regions of origin serve as these marks of quality, since these places were well known for their specialization in a particular foodstuff. Products were even named for their place of origin, as with port, marsala, and burgundy. Later in the nineteenth century, countries become more prominent than particular places or regions, so American bacon, French wine, and Scottish herring were common marks of quality. By the end of the century, individual companies established export brands (often these were initially based on country names, as with Anglo-Swiss milk). Many of these, like Beck's beer, Swift's meats, and Huntley and Palmer biscuits are still with us.

The ecological consequences of the luxury export trade are very difficult to track, as the sources of supply and fashionable goods shifted constantly. Sometimes the origins of goods are obscure, as with the reindeer tongues in an advertisement from 1840. Later these were supplanted by buffalo tongues, presumably from the slaughter on the North American Great Plains, and finally these gave way to lamb tongues from New Zealand and Australia. Today Danish canned pig tongues are still imported to Belize, along with plastic buckets of Canadian salted pigtails. Large-scale production of glass bottles, stoneware jugs, wooden barrels, kegs, firkins, and other packaging undoubtedly contributed to the demand for wood that deforested much of Europe, as did the distilling and baking industries.

Even so minor a luxury condiment as the anchovy, given a steady market dispersed among Europeans throughout the world, could become a major industry of huge local importance. In 1859 Simmonds reported that anchovies came mostly from Brittany. Entering world commerce preserved in oil or salt in small kegs, weighing about 12 lbs. each, 50 to 100 tons were imported into England per year, and in 1852,

> 576 millions of sardines were taken on the coast of Brittany. . . . Half of these were sold fresh and the other half preserved. . . . 160 vessels manned by 3500 sailors and fishermen are engaged in the trade. The preparation, transport, and sale of the fish employ 10,000 persons. 9000 of these, of whom one half are females, are occupied all the winter in making and mending the nets. (Simmonds 2001:252)

For the most part luxury export production in Europe and North America was spatially dispersed, and drew on a huge number of different resources, some of which were gathered and traded from far away. The commodity chains were often incredibly complex and tangled. Just to give one example, a substance called isinglass was used in the nineteenth century to clarify wine and beer for export (it was also used to make jellied desserts, and in medicinal plasters). It was extracted from swim bladders in fish-processing factories on the north Atlantic coast of Canada and New England. Some of it came from a fishery for a small shark, the spotted dogfish, which were primarily fished for their livers, which were rendered into a popular medicinal oil. The rest of the shark was dried and fed to hogs, yet another export commodity (see Simmonds 2001).

Direct Impacts on the Local Environment

It is much easier to trace the dramatic effects of ravenous crews of extractive workers on the local environments where they worked. Miners, loggers, whalers, trappers, and fishermen did not just subsist on rations. They constantly supplemented their diet, both trading with local people, and hunting and fishing on their own for whatever fresh meat they could find.

While indigenous people's exploitation of wild animal foods was limited by population, technology, and common property regimes designed to limit access and control harvest, mobile groups of extractivists knew no such limits. By their very nature they were nonterritorial, and their lifestyle was built on a different relationship to resources from that of settled people who had developed systems of property rights and controlled access.

The very nature of most early extractive economies was their marginal position in relation to state regimes. They were almost entirely unsupervised by any European power that might have an interest in conservation of resources for the long term, and their social organization and technology enabled them to ignore any local system that might limit their pillage. Most of the men in the extractivist workforce came from European lower classes, in a society where hunting and fishing were highly regulated privileges, and poaching was a serious crime. In the eighteenth and early nineteenth centuries many men arrested for poaching in rural parts of England were sold or indentured and transported abroad, and of these a proportion would have ended up as extractive workers. So consuming wild game had symbolic as well as nutritional significance, as a way to reclaim what had become the privilege of the elite in Europe. More than one traveler in Belize remarked that local laborers ate fish and game that would have graced the tables of only the wealthiest of European nobility.

The social and working lives of extractivists also had a strong effect on their relationship to wild animals. If workers were not themselves slaves, they tended to work under some other sort of coercive regime, including debt servitude or indenture. Their work was physically dangerous—whalers for example had notoriously high mortality rates, and Alaskan offshore crabbing is still the most dangerous occupation in the United States. If they were not outlaws, like many Caribbean buccaneers, turtlers, and loggers, they lived in lawless places, where possession was always uncertain and life was cheap.

Most extractive industries had a predominantly male work environment. The intense solidarity of work groups was built and maintained through practices of obligatory generosity. When men had money, drink, or other resources, they were expected to share generously until it was gone, a pattern that has been called "crew culture" (Belich 1996:430–437; Wilson 1973) This provided the basic dynamic for what I have called a "binge economy," built around a rhythm of hard work alternating with release (Wilk n.d.). Long periods in the mines, or forests, or out at sea, living on rations while doing arduous, dangerous labor were punctuated by wild binges of sex, drink, feasting, gambling, and spending. Wild boomtowns, red light districts, frontier settlements, and ports grew up around the world, devoted to serving up these entertainments, draining the workers' purses. Then broke, they headed back to work.

Exotic game often filled the menu when men were on a binge. Local populations of favored species were often depleted quickly to meet the demand for these feasts. Manatees quickly disappeared from the parts of Jamaica near the pirate haven of Port Royal; within two years of the beginning of the California gold rush, San Francisco Bay had been swept clean of oysters (Margo 1947).

This was an economy without accumulation, where the time horizons for economic decisions were extremely short. Workers, especially when young, rarely planned anything beyond the next port, paycheck, or lucky strike. Individuals and groups were highly mobile, and their occupation of any one place was always temporary. Extractivism thrived on expanding economic and colonial frontiers, often laying the groundwork for a more permanent economic system, which would then drive the extractivists out and force them to move on to new areas. One could hardly think of a group less likely to develop a long-term sustainable relationship to a resource base. Instead, in a highly competitive environment, the rule was to take all that was available, since if you did not someone else would.

This is not to say that extractivists did not regulate themselves in any way, and that the rule was always cutthroat competition. Many groups developed rules to regulate competition and maintain peace and order among themselves. Even Caribbean pirates worked under signed articles that specified how spoils would be divided. Another example comes from seabird-egg harvesting, a large business in many parts of the world right up through the beginning of the twentieth century. On the Pedro Keys in the Caribbean, egg gathering was regulated by a

> custom which recognises the first coming vessel as commanding for the season. The second vessel in seniority is called the Commodore, the first being styled the Admiral. They have a code of laws, to which, in a spirit of honourable compliance, all are expected to show obedience; and in case of any infraction of the obligations thus voluntarily imposed upon themselves, a jury selected from the several vessels tries complaints, and with due formality inflicts punishment for offenses. (Simmonds 2001:166)

It is important to note that these regulations had nothing whatsoever to do with limiting the harvest; only to keeping the peace so that all could gather more effectively. The rules merely codify general principles that tended to characterize most extractive economies, which can be summarized as "finders keepers," "first come, first served," and "free-for-all." This economy provided a huge incentive to explore and look for new resources, since the old ones are already split up, and latecomers get poorer access.

The effects of this open access on the animal life of the regions where extractivists worked and traveled were drastic, especially on fragile island ecosystems. The millions of sea turtles that teemed in the Caribbean Sea almost became extinct (Jackson 1997). Sailors, hunters, sealers, and fishermen dined freely on tortoises in the Galapagos, dodos on Mauritius, and baby seals in Alaska. Extractivists hunted and ate an amazing variety of birds and mammals, from penguins to porpoises, albatrosses to walrus.

Hunting was, for many extractivists, the only available form of recreation, which they pursued with enthusiasm and a competitive spirit. Accounts mention times when men engaged in contests to see who could kill the most animals, even when there was no particular need for meat. In Belize, for example, the fun of a parrot hunt would result in nothing more than a parrot-tongue pie. At times hunting could also produce a nice supplementary income for extractivists. In Belize, turtlers, chicle gatherers, fishermen, and loggers often killed crocodiles for their skins, macaws for feathers, jaguars and ocelots for pelts, and manatees for meat that could be salted, and especially their fins, which were pickled and considered a great delicacy.

Since they moved often between city and country, extractivists informally traded many other kinds of wild foods and resources to elite urban consumers, in a trade that usually went unreported and unremarked, but which nevertheless had a dramatic effect on nature. To mention just a few examples, in Belize loggers and other extractivists brought to the city such things as live baby animals for pets, palm hearts, the salted roe of freshwater fish like tarpon and snook, iguana and turtle eggs, river turtles, crabs, and crayfish, wild allspice, sarsaparilla, and a large variety of other medicinal leaves, roots, bark, and seeds. Since we know nothing of what the wild flora and fauna populations were like before the time of the extractive economy, it is impossible to assess the effects of all these activities. Whatever the scale, this trade certainly undermines the use of the terms "untouched" and "primeval" for the Belizean rainforests, words in common use among international and local conservationist groups. (And the forests exploited by extractivists were the anthropogenic product of at least four thousand years of indigenous occupation as well.) It is often hard to tell which did more damage—the indiscriminate introduction of European animals and pests, the destruction of indigenous people and their knowledge of local ecologies, or the way the extractivists treated every place they stopped as a food bank to be robbed and abandoned.

Nature as the Enemy

The work environment and social lives of extractive workers varied widely, according to local circumstances, countries of origin, and mode of extraction. But my comparison of very different extractivist groups, separated in time and space, discloses a consistent pattern in the way they related to nature and the natural world. In simple terms, extractivists see nature as a dangerous enemy, which needs to be fought for survival.

From the vantage point of an educated middle-class academic, it is almost impossible to imagine living in the intensely male culture that developed among extractivist groups. These men developed their own argot, mostly unintelligible to outsiders and initiates (though it was a continual source of slang impressions in common speech [Grose 1811]). The work regimen required high degrees of physical strength and skill, and a physical adaptation that left a permanent mark on men's bodies. One could identify a logger, a sailor, or a fisherman just by looking at their hands, gait, and posture. They adopted particular modes of dress, grooming, and body modification that were themselves a lasting physical language of identification.

Men in extractive work groups depended on each other to an extraordinary degree. One man's error could kill or maim an entire crew. Apprenticeship and entry into the crew was therefore not easy; it required testing that proved a new member's ability. But once in the group, men treated each other with intense loyalty and care. While showing nothing but toughness and even violence toward outsiders, members of work crews were often tender and caring with each other, and they often claimed kinship closer than blood. Recent scholars have speculated about the possibility of sexual relationships in the isolated homosocial environment on board ships and in camps (Burg 1983; Linebaugh and Rediker 2000).

This social environment meant that danger was usually externalized; within the group a man was safe, but outside, among other people or in nature, there was constant peril. From our modern analytical standpoint we can see how most extractive workers were oppressed by a ruthless economic system; work discipline was often harsh, and laborers had few rights or protections (Linebaugh and Rediker 2000). So-called free laborers were often treated worse than slaves, who at least had commodity value. But while extractivists did resist their exploitation through violent rebellion, theft, and daily subversive acts, they were not organized as a class, and they recognized no solidarity with other workers. Instead, within a masculine workplace culture, they developed a fierce pride in their own abilities and skills, and each crew or work group was highly competitive, if not hostile to others. Fights between different logging crews, for example, or between loggers and men of other occupations, were common.

The fear and anger provoked by their exploitation was aimed to some extent, therefore, at rival groups, but more often the main focus was nature itself, which presented daily challenges and dangers. Bosses, supervisors, merchants, and other crews were predictable and were therefore treated as risks of the job. Nature, on the other hand, was fickle and unpredictable, so it was a source of true uncertainty. Aspects of nature like violent weather, poisonous plants and animals, and dangerous crossings were objectified and often named; encounters were seen as gambles ruled by luck and the supernatural. Ahab's foe was the killer white whale, not the merchants and bankers who drove the whaling industry so far into foreign waters that a single voyage could take three or four years (Philbrick 2000).

My point is that extractive workers, often the first and only Europeans to enter many ecologically unique areas of the world, were the least likely possible group to treat those resources with respect or stewardship. The popular literature tends to portray the extractive working classes as a disorderly rabble of greedy and lawless wastrels, destructive by their very nature. Instead, I would argue, there are very good reasons why they took whatever they wanted from nature, without thought for the future. Many of them knew that they had no future, that their lives were likely to be short. Their claims on particular resources, as in the case of placer gold miners, were impossible to defend. And both the social lives and cultural milieu of the extractivists provided incentives to treat the world as a place to be plundered rather than cultivated.

Conclusion

While the heyday of extractive economies was the nineteenth century, many can still be found that share, to greater or lesser extent, the same set of social and economic characteristics. Spike Walker's recent popular book *Working on the Edge* describes the life of king crab fishermen in Alaska in terms that would be entirely familiar to a Belizean logger in the 1850s. Workers endure a difficult initiation, long periods of arduous, dangerous labor, and then they binge on liquor, sex, drugs, and high-cost luxury consumer goods. They are both highly competitive and highly protective of their crewmates in the face of common danger. The same can be said for offshore oil workers, longline open ocean fishermen, and contemporary rainforest loggers. Nothing could be more different from the kind of stable, settled, and sustainable extractive economy represented by the lobster fishery in New England, as described by Acheson (2003). Lobster fishermen have recognized territories close to their homes, live in conjugal families in stable communities, and tend their resource in a manner more like farming than extractivism.

The Alaskan crabbers, on the other hand, are engaged in what will probably prove an unsustainable fishery, despite government regulation. Like most mobile extractivists, the king crab fishers are likely to push the resource over the edge, and then move on to another lucrative short-term fishing boom. It is important to recognize that the unsustainability of the fishery is not a product of the social or cultural lives of the workers themselves, though they are easy to blame. As in logging, mining, whaling, and other enterprises, the largest share of the profits in the system goes to the contractors and employers, the suppliers, merchants, and providers of red-light services. This entire superstructure is ultimately dependent on the hides, oil, wood, metals, and other commodities that flow from extraction, but unlike the laborers themselves, those who run the superstructure have no direct contact with the natural environment where the extractive labor takes place. They are in no position to judge for themselves the state of the resource; instead they have to depend on secondary indicators, and on what the workers tell them. Those who profit from the exploitation of both nature and the extractive workers are therefore in a poor position to judge the sustainability of the enterprise. The workers themselves may be well aware that the whales are getting scarce, the seals are no longer coming ashore, or the trees are getting farther and farther from the river. But given their circumstances, their only option is to sail farther, go up new rivers, work longer hours, and kill the last dodo for dinner.

The extractive economy I have discussed here did not have clear edges, and many occupations resemble extractive work to a greater or lesser degree. The cowboys of the American west, or the gauchos of the Argentine pampas, were extractivists only in an indirect sense, but their diets, social organization, and environmental effects were much like those of miners and loggers. Some extractive industries were more mobile than others, and it was not unusual for frontier camps full of men to gradually become more like a normal community with conjugal families and households. While it will take some time to work out a full comparative typology of different kinds of extractive economies, it is not too soon to point out the degree to which the extractive way of life became an object of the popular imagination. This helps to account for the persistence of elements of the extractivist culture among descendant communities that have long since turned to other occupations.

Notes

1. Waste from slaughterhouses, the lees left over from brewing, and by-products from dairies, grist mills, and a host of other industries were fed to pigs.

2. One significant exception was Argentina, which produced wheat and salted beef at prices competitive with North America, largely through the same methods of appropriating virgin farmland from aborigines.

3. Of course, the extractive workforce also needed clothes and tools, which required another entire commodity chain of raw material production, processing, and transport, involving still more labor forces, and widespread ecological consequences. Rough cotton cloth and other coarse fibers were consumed in huge quantities by extractivists, but I have not yet traced the complex connections.

References

Acheson, J. M. 2003. *Capturing the commons: Devising institutions to manage the Maine lobster industry.* Hanover, N.H.: University Press of New England.

Belich, J. 1996. *Making peoples: A history of the New Zealanders.* Honolulu: University of Hawaii Press.

Burg, B. 1983. *Sodomy and the pirate tradition.* New York: New York University Press.

Crosby, A. 1973. *The Columbian exchange: Biological and cultural consequences of 1492.* Westport, Conn.: Greenwood.

Falconer, W. 1815. *A new universal dictionary of the marine.* London: T. Cadell.

Grose, Captain, et al. 1811. *A dictionary of puckish slang, university wit, and pickpocket eloquence.* www.ibiblio.org/gutenberg/etext04/dcvgr10.txt.

Jackson, J. B. C. 1997. Reefs since Columbus. *Coral Reefs* 16:S23–S32.

Linebaugh, P., and M. Rediker. 2000. *The many-headed hydra.* Boston: Beacon.

Marx, R. 1973. *Port Royal rediscovered.* Garden City, N.Y.: Doubleday.

Margo, J. 1947. The food supply problem of the California gold mines, 1848–1855. MA thesis, Stanford University.

McCusker, J., and R. Menard. 1991. *The economy of British America, 1607–1789.* Chapel Hill: University of North Carolina Press.

Meillassoux, C. 1981. *Maidens, meal and money.* Cambridge, U.K.: Cambridge University Press.

Nelson, A. 2001. *The Tudor navy: The ships, men, and organization, 1485–1603.* Washington, D.C.: U.S. Naval Institute.

Philbrick, N. 2000. *In the heart of the sea.* New York: Penguin.

Rediker, M. B. 1987. *Between the devil and the deep blue sea: Merchant seamen, pirates, and the Anglo-American maritime world, 1700–1750.* Cambridge, U.K.: Cambridge University Press.

Roth, J. P. 1998. *The logistics of the Roman army at war (264 BC–AD 235).* Leiden: Brill.

Sauer, C. 1992. *The early Spanish main.* Berkeley: University of California Press.

Simmonds, P. 2001 (1859). The curiosities of food. Berkeley, Calif.: Ten Speed Press.

Tannahill, R. 1988. *Food in history.* New York: Three Rivers.

Wilk, R. n.d. The binge economy. Paper presented at the Conference on Culture and Consumption, Paris, June 2001.

Wilson, P. 1973. *Crab antics.* New Haven, Conn.: Yale University Press.

Yellow Jack and Geopolitics: Environment, Epidemics, and the Struggles for Empire in the American Tropics, 1640–1830   **10**

J. R. MCNEILL

L INKING THE ECOLOGICAL and the political is anything but original. Chinese emperors for more than two millennia demonstrated that they enjoyed the mandate of heaven by their successful management of the environment. Excessive flood or drought called their authority into question. Likewise, many African kings and chiefs derived part of their legitimacy from perceived skill in rainmaking. Emperor Louis Napoleon in 1857 addressed the French parliament with the great Alpine floods of 1856 as well as the uprisings of 1848 on his mind: "By my honor, I promise that rivers, like revolution, will return to their beds and remain unable to rise during my reign" (Bess 2003:57). Linkages between the ecological and political realms of course were not merely magical and imaginary. They existed and exist on the most basic material levels.

In this chapter I attempt to join ecological and epidemiological history to one of the most venerable of historical interests, international and military competition, in the context of European imperial struggles, and American anti-imperial struggles, in the lowland tropics of Atlantic America. The essay focuses on the geopolitical impacts of yellow fever, and in so doing explores a world now mercifully vanished. Today yellow fever is almost a trivial disease, perhaps accounting for about twenty thousand or thirty thousand deaths per year according to the World Health Organization (although the officially recorded figure is usually around five thousand). By comparison, malaria kills 2–3 million people per year today. But before the twentieth-century medical interventions that led to mosquito control and vaccination, yellow fever was a fearsome scourge in the tropical Atlantic world. It was above all else the ecological and social revolutions of the sugar plantation that opened yellow fever's reign of terror in the Americas.

Here I will argue that the sugar revolution created new environmental conditions extremely propitious for the propagation of yellow fever, and that in so doing, it created a new set of governing conditions for geopolitics in the American tropics. A lot of Latin America stayed Latin because of these new conditions, despite predatory ambitions of the British, Dutch, and occasionally French. Moreover, much of tropical America acquired independence after the 1770s because of canny exploitation of these conditions by people born and raised in the American tropics and hence often resistant to yellow fever. Those little Amazons, the female mosquitoes *Aedes aegypti*, vectors of yellow fever, underpinned the geopolitical order of the American tropics from 1660 to 1780. After 1780 they undermined it. But for mosquitoes and viruses to exert such influence over the course of history, governments, militaries, and people had to conduct their affairs in certain very specific ways: nature makes its own history, but it does not make it just as it pleases.

Sugar, Slaves, and Sieges

With decisive help from Eurasian diseases (Cook 1998; Alchon 2003), Spain acquired a loose but lucrative empire in the Americas after 1492. By 1600 the lowland tropical segments of that empire were depopulated backwaters, but great riches flowed from silver mined in the Andes and highland Mexico. To get silver to Spain, it had to pass through choke points in the tropical lowlands and the Caribbean Sea, such as the isthmus of Panama or the port of Veracruz, and, invariably, the port of Havana. That fact, and the hope that great wealth might lie elsewhere in the American tropics, inspired England, France, and Holland to contest these Spanish dominions. They acquired several Caribbean islands and a few stretches of coastline by 1655, usually via conquest and settlement involving, initially, only a few hundred people per adventure. This was the age of buccaneers, when even modest efforts with minimal support from European states could change the political map of the Caribbean. That age ended when three things came to the Atlantic American tropics: sugar, slaves, and sieges.

Sugar made its first major impact in the Americas in northeastern Brazil. When the Portuguese expelled the Dutch (who controlled part of Brazil 1630–1654), the Dutch (and Luso-Brazilian Sephardic Jews) brought sugar and the latest in sugar-refining technology to the Caribbean, beginning in Barbados in the 1640s. A social revolution followed, as the plantation complex, to use Philip Curtin's (1991) phrase, spread throughout suitable lowland regions. Eventually, after an experiment with indentured labor from Europe failed, planters turned to mass importation of slaves from West Africa. This soon created politically unreliable majorities on many islands and coastlands, changing the nature of war and politics. The comparative scarcity of whites and their appropriate fear of arming blacks led to a pattern of warfare by European expeditionary forces. To protect their colonies, all European empires upgraded their fortifications. Spanish silver and everyone's sugar made it possible to afford such investments in the seventeenth century, and made many colonies and ports too valuable not to fortify. Spain in particular relied on masonry and local militias, more than upon naval power, for imperial defense. Thus the Vauban revolution in fortification (named for the French military engineer, Sebastien le Prestre de Vauban [1633–1707]) came to the Americas, and with it, the pattern of prolonged siege warfare.

Siege warfare in the Atlantic American tropics proceeded under conditions very different from those prevailing within Europe, along its Habsburg-Ottoman frontier, or at the scattered European outposts elsewhere around the world. A Vauban fortress in Europe was intended to be able to hold out for six weeks, by which time, the theory went, relief columns might march to the rescue (Duffy 1979; Parker 1996). In the far-flung Portuguese, Dutch, and British strongholds in the Indian Ocean, relief could never arrive in time, and so besiegers often succeeded. But in the tropical Atlantic, siege warfare after 1655 favored the defenders.

In 1655 the English took Spanish Jamaica, part of Oliver Cromwell's "Western Design," intended to weaken Spain. This conquest involved a force of some seven thousand men, far more than had taken part in any previous campaign in the Caribbean. The days of buccaneers were passing, although another seventy years would elapse before they were finally extinguished. The era of expeditionary forces, of systematic and large-scale warfare around the Atlantic, was beginning. It took Cromwell's legions a day to take the main Spanish settlement on Jamaica, and a week to control the entire island (although guerrilla resistance flickered on). But after this easy conquest, very few successful invasions took place in tropical America, despite repeated war and upward of fifty attempts (Buchet 1991; Butel and Lavallé 1996; Zapatero 1964). The main reason for this lies in another unsuspected consequence of the arrival of sugar: yellow fever.

Aedes aegypti and Yellow Fever

Native to tropical West Africa, yellow fever is a viral infection, of the genus flavivirus that also includes dengue fever, West Nile virus, and Japanese encephalitis, among others (Strode 1951; Vainio and Cutts 1998; Monath 1999; Cooper and Kiple 1993; Barrett and Monath 2003; da Costa Vasconcelos 2003). It, like all other in its genus, is an arbovirus, meaning it is communicated by mosquitoes or ticks. Its symptoms can be mild or serious, and in fortunate cases consist of high fever, muscular pains, and headache that last for three or four days but then disappear. In serious cases, these symptoms abate, then recur, joined by jaundice and internal hemorrhage. In the latter stages of lethal cases, the victim vomits up partially coagulated blood, roughly the color and consistency of coffee grounds, which symptom gave the disease one of its several nicknames: the black vomit. When this happens, death is near. The gruesome symptoms of yellow fever have the happy effect of making historical diagnosis less problematic than in most other cases. Whereas from seventeenth- and eighteenth-century descriptions it is normally impossible to tell a case (or an epidemic) of malaria from one of typhus, the black vomit is a distinctive signature.

Yellow fever kills people through organ failure, normally the liver, and by circulatory collapse. Typically the immune system forms antibodies within a week, but that does not always help. Indeed "it is unclear whether immune mechanisms during the acute stage of the disease contribute to pathogenesis" (Monath 1999:1262). In vulnerable human populations in times past, case mortality may have been as high as 85 percent, although today the range seems to be much lower, never more than 30–50 percent (Mandell, Bennett, and Dolin 2000: vol. 2, 1716). Perhaps in the past reporting was so poor than many who had the disease but recovered went unnoticed; perhaps nowadays the virus no longer gets the chance to run amok among highly susceptible populations. Additionally, it may be that the virus has evolved so as to be less virulent in recent centuries, although the evidence from analysis of the virus's genome implies it has been genetically very stable: the American yellow fever virus is extremely close to the West African one, and the symptoms of the disease are identical everywhere. That suggests the virus has remained genetically stable since its transmission from Africa to the Americas. It also confirms the West African origin of the virus, which had formerly been a controversial question. Dengue, a sister virus, has in contrast evolved rapidly in the past two hundred years (Tsai 2000; Tabachnik 1998:413).

Young adults are the most at risk to yellow fever—which suggests that an overvigorous immune system response may indeed sometimes contribute to the lethality of yellow fever. Once one has the virus, even today there is nothing much doctors can do, and in the seventeenth and eighteenth centuries what they tried, such as bleeding patients, likely hurt more than it helped. Children normally experience it only mildly, a common pattern among infectious diseases, and their prospects for survival are excellent. In survivors, it produces lifelong immunity. Seventeenth- and eighteenth-century observers sometimes claimed the disease struck men more seriously than women, but this was probably a matter of exposure rather than pathology. The modern medical literature makes no mention of any differential risk among males and females. A very effective vaccination has been available since 1936.

The yellow fever virus has long been endemic in tropical African forests, and is now endemic in tropical American ones as well, circulating among monkeys and species of mosquito that are not much attracted to human blood. Today, as in the past, it is primarily a disease of tree-dwelling monkeys, lethal to howler monkeys but not to most other monkey species. Its mosquito vectors, which carry it from monkey to monkey, live in the forest canopy, and rarely take a human blood meal. It strikes individuals who venture into tropical forests, especially loggers who cut down trees and stir up mosquitoes. Usually these are isolated cases (sometimes called "sylvan yellow fever") and do not trigger epidemics because too few people are within range of infected mosquitoes, and the forest mosquitoes prefer monkey blood anyway. Yellow fever becomes epidemic among humans when it circulates among urban populations via the vector *A. aegypti*, which does find human blood appealing. (Happily this has happened only once in the Americas since 1954.) Urban, epidemic yellow fever is the same disease as sylvan yellow fever, caused by the same virus, but communicated by a different mosquito and circulating among a larger human population.

Yellow fever's geographic range and distribution is determined mainly by characteristics of the vector, *A. aegypti*. The virus spends most of its life in the salivary glands of mosquitoes; human bloodstreams and livers are merely the principal means by which the virus gets from mosquito to mosquito. Recent research shows that human bodies are not the only means: *A. aegypti* mothers can transmit the virus directly to their daughters ("vertical transmission"), although this is apparently very rare (Vainio and Cutts 1998:30; Monath 1999:1263). The *A. aegypti*, of African origin, is a domestic mosquito that lives close to humans and breeds mainly in water containers, and according to some reports, preferably clay-bottomed ones (Ramenofsky 1993:325, citing Carter 1931). Unlike many mosquitoes, it needs clean, unpolluted water for its eggs to become larvae, pupae, and then to become fledgling mosquitoes. Once mature and aloft, it likes to stay close to the ground, and bites people mainly on the ankles and calves, generally at dusk or dawn. Unlike its buzzing brethren, it is a silent mosquito. It can suck up two or three times its weight in human blood (only in desperation will it bite other mammals) in ninety seconds. It is attracted to motion, to heat, and to exhalations of water vapor, carbon dioxide, and lactic acid (Christopher 1960; Clements 2004). A hardworking body low to the ground, say a sugarcane cutter or a digging soldier, was catnip for a female *A. aegypti* (Black 2003:51). The mosquito rarely travels more than 300 meters from its birthplace, except on ships (or airplanes). It needs temperatures above 10°C to survive, above 17°C to feed, and above 24°C to prosper. It also needs liquid every few days. Hence yellow fever is and always has been a disease of the humid tropics and especially of preferred habitats of the *A. aegypti*, although it used to make seasonal forays to temperate ports around the Atlantic basin, occasionally as far north as Quebec, in summer months when infected mosquitoes stowed away on board sailing ships.

Epidemic yellow fever has other, more stringent, requirements. The virus must establish a cycle that allows indefinite transfer from mosquito to human host to mosquito. This requires a lot of mosquitoes, the more so because (nowadays at any rate) only about 60 percent of *A. aegypti* are able to transmit the virus (Cohen and Crane-Kramer 2003:88). Without plentiful vectors, the virus will not move from person to person rapidly enough: people have the disease only seven to ten days, after which time they are either immune or dead, in either case no longer capable of hosting the virus. Victims' blood is infective for only three to six days. The transmission cycle also needs a favorable ratio of nonimmune to immune people available for mosquitoes to bite. To perpetuate the cycle, an infected *A. aegypti* must behave a bit like Count Dracula: it must find virgin blood and find it fast. The mosquito lives a few weeks at most. Immune people are virus-killers: the cycle of transmission is broken when mosquitoes inject the virus only into immunized bloodstreams. So a yellow fever epidemic requires suitable vectors in sufficient quantity and susceptible hosts in both sufficient quantity and proportion. From the virus's point of view, its opportunities are sadly limited by the fragility of this cycle. Indeed, despite the warmth and rainfall, conditions in the Atlantic American tropics before 1640 left a lot to be desired: not enough clay-bottomed water vessels, not enough (if any) *A. aegypti*, not enough human bloodstreams, and among those bloodstreams, not enough who spent their childhoods in places where cold temperatures precluded exposure and therefore immunity to the virus.

But after 1640 sugar and geopolitics set the table very nicely for the yellow fever virus. Sugar wrought an ecological revolution on dozens of islands and numerous patches of adjacent continental lowlands. Soon, armies of slaves hacked down and burned off millions of hectares of forest in order to plant cane (Funes Monzote 2004). Their efforts led to multiple ecological changes (Watts 1987:219–223, 399–405, 434–443). Soil erosion accelerated. Wildlife vanished. More important from the human point of view, as plantations replaced forest, conditions came to favor the transmission of yellow fever. Falling trees brought canopy-dwelling mosquitoes down to ground level, where their chances of biting a person improved. This meant sylvan yellow fever, if it existed on the sugar islands at all, could more easily ignite an epidemic. Deforestation meant fewer birds, and fewer birds meant fewer predators for all mosquitoes. However, for mosquito population dynamics breeding conditions matter more than predation, so by far the most crucial ecological development was what replaced the felled forests: the sugar plantations themselves.

Plantations made excellent *A. aegypti* incubators. Sugar production in the seventeenth and eighteenth centuries involved initial refining on the spot (Ligon 1657; Moreno Fraginals 1978). Part of the process required putting partially crystallized sugar in clay pots for a few months. The pots had holes in them to let the molasses drain out, leaving semirefined sugar. A small plantation needed hundreds of clay pots. A big one used tens of thousands of them. They were empty except for three or four months after the harvest. Presumably they often broke, as they were of clay and roughly handled by people who had no interest in their preservation. Clay pots and fragments of clay pots caught the rain and made ideal homesteads for *A. aegypti*, contributing mightily to mosquito numbers (Goodyear 1978). In any case, whether clay contributed to mosquito nutrition or not, clay pots contributed mightily to mosquito numbers. With the spread of sugar eventually many ports (and forts) were ringed by plantations producing tons of sugar and clouds of *A. aegypti*. The mosquito may have successfully colonized the Atlantic American tropics before 1640, but after 1640 appropriate breeding grounds were far easier to find.

So was good food. *A. aegypti* prospered after 1640 because human blood and sugarcane juice got easier and easier to find. Sugar meant slaves, and population growth. Caribbean population had crashed after 1492, and by 1640 was perhaps two hundred thousand. By 1800 it had surpassed 2 million, improving mosquito nutrition handsomely. Beyond blood, *A. aegypti* can also eat sucrose. It likes sweet fluids, the sweeter the better. It can live off honey or sugar alone, although that diet is insufficient for the female of the species to sustain ovulation. So while individual mosquitoes could live well tapping the abundant cane juice on Caribbean plantations, sustainable *A. aegypti* populations required human blood meals as well. After 1640 there was more and more sugar, more and more human blood, and more and more water vessels in the Atlantic American tropics. For that matter, there were more and more slave ships arriving from West Africa, bringing as stowaways more and more mosquitoes. Things were looking up for *A. aegypti* in the Americas.

Conditions for the yellow fever virus improved too, with one catch that geopolitics soon addressed. More mosquitoes, more human bloodstreams, and more ships from Africa favored the establishment of the yellow fever virus in the neotropics. Indeed, the first clear epidemic of yellow fever in the Americas came in 1647, striking Barbados—then the main sugar island—first, and over the ensuing months and years, Guadeloupe, St. Kitts, Cuba, Yucatán, and the east coasts of Central America generally. It killed perhaps 20–30 percent of local populations. But after this outbreak, yellow fever disappeared for almost forty years (Kiple 1993; cf. Guerra 1993, who believes earlier epidemics were yellow fever). Presumably, it worked its way through the susceptible hosts, leaving behind a higher proportion of immunes. It could not flourish again without a sufficient proportion of nonimmunes. This, for the yellow fever virus, was problematic.

The virus's problem was compounded by the resistance of West Africans. Yellow fever confers immunity on all survivors. Almost all slaves arriving in the Caribbean from Africa had grown up in endemic yellow fever zones, and hence were immunes and virus stoppers. Beyond that, West Africans and people of West African descent may carry an inherited partial immunity to yellow fever whether or not they carry conferred immunity (Vainio and Cutts 1998:30; Kiple 1985:163). So while the population growth of the sugar zones helped the mosquitoes find food, it did not provoke many epidemics because so many of the people bitten by mosquitoes were West Africans (or, possibly, because so many were of West African descent). Raging epidemics required an influx of inexperienced immune systems. This is what expeditionary warfare provided.

Differential Immunity and Expeditionary Warfare

Participants and observers in the interimperial wars of the seventeenth and eighteenth centuries normally regarded yellow fever epidemics as acts of God. Modern military historians tend to see them as random events. But differential immunity made yellow fever decidedly and systematically partisan.

Yellow fever went easy on entire populations that included numerous individuals with either conferred or (if it existed) inherited immunity. In this way, a large contingent of Africans or, perhaps somewhat less effectively, of Caribbean-born whites, could serve as a shield for individuals highly vulnerable themselves to yellow fever, by interrupting the transmission cycle (this is known as "herd immunity" to epidemiologists). The conditions strongly favored local populations over invaders and immigrants, strongly favored populations with West Africans as opposed to those without them, and even favored populations with children as opposed to those made up exclusively of adults. Yellow fever was most dangerous to unadulterated populations of young adult Europeans: precisely the composition of expeditionary forces.[1]

After the one-week conquest of Jamaica in May 1655, the English troops fell victim to disease. By November, 47 percent were dead, and half the remainder were ill (Buchet 1991:1129). Henceforth British garrisons in Jamaica died off at a rate of about 20 percent annually in peacetime, almost entirely from diseases (malaria and others as well as yellow fever). This was about seven times the peacetime death rate of British garrisons in Canada. But in 1655 English soldiers conquered the island before disease conquered them. After 1655, the reverse was the rule.

Beginning in the 1680s, in the context of the struggles between England and Louis XIV's France, expeditions to the West Indies became more frequent and thus so did yellow fever outbreaks. Before 1713, Spain often fought on the same side as Britain, but after the accession of a Bourbon king in Madrid, Spain normally allied with Bourbon France against Britain. Most West Indies expeditions were British, but some were French, especially before Louis XIV scaled back his navy in the 1690s. Almost all were failures. After the successes, victors usually evacuated quickly, suffering from epidemics, and at the next peace treaty conquered ports were restored to their previous masters.

In 1689, at the outset of the War of the League of Augsburg (1689–1697), an English expedition against Guadeloupe failed, losing half its men to diseases. In 1692, Commodore Wrenn's force lost more than half its number to yellow fever. In 1693, another expedition lost 50 percent of its soldiers and sailors in failing to take Martinique. In 1695 a combined English and Spanish force lost 61 percent of the soldiers it disembarked in a doomed effort to dislodge the French from settlements that would at the next peace treaty be recognized as St.-Domingue. In 1697 a French expedition under Baron de Pointis failed to take Cartagena from Spain, losing 24 percent of its men to disease (Buchet 1991:730, 783–784). These figures refer only to deaths: In all of these expeditions yet more men were unfit for service because of disease. A deadly pattern had begun to assert itself. That it continued was due to a combination of ignorance and callousness on the part of those charged with crafting grand strategy.

The War of the Spanish Succession (1701–1713) was a Spanish success in the American tropics. France and Britain mounted nineteen cruises or expeditions; serious disease mortality hampered or destroyed at least fourteen of them, possibly as many as eighteen. Of only one is there clear evidence that fewer than 10 percent of the troops died from disease. The War of Jenkins' Ear and the War of the Austrian Succession (together 1739–1748) presented much the same picture. In a famous expedition in 1739–1742 Admiral Edward Vernon took Portobelo and Chagres, ill-defended ports each of which surrendered within two days of sighting Vernon's fleet. He arrived in November, well before the rains that normally presaged a population explosion of *A. aegypti*. He had the largest force ever seen in these seas, nearly twenty-five thousand, counting sailors and soldiers. In April 1741 he tried to take Cartagena but lost 41 percent of all men under his command, 70 percent of all disembarked soldiers, and 77 percent of those hailing from Britain (thirty-six hundred colonial troops fared slightly better). Only about 650 died in combat. Fleeing Cartagena, Vernon attempted to take Santiago de Cuba as a consolation prize, and lost 50 percent of his surviving troops to yellow fever. In all Vernon lost about three-fourths of the men under his command in 1740–1742; fewer than one thousand of these died in combat (Harding 1991:3–4; Buchet 1991:515–526).[2]

The Seven Years' War, the War of the American Revolution, and the Napoleonic Wars included numerous further episodes along these lines. I will mention only two, one for its anecdotal quality and the other because it is an important exception to the grisly rule. The anecdote comes from a British expedition against Fort San Juan in Nicaragua in 1780. Fevers, including yellow fever but probably not confined to it, killed 77 percent of its men and forced the abandonment of an initially successful campaign. One of the few survivors was twenty-one-year-old Horatio Nelson, future hero of Trafalgar: among his other strengths, it seems, was his immune system (Dancer 1781).[3]

The exception came in 1762, when Admiral George Pocock, Lord Albermarle, and fourteen thousand men besieged Havana. Havana was the key to Spain's strategic position in the Americas, the port from which ships bound for Spain departed the Indies, as well as the most important naval shipbuilding center in the Spanish Empire. It was well fortified and generally regarded in Spain as impregnable.[4] Spanish authorities anticipated an attempt on Havana, and in the summer of 1761 reinforced it with about one thousand men—of whom 138 promptly died of yellow fever. But the thousand reinforcements were too few to sustain an epidemic, and by late 1761 Havana's defenders and population—then about thirty-five thousand people—enjoyed good health. They were busily strengthening the city's fortifications, intent on slowing the besiegers' progress and exposing them to the dangers of the local disease environment (Parcero Torre 1998:48, 60–62). But when the British landed, on 7 June 1762, they were masters of the city in nine weeks. The Spanish governor, Juan de Prado, after a bombardment that tore a hole in the city's walls, surrendered just as yellow fever took hold among the besiegers.[5] Shortly after the conquest, Pocock had lost 41 percent of his men, 34 percent of them to yellow fever (only 7–8 percent died in combat or of other causes), and another 37 percent were ill. Only 21 percent were fit to bear arms. On 18 October the expeditionary force reported that 305 men had died in combat, 255 from wounds, and 4,708 from sickness.[6] More still would die before Britain evacuated Havana in mid-1763. The British army lost more men to yellow fever in thirteen months at Havana than in all the campaigns of the Seven Years' War in North America put together. Lord Albermarle had to abandon plans to move from Havana to a conquest of Louisiana because of a shortage of able-bodied men. Although they at first intended to remain, and spent money rebuilding Havana's fortifications, they gave it back to Spain at the Peace of Paris in 1763 and evacuated in July of that year.[7] Samuel Johnson wrote: "May my country be never cursed with such another conquest!" (Johnson 1977:374). Yellow fever kept Cuba Spanish even though Havana fell before the virus could work its mischief.

The power of yellow fever was such that defenders, if comprised of local troops with hardened immune systems, generally had only to hold out for three to six weeks to be assured of victory. Their chances improved if the siege took place during the rainier parts of the year (May–November in the Caribbean), when *A. aegypti* strength peaked. Expeditionary fleets tried their best to avoid the hurricane season (July–October) in the American tropics. Strategists in Europe well knew (at least from the 1690s) that prospects for success receded if one failed to get the troops to the scene between December and May. But organizing and victualling a force according to schedule was no easy business in an age of private contracting and uncertain stocks of food and ships. Finding men willing to take the king's shilling proved especially challenging if prospective recruits thought their destination might be the Caribbean. Hence many expeditions arrived later than planned, and suffered the consequences. At any time of year, one had to be quick. As Admiral Charles Knowles wrote in 1747, "Whatever is to be effected in the West Indies must be done as expeditiously as possible, or the climate soon wages a more destructive War, than the Enemy."[8] Amphibious expeditions and siege warfare worked in the Indian Ocean, where there was malaria but no yellow fever. In the Caribbean, with rare exception, they did not.

Revolutions, Canals, and Fevers

The geopolitical significance of yellow fever in the Americas changed toward the end of the eighteenth century. The restiveness of slave populations acquired more political forms and more often led to organized violence. An illustrative example of this came in Surinam in the 1770s. There Dutch planters had lived sumptuously if unhealthily amid a slave majority, but by 1772 maroon communities had grown powerful enough to threaten Surinam's plantation society. The Dutch government sent about 1,650 men from Europe in two contingents to do battle with the maroons. They succeeded in driving the maroons deeper into the forests and away from the plantations, but only about two hundred soldiers lived to return to Europe (Price and Price 1988:xxvi, lxxxvi).[9] A Scot who served with the Dutch in Surinam observed that by the end "not 20 were to be found in perfect health." He also detected the impact of differential disease immunity, noting that: "amongst the Officers and Private men who had *formerly* been in the West Indies, none died at all, while amongst the whole number of near 1200 together I Can Recollect one Single marine who Escaped from Sickness" (Stedman 1988:607). Once people of West African origin began to make war on their own behalf in the American tropics, their relative immunity to yellow fever (and to falciparum malaria), if shrewdly exploited, magnified their power. That power soon shook the foundation of the imperial order in the American tropics. The maroons of Surinam lived to fight another day but were too few to take over their country.

In Haiti, both the scale and the agenda were larger. In the French colony of St.-Domingue by 1790 there were about half a million slaves, forty thousand French, and thirty thousand free people "of color." Taking advantage of and inspiration from events in France, slaves and former slaves engineered a revolution against French planters, beginning in 1791, which the French, then the British, then the French again attempted to undo. In 1792 slaves prevented a small French force from reestablishing control. In 1794 British redcoats occupied the major ports. They found themselves, together with their Spanish allies, at war with Toussaint L'Ouverture (1743–1803) and his ill-equipped Haitian army. In the course of their stay in St.-Domingue, British forces lost about fifty thousand men, the majority falling to yellow fever. Britain lost about sixty-five to seventy thousand in all West Indian campaigns, 1793–1796, mainly to diseases, of which yellow fever was the greatest menace (Duffy 1987:334). After the British gave up, the French tried to reclaim Haiti. In 1802 Napoleon sent his brother-in-law and fifty-eight thousand soldiers to subdue Toussaint. Initially they met with military success as Toussaint prudently refused to commit large forces in a decisive battle. Over the next eighteen months, some fifty thousand Frenchmen died in Haiti, the French surrendered, and the survivors departed. Toussaint was no fool: he knew that if he did not give battle yellow fever would destroy the French, as it had done the British. His lieutenant and successor, Jean-Jacques Dessalines, knew it too: he told his followers to take courage, that "The French will not be able to remain long in San Domingo. They will do well at first, but soon they will fall ill and die like flies" (James 1989:314).[10] And this is exactly what happened. Toussaint and Dessalines would have been poor commanders indeed not to shape their strategy to exploit the overwhelming power of their insect and viral allies. Napoleon's defeat in Haiti led him to sell Louisiana to the United States in 1803. France finally recognized Haitian independence in 1825.

In the cases of Surinam and Haiti, the military impact of differential immunity was especially strong, because one of the combatant forces in each case consisted mainly of West Africans. But American-born whites, called creoles in the Spanish empire, also enjoyed military advantages derived from the antibodies in their bloodstreams. Like Toussaint, they learned how to exploit it without understanding it.

When Napoleon invaded Spain in 1808, most of Spanish America took the opportunity to declare independence. Vicious civil wars followed in many settings. After the Spanish, with British help, ejected Napoleon from Iberia the restored Spanish monarchy sought to reclaim its American empire, and to this end shipped out over forty thousand soldiers. Very few ever returned. The largest contingent, some ten thousand men under General Pablo Morillo, went to the former viceroyalty of New Granada, today's Colombia and Venezuela, in 1815. They successfully besieged Cartagena in a fifteen-week campaign, but their luck ended there. By 1817 a third of Morillo's men were dead from disease. Reigning ideas held that yellow fever (and malaria) came from "miasmas" arising from swamps, but Morillo was ahead of his time. He wrote to the minister of war, "The mere bite of a mosquito often deprives a man of his life," an observation that anticipated the discovery of the etiology of yellow fever by eighty years (Rodríguez Villa 1908–1910:442–443).[11] Of all the men who served Spain in Venezuela and Colombia, between 90 and 96 percent died there, mainly from disease (Albi 1990:403–405). Yellow fever and malaria also afflicted soldiers fighting for independence, but not nearly as seriously. Simon Bolívar, while lamenting the "infinite" illness that beset his troops, noted that royalist troops suffered even more from disease, on account of their "nature" and their positions. What he observed, but did not recognize, was that the soldiers' place of origin, rather than their nature, determined their level of susceptibility. But the result was the same: Spain could not maintain an army in New Granada, because soldiers died far faster than replacements could be found. Morillo recruited local men, but they deserted en masse, sometimes for political reasons, sometimes to avoid the epidemics that beset the Spanish troops. With its army melting away, Spain could not resist the revolution.

While it is true that the Spanish American revolutions succeeded in Buenos Aires and elsewhere in the absence of serious epidemics, the events in New Granada affected all of Spanish America. The Crown unwisely chose to concentrate its military efforts there, and thereby exposed the greater part of its forces to tropical fevers. This meant fewer troops could be spared for Chile, Peru, and elsewhere. And it further meant that recruiting new soldiers in Spain would be even more difficult. Contingents bound for New Granada had to be told they were headed to Buenos Aires lest they mutiny. According to one British account, rebellious Buenos Aires was ripe for reconquest in 1819–1820. But Spain could not get an army to the scene in order to take advantage of the situation. An army of fourteen thousand assembled in Cadiz in 1820 threw its weight behind a revolution rather than go to fight in America. Its officers had the salutary experience of observing some of the few survivors of Morillo's Colombian campaigns (who apparently sparked a yellow fever epidemic in Cadiz) shortly before they joined the revolution of 1820 (Woodward 1968).

On several other occasions in the nineteenth century yellow fever affected military campaigns in the greater Caribbean, and settlement patterns as well. Perhaps its most significant impact was in preventing a French Panama Canal. In 1879 Ferdinand de Lesseps, the French diplomat who had organized the Suez Canal project a decade before, formed a company to build a canal across the isthmus of Panama. After his bankruptcy in 1889, a successor company carried on the work. Between 1881 and 1903 de Lesseps and his followers recruited tens of thousands of laborers to Panama, half of them from Jamaica, many of the rest from elsewhere in the Americas, but a few thousand luckless souls from Europe. Among the Frenchmen who went to dig in Panama, 67 percent died there. An inspector general, Jules Dingler, declared on arrival in 1883 that only dissipated drunks died of yellow fever. Within months his son and daughter died of the disease, then his wife. Dingler himself returned to France in 1884. The annual death rate for all men on the canal project was about 6–7 percent, and in all twenty-two thousand died failing to finish a canal. In the hospitals the French built, more than three-quarters of all patients suffered from yellow fever or malaria. To prevent ants and other crawling insects from feasting on hospital patients, French doctors tried to ensure that each hospital bed's legs were inserted into pots of water, creating ideal breeding habitat for the silent angels of death, *A. aegypti*. The French finally gave up, leaving the Panama Canal to the Americans. With the help of newly acquired knowledge of the transmission cycle of yellow fever, and with energetic mosquito control, the United States in 1914 succeeded where France had failed, ensuring American control of the canal for some eighty years to come (Le Prince and Orenstein 1916; Gorgas and Hendrick 1924).

Conclusion

A grass from New Guinea (sugarcane) and a mosquito and a virus from Africa, after the mid-seventeenth century wrought an ecological transformation that for 130 years stabilized the geopolitics of the Caribbean basin. They helped keep the Spanish Empire intact after 1655, and prevented first France and then Britain from acquiring a choke hold on Spanish silver and a near monopoly position on American sugar. Either one—more silver or more sugar—might have made Louis XIV more successful in his bid for European hegemony, or Georgian Britain still more successful in its subsequent expansion. After the 1770s, differential disease immunity assisted insurgent populations of the American tropics as they sought to end European empires in the New World. In the environmental and epidemiological changes these empires wrought they sowed the (slow-germinating) seeds of their own destruction. A century later, after 1898, a new empire arose in the Caribbean, made possible (or at least inexpensive) by further environmental and epidemiological change: the mosquito control and yellow fever prevention undertaken by the U.S. Army.

Notes

This chapter is a revised version of an article published in *Review* 27(4): 343–364 (2004).

   1. To be more exact, the most vulnerable were populations of young adults who had grown up, and whose ancestors for millennia had grown up, outside of yellow fever zones and possibly dengue fever zones. Apparently there is some "cross-protection" for survivors of one or another of the flaviviruses (Vainio and Cutts 1998:30; Tsai 2000:272–275). There is some evidence that southern Chinese, who have no experience of yellow fever but have survived dengue fever, are also resistant to yellow fever. People from India, when translated to the Caribbean in the nineteenth century, seem to have shown greater resistance to yellow fever. Yellow

fever has never been recorded anywhere in Asia or the South Pacific, for which there is no explanation. Perhaps it is connected to the prevalence of dengue: just as in the Caribbean populations who came from dengue zones seem to have shown a stronger resistance to yellow fever, so possibly dengue survivors carry sufficient cross-protection against yellow fever that the disease could not establish itself in Asia.

2. De Zulueta (1992) takes the view that yellow fever did not decide the battle, which was won by Spanish tenacity and lost by British blundering. He argues that yellow fever became truly serious among British troops only after they had failed in an attempt to take one of Cartagena's forts by storm. True enough, but they attempted it rashly, without proper preparation, because of Vernon's dread of the building epidemic. The mortality among the colonials continued after Cartagena. Gallay (1996:105) says less than 10 percent of the colonials returned home. Among the survivors under Vernon's command was a Virginian named Lawrence Washington, whose plantation—Mt. Vernon—he named for his admiral before he passed it on to his more famous half-brother George.

3. Public Record Office (P.R.O.), ADM 101/102/9 "Diary of Surgeon Leonard Gillespie on HMS Majestic at Martinique 1794–1795," also relates the disease experience of the San Juan expedition.

4. Biblioteca Nacional (Madrid), ms 10, 421, "Processo dada al Gobernador de la Habana Juan de Prado" (1765). In the 192 folios recording this trial the view was repeatedly expressed that Havana, if competently defended, would withstand all attacks, e.g. fol. 140: "invencible seguridad de la Plaza."

5. Forty-four letters from de Prado are in Seville's Archivo General de Indias, Sección Ultramar, legajo 169. His siege diary appears in de la Pezuela (1863:vol. 3, 27–51).

6. P.R.O., CO 117/1, f. 155, "General Return of Officers, Sergeants, Drummers, and Rank and File . . . from the 7th June to eighteenth October 1762."

7. P.R.O., CO 117/1, f. 275, "Estimate of the Expenses of the Fortifications at the Havana."

8. British Library, Additional Mss. 23,678, fol. 17 (1747).

9. Figures vary. Stedman himself (1988:607) thought that only a hundred of twelve hundred survived. The Dutch forces numbered closer to 1,650 than 1,200 (Hoogbergen 1990:104).

10. See James (1989:299) for Toussaint's statement: "the rainy season will rid us of our foes." James provides no sources for these quotations. Laurent-Ropa (1993:323) gives fifty-four thousand as the total number of French troops lost in Haiti, with eight thousand survivors. A contingent of Swiss mercenaries some eight hundred strong lost all but eleven men; Swiss mercenaries never consented to go overseas again (Anex-Cabanis 1991:187).

11. According to Elvin (2004:262), the Bai people of Yunnan (southwestern China) understood that there was a link between anopheles mosquitoes and malaria during the Ming dynasty, and some Chinese learned of it too. Iliffe (1995:58) says

Ethiopians from very early (it is unclear just what this means) associated malaria with mosquito bites. The scientific recognition of the role of mosquitoes as transmitters of infection came only at the end of the nineteenth century.

References

Albi, J. 1990. *Banderas olvidadas: El ejército realista en América.* Madrid: Ediciones de Cultura Hispánica.

Alchon, S. A. 2003. *A pest in the land: New World epidemics in a global perspective.* Albuquerque: University of New Mexico Press.

Anex-Cabanis, D. 1991. Mort et morbidité aux Antilles lors de l'expédition de Saint-Domingue: Notes à propos des mercenaires suisses. In *Mourir pour les Antilles,* ed. M. Martin and A. Yacou, 181–188. Paris: Editions Caribéennes.

Barrett, A. D., and T. Monath. 2003. Epidemiology and ecology of yellow fever virus. *Advanced Virus Research* 61:291–315.

Bess, M. 2003. *The light-green society: Ecology and technological modernity in France, 1960–2000.* Chicago: University of Chicago Press.

Black, W. C. 2003. Evolution of arthropod disease vectors. In *Emerging pathogens: Archaeology, ecology, and evolution of infectious disease,* ed. C. Greenblatt and M. Spigelman, 49–63. New York: Oxford University Press.

Buchet, C. 1991. *La lutte pour l'espace caraïbe et la façade atlantique de l'Amérique centrale et sud.* Paris: Librairie de l'Inde.

Butel, P., and B. Lavallé, eds. 1996. *L'espace caraïbe: Théâtre et enjeu des luttes impériales, XVIe–XIXe siècle.* Bordeaux: Maison des Pays Ibériques.

Carter, H. R. 1931. *Yellow fever: An epidemiological and historical study of its place of origin.* Baltimore: Williams and Wilkins.

Christopher, R. C. 1960. *Aedes aegypti, the yellow fever mosquito: Its life history, bionomics, and structure.* Cambridge, U.K.: Cambridge University Press.

Clements, A. N. 2004. *The biology of mosquitoes.* 2 vols. Dordrecht: Kluwer Academic.

Cohen, M. N., and G. Crane-Kramer. 2003. The state and future of paleoepidemiology. In *Emerging pathogens: Archaeology, ecology, and evolution of infectious disease,* ed. C. Greenblatt and M. Spigelman, 79–91. New York: Oxford University Press.

Cook, N. D. 1998. *Born to die.* New York: Cambridge University Press.

Cooper, D., and K. Kiple. 1993. Yellow fever. In *Cambridge world history of human disease,* ed. K. Kiple, 1100–1107. New York: Cambridge University Press.

Curtin, P. 1991. *The plantation complex.* New York: Cambridge University Press.

da Costa Vasconcelos, P. F. 2003. Febre amarela. *Revista da Sociedade Brasileira de Medicina Tropical* 36:275–293.

Dancer, T. 1781. *A brief history of the late expedition against Fort San Juan, so far as it relates to the diseases of the troops.* Kingston: Douglas and Aikman.

De la Pezuela, J., ed. 1863. *Diccionario geográfico, estadístico, histórico de la Isla de Cuba.* Vol. 3. Madrid: Mellado.

De Zulueta, J. 1992. Health and military factors in Vernon's failure at Cartagena. *Mariner's Mirror* 78:127–141.

Duffy, C. 1979. *Siege warfare: The fortress in the early modern world, 1494–1660.* London: Routledge.

———. 1987. *Soldiers, sugar, and seapower: The British expeditions to the West Indies and the war against revolutionary France.* Oxford: Oxford University Press.

Elvin, M. 2004. *The retreat of the elephants: An environmental history of China.* New Haven, Conn.: Yale University Press.

Funes Monzote, R. 2004. *De bosque a sabana. Azúcar deforestación y medio ambiente en Cuba, 1492–1926.* Mexico City: Siglo Veintiuno.

Gallay, A., ed. 1996. *Encyclopedia of colonial wars of North America.* New York: Garland.

Goodyear, J. 1978. The sugar connection: A new perspective on the history of yellow fever. *Bulletin of the History of Medicine* 52:5–21.

Gorgas, M. D., and B. J. Hendrick. 1924. *William Crawford Gorgas: His life and work.* New York: Doubleday.

Guerra, F. 1993. The European-American exchange. *History and Philosophy of the Life Sciences* 15:313–327.

Harding, R. 1991. *Amphibious warfare in the eighteenth century: The British expedition to the West Indies, 1740–1742.* London: Royal Historical Society.

Hoogbergen, W. 1990. *The Boni maroon wars in Suriname.* Leiden: Brill.

Iliffe, J. 1995. *Africans: The history of a continent.* Cambridge, U.K.: Cambridge University Press.

James, C. L. R. 1989. *The black Jacobins.* New York: Vintage Books.

Johnson, S. 1977. Thoughts on the late transactions respecting Falkland's islands. In *Political writings*, ed. D. Greene, vol. 10. New Haven, Conn.: Yale University Press.

Kiple, K. 1985. *The Caribbean slave: A biological history.* New York: Cambridge University Press.

———. 1993. Disease ecologies of the Caribbean. In *Cambridge world history of human disease*, ed. K. Kiple, 497–513. New York: Cambridge University Press.

Laurent-Ropa, D. 1993. *Haiti: Une colonie française, 1625–1802.* Paris: L'Harmattan.

Le Prince, J. A., and A. J. Orenstein. 1916. *Mosquito control in Panama.* New York: Putnam.

Ligon, R. 1657. *A true and exact history of Barbadoes.* London: Parker.

Mandell, G. L., J. E. Bennett, and R. Dolin. 2000. *Principles and practice of infectious disease.* 2 vols. Philadelphia: Churchill Livingstone.

Monath, T. P. 1999. Yellow fever. In *Tropical infectious diseases*, ed. R. Guerrant, D. H. Walker, and P. F. Weller, 1253–1264. Philadelphia: Churchill Livingstone.

Moreno Fraginals, M. 1978. *El ingenio: Complejo económico-social cubano del azucar.* Havana: Editorial de Ciencias Sociales.

Parcero Torre, C. M. 1998. *La pérdida de la Habana y las reformas borbónicas en Cuba (1760–1773).* Madrid: Junta de Castilla y León.

Parker, G. 1996. *The military revolution: Military innovation and the rise of the west, 1500–1800*. Cambridge, U.K.: Cambridge University Press.

Price, R., and S. Price. 1988. Introduction. In *Narrative of a five years expedition against the revolted negroes of Surinam*, by J. G. Stedman. Baltimore: Johns Hopkins University Press.

Ramenofsky, A. 1993. Diseases of the Americas, 1492–1700. In *Cambridge world history of human disease*, ed. K. Kiple, 317–327. New York: Cambridge University Press.

Rodríguez Villa, A. 1908–1910. *El teniente general Don Pablo Morillo, primer conde de Cartagena, marqués de la Puerta (1778–1837)*. Madrid: Editorial América.

Stedman, J. G. 1988. *Narrative of a five years expedition against the revolted negroes of Surinam*. Baltimore: Johns Hopkins University Press.

Strode, G. K., ed. 1951. *Yellow fever*. New York: McGraw-Hill.

Tabachnik, W. J. 1998. Arthropod-borne emerging disease issues. In *Emerging infections*, ed. R. M. Krause, 411–430. San Diego: Academic.

Tsai, T. 2000. Yellow fever. In *Hunter's tropical medicine and emerging infectious diseases*, ed. G. T. Strickland, 272–275. Philadelphia: Saunders.

Vainio, J., and F. Cutts, eds. 1998. *Yellow fever*. Geneva: World Health Organization.

Watts, D. 1987. *The West Indies: Patterns of development, culture and environmental change since 1492*. Cambridge, U.K.: Cambridge University Press.

Woodward, M. L. 1968. The Spanish army and the loss of America, 1810–1824. *Hispanic American Historical Review* 48:586–607.

Zapatero, J. 1964. *La guerra del Caribe*. San Juan: Instituto de Cultura Puertoriqueña.

ECOLOGY AND UNEQUAL EXCHANGE: UNRAVELING ENVIRONMENTAL INJUSTICE IN THE MODERN WORLD

II

Marxism, Social Metabolism, and International Trade

11

JOAN MARTINEZ-ALIER

I N THE EARLY TWENTIETH CENTURY, there was resistance from social scientists and economists (Max Weber, F. A. von Hayek) against authors (Wilhelm Ostwald, Otto Neurath) who emphasized the flow of energy in the economy. This debate between the money-focused view and the ecological view of the economy is now more relevant than ever. It has produced the schools of ecological economics and industrial ecology, which look at the economy in terms of "social metabolism." Even Marx (inspired by Moleschott and Liebig) used the word "metabolism," but Marxist historians conducted no systematic calculations of energy and material flows. This chapter introduces the agricultural energetics of S. A. Podolinsky, rejected by Engels in 1882 but adopted by Vladimir Vernadsky in 1924. It also presents the framework for calculations of material flows that was proposed by Patrick Geddes in 1884 as an argument against neoclassical economics, and that provides a basis for modern theories of ecologically unequal exchange.

In the 1970s, the systematic study of human society and economy from a physical point of view (i.e. in terms of flows of materials and energy) began to be practiced by several research groups. Some authors wrote histories of the use of energy in human economies (Cipolla 1974 [1962]; Sieferle 1982; Debeir, Deléage, and Hémery 1986; Hall, Cleveland, and Kaufman 1986). Other authors also looked at the use of materials and water, and at the human influence on the carbon cycle and other biogeochemical cycles (McNeill 2000). The notion of energy return on energy input (EROI) to the economy was applied in the 1970s by Charles Hall and other ecologists. Authors working on "industrial metabolism" (Ayres 1989) or "social metabolism" (Fischer-Kowalski 1998; Haberl 2001) have looked at modern economies in terms of flows of energy and materials. In this chapter, I shall show how this view of the economy has intellectual roots in some nineteenth-century natural scientists (Martinez-Alier 1987), whereas economists, on the contrary, refused to adopt a sociometabolic view. Only much later, in the late twentieth century, some natural scientists and also some dissident economists such as Nicholas Georgescu-Roegen, Kenneth Boulding, K. W. Kapp, and Herman Daly began to view the economy as a subsystem embedded in a biophysical system that can be described in terms of flows of materials and energy. This perspective has given rise to the schools of ecological economics and industrial ecology.

Marxist scholars working on economic and social history have generally not been concerned with material and energy flows. However, Marx and Engels had shown a profound interest in the metabolic relation between the human economy and the natural environment, particularly as regards capitalist agriculture. This was expressed in Marx's use, after 1857–1858, of the notion of "metabolism" (*Stoffwechsel*) between human society and Nature. The Marxist concept of "metabolism" became widely known with Alfred Schmidt's (1978) work. Schmidt acknowledged Moleschott's and Liebig's influences, and also Marx's substantive use of the term in his discussion of the cycling of plant nutrients (Schmidt 1978:86–89; Martinez-Alier 1987:220–226). Marx became so keen on the concept of metabolism that, in a letter to his wife on June 21, 1856, he wrote that what made him feel like a man was his love for her, not his love for Moleschott's metabolism or for the proletariat.

Marx and Engels were one generation younger than the agricultural chemists Liebig (1803–1873) and Boussingault (1802–1887), who from 1840 onward published their findings on the cycles of plant nutrients (phosphorous, nitrogen, potassium), influenced by the debates on the threat of decreasing agricultural yields and by the wholesale imports of guano from Peru, an essential bulk commodity. About 11 million tons of guano were exported from Peru in four decades (Gootenberg 1993). The analyses of the composition of imported guano, and also of other manures and fertilizers, such as bones, already known to farmers, laid the foundations for agricultural chemistry. Liebig's name was associated, according to his own wishes, with a new and expansive sector of the economy, the fertilizer industry. Liebig can also be seen as one of the founders of ecology before the name itself was invented (Kormondy 1965). Politically he developed an argument against large-scale export agriculture because it would not allow the plant nutrients to return to the soil. He was in favor of small-scale agriculture and dispersed settlements. Marx quoted this opinion favorably on several occasions.

Marx found Liebig supremely relevant because he discussed the natural conditions of agricultural fertility and promoted the development of the productive forces through the fertilizer industry. This was useful for the polemics against Malthus, and for the theory of land rent. Foster (2000), who rediscovered Marx's "metabolism," analyzed in great depth Marx's debt to Liebig, though he wrongly dismissed Moleschott's influence, failing to quote Moleschott's books of 1851 and 1852 on the "circle of life" and the physiology of metabolism in plants and animals.

Marx was a historian and an economist, but also a student of agriculture and agricultural chemistry, adopting the notion of "metabolism" between human society and Nature. The material flows between humans and Nature were mobilized by human labor, except perhaps in hunting-and-gathering societies. The development of tools was essential for this metabolism. As Marx did not consider the flow of energy in agriculture and in industry, he could not trace a fundamental distinction (as Lotka was to do in 1911) between endosomatic and exosomatic use of energy. This difference between biometabolism and technometabolism is crucial for human ecology. The human species has genetic instructions regarding endosomatic energy use, but not for exosomatic energy use, which can only be explained by history, politics, economics, culture, and technology.

Marx wrote to Engels on February 13, 1866, that Liebig's agricultural chemistry was more important for the discussion on decreasing returns than all the economists put together. Marx dismissed the notion of decreasing returns in agriculture, praising Liebig's chemistry and its promise of artificial fertilizers, and arguing that it did not make sense to assume, for example in Britain, that the produce of the land would increase in a diminishing ratio to the increase of the laborers employed, because in reality there was both an increase in production and an absolute decrease in the number of laborers (Marx 1969 [1867]:ch. 13). Marx was not worried about crises of subsistence. He attacked Malthus for suggesting that to improve the situation of the poor was counterproductive, since the result would be that they would have more children. There were many debates around 1900 on "how many people could the Earth feed" (Pfaundler 1902; Cohen 1995). Some Marxists (Lenin 1913) attacked not only Malthus but also the neo-Malthusians of the late nineteenth century and early twentieth century, who were often political radicals and feminists like Paul Robin and Emma Goldman (Gordon 1976; Ronsin 1980; Masjuan 2000).

Podolinsky's Agricultural Energetics

The link between material metabolism (*Stoffwechsel*, literally the exchanges of materials) and the flow of energy at the level of cells and organisms was made in the 1840s. It was then acknowledged that agriculture implied changes in the flow of energy and not only in the cycling of plant nutrients. Mayer (1845), in fact, used the concept of *Stoffwechsel* for energy flow. Metabolism was recognized as comprising not only materials but also energy (Haberl 2001). The difference, of course, is that materials can be cycled, while energy can not. Recognition of the unilinear flow of energy was developed after 1850 and the establishment of the Second Law of Thermodynamics.

As is evident from their correspondence (Marx and Engels 1976), Marx and Engels were interested in energy. For instance, Engels wrote to Marx on July 14, 1858, commenting on Joule's work in 1840 on the conservation of energy as something that was well known to them. Marx was keen on new sources of energy. One example will suffice: it was already discussed at this time whether hydrogen could be a net source of energy, depending on the energy requirement for electrolysis. Marx wrote to Engels on April 2, 1866, that a certain M. Rebour had found the means of separating the oxygen from hydrogen in water at very little expense. However, in his published work, Marx did not refer to the flow of energy as metabolism.

As Engels became aware of Clausius's concept of entropy, he wrote to Marx (March 21, 1869):

> In Germany the conversion of the natural forces, for instance, heat into mechanical energy, etc. has given rise to a very absurd theory—that the world is becoming steadily colder... and that, in the end, a moment will come when all life will be impossible.... I am simply waiting for the moment when the clerics seize upon this theory.

Indeed, not only the clerics but also W. Thomson (Lord Kelvin) brandished the Second Law in his religious tirades about the "heat death," although he could have no inkling of the source of solar energy in nuclear fusion. One may sympathize with Engels's dislike for the use to which the Second Law was put. Josef Popper-Lynkeus (1838–1921), who with Ernst Mach exerted a major influence on the analytical, antimetaphysical philosophy of the Vienna Circle, complained in 1876 about W. Thomson's "theological handling of Carnot's law" (Martinez-Alier 1987:197). However, Engels's dislike of the Second Law was not only motivated by its religious abuse. He believed, in fact, that ways would be found to reuse the heat radiated into space.

Another interesting point is Engels's negative reaction in 1882 (in letters to Marx) regarding Podolinsky's work. Podolinsky had studied the entropy law and the economic process, and he tried to convince Marx that this could be brought into the Marxist analysis. Politically he was not a Marxist, but a Ukrainian federalist *narodnik*. He complained about Marx's dominating behavior at the congress of the International of 1872, praising the anarchist James Guillaume. However, he saw his own work on agricultural energetics as a contribution to Marxism. In a letter to Marx dated April 8, 1880, he wrote: "With particular impatience I wait for your opinion on my attempt to bring surplus labour and the current physical theories into harmony" (Podolinsky's correspondence at the Institute of Social History, Amsterdam). In an article published in Russian in 1880 and in German in 1883, and in shorter French and Italian versions in 1880 and 1881, Podolinsky (1880a) began by explaining the laws of energetics, quoting from Clausius that although the energy of the universe was constant, there was a tendency toward the dissipation of energy or, in Clausius's terminology, there was a tendency for entropy to increase. He did not discuss the difference between open, closed, and isolated systems, but stated explicitly, as the starting point of his analysis, that the earth was receiving enormous quantities of energy from the sun, and would do so for a very long time. All physical and biological phenomena were expressions of the transformations of energy. He did not enter into the controversies regarding the creation of the universe and its "heat-death," nor did he discuss the relations between thermodynamics and the theory of evolution. In March 1880 he published an article criticizing social Darwinism (Podolinsky 1880b). He certainly realized that the availability of energy was a crucial consideration for demography, defining the feasibility of an increase in population. However, he argued that the distribution of production was explained by the relations between social classes: "In the countries where capitalism triumphs, a great part of work goes towards the production of luxury goods, that is to say, towards a gratuitous dissipation of energy instead of towards increasing the availability of energy" (Podolinsky 1880b).

Podolinsky explained that plants assimilated energy, and animals fed on plants and degraded energy. This formed the *Kreislauf des Lebens*:

> We have in front of us two parallel processes which together form the so-called circle of life. Plants have the property of accumulating solar energy, but the animals, when they feed on vegetable substances, transform a part of this saved energy and dissipate this energy into space. If the quantity of energy accumulated by plants is greater than that dispersed by animals, then stocks of energy appear, for instance in the period when mineral coal

was formed, during which vegetable life was preponderant over animal life. If, on the contrary, animal life were preponderant, the provision of energy would be quickly dispersed and animal life would have to go back to the limits determined by vegetable wealth. So, a certain equilibrium would have to be built between the accumulation and the dissipation of energy. (Podolinsky 1883:420, my translation)

Not only plants, but also human labor had the capacity to retard the dissipation of energy. Human labor achieved this through agriculture, although the work of a tailor, a shoemaker, or a carpenter would also qualify, in his view, as productive work, since they afforded "protection against the dissipation of energy into space." The energy available for humankind came mainly from the sun, and Podolinsky provided figures for the solar constant. He explained how coal and oil, wind energy, and water power were transformations of solar energy. He mentioned tides as another possible source of energy. He then turned to his analysis of agricultural energetics, remarking that only a tiny proportion of the sun's energy was assimilated by plants.

Human work, together with the work of animals controlled by humans, could increase the availability of energy through agricultural activity. Podolinsky showed this in France. Table 11.1 summarizes his data (cf. Martinez-Alier 1987:48, for information on sources).

Podolinsky compared wheat agriculture and sown pastures with natural pastures and forests, concluding that production was higher when there was an input of human and animal work. Thus, comparing wheat agriculture to natural pastures, each kcal put in contributed to an increase of 22 kcal of production. Compared to forests, the energy productivity of human and domestic animal work was even higher. Notice that Podolinsky was counting human and animal *work*, that is, not the food intake but the work done. He

Table 11.1.   Average annual production and energy input (through the work of humans and domestic animals) per hectare in France in 1870, according to Podolinsky

	Production (kg)	Production (kcal)	Energy input (kcal)
Forest	900 (dried wood)	2,295,000	Nil
Natural pastures	2,500 (hay)	6,375,000	Nil
Sown pastures	3,100 (hay, excluding seed)	7,905,000	37,450 (50 horse-hours and 80 man-hours)
Wheat	800 (wheat) and 2,000 (straw) (excluding seed)	8,100,000	77,500 (100 horse-hours and 200 man-hours)

Note: Energy values of wood, hay, and straw: 2,550 kcal/kg; of wheat: 3,750 kcal/kg. Hours of work converted into kcal: 645 kcal/hour of horse-work, 65 kcal/hour of man-work.

did not include solar radiation in the input of energy, because he was writing as an ecological economist. Solar radiation is indeed a free gift of Nature (so far without an owner, so that there is no payment of rent).

The conclusion was that work could increase the "accumulation of energy on earth." Although he mentioned guano, and although he must have been keenly aware of the war then raging for Peruvian or Chilean saltpeter (another early bulk commodity), he did not subtract from the output, or include in the input, the energy contents and cost of fertilizer. Nor did he consider the energy spent by steam engines in threshing. His methodology is nevertheless basically the same as that used later for establishing the energy balance of particular crops, or for small-scale societies, or for the entire agricultural sector of particular countries (Cottrell 1955; Rappaport 1967; Odum 1971; Pimentel et al. 1973; Pimentel and Pimentel 1979; Leach 1975; Fluck and Baird 1980).

Podolinsky then went on to explain the capacity of the human organism to conduct work. Otherwise "it would be difficult to explain the accumulation of energy on the surface of the earth under the influence of labour" (Podolinsky 1880b). Quoting from Hirn and Helmholtz, he correctly concluded that "man has the capacity to transform one-fifth of the energy gained from food into muscular work," giving to this ratio the name of "economic coefficient" and remarking that man was a more efficient transformer of energy than a steam engine. He then used a steam-engine metaphor to express a general theoretical principle on the natural conditions of human existence, from an energy point of view. He wrote that humanity was a "perfect machine" in Sadi Carnot's sense: "Humanity is a machine that not only turns heat and other physical forces into work, but succeeds also in carrying out the inverse cycle, that is, it turns work into heat and other physical forces which are necessary to satisfy our needs, and, so to speak, with its own work turned into heat is able to heat its own boiler" (Podolinsky 1880b).

For humanity to ensure its elementary conditions of existence, argued Podolinsky, each calorie of human work must yield (i.e. produce or provide access to) several calories of food energy. Taking into account that not everybody is able to work (e.g. children, old people) and that there are other energy needs than food energy, the necessary minimum productivity would be in the order of ten or more. If that minimum is not achieved, "scarcity appears and, many times, a reduction of population" (Podolinsky 1880b). Podolinsky thus established the basis for a view of the economy in terms of energy metabolism, looking at the energy return to energy input as a foundation for the reproduction of the social system. He thought that he had reconciled the Physiocrats with the labor theory of value, although the eighteenth-century Physiocrats had not been able to see the economy in terms of energy flow.

Podolinsky emphasized the difference between using the flow of solar energy and the stock of energy in coal. The task of labor was to increase the accumulation of solar energy on Earth, rather than the simple transformation into work of energy already accumulated on Earth, considering that work done with coal was inevitably accompanied by a great dissipation of heat-energy into space. The energy productivity of a coal miner was much larger than that of a traditional farmer, but this energy surplus from coal was ephemeral. Moreover, Podolinsky added in a footnote, there was a theory that linked climatic changes to concentrations of carbon dioxide in the atmosphere, as Sterry Hunt had explained at a meeting of the British Society for the Advancement of Science in the autumn of 1878. The emphasis here is not on capital accumulation in the sense of an increased stock of means of production, and even less in financial terms, but on increasing the availability of energy. This is an early example of "non-equivalent descriptions" of the same economic reality in terms of both economic and energy magnitudes (Giampietro 2003).

Podolinsky was not pessimistic about the prospects for the economy, however. He was optimistic about the direct use of solar energy for industrial purposes, referring to the "solar engine of M. Mouchot" (cf. Mouchot 1879 [1869]). He also envisaged that one day solar energy would be used directly for chemical syntheses of nutritive substances, bypassing agriculture. Thus, he argued, a proper discussion of the demographic question should take into account the relation between the quantity of energy available on the earth and the quantity of people who live on it, a perspective more relevant than the Malthusian prognosis. As he had written to Marx on March 30, 1880, he also hoped to develop applications of his energy accounts to different modes of production.

Podolinsky's work is important, not only in the Marxist context, but in its own right, apart from his encounters with Marx and Engels. Podolinsky is more relevant for ecological economics than Marx and Engels, because he conducted a concrete study (perhaps the first one) of "social metabolism" in terms of energy. Although he had a short life and was severely ill for his last ten years, he left a strong trace in Ukrainian federalist politics as a friend of Mikhail Drahomanov (1841–1895) and also in the *narodnik* movement against the Russian autocracy. He was trained as a medical doctor and physiologist. His work on energy and the economy was praised by Vernadsky in a section of *La Géochimie* (1924). Several authors (e.g. Felix Auerbach,

John Joly) had explained life as a process that reversed or slowed down the dissipation of energy. Vernadsky (1924:334–335) added that Podolinsky had studied the energetics of life and tried to apply his findings to the study of the economy.

The notion of a link between the use of energy and human society, in the form of "social energetics," became well established and debated in Europe around 1900. Some Marxist authors like A. Bogdanov (1873–1928) and N. I. Bukharin (1888–1938) adopted this outlook, and their work has been viewed as an anticipation of von Bertalanffy's (1968) systems theory, which grew out of the links between thermodynamics and biology (Susiluoto 1982). However, there is no line of ecological Marxist history based on quantitative studies of material and energy flows.

Otto Neurath's *Naturalrechnung*

In my 1987 book with Klaus Schlüpmann, the links between Marxism and a biophysical approach to the economy were discussed mainly by looking at Podolinsky's agricultural energetics and Engels's negative reaction to it. We also called attention to the ecological aspects of Otto Neurath's position in the Socialist Calculation debate of 1919 and the following years. Otto Neurath (1882–1945) was a logical empiricist philosopher of the Vienna Circle, but also an economist or economic historian, and a Marxist in at least two senses. First, in the Socialist Calculation debate he defended a democratically planned economy based on physical accounting in energy and material terms (*Naturalrechnung*). In this respect, he was influenced by Josef Popper-Lynkeus's and Karl Ballod-Atlanticus's quantitative "utopias." He introduced the idea of incommensurable values in the economy (Martinez-Alier 1987; O'Neill 1993, 2002, 2004; Martinez-Alier, Munda, and O'Neill 1998; Uebel 2005). Second, in the context of the Vienna Circle's project of compiling an encyclopedia of unified science, Neurath in the 1930s and 1940s defended a dialectical view of history (although he did not like the word "dialectics") as the integration of findings from different sciences regarding concrete processes and events. The findings of one science regarding a particular process or event, he argued, should not be contradicted by the findings of another science also represented in the encyclopedia, leaving things at that. Resolution of the contradiction should be attempted. To use Edward Wilson's word from our own time, "consilience" should be the rule of the encyclopedia.

To grasp the political relevance of Otto Neurath's work, one must understand that Hayek's (1979 [1952]) strong critique of "social engineering" was directed not only against thinkers of the past such as C. H. Saint-Simon, but also against authors who had a sociometabolic vision of the economy. As John O'Neill has put it, Hayek's criticism was directed at the whole tradition, now called ecological economics, which attempts to understand the ways in which economic institutions and relations are embedded within the physical world and have real physical preconditions, and which is consequently critical of economic choices founded upon purely monetary valuation (O'Neill 2002, 2004). While Patrick Geddes, Wilhelm Ostwald, Lancelot Hogben, Frederick Soddy, and Lewis Mumford were all rudely dismissed by Hayek because they viewed the economy in sociometabolic terms, Neurath's *Naturalrechnung* as a tool for democratic planning was Hayek's main target.

One is also reminded of Max Weber's critical comments on Neurath in *Economy and Society*, and even more of his critique of Wilhelm Ostwald in 1909. Ostwald, who was a well-known chemist, interpreted human history in terms of the use of energy, influencing many authors, among them Henry Adams (1838–1918), who believed that there was a "law of acceleration" of the use of energy: "The coal output of the world, speaking roughly, doubled every ten years between 1840 and 1900, in the form of utilized power, for the ton of coal yielded three or four times as much power in 1900 as in 1840." One hundred years later, research shows the close relation between economic growth and the use of energy in the economy, or rather "physical work output as distinguished from energy (exergy)" (Ayres and Warr 2003). The links between energy and economy are more relevant than ever as we anticipate the patterns of economic growth of India, China, and other countries, their effects on the prices of oil and gas, the increased human use of biomass as fuels to the detriment of other species, and the increased use of coal and its implications for the greenhouse effect.

Ostwald had proposed two simple laws, which might act in opposite directions. First, the growth of the economy implied the use of more energy, and the substitution of other forms of energy for human energy. Second, there was a trend toward higher efficiency in the transformation of energy in particular technologies and processes. Max Weber (1909) wrote an ironic review of Ostwald's views, where he defended the separation between sciences, insisting that chemists should not write on the economy. This review was praised by Hayek (1979 [1952]:171) in the 1940s. Weber's basic point (cf. Martinez-Alier 1987:ch. 12) was that economic decisions by entrepreneurs on new technologies or new products were based on costs and prices. Even if a production process was less efficient in energy terms, it would nevertheless be adopted because it was cheaper. Energy accounting was irrelevant for the economy. Weber did not question energy prices as we do now, when the greenhouse effect and the intergenerational allocation of exhaustible resources are taken into account.

Marx's doubts on the benefits of economic growth, clearly expressed in his ecological critique of capitalist agriculture, were not forgotten within the Marxist tradition, but the technological optimists, who believed in the development of the productive forces, predominated. One of the most influential technological optimists of the twentieth century was the Marxist historian of science J. D. Bernal. In the 1950s he was totally in favor of the "civil" use of nuclear energy, which Lewis Mumford was strongly critizicing at the time (Thomas et al. 1956:1147). Mumford, described by Ramachandra Guha as the "forgotten American environmentalist" (i.e. compared to G. P. Marsh, John Muir, Gifford Pinchot, Aldo Leopold, Rachel Carson, etc.), was heir to Patrick Geddes, William Morris, and John Ruskin, rather than a part of the Marxist tradition.

Ecologically Unequal Exchange

Mumford's mentor, Patrick Geddes (1854–1932), a biologist and urban planner, did not discuss Marx, but attacked neoclassical economists such as Walras because they did not count flows of energy, materials, and waste (Martinez-Alier 1987:ch. 6). Geddes (1885) constructed a sort of input-output table inspired by the *Tableau Economique* of the Physiocrat François Quesnay. The first column would contain the sources of energy as well as the materials used, not for their potential energy, but for their other properties. Energy and materials, in this model, are transformed into products through three stages: extraction, manufacture, and transport and exchange. Estimates should be made of the losses through dissipation and disintegration at each stage. The quantity of the final product (or "net" product, in Physiocratic terms) seems small in proportion to the gross quantity of potential product, but the losses at each stage are not accounted for in economic terms. The final product, in this perspective, is not "added value" at all, but the value remaining from the energy and materials that were available at the beginning.

Geddes's scheme is relevant to the attempts today to develop a theory of ecologically unequal exchange between metropolitan centers and their global peripheries. In neoclassical economics, provided that markets are competitive and ruled by supply and demand, there cannot be unequal exchange. This could only arise from monopoly or monopsony conditions, or because of noninternalized externalities or excessive discounting of the future. In an ecological-economics theory of unequal exchange, one could say that the more of the original exergy (available energy or "productive potential" in the raw materials) that has been dissipated in producing the final products or services, the higher the prices of these products or services will have to be (Hornborg 1998; Naredo and Valero 1999; Naredo 2001). This was indeed implied by Geddes with different words. Thus, Hornborg concludes, "market prices are the . . . mechanism by which world system centres extract exergy from . . . their peripheries" (Hornborg 1998:131–132).

At the beginning of European colonization, the goods imported to Europe were mainly what Immanuel Wallerstein has called "preciosities" like silver and pepper. The means of transport at the time were such that bulky trade was not possible. Such goods, characterized by high exchange value per kilogram, are still traded, of course. The effects on the ecology and human livelihood in the exporting countries might be terrible, but such trade is nevertheless marginal for the social metabolism of the importing countries. Consider, for instance, the heavy local ecological impacts of exports of ivory or tiger skins, compared to the irrelevance of such trade for the importing countries' metabolism. "Preciosities" like gold may be crucial for the relations of some social groups, but the impacts of gold extraction through opencast mining, using much water and cyanide, will be felt in distant localities, not in the importing countries.

Sugar was initially a "preciosity." It later became a bulk commodity that played a great role, as Sidney Mintz (1985) has shown, in the biometabolism of the English working class. Other bulk commodities, like guano and Chilean saltpeter between 1840 and 1914, and certainly wood, oil, and gas today, became decisive in the sociometabolism of the importing countries. In this sense, Europe is now more colonial than ever. Gasoline stations in central Europe might have signs reading "*Kolonialwaren.*" In the nineteenth and early twentieth centuries, the countries of what today is the European Union largely depended on their own coal and biomass as energy sources, but now the European Union is a large net importer of oil and gas. Taking the weight of all materials together (energy carriers, minerals, metals, biomass), the European Union imports about four times more than it exports. Meanwhile, Latin America appears to be exporting six times more than it imports (Giljum and Eisenmenger 2004). Moreover, exports from the South often carry heavier "ecological rucksacks" than its imports. This is shown by research on the energy and carbon intensity of Brazilian trade, that is, the energy dissipated and carbon dioxide produced by each dollar of exports and imports (Machado, Schaeffer, and Worrell 2001), and by research on the "environmental pollution terms of trade" for several metals (Muradian, O'Connor, and Martinez-Alier 2002). Pengue (2005) has similarly calculated the loss of nutrients, soil erosion, and "virtual water" as hidden exports in the soybean trade of Argentina.

The United States, having reached the peak of the internal Hubbert curve in the 1970s, now imports more than half the oil that it consumes. These imports are over 10 mbd, that is 500 million tons per year, or 2 tons per person per year. In comparison, research on material flow accounting shows that in the poorest countries, the total tonnage of materials mobilized internally and through trade per person per year (including biomass and all other materials) is of the order of 3 tons.

Pérez-Rincón (2006) has found that Colombia exports about 70 million tons per year compared to 10 million tons of imports. He shows that Prebisch's (1949) approach was based on the notion of a global system that defines a historical division between *periphery* countries specialized in exporting primary goods and *center* countries that export industrial goods. This specialization tends to entrench the role of peripheral regions as suppliers of resources extracted to satisfy the requirements of the center. The theory of the deterioration of terms of trade in developing countries was formulated in parallel by Prebisch (1949) and Singer (1950). The center-periphery division does not only have monetary implications for the terms of trade, but also physical implications: southern regions typically provide materials and energy so that the north can maintain and develop its socioeconomic metabolism. Such sociometabolic aspects were not yet considered by Prebisch. An "ecological Prebisch" would propose new economic instruments such as "natural capital depletion taxes." A discussion is also needed on the claims for repayment of an "ecological debt." Not all developing countries are net physical exporters: India and China are probably net importers of energy and materials, mainly because of oil imports. Internally, however, some areas in India and China provide bulk materials such as coal and other minerals.

Whatever the historically changing positions of different countries and regions, the metabolic processes that maintain the centers of the world-system are guaranteed by ecologically unequal exchange, deteriorating terms of trade for natural resources, and sometimes by military power. The deterioration of terms of trade means that an increasing quantity of primary exports is needed to obtain a given amount of imported goods. This phenomenon gave rise to the concept of economically unequal exchange and to Prebisch's doctrines, which were popular in the 1950s and 1960s. Marxists added that exports from poor countries were often more intensive in underpaid human labor than imports, so that there was an unequal exchange in terms of embodied labor (Emmanuel 1972). In this chapter, the environmental aspects have been added to the discussion on unequal exchange by looking at net physical flows and the environmental impacts of trade.

A sociometabolic perspective shows that capital accumulation does not take place on its own, and is not only based on the exploitation of labor and technical change. Industrial capitalism advances into commodity frontiers because it uses more and more materials and energy, produces more and more waste, and thus undermines not only its own conditions of production but the conditions of existence of peripheral peoples, who complain accordingly. Such ecological conflicts are becoming increasingly visible (Martinez-Alier 2002).

References

Ayres, R. U. 1989. Industrial metabolism. In *Technology and environment*, ed. J. Ausubel, 23–49. Washington, D.C.: National Academy Press.

Ayres, R. U., and B. Warr. 2003. Accounting for growth: The role of physical work. In *Advances in energy studies*, ed. S. Ulgiati. Padua: SG Editoriali.

Cipolla, C. 1974 (1962). *The economic history of world population*. 6th ed. London: Penguin.

Cleveland, C. J. 1987. Biophysical economics: Historical perspectives and current recent trends. *Ecological Modelling* 38:47–73.

Cohen, J. 1995. *How many people can the Earth support?* New York: Norton.

Cottrell, F. 1955. *Energy and society: The relations between energy, social change and economic development*. New York: McGraw-Hill.

Debeir, J. C., J. P. Deléage, and D. Hémery. 1986. *Les servitudes de la puissance: Une histoire de l'energie*. Paris: Flammarion.

Emmanuel, A. 1972. *Unequal exchange: A study of the imperialism of free trade*. New York: Monthly Review Press.

Engels, F. 1972 (1925). *Dialektik der Natur*. Marx Engels Werke, vol. 20. Berlin: Dietz Verlag.

Fischer-Kowalski, M. 1998. Society's metabolism: The intellectual history of material flow analysis, Part I, 1860–1970. *Journal of Industrial Ecology* 2 (1): 61–78.

Fischer-Kowalski, M., and W. Huettler. 1998. Society's metabolism: The intellectual history of material flow analysis, Part II, 1970–1998. *Journal of Industrial Ecology* 2 (4): 107–136.

Fischer-Kowalski, M. and C. Amann. 2001. Beyond IPAT and Kuznets curves: Globalization as a vital factor in analysing the environmental impact of socio-economic metabolism. *Population and Environment* 23 (1):7–49.

Foster, J. B. 2000. *Marx's ecology: Materialism and nature*. New York: Monthly Review Press.

Fluck, R. C., and D. C. Baird. 1980. *Agricultural energetics*. Westport, Conn.: AVI.

Geddes, P. 1885. An analysis of the principles of economics. Proceedings of the Royal Society of Edinburgh, 17 March, 7 April, 16 June, 7 July 1884. London: William and Norgate.

Giampietro, M. 2003. *Multiple-scale integrated assessment of agroecosystems.* Boca Raton, Fla.: CRC Press.

Giljum, S., and N. Eisenmenger. 2004. North-South trade and the distribution of environmental goods and burdens. *Journal of Environment and Development* 13 (1):73–100.

Gootenberg, P. 1993. *Imagining development: Economic ideas in Peru's "fictitious prosperity" of guano, 1840–80.* Berkeley: University of California Press.

Gordon, L. 1976. *Woman's body, woman's right: A social history of birth control in America.* New York: Grossman.

Haberl, H. 2001. The energetic metabolism of societies, pt. 1, Accounting concepts, the energetic metabolism of societies, pt. 2, Empirical examples. *Journal of Industrial Ecology* 5 (2):11–33.

Hall, C., C. J. Cleveland, and R. Kaufman. 1986. *Energy and resources quality: The ecology of the economic process.* New York: Wiley.

Hayek, F. A. 1979 (1952). *The counter-revolution of science: Studies on the abuse of reason.* 2nd ed. Indianapolis: Liberty.

Hornborg, A. 1998. Toward an ecological theory of unequal exchange: Articulating world system theory and ecological economics. *Ecological Economics* 25 (1): 127–136.

Kormondy, E. J. 1965. *Readings in ecology.* Englewood Cliffs, N.J.: Prentice-Hall.

Leach, G. 1975. *Energy and food production.* Guildford, U.K.: IPC Science and Technology Press.

Lenin, V. I. 1913. The working class and neomalthusianism. *Pravda* 137 (June 16).

Machado, G., R. Schaeffer, and E. Worrell. 2001. Energy and carbon embodied in the international trade of Brazil: An input-output approach. *Ecological Economics* 39 (3): 409–424.

Martinez-Alier, J. 1987. *Ecological economics: Energy, environment and society,* with K. Schlüpmann. Oxford, U.K.: Blackwell.

———, ed. 1995. *Los principios de la economia ecologica.* Madrid: Argentaria-Visor.

———. 2002. The environmentalism of the poor: A study of ecological conflicts and valuation. Cheltenham, U.K., and Northampton, Mass.: Edward Elgar.

Martinez-Alier, J., G. Munda, and J. O'Neill. 1998. Weak comparability of values as a foundation for ecological economics. *Ecological Economics* 26:277–286.

Marx, K. 1969 (1867). *Das Kapital.* Vol. 1. Frankfurt, Vienna, and Berlin: Ullstein Verlag.

Marx, K., and F. Engels. 1976. *Lettres sur les sciences de la nature et les mathematiques.* Paris: Mercure de France.

Masjuan, E. 2000. *La ecología humana y el anarquismo ibérico: El urbanismo "orgánico" o ecológico, el neo-Malthusianismo y el naturismo social.* Barcelona: Icaria.

Mayer, J. R. 1845. *Die organische Bewegung in ihrem Zusammenhang mit dem Stoffwechsel.* Heilbronn. (Published also in *Die Mechanik der Wärme: gesammelte Schriften.* Stuttgart, 1893; and in W. Ostwald, *Klassiker der exacten Naturwissenschaften.* Leipzig: Akademische Verlag, 1911.)

McNeill, J. R. 2000. *Something new under the sun: An environmental history of the twentieth-century world.* New York: Norton.

Mintz, S. 1985. *Sweetness and power: The place of sugar in modern history.* New York: Penguin.

Moleschott, J. 1850. *Lehre der Nahrungsmittel: Für das Volk.* Enke, Erlangen.

———. 1851. *Physiologie des Stoffwechsels in Planzen und Thieren.* Erlangen.

———. 1852. *Der Kreislauf des Lebens, Von Zabern.* Mainz.

Mouchot, A. 1879 (1869). *La chaleur solaire et ses applications industrielles.* 2nd ed. Paris: Gauthier-Villars.

Muradian, R., M. O'Connor, and J. Martinez-Alier. 2002. Embodied pollution in trade: Estimating the "environmental load displacement" of industrialized countries. *Ecological Economics* 41 (1): 51–67.

Naredo, J. M. 2001. Quantifying natural capital: Beyond monetary value. In *The sustainability of long-term growth: Socioeconomic and ecological perspectives*, ed. M. Munasinghe and O. Sunkel. Cheltenham, U.K., and Northampton, Mass.: Elgar.

Naredo, J. M., and A. Valero. 1999. *Desarrollo económico y deterioro ecológico.* Madrid: Argentaria-Visor.

Odum, H. T. 1971. *Environment, power and society.* New York: Wiley.

O'Neill, J. 1993. *Ecology, policy and politics.* London: Routledge.

———. 2002. Socialist calculation and environmental valuation: Money, markets and ecology. *Science and Society* 66 (1): 137–151.

———. 2004. Ecological economics and the politics of knowledge: The debate between Hayek and Neurath. *Cambridge Journal of Economics* 28:431–447.

Pengue, W. A. 2005. Transgenic crops in Argentina: The ecological and social debt. *Bulletin of Science, Technology and Society* 25 (4): 314–322.

Pérez-Rincón, M. A. 2006. Colombian international trade from a physical perspective: Towards an ecological "Prebisch thesis." *Ecological Economics*, in press.

Pfaundler, L. 1902. Die Weltwirtschaft im Lichte der Physik. *Deutsche Revue* 22 (April–June): 29–38, 171–182.

Pimentel, D., et al. 1973. Food production and the energy crisis. *Science* 182:443–449.

Pimentel, D., and M. Pimentel. 1979. *Food, energy and society.* London: Arnold.

Podolinsky, S. A. 1880a. Le socialisme et la théorie de Darwin. *Revue Socialiste*, March 1880.

———. 1880b. Trud cheloveka i ego otnoshenie k raspredeleniiu energii [Human labor and its relations to the distribution of energy]. *Slovo* 4 (5): 135–211. (German translation, Menschliche Arbeit und Einheit der Kraft, *Die Neue Zeit*, vol. 1, March-April 1883; Spanish translation in Martinez-Alier 1995.)

Prebisch, R. 1949. *El desarrollo económico de la América Latina y algunos de sus principales problemas.* Santiago: ECLAC. (*The economic development of Latin America and its principal problems.* New York: UNECLAC, 1950.)

Rappaport, R. 1967. *Pigs for the ancestors: Ritual in the ecology of a New Guinea people.* New Haven, Conn.: Yale University Press.

Ronsin, F. 1980. *La grève des ventres: Propagande néo-malthusienne et baisse de la natalité en France, 19–20 siècles.* Paris: Aubier-Montagne.

Schmidt, A. 1978. *Der Begriff der Natur in der Lehre von Marx.* 3rd ed. Frankfurt-Cologne: EVA.

Sieferle, R. P. 1982. *Der unterirdische Wald: Energiekrise und industrielle Revolution.* Munich: Beck. (English trans., Cambridge, U.K.: White Horse Press, 2001.)

Singer, H. W. 1950. The distribution of the gains between investing and borrowing countries. *American Economic Review* 40:473–485.

Susiluoto, I. 1982. *The origins and development of systems thinking in the Soviet Union: Political and philosophical controversies from Bogdanov and Bukharin to present-day reevaluations.* Helsinki: Suomalainen Tiedeakatemia.

Thomas, W. L., C. O. Sauer, M. Bates, and L. Mumford, eds. 1956. *Man's role in changing the face of the earth.* Chicago: University of Chicago Press.

Uebel, T. E. 2005. Incommensurability, ecology and planning: Neurath in the socialist calculation debate, 1919–1928. *History of Political Economy* 37 (2): 309–342.

Vernadsky, V. 1924. *La géochimie.* Paris: Alcan.

Von Bertalanffy, L. 1968. *General system theory.* Harmondsworth, U.K.: Penguin.

Weber, M. 1909. Energetische kulturtheorien. *Archiv für Sozialwissenschaft und Sozialpolitik* 29. Repr., Max Weber, *Gessamelte Aufsätze zur Wissenschatslehre,* 3rd ed. Tübingen: Mohr (Paul Siebeck), 1968.

White, L. 1943. Energy and the evolution of culture. *American Anthropologist* 45 (3): 335–356.

———. 1959. The energy theory of cultural development. In *Readings in anthropology,* vol. 2, ed. M. H. Fried, 139–146. New York: Thomas Y. Cromwell.

Natural Values and the Physical Inevitability of Uneven Development under Capitalism

12

STEPHEN G. BUNKER

EXPLANATIONS OF UNEVEN DEVELOPMENT under capitalism routinely invoke different rates of capital accumulation and differential productivity of labor across economic sectors and geographical regions, ignoring that uneven development also responds to immutable physical laws. Production involves the transformation of matter and energy, which can neither be created nor destroyed and whose transformation always creates entropy, or the loss of potential energy to kinetic energy or heat (Bunker 1985; Martinez-Alier 1987; Hornborg 2001). Social production, in which labor redirects the transformation of matter and energy, requires extraction, in which labor appropriates naturally produced material and energetic forms. The productivity of labor can only be increased by simultaneously increasing the appropriation and transformation of energy stored in material forms produced in nature, that is, without human intervention or direction.

Extraction, Production, and Uneven Development

In simple economies, extraction and production often occur in close proximity; individuals and groups typically engage in both activities. As social production expands under capitalism, both the amount and the variety of material and energetic forms consumed in its concentrated industrial loci increase. Natural production, however, does not increase or diversify at the same rate as social production. Indeed, many particular material forms are naturally produced only within particular ecosystems in specific locations, and extraction usually leads to a depletion or reduction of natural products

239

in these specific locations (Jalee 1969; Caldwell 1977; Bunker 1985, 1992; Bunker and Ciccantell 2003).

Economies of scale reduce the unit costs of production through the use of more powerful and efficient technologies. The new technologies are costly to implement, and must operate at or near full capacity to return the investments they require. Their maintenance and repair may require special machines and labor skills. All of these conditions tend increasingly to agglomerate production in concentrated spaces as technology becomes more efficient and costlier. The new technologies can only achieve their intended results, though, by transforming more matter and energy into more commodities. In addition to needing greater volumes of raw materials, these more powerful technologies tend to require raw materials with more precisely specified physical and chemical characteristics and hence only available in a reduced number of specific locations.

Productive expansion can only occur, therefore, through the proliferation of extractive economies in geologically and climatologically distinct ecosystems dispersed at greater distances across broader space (cf. Lenin 1965 (1916); Luxemburg 1968; Bunker and Ciccantell 2005). In this sense the expansion of industrial production entails, as a physical necessity, the widening spatial and temporal separation of extraction and production.

Historically, the instruments of trade and of war, and particularly the means of transport they required, together with the growing power and consumption of classes that organized and dominated trade and violence, vastly expanded the need for raw materials. The search for raw materials, in turn, drove the expansion of early states and empires and extended trading networks (Ekholm and Friedman 1982:97; Diakonoff 1969:28, 1982:78; McNeill 1963:71–74; Adams 1977:165–174; Drennan 1984; Chaudhuri 1985:203–204). Nonetheless, with the notable exceptions of timber for ships, metals for arms, and stones for building, most of the matter socially transformed was extracted close at hand. It was not until the conquest of the New World that extracted matter in large quantities was transported between widely distant regions, as gold and silver, cacao, animal oils, and spices fueled the surge of commerce in bulkier, less precious commodities, such as fish, wheat, and wood, that enabled Holland to rise to trade dominance by becoming the most efficient carrier in the sixteenth-century world. Commerce in low-value/high-volume goods surged again as Britain developed a coal-based industry in the seventeenth century that by the eighteenth century had spawned the Industrial Revolution and the internalization of production that it made possible (Arrighi 1994).

The emergence and evolution of the capitalist mode of production set in motion the social processes that made the progressive spatial separation of extraction and production physically inevitable. Central among these processes was the shift from organic to inorganic and from vegetable to metal as the most voluminously used forms of energy and matter in social production. This shift provided both the means and the motives for accelerating economies of scale in extraction, in transport, and in production. Increasingly powerful technologies of smelting and casting made possible larger and stronger constructions than possible with woods, and greater speeds and forces and straighter lines of sail than possible with wind. Where vegetable fibers required separate space for each plant unit as it grew, so that increased production occupied more horizontal ground, minerals accumulated and were stored vertically (Mumford 1961; Hugill 1994). Mineral extraction was thus far more amenable to technical economies of scale, though mining becomes more expensive as a deepening mine engenders progressively more difficult conditions for labor, including the need to pump water out and air in. Lifting weight vertically is obviously more costly than moving it horizontally. On the other hand, the growing demand for metals that the new economies of scale made possible, and the utility of metals for constructing technical fixes for the problems that deep mining encountered, generated innovations such as the steam engine. Many of these could be applied directly to transport and production as well as to extraction, and so drove simultaneously further economies of scale, increased levels of production and consumption, and even greater volumes of extraction and transport.

The transition to metals, accelerated by the ease of national access to coal, started in Britain as early as the seventeenth century, but it was not until the nineteenth century that the technologies developed and the capital accumulated in industrial production fed back into the rapid advances in fossil-fuel driven transport in steel-constructed vessels and frames on steel-constructed infrastructure. These developments so reduced transport costs that a wide range of material and energetic forms once too bulky for profitable exchange could now move, in large quantities, across great distances. This, in turn, allowed for tremendous increases in the mass of matter and energy transformed by industry. It also intensified its inherent tendencies to spatial concentration.

An important difference leading to uneven development is that the dynamics of scale function inversely in extractive and productive economies. The forces of production develop progressively in industrial systems because the unit costs of commodity production tend to fall as the scale of production increases. In extractive systems, unit costs tend to rise as the scale of extraction increases. Extraction usually starts by appropriating the most accessible sources. Greater amounts of any extractive commodity can be obtained only by exploiting increasingly distant or difficult sources. Though technological innovation may reduce costs of some extractive processes in the short run, unit costs of extraction continue to rise in the long run. Therefore, when extractive systems respond to increased external demand or internal pressures to increase profits, they tend to impoverish themselves, (1) by depleting easily accessible non-self-renewing resources or (2) by exploiting the most proximate self-renewing resources beyond their capacities for regeneration, thereby (3) requiring more labor and capital per unit extracted and so (4) forcing the unit cost of the extracted resources to rise so high that the development of synthetic or cultivated alternatives in other regions becomes cost effective. Alternately, technologies or products using other raw materials from other regions may become competitive in the productive economy.

The rising unit costs of extraction make extractive economies highly unstable: if high demand and expanded scale increase unit costs of extraction by depleting the most accessible resources, entrepreneurs will either search for more accessible sources in other regions or attempt to domesticate or to synthesize agricultural or industrial substitutes and to transform the extractive economy into a productive one. Capitalism generates the research and technical capacities required for plant domestication and transfer and for synthetic substitutions of vegetable matter. Brockway (1979) has shown how the development of the botanical and related sciences in nineteenth-century Britain responded to rising unit costs in Latin American extractive economies. British capital and the British state promoted the domestication, genetic adaptation, and transfer of cultigens extracted there to Asian and African colonies where the British controlled the land and labor necessary to transform them into plantation crops. Successful transformation to a plantation system brought rubber and chinchona into a mode of production in which increased scale progressively reduced unit costs to levels at which extractive systems could no longer compete. These plantation systems were eventually impoverished by industrial production of synthetic substitutes. Modern searches for oil substitutes—whether nuclear, solar, or agricultural—respond similarly to rising capital and labor costs as the most accessible oil sources are depleted.

Special Cases: The Developmental Paths of Particular Extractive Economies

Some extractive economies have replicated the integration of extraction and production which characterized precapitalist and early capitalist economies. The potential for such development depends in part on the spatial location of the resource, in part on its natural, or physical characteristics, and in part on the degree of capital concentration and intensification in the economic sector that uses or consumes the resource (North 1961). Because of the general tendency for capital to concentrate and intensify in all productive sectors over time, and for materials to be used in more and more costly machines, these possibilities for productive economies to emerge from extraction diminish as capitalism evolves (Mandel 1975). Capital accumulation and technological advances in productive economies also work directly to restrict such possibilities; as transport technologies improve and lower the costs for bulk movements of matter, the marginal price advantage that preliminary processing to reduce bulk provides to the extractive region is pushed back toward pure extraction (cf. de Silva 1982:78). Even the exceptional cases of production emerging from extraction illustrate these principles.

The development of a ship-building industry in colonial New England resulted from the coincidence of that region's relative advantages in two extractive industries—fishing and lumbering—with the burgeoning triangular trade between the West Indies, Britain, and North America (Clark 1916; Shepherd and Walton 1972; both cited in Chase-Dunn 1980). Chase-Dunn points out that the development of the shipping industry occurred during a period of rapid expansion in the entire world economy and of intense political struggle in the more advanced industrial centers in Europe. Later, the development of steamships—a new technology requiring a greater concentration of capital and articulation with a longer, more complex chain of labor and material transformations—returned the advantage in ship-building to Britain (Bunker and Cicantell 2005). In the meantime, though, productive economies had emerged, and sufficient industrial capital had been accumulated for productive growth to continue in America. The linked industries that developed—sugar refineries, distilleries, lumber and flour mills, tin plate and bottling plants—were not so capital intensive as to be beyond the reach of rapidly accumulating local capitals (Emmanuel 1972; de Silva 1982:76; Meinig 1986; Parker 1991). Mandel (1975:50–52) characterizes this period, especially from 1848 to the 1860s, as a time in which capital accumulation in Great Britain, France, and Belgium had not yet proceeded sufficiently to establish factories in other parts of the world and transport was still too costly to allow the bulk shipment of cheap goods. He concludes that "those economies which were themselves pressing toward a capitalist mode of production were on the whole left unlimited scope for primitive accumulation of indigenous national capital." This was clearly as much the case for nascent North American industries as it was for the Italian, Russian, Japanese, and Spanish economies that Mandel describes in these passages.

De Silva (1982) suggests that a burgeoning domestic market for manufactured goods complemented primitive accumulation in North America. Chase-Dunn (1980) argues that during this period of North American industrial development, European immigrants brought with them a steady influx of technical knowledge and skills from the most dynamic industrial economies and that commonalities of language and culture facilitated access to the scientific and technical knowledge generated by European development. Parker (1991) shows how the American Midwest's political economy evolved in the interaction between these immigrant groups' different technical and cultural attributes and the challenges and opportunities presented by the natural environment.

Once productive industrialization commences, and as it expands through multisectoral linkages, access to natural products can provide it with a series of savings that make local industries more competitive and allow for higher wages. These high wages, in turn, amplify the local market and provide expansive opportunities to realize surplus value though growing industrial production.

The rush of men seeking gold in California during this same period had similar effects there. Numerous small capitals and technical skills were carried there, as most of these prospectors had to pay their own way. The resulting demand for implements, services, shelter, and so forth set up a huge network of lateral linkages, which the agricultural and forestry potential of the region helped to maintain. Paul (1963:15–16), who estimates that the gold rush took the non-Indian population of California from 14,000 in 1848 to 380,000 in 1860, calculates that even at the height of the boom, less than half of the men were actually working in the mines. He quotes an early miner who spoke of "the crowds of lawyers, small tradesmen, mechanics, and others who swarm in every little camp, even of the most humble description, soliciting the patronage of the public." Paul goes on to suggest that the miner might well have included the "wondrous" numbers of hotels, restaurants, brothels, and "hurdy-gurdy" houses.

Farming and forestry developed rapidly to provide the raw materials that this population, and the mining infrastructure itself, required. Later, high wages and the depletion of placer deposits and easily accessible lodes fostered more mechanical, capital-intensive means of mining. These required elaborate sluices and metal pipes; more sophisticated means of industrial production began to emerge to meet this demand.

Agriculture and forestry have survived the decline of gold mining and continue to complement the industrial economies of the American West Coast. Extractive economies, however, are far less articulated with production in the former mining areas of the southwest and northwest, which did not offer California's favorable combinations of good soils, irrigable valleys, and easy communication.

The development of industrial production along different parts of the Canada-U.S. border out of earlier extractive economies reflected not only the extraordinarily favorable natural transport facilities of these regions, but also the fact that locally dominant classes were able to accumulate the capital and to develop the technologies necessary to control the transformation of the materials extracted—ore, coal, and timber. The technologies and markets for manganese and bauxite, in contrast, are not nearly as accessible to populations in the Brazilian Amazon, nor has the productive transformation of tin, copper, or antimony been accessible to the Andean and African populations that have mined it. The steady rise in the scale of industrial and transport technology, and in the organic composition of capital, progressively reduces the opportunities to develop production out of extraction.

It is also possible that the national state may intervene to redirect profits from extraction into production (Becker 1985; Stephens and Stephens 1985; Coronil 1997), but usually this involves taxing the extractive region's economy in favor of a widely distant productive region, as occurs in Brazil (Bunker 1985) and South Africa (Wolpe 1980; Legassick 1977). This essentially amounts to a double extraction, first as raw materials, second as revenue, from the extractive regional economy, and simply aggravates its impoverishment (Bunker 2000).

There are, however, especially in Europe and America, cases of successful transition from extraction to production. Until the resources extracted are depleted, the extractive economy located near a productive center may enjoy many of the latter's inherent locational advantages. It tends to be less exploitative of labor as a result and therefore tends more to capital-intensive technologies and environmental safeguards. The off-shore oil wells near Santa Barbara, California, in recent years, and the Sacramento Valley farmers' effective resistance to the environmentally destructive hydraulic mining practiced by large corporations in the 1880s (Kelley 1956, 1959) provide examples of how the development of productive economies can limit the deleterious effects of extractive economies.

If farmers lack the political power and linkages necessary to confront extractive capitalists, however, the destruction of their environmental base can make them dependent on extractive wages, as happened in Peru's Cerro de Pasco mine (Flores Galindo 1974) and in Appalachian Kentucky (Gaventa 1980).

Cases of production emerging from extraction, whether in the central economy or in the semiperipheral economies associated with dependent development (Evans 1979) finally mean that matter and energy from other extractive economies now flow toward an emerging center of production. Uneven development continues, though its loci shift.

Productive Expansion, Extractive Decline, and the Problem of Value

Within any ecosystem and for any species, there are rates of harvest that, if performed without destroying or too greatly reducing other species, would allow indefinitely sustained yield. The expansive logic of capitalist production, however, usually precludes such careful calculation of harvest rates. Instead, extraction rates respond to opportunities for profit set by production-driven demand. Pressures to maximize profits from extraction, therefore, typically lead to extraction rates that cannot be sustained, so the extraction of both nonrenewable and renewable resources tends to impoverish their regional economies.

The combination of (1) factors that lead to the eventual impoverishment or collapse of extractive economies in specific regions or subregions with (2) factors that prevent extractive economies based on remote resources from sharing with other enterprise the locational advantages of population centers and a socially built environment creates cycles in which costly infrastructure and human settlements are periodically abandoned or suffer severe reduction in economic utility. Economic and social development based on extractive economies thus tends to be discontinuous in time and space. Production systems build a social and physical environment shared by multiple enterprises. These enterprises suffer the effects of technological and demand changes at different times and rates, so a production system as a whole tends to be more stable and continuous than an extractive one. Production systems' locational advantages of shared labor pools and infrastructure are much more likely to allow adaptation to changing technologies and markets. The fact that most of the infrastructure developed for extractive export economies is specific to the requirements of resource removal and transport exacerbates their loss of utility as the extracted resource is exhausted or substituted (Barham and Coomes 1994).

Predominantly extractive economies disrupt human communities and the natural environment in ways that destroy values and limit productivity in both. Because extraction forces out or prevents the social and political articulation of extractive labor with other organizational or economic forms, local populations have no effective means to oppose or resist entrepreneurs or dependent national states whose quest for rapid profits is realized through the destruction of local productive systems—natural and social. Thus, extractive economies tend toward eventual stagnation, broken by new extractive cycles if new demands emerge for other material resources available in the region (Bunker 1985, 2003; Karl 1997; Coronil 1997).

The flow of matter and energy from extractive economies and its heat-releasing conversion in socially manipulated transformation adds organic and inorganic matter that disrupts the natural energetic cycles in the productive economies' environments. Capitalist expansion accelerates this process. This disruption imposes costs on the productive society as a whole rather than directly on private capital, but it does raise the costs of production and reproduction. Solutions to these disruptions require intensified human intervention in the maintenance of the built environment. This intervention consumes further amounts of matter and energy, and so contributes to the acceleration of extraction. Ironically, it also provides opportunities for private profit.

Conventional theories of value, production, and exchange, and the models of development that draw on those theories, have not adequately recognized the absolute physical dependence of production on extraction or the inevitable loss of value in the extractive economy (Martinez-Alier 1987). Nor have they accounted for the ways that the extraction, transport, and use of natural resources and the social formations that emerge around these processes affect the subsequent developmental potential of the environments from which resources are extracted. Instead, most theorists of development have attempted to extend models derived from systems of industrial production to nonindustrial systems for which they have only limited relevance. Socioeconomic models of uneven development and unequal exchange based exclusively on comparisons of labor productivity or labor values cannot adequately explain the underdevelopment of extractive economies, because the exploitation of natural resources uses and destroys values that cannot be calculated merely in terms of labor or capital.

Any theory of value based exclusively on labor requires concepts of abstract labor that are theoretically coherent only within a fully capitalist economy (see de Janvry 1981:79). Such economies cannot exist in isolation, or as closed systems, because of their dependence on resource extraction from naturally occurring transformations of matter and energy. Theories of value based exclusively on labor neglect the usefulness to continued social reproduction of energy transformations in the natural environment (Bunker 1986). They cannot account for the uneven development and accumulation in the value of the ideas, beliefs, and information that underlie the divergent human social organization in productive and extractive economies (Hornborg 2001).

The Limitations of a Labor Theory of Value

Capitalism as a system produces an ideology that focuses on the value of labor, as this value fundamentally affects both the cost of production and the potential for consumption. The individual capitalist can legitimate his control and increase his profits to the extent that prevailing ideologies relegate natural products to the status of a free gift or a right of property (Wittfogel 1985 [1929]:40). Marx's labor theory of value is an appropriate description of value as it is socially conceived under capitalism. It is obviously crucial to understand how this social attribution works within the capitalist system. We must be very careful, however, not to allow a theory of exchange value produced and maintained by the predominant mode of production within specific social formations to become a general analytical standard of value.

Marx was clearly aware of the central importance of nature, but his ideas on nature remained for the most part abstract, limited to scattered references rather than systematically developed. Schmidt (1971), Smith (1984), Foster (2000), Moore (2003) and, much earlier, Wittfogel (1985 [1929]) have pulled these references together sufficiently to dismiss the still current notion that Marx was unconcerned with environmental processes (see Redclift 1984), but we must acknowledge that he wrote without the benefit of much that has been discovered about ecosystems.

Marx carefully limited his discussion of value, making it clear that both his labor theory of value and his theory of rent are impossible where "capital has not yet completely, or even sporadically, brought social labor under its control" (1967: vol. 3, 783, 787n). My argument is not so much against Marx's carefully delimited labor theory of value, as against the unqualified use that theorists of underdevelopment have made of it in contexts other than that for which it was intended. A brief review of Marx's writings on value shows why his theory does not work for analyses of extractive exports to an industrially dominated world market.

Marx included "natural forces" or "natural powers" (see Wittfogel 1985 [1929]) in his concept of use-value, although at times he called them also means of production, depending on the way they enter the production process. Neither formulation, however, adequately accounts for the social and environmental costs of extractive export economies, because Marx did not elaborate a comprehensive theory of how use-values are produced. Rather, he consistently subordinated use-value to the labor values incorporated in commodities. "A thing can have use-value, without having value. This is the case whenever its utility to man is not due to labour. Such are air, virgin soil, natural meadows, etc." (1967: vol. 1, 40) even though "the increased productiveness of the labour used . . . arises from the greater natural productiveness of labour bound up with the application of a force of nature" (1967: vol. 3, 645). The notion that use-value is not value and that only human labor incorporated in commodities creates value appears also in his discussion of natural forces and resources as means of production:

> The means of production never transfer more value to the product than they themselves lose during the labour-process by the destruction of their own value. If such an instrument has no value to lose, in other words, if it is not the product of human labour, it transfers no value to the commodity. In this class are included all means of production supplied by Nature without human assistance, such as land, wind, water, metals in situ, and timber in virgin forests. (1967: vol. 1, 204)

The implication of these passages should be clear: the attribution of value exclusively to labor is definitional, and therefore arbitrary. Furthermore, the definition is useful only from the perspective of capitalism as a system into which raw materials are incorporated through the mechanism of rent, which is merely a social relation of appropriation, and does not specify the processes that actually produce the use-values appropriated by private ownership.

Capitalism is the only mode of production based completely on the production and circulation of exchange values, therefore value in Marx's terms can only occur in capitalist modes of production. Natural resources can be monopolized. This monopoly creates the basis of rent. Rent assigns prices to natural resources, but the resources themselves have no value. Their prices siphon off surplus profits, but they remain outside the essential labor-capital relation to which Marx applies his theory of value. As a result, the argument that only labor creates value is tautological within Marx's particular set of definitional assumptions.

These assumptions work well to describe the relation of labor to capital within a system conceived as closed, and whose laws of motion depend completely on the production and circulation of commodities. It is impossible, however, to use this particular, and arbitrary, definition of value to calculate the inequality of exchange that a raw-material exporting region suffers. Resource extraction imposes demonstrable environmental losses; these losses demonstrably limit the future productivity of human labor, whether it is incorporated in use-values or commodities exchanged for profit. To calculate the effects of these losses, we must be able to attribute some value to them, quite independent of labor. To understand their value, we must know how they are produced. Hence the notion of value produced in nature is an essential complement to the concept of values produced by labor.

Marx was generally aware of this problem, but his formulation of value does not solve it. He recognized that labor productivity depended on the "power of nature," and that extraction diminished this power. He distinguished extractive economies as a special problem in his general labor theory of value, (see, e.g. 1967: vol. 1, 40, 104, 181) and tried to deal with them in his theory of rent. Nwoke (1984:47) describes Marx's theory of rent as a necessary qualification of the law of value in extractive economies:

> In essence, the law of value is, according to Marx, subject to two modifications in the extractive sphere. First, the impossibility of generalizing the productivity of labor, which in this sphere depends on the power of nature, therefore leads to the limitation of competition. . . . Second, landed property's rent will set limits to competition in the extractive sphere.

The values extracted from nature, however, cannot be subsumed within the concept of rent, because rent refers only to the monetary form of their appropriation into capitalist production and cannot describe the process by which they are produced. Furthermore, rent, as Marx described it, depends on property relations and institutions characteristic of capitalism, and much extraction occurs in regions where these relations and institutions have not emerged, and indeed often cannot emerge because of the constant disruption of social organization in extractive economies (Bunker 1985).

Rent theory is only appropriate to analyze the relation of extraction to production where both occur together in capitalist social formations. Pure extractive economies are the extreme case of human appropriation of natural values, but many apparently productive processes include elements of extraction. Different agricultural and pastoral economies, for example, present a gradient of the proportions of human labor and natural values incorporated into the final product, ranging from the minimal modifications of the natural environment in ecologically complex swidden systems to the energy-intensive manipulations and simplifications of bounded ecosystems in large-scale monocropping systems. Forestry exhibits similar gradations. Factories need air, space, and water even in highly capitalist economies. Much of social production continues to entail complex and variable combinations of natural and labor values. Rent theory explains the portion appropriated by owners in capitalist modes of production, but even there leaves out the question of how natural values are produced.

In short, Marx's labor theory of value is an elegant definitional device that works well within the problem Marx set himself, that is analysis of the capitalist mode of production of exchange values as a closed system. The assumption that the system is closed, that is, that all values are produced within the capitalist mode of production, is a heuristic device that diverges from historical reality (Marx 1967: vol. 3, 782–788) and from the physical fact that much of the matter and energy whose expanded and accelerated consumption is necessary for capitalism's "laws of motion" come from non-capitalist extractive economies.

The diversity and interdependence of material and energetic forms force us to recognize that there is no possible unidimensional calculus of value. The long-term maintenance of human life depends on energy transformation processes of which we are not yet aware. We cannot yet measure all of the complex energy exchanges in the biotic chains that make up the ecosystems in which we participate. Nor can the value of human organization and knowledge that emerge from our earlier uses of matter and energy be directly measured. Even without a unidimensional calculus of value, however, we can analyze the very different potentials for social organizational, infrastructural, and economic development in the societies that concentrate energy from outside and the societies that lose energy to them. We can then also explain how the dominance of productive systems accelerates extraction and ecological destruction.

Extraction, Value, and Unequal Exchange

Consideration of naturally as well as socially produced values can solve some of the problems in theories of unequal exchange. These theories have distorted Marx's more careful analyses. Emmanuel (1972) invokes wage differentials; Mandel (1975) stresses the differential productivity of labor; de Janvry and Kramer (1979) criticize both; but in one way or another all focus on inequalities of labor incorporated in exchange values even when they discuss raw materials exports.

The fundamental values in timber, minerals, oil, fish, and so forth are predominantly in the good itself, rather than in the incorporated labor. Additional value is created when these materials are transformed by labor. The important point, however, is that this additional value is generally realized in the industrial center, rather than in the extractive periphery. Thus, there are multiple inequalities in international exchange. One results from the differential wages of labor. Another emerges from the transfer of the natural value in the raw, unlabored resources from periphery to center. Another resides in the full realization of exchange value in the center, rather than in peripheral sources of material commodities. The ultimate inequality is in the thermodynamic requirement of a reduction of natural and social productivity in the extractive economy in order to sustain the growth of social productivity in the industrial economy. The use of labor as a standard of value for unequal exchange ignores the multiple inequalities inherent in the subordination of extractive economies to productive economies when value in nature is appropriated in one region and labor value is incorporated in another.

We must consider the effects of the exploitation of labor and the exploitation of entire ecosystems as separate but complementary phenomena, both of which affect the development of particular regions. We can therefore reject Amin's (1977) arguments that unequal exchange occurred only after center wages started to rise above subsistence levels as the result of imperialist strategies that opened world markets and world sources of raw materials for capitalist exploitation. The appropriation of values in nature from the periphery initiated unequal exchange between regions and ecosystems long before the rise of wages and the expansion of consumer demand in the core. Examination of the ecological effects of the ivory trade (Soremekun 1977) and of the demographic effects of the slave trade on large parts of Africa (Rodney 1972) demonstrates the impact of exploitation between "geographic" areas, as well as between classes, on the evolution of unequal exchange.

Most of the theorists of unequal exchange have not understood how carefully Marx pointed out that the quantity and quality of "natural forces" affect the productivity of social labor. Instead of trying to extend or systematize Marx's incomplete discussion, they have ignored the limitations he himself recognized, and have attempted to use an unqualified labor theory of value to explain how commerce between capitalist and noncapitalist social formations leads to the underdevelopment of the latter.

The central flaw in labor-based theories of unequal exchange is that they must finally assume reciprocal, but unbalanced, flows of comparable exchange values. Exchange values cannot be compared between extractive and productive economies, because they are neither produced nor appropriated in the same way. In the capitalist economy, exchange value is produced in the relation between capitalist and labor. In Marx's definition all exchange value is borne by use-values; because all production is assumed to be commoditized, the use-values are produced in order to realize exchange values. In the extractive economy organized to export natural products, the production of the use-value itself occurs in nature, not through labor. Labor is organized to appropriate this use-value from nature. Exchange value is produced by extractive labor only in the removal and transport of the use-value. Transport does not add to use-value, it simply changes the locus in which this value is realized, which means that it is lost in one place and gained in the other (cf. Harvey 1982; Smith 1984:81–83). The fundamental separation of the production and realization of use-values and exchange values in extractive economies is therefore a different process and a different relation than their fundamental articulation in productive economies. The attempt to transpose Marx's theory to the problem of the despoliation of those parts of the periphery that provide the core with raw materials shackles and distorts the analysis of uneven development and legitimates capitalism's continued undervaluation and waste of peripheral ecosystems.

Conclusion

The world economy functions through exchange, and the capitalist system based on the production of exchange values affects the noncapitalist economies with which it is articulated through exchange. A theory of value grounded in the assumption that labor is directed to the production of exchange values works well for a systematic analysis of capitalism as a closed system, but it cannot work for either natural or social systems in which all or a major part of production is not directly aimed at exchange, or clearly, in a system in which production is not intentionally directed. To understand the world economy and its future, we need to explain systematically not just the production of exchange values, but also the production of use-values. This requires perceiving nature not as object, subject, or plastic source of raw materials and natural forces, but as process and system of production that follows its own laws and forces society to do the same, even though social intentionality and directed cooperation create society's distinct productive dynamic.

To understand the world economy as a whole and uneven development within it, we must generate models of natural production that allow us to trace the multiple interacting effects of natural and social systems. In other words, we must accord to the production of use-values a theoretical elaboration equal to that which Marx and others have developed for the production of exchange values. Only then can we understand the full complexity, interaction, and interdependence of both kinds of value. It bears repeating, however, that such an endeavor can never yield the unidimensional standard of value that is assumed in the labor-based theories of unequal exchange. In both social and natural systems, the production of value involves complex interactive processes that escape accounting of directly comparable measures. Fundamentally different dynamics in natural and social productive and in social extractive processes, rather than merely different amounts of energy—human or nonhuman—embodied in particular objects or commodities, underlie uneven development. The differential wages of labor and prices of resources within a particular social formation emerge from these processes and affect their subsequent developments, interactions, rates, and intensities, but cannot fully account for the unbalanced interactions between them.

A labor theory of value and models of unequal exchange of labor between regions are inadequate to explain the loss of value and consequent underdevelopment in extractive economies, but an insistence on natural value does not mean we can ignore the role of labor. It is precisely because the use-values of extracted goods are produced in nature, but are considered to be the property of extractive entrepreneurs (see Wittfogel 1985 [1929]:40) that the small portion of extractive labor that contributes to their value and to their utility can be exploited without regard to labor's reproduction. During brief extractive booms, labor not directly involved in the process is usually "in the way" (see Gaventa 1980). The rapid geographical shifts of extractive location, the investment of surplus capital in transport and exchange infrastructure, and the logic of exploiting available resources quickly as demand rises, all militate against the establishment of linkages to local productive communities, even though their absence does raise labor maintenance costs. Labor is expendable in the short-run, profit-maximizing logic of extractive export economies. The continued disruption of populations, however, accelerates the eventual collapse of each particular extractive cycle by contributing to rising labor costs, and constitutes a major component of the labor shortages or maldistributions that cause progressive impoverishment across sequential extractive cycles (Bunker 1985).

Extraction and production originally occurred together in social formations bounded by a single regional ecosystem. In such conditions human needs usually distributed extractive activity across a wide range of species and minerals; relatively little matter and energy were extracted from each of a large number of forms, so biotic chains could reproduce themselves stably. Since the profit-maximizing logic of extraction for exchange value across regional ecosystems was introduced, however, price differentials between extractive commodities, and the differential return to extractive labor, stimulate concentrated exploitation of a limited number of resources at rates that disrupt both the regeneration of these resources and the interactions within biotic chains of coevolved species and associated geological and hydrological regimes. Industrial modes of production depend on this self-depleting form of extractive activity, and therefore inevitably undermine the resource bases on which they depend. Industrial modes of production have evolved the social organizational and the infrastructural capacity to change their own technologies and thereby to find substitutes for essential resources as they are depleted. This process is necessarily finite, however, as each new technology requires other resources from what are, ultimately, either limited stocks or vulnerable ecosystems.

Social production, natural production, and the extraction that mediates between them are inextricably linked, but once the exchange of commodities breaks out of the boundaries of single ecosystems and allows social production to draw on energy and matter produced in multiple ecosystems, the logic and dynamic of the three processes become increasingly distinct. Despite the crucial element of human intentionality, however, social production remains bound by natural production processes. It cannot create the matter and energy that it transforms, and its technologies must be devised in ways compatible with the material forms in which nature transforms and stores energy. The idea that nature can be socially created is thus a peculiar illusion based on a partial vision. It emphasizes only the extraordinary growth of the social forces of production and destruction and ignores the inexorable and reciprocal determinancy of natural forces of production. The ultimate unity of nature is confirmed in the intertwining of the effects and dynamics of all three processes, rather than in models of each separate process that attempt to incorporate the logics of the other into a single dynamic.

Note

Lengthy discussions and correspondence with Richard N. Adams, Kevin Archer, Robert Bunker, Christopher Chase-Dunn, Michael Johns, Richard Norgaard, Linda Seligmann, and Charles H. Wood have been invaluable to the formulation of these arguments. I am most grateful as well to Richard Peet for his encouragement and for some very important bibliographical suggestions. (The editors are grateful to Dena Wortzel, Denis O'Hearn, and Paul Ciccantell for checking this much abbreviated, final version.)

References

Adams, W. Y. 1977. *Nubia: Corridor to Africa.* Princeton, N.J.: Princeton University Press.

Amin, S. 1977. *Imperialism and unequal development.* New York: Monthly Review Press.

Arrighi, G. 1994. *The long twentieth century*. London: Verso.

Barham, B., and O. Coomes. 1994. Reinterpreting the Amazon rubber boom: Investment and the role of the state. *Latin American Research Review* 29 (2): 73–109.

Becker, D. G. 1985. Nonferrous metals, class formation, and the state in Peru. In *States versus markets in the world-system*, ed. P. Evans, D. Rueschemeyer, and E. H. Stephens, 67–90. Beverly Hills, Calif.: Sage.

Brockway, L. 1979. *Science and colonial expansion: The role of the British royal botanic gardens*. New York: Academic Press.

Bunker, S. G. 1985. *Underdeveloping the Amazon: Extraction, unequal exchange, and the failure of the modern state*. Urbana: University of Illinois Press.

———. 1986. On values in modes and models: Reply to Volk. *American Journal of Sociology* 91 (6): 1437–1444.

———. 1992. Natural resource extraction and power differentials in the world economy. In *Understanding economic process*, ed. S. Ortiz and S. Lees, 61–84. Washington, D.C.: University Press of America.

———. 1994. Flimsy joint ventures in fragile environments. In *States, firms, and raw materials: The world economy and ecology of aluminum*, ed. B. Barham, S. G. Bunker, and D. O'Hearn, 261–296. Madison: University of Wisconsin Press.

———. 2000. *Notas sobre a renda do solo e a tributacao*. Belém, Brazil: Papers do Nucleo de Altos Estudios Amazonicos, Universidade Federal do Pará.

———. 2003. Matter, space, energy and political economy: The Amazon in the world system. *Journal of World-System Research* 9 (2): 218–258.

Bunker, S. G., and P. Ciccantell. 2003. Generative sections and the new historical materialism: Economic ascent and the cumulatively sequential restructuring of the world economy. *Studies in Comparative International Development* 37 (4): 3–30.

———. 2005. *Globalization and the race for resources*. Baltimore: Johns Hopkins University Press.

Caldwell, M. 1977. *The wealth of some nations*. London: Zed.

Chase-Dunn, C. 1980. The development of core capitalism in the antebellum United States: Tariff politics and class struggle in an upwardly mobile semiperiphery. In *Studies of the modern world-system*, ed. A. J. Bergesen, 189–230. New York: Academic Press.

Chaudhuri, K. N. 1985. *Trade and civilisation in the Indian Ocean: An economic history from the rise of Islam to 1750*. Cambridge, U.K.: Cambridge University Press.

Clark, V. S. 1916. *History of manufactures in the United States, 1607–1860*. Washington, D.C.: Carnegie Institute of Washington.

Coronil, F. 1997. *The magical state: Nature, money, and modernity in Venezuela*. Chicago: University of Chicago Press.

De Janvry, A. 1981. *The agrarian question and reformism in Latin America*. Baltimore: Johns Hopkins University Press.

De Janvry, A., and F. Kramer. 1979. The limits of unequal exchange. *The Review of Radical Political Economy* 2 (4): 3–15.

De Silva, S. B. D. 1982. *The political economy of development*. London: Routledge and Kegan Paul.

Diakonoff, I. M. 1969. Main features of the economy in the monarchies of ancient western Asia. *Ecole Practique des Hautes Etudes–Sorbonne, Congrès et Colloques* 10 (3): 13–32. Paris and The Hague: Mouton.

———. 1982. The structure of near eastern society before the middle of the 2nd millenium B.C. *Oikumene* 3:7–100. (Publishing house of the Hungarian Academy of Sciences.)

Drennan, R. D. 1984. Long-distance movement of goods in the Mesoamerican formative and classic. *American Antiquity* 49 (1): 27–43.

Ekholm, K., and J. Friedman. 1982. Capital imperialism and exploitation in ancient world-systems. *Review* 6 (1): 87–110.

Emmanuel, A. 1972. *Unequal exchange: A study in the imperialism of trade*. New York: Monthly Review Press.

Evans, P. 1979. *Dependent development: The alliance of multinational, state, and local capital in Brazil*. Princeton, N.J.: Princeton University Press.

Flores Galindo, A. 1974. *Los mineros de la cerro del Pasco*. Lima: Pontificia Universidad Catolica del Peru.

Foster, J. B. 2000. *Marx's ecology: Materialism and nature*. New York: Monthly Review Press.

Gaventa, J. 1980. *Power and powerlessness: Quiescence and rebellion in an Appalachian Valley*. Urbana: University of Illinois Press.

Harvey, D. 1982. The spatial fix: Hegel, von Thünen, and Marx. *Antipode* 13 (3): 1–12.

Hornborg, A. 2001. *The power of the machine: Global inequalities of economy, technology, and environment*. Walnut Creek, Calif.: AltaMira.

Hugill, P. 1994. *World trade since 1431*. Baltimore: Johns Hopkins University Press.

Jalee, P. 1969. *The third world in the world economy*. New York: Monthly Review Press.

Karl, T. L. 1997. *The paradox of plenty: Oil booms and petro-states*. Berkeley: University of California Press.

Kelley, R. L. 1956. The mining debris controversy in the Sacramento Valley. *Pacific Historical Review* 25 (November): 331–346.

———. 1959. *Gold vs. grain: The hydraulic mining controversy in California's Sacramento Valley: A chapter in the decline of laissez-faire*. Glendale, Calif.: Clark.

Legassick, M. 1977. Gold, agriculture, and secondary industry in South Africa, 1885–1970: From periphery to sub-metropole as a forced labour system. In *The roots of rural poverty in central and southern Africa*, ed. R. Palmer and N. Parson, 175–200. Berkeley: University of California Press.

Lenin, V. I. 1965 (1916). *Imperialism: The highest stage of capitalism*. Peking: Foreign Languages Publishing House.

Luxemburg, R. 1968. *The accumulation of capital*. New York: Monthly Review Press.

Mandel, E. 1975. *Late capitalism*. London: New Left Review Editions.

Martinez-Alier, J. 1987. *Ecological economics: Energy, environment and society.* Oxford, U.K.: Blackwell.

Marx, K. 1967. *Capital.* Vols. 1 and 3. New York: International Publishers.

McNeill, W. 1963. *The rise of the west: A history of the human community.* Chicago: University of Chicago Press.

Meinig, D. W. 1986. *Atlantic America, 1492–1800.* Vol. 1 of *The shaping of America: A geographical perspective on 500 years of history.* New Haven, Conn.: Yale University Press.

Moore, J. W. 2003. Nature and the transition from feudalism to capitalism. *Review* 26 (2): 97–172.

Mumford, L. 1961. *The city in history: Its origins, its transformations, and its prospects.* New York: Harcourt, Brace, and World.

North, D. C. 1961. *Economic growth of the United States: 1790–1860.* Englewood Cliffs, N.J.: Prentice Hall.

Nwoke, C. N. 1984. World mining rent: An extension of Marx's theories. *Review* 8 (Summer): 29–89.

Parker, W. N. 1991. *America and the wider world.* Vol. 2 of *Europe, America and the wider world.* Cambridge, U.K.: Cambridge University Press.

Paul, R. W. 1963. *Mining frontiers of the far west, 1848–1880.* New York: Holt, Rinehart and Winston.

Redclift, M. 1984. *Development and the environmental crisis: Red or green alternatives?* London: Methuen.

Rodney, W. 1972. *How Europe underdeveloped Africa.* Dar es Salaam: Tanzania Publishing House.

Schmidt, A. 1971. *The concept of nature in Marx.* London: New Left Books.

Shepherd, J. F., and G. M. Walton. 1972. *Shipping, maritime trade and economic development of colonial North America.* Cambridge, U.K.: Cambridge University Press.

Smith, N. 1984. *Uneven development: Nature, capital, and the production of space.* Oxford: Basil Blackwell.

Soremekun, F. 1977. Trade and dependency in central Angola: The Ovimbundu in the nineteenth century. In *The roots of rural poverty in central and southern Africa,* ed. R. Palmer and N. Parsons, 82–95. Berkeley: University of California Press.

Stephens, E. H., and J. D. Stephens. 1985. Bauxite and democratic socialism in Jamaica. In *States versus markets in the world system,* ed. P. Evans, D. Rueschemeyer, and E. H. Stephens, 33–66. Beverly Hills, Calif.: Sage.

Wittfogel, K. A. 1985 (1929). Geopolitics, geographical materialism and Marxism. Trans. G. L. Ulmen. *Antipode* 17 (1): 21–72.

Wolpe, H. 1980. Capitalism and cheap labour-power in South Africa: From segregation to apartheid. In *The articulation of modes of production,* ed. H. Wolpe, 289–320. London: Routledge and Kegan Paul.

Footprints in the Cotton Fields: The Industrial Revolution as Time-Space Appropriation and Environmental Load Displacement

13

ALF HORNBORG

F
OR MANY YEARS I have been pursuing an understanding of industrial capitalism as more of a global zero-sum game than a national
cornucopia (Hornborg 1992, 1998, 2001). In this work I have been
using the Second Law of Thermodynamics (the so-called Entropy Law) as a
point of departure, arguing that the build-up and maintenance of industrial
infrastructure necessarily requires a continuous net input of free or available
energy (technically referred to as "exergy," and closely related to the concept
of "negative entropy"; cf. Schrödinger 1944; Georgescu-Roegen 1971).
Purely analytically, it is possible to conclude that industrial infrastructure—
whether a factory, an industrial city, or the global "technomass"—must
maintain an unequal exchange of free energy with its hinterland in order
to survive and grow. It is also possible to analytically conclude that, under
market conditions, this unequal exchange will be orchestrated by the terms
of trade between industrial and extractive sectors of the national and global
economy, that is, the rate at which industrial manufactures are exchanged
for fuels and raw materials. The concept of "unequal exchange" in this
sense is objectively specified rather than normative, and can be applied to
several other possible metrics of trade, including material flows (Fischer-
Kowalski 1998). Georgescu-Roegen (1971) argued that not only energy
but materials, too, suffer irreversible dissipation in economic processes, and
that the concept of entropy applied to such processes should be understood
in terms of the generation of increasing energetic and material "disorder"
as a by-product of the local creation of cultural and technological "order"
or structure. Prigogine's concept of "dissipative structures" has been applied

to the asymmetric flows of entropy and negative entropy between different sectors of global society (Hornborg 1992; Clark 1997).

Combined with a world-systems perspective (Frank 1966; Wallerstein 1974–1989), such an understanding of industrial capitalism would provide a theoretical framework for interpreting the socioecological logic by which environmental problems tend to be unequally distributed between different sectors of the global population (Martinez-Alier 2002). What Clark (1997:8–10) calls the "entropic costs" of industrial metropoles should be clarified as comprising two dimensions: (1) the appropriation of "negative entropy" (accessible, high-quality energy and materials) from elsewhere, and (2) the displacement of entropy (energetic and material disorder) elsewhere. In the present world order, the first could be exemplified by the struggle of industrial powers to control crucial sources of fossil fuels (Klare 2001), the second by controversies over various kinds of "ecological distribution conflicts" (Martinez-Alier 2002:258–260), recently perhaps best illustrated by the "disproportionate" use of sinks for carbon dioxide—and share of the burden of its climatic consequences—emitted in the unequally distributed consumption of these fuels (Martinez-Alier 2002:213–233).

An important justification for this kind of perspective is that it can help explain widening gaps in technological development and economic growth between different sectors of national and international economies, as the continuous net input of natural resources into industrial sectors—in yielding further technological development—will improve their efficiency and economies of scale so as to increase the asymmetries in exchange in a self-reinforcing manner (Bunker 1985). Seen in this light, the accumulation of capital is recursively connected with unequal exchange. Another important consideration is the extent to which technological development in industrial sectors, while giving the illusory appearance of liberation from material constraints (as expressed in neoclassical economic notions of substitutability of factors of production,[1] and recently also in the notion of "dematerialization"), in fact represents a displacement of environmental loads to extractive sectors (Muradian and Martinez-Alier 2001). Richard Wilkinson (1973) has shown that the imperative of substituting for dwindling resources was an important incentive for early British industrialization, prompting exploitation not only of, for example, new, subterranean energy resources within Britain itself, but increasingly also of natural resources on other continents (cf. Pomeranz 2000). The reliance of the industrialized North on natural resources from its global periphery has become increasingly obvious in recent decades (cf. Klare 2001).

Owing largely to its foundation in thermodynamics, this analytical work has been difficult to translate into quantitative, empirical research. Actually traded quantities of exergy and negative entropy, as embodied in commodities, are inherently difficult to estimate. It should nevertheless be possible to detect such structural asymmetries in trade by converting statistics on commodity flows into quantities of "embodied land" and "embodied labor." Both these factors of production can be sources of exergy for the accumulation of capital, but have the advantage of being quantifiable, for example in annual hectare yields and in hours of human labor. Whether or not the traded commodities are actual physical sources of exergy for capital (e.g. fuels, labor, food), it should be illuminating to calculate net transfers of embodied labor and land in relation to exchange values. The simpler a system of trade relations is, the easier it should be to make such calculations. I have thus chosen to investigate, from this perspective, certain aspects of British overseas trade in the mid-nineteenth century. The years around 1850 are particularly interesting in that it is possible to obtain a wide range of fairly reliable data for these years, during what is a comparatively early and expansive period in British industrialization. These data have the advantage not only of being fairly simple and easy to synthesize, in comparison with modern trade, but also of illuminating the very origins of industrial capitalism. It is not unreasonable to propose, as a hypothesis requiring further methodological refinement, that global patterns of asymmetric resource exchange established in the early phases of industrialization have continued to reinforce themselves through the continuing technological superiority (i.e. the accumulation of capital) that they engendered in northwestern Europe. Recent statistics supporting such an interpretation include estimates of so-called ecological footprints of different nations (Wackernagel and Rees 1996).[2]

In approaching the statistics on nineteenth-century British trade, I initially posed the following questions:

1. How many annual hectare yields and hours of human labor were embodied in the British imports of raw cotton, wheat, and other commodities?

2. How many annual hectare yields and hours of human labor were embodied in the British production of textiles, and at which rates were they exchanged for those embodied in imports?

3. How many domestic (British) annual hectare yields and hours of human labor were liberated for other purposes by the displacement of land and labor inputs to other nations?

The answers to these questions are not as readily available in the standard literature on British economic history as I had anticipated, which suggests that such questions have been far from prominent, to say the least, in the voluminous research on the Industrial Revolution. In fact, my impression is that the conventional economic discourse on industrialization conspires to keep such questions—and their answers—out of view.

The figures that I have finally arrived at, often through convoluted deductions from statistics assembled to illuminate very different issues, are presented in table 13.1. For each calculation I have provided a footnote explaining how the figures were calculated. Some of these figures may seem fraught with uncertainty, but in this first approximation I consider the questions posed and methodology used more important than the minute details of mathematical accuracy. I would welcome suggestions on how to improve accuracy in these estimates, whether by consulting other sources or applying other methods of calculation. The results arrived at, however, are probably not so far off the mark as to lack significance for a rethinking of industrialization (capital accumulation) in terms of the appropriation of land and labor from elsewhere.

Discussion

From these data, a number of observations can be drawn about the global economies of (natural) space and (human) time that were—and probably continue to be—recursively linked with technological development, or capital accumulation. To begin with, we can now provide provisional answers to the three questions raised at the outset.

1. The 1850 import of 223,623 tons of raw cotton from the American South represented over 616 million hours of (mostly slave) labor and the annual yield of over 1.1 million hectares of agricultural land. If projected onto total imports (254,921 tons), the flow of raw cotton to England in 1850 embodied over 702 million hours of labor and 1.26 million hectare yields. If British figures on wool production are generalized to apply also to imported raw wool, wool imports in 1850 (27,170 tons) represented over 26.8 million hours of labor and 0.75 million hectares. In the same year, imports of wheat represented over 985 million hours and the productivity of 2.95 million hectares abroad. Imports of these three commodities alone—cotton, wool, and wheat—in 1850 represented 1,714 million hours of labor and a year's harvest from almost 5 million hectares of land.[3]

2. The 1850 production of cotton manufactures in Britain (226,879 tons) represented around 272 million hours of British labor. The production of

Table 13.1. Estimates of inputs of land and labor in some key commodities in British overseas trade around 1850. Measures are in hectares, hours, metric tons, and British currency ca. 1850

Cotton	Years		Wool	Years		Wheat	Years	
Hours of labor required for production of one ton of raw cotton in American South[1]	1850	2,755	Hours of labor required for production of one ton of raw wool in England[2]	1850	988	Hours of labor required for production of one ton of wheat imported to England[3]	1850	1,144
Hectares of land required for production of one ton of raw cotton in American South[4]	1850	4.95	Hectares of land required for production of one ton of raw wool in England[5]	1867	27.7	Hectares of land required for production of one ton of wheat imported to England[6]	1850	3.43
Tons of raw cotton imported from American South to England[7]	1815 1850	24,494 223,623	Tons of raw wool produced in England[8]	1800–1819 1850–1854	45,360 61,236	Hectares of land required for production of one ton of wheat in England[9]	1851	1.14
Tons of raw cotton imported to England (total)[10]	1800 1815 1850 1854	25,213 45,813 254,921 396,131	Tons of raw wool imported to England[11]	1800 1820 1830 1850 1854	3,818 4,399 14,333 27,170 47,376	Tons of wheat imported to England[12]	1850	861,790
Hours of labor required for production of one ton of cotton manufactures in England[13]	1819–1821 1829–1831 1849–1851	5,172 3,225 1,200	Hours of labor required for production of one ton of woolen manufactures in England[14]	1850	6,968	Hours of labor required for production of one ton of wheat in England[15]	1851	394
Quantity of cotton yarn produced in England from one ton of raw cotton[16]	1828–1861	890 kg	Quantity of woolen manufactures produced from one ton of wool[17]	1741	750 kg	Tons of wheat harvested in Gt. Britain[18]	1849–1854	3,620,000

(Continued)

Table 13.1. (Continued)

Cotton	Years		Wool	Years		Wheat	Years	
Tons of cotton manufactures produced in[19] (and exported from[20]) England	1850	226,879 (168,910)	Tons of woolen manufactures produced in England[21]	1741 1799 1805 1850	28,541 33,339 34,700 66,303	Tons of guano imported to England[22]	1851–1853	165,350
Exchange value of one ton of raw cotton[23]	1850 1854	£84.46 £50.94	Exchange value of one ton of raw wool[24]	1850 1854 1854–1860	£71.88 £137.18 £154	Exchange value of one ton of guano[25]	1851–1853	£15.89
Exchange value of one ton of cotton manufactures exported from England[26]	1840 1850	£322 £293	Exchange value of one ton of woolen manufactures exported[27]	1805 1854 1854–1860	£533 £342 £385	Exchange value of one ton of wheat imported to England[28]	1849–1854	£222

Notes:

1. McDonald and McWhiney (1980:1098) provide the figure 0.8 hand-hours to produce a pound of cotton on an Alabama plantation in 1850. 1 ton = 2,204 lbs. = 2,755 hours.

2. The average weight of a fleece of wool (presumably an average for ewes and lambs, i.e. sheep under one year old) in 1688–1695 was estimated at 4 lbs. (209) or 1,81 kg, while a more conservative estimate in 1741 suggests 3.5 lbs. (Deane 1957:211) or 1.58 kg. Modern averages from British breeds and two shearings annually suggest a wool harvest of 4.2 kg per ewe (Sjödin 1974:384). One way of estimating actual wool output is to use data on numbers of sheep and total wool clip from a year (1867) when both figures are available. Mitchell (1962:82, 84, 190) gives 28,919,000 sheep (ewes and lambs) in Great Britain and 4,836,000 in Ireland in 1867 and a domestic wool clip in the United Kingdom of 163,000,000 lbs. = 73,936,800 kg. A total of 33,755,000 sheep in the United Kingdom thus yielded 4.8 lbs. = 2.1 kg of wool per sheep. The total clip divided by 20,483,000 ewes gives 3.6 kg of wool per ewe and 278 ewes per ton of wool produced. Labor input per ewe has been estimated at 4 hours per ewe (Sjödin 1974:400) or 1,112 hours for animal care and 864 hours for fodder production and fencing. The latter figure builds on Collins' (1969:460) estimate of mowing rate with scythe (albeit for corn rather than hay) at around 1 acre per worker-day, plus an estimated additional day per acre for drying and harvesting = 2 days/acre = approximately 5 worker-days per hectare, and a requirement of 1.5 kg hay per ewe for 120 days x 278 ewes = 50 tons of hay. With worker-days estimated at 10 hours and average hay yields at 1.4 tons per acre = 3.45 tons per hectare in 1885 (Mitchell 1962:90), this means about 724 hours in fodder production per ton wool produced. With an approximated additional two weeks (120 hours) spent annually on mending fences, this gives 864 hours, and a total of 1,976 hours for 278 ewes. This latter estimate is based on commodity prices for 1854–1860 provided by Schlote (1952:116), according to which wool was valued at £7 per 100 lbs. = £0.154 per kg or £0.55 per ewe and year. The value of meat production per ewe and year has been estimated at around £0.7, based on a yield of 20 kg x £0.035. This estimate is based on a comparison of meat prices as given by Schlote (1952:116): Bacon = £2.6/cwt; ham = £3.2/cwt; salt beef = £2/cwt; salt pork = £2.4/cwt. Mutton has been estimated at £1.8/cwt. One hundredweight (cwt) = 50.8 kg.

3. Mitchell (1962:100) lists the principal sources and quantities (in thousands of hundredweights) of wheat imports to the United Kingdom in 1850: Russia = 2,766,000 cwt, Prussia = 3,609,000 cwt, Canada = 38,000 cwt, United States = 436,000 cwt. If 1 cwt = 50.8 kg, the metric equivalents are: Russia = 140,512 tons, Prussia = 183,337 tons, Canada = 1,930 tons, United States = 22,148 tons. Clark (1993:228) estimates the output per worker in bushels of wheat in Germany in 1850 as 113 bushels and in Russia in 1870 as 80 bushels. Using the average conversion factor from bushels to hundredweights of wheat (1.81 bushel = 1 cwt) in the period 1910–1939 (Mitchell 1962:90, 102), I have counted 1 bushel of wheat as equivalent to 28 kg. This gives an output per worker in Germany of 3,164 kg and in Russia of 2,240 kg. Assuming 3,000 hours per work-year, this would mean 949 hours per ton of wheat in Germany and 1,339 hours per ton in Russia. Considering that British wheat imports from Prussia and Russia are of similar proportions, whereas imports from North America are still marginal in 1850, I have entered the average of Prussian and Russian conditions = 1,144 hours per ton.

4. According to McDonald and McWhiney (1980:1096), the average yield per acre for the American South as a whole in 1850 was about 180 pounds of ginned lint. 180 lbs./acre = 201.67 kg/ha = 4.95 ha/ton.

5. Modern agricultural handbooks estimate 6.2 ewes per hectare pasture and hay (Sjödin 1974:384). I have reduced this figure to 5 ewes per hectare in the mid-nineteenth century. One way to calculate the number of hectares required per ton of wool would be to simply divide 278 ewes by 5, which gives 55.6 hectares. If we divide the total number of ewes in the United Kingdom in 1867 (20,483,000) by 5, we get 4,096,600 as an approximate number of hectares (pasture and hay) allocated to sheep. As the total clip in 1867 was 73,936,800 kg, the amount of wool produced per hectare can then be estimated at 18 kg, which again gives 55.6 hectares per ton of wool. Estimating the value of wool as about 50 percent of total output of sheep in monetary terms, the number of hectares should be reduced by half to 27.7.

6. Clark (1993:228) estimates the output of wheat per acre in Germany in 1850 at 7.1 bushels and in Russia in 1870 at 3.0 bushels. Converted to kilograms and hectares, this means 2.03 hectares/ton in Germany and 4.83 hectares/ton in Russia. As wheat imports from these two countries dominate the statistics and are of similar proportions in 1850, I have entered their average = 3.43 hectares per ton.

7. Mitchell (1962:180) provides the following figures for imports of raw cotton from the United States to the United Kingdom: 1815 = 54,000,000 lbs. = 24,494 tons; 1850 = 493,000,000 lbs. = 223,623 tons.

8. Mitchell (1962:190) estimates the average domestic wool clip of the United Kingdom in 1800–1819 at 100,000,000 lbs. = 45,360 tons and in 1850–1854 at 135,000,000 lbs. = 61,236 tons.

9. Clark (1993:228) estimates the output of wheat in Britain in 1851 at 12.6 bushels per acre. Converted to kilograms and hectares, this gives 1.14 hectares per ton.

10. Schumpeter (1960:59) for 1800 estimates 55,586,341 lbs. = 25,213 tons. Mitchell (1962:180) gives 1815 = 101,000,000 lbs. = 45,813 tons; 1850 = 664,000,000 lbs. = 254,921 tons. Schlote (1952:21) gives 396,131 tons for 1854.

11. Mitchell (1962:191) provides the following figures for raw wool imports to Great Britain in 1800: 8,418,000 lbs. = 3,818 tons. The remaining figures (Mitchell 1962:192) are for the United Kingdom, with reexports subtracted: 1820 = 9,700,000 lbs. = 4,399 tons; 1830 = 31,600,000 lbs. = 14,333 tons; 1850 = 59,900,000 lbs. = 27,170 tons. Schlote (1952:21) gives 47,376 tons in 1854.

12. Mitchell (1962:98) gives net imports of wheat and wheat meal and flour (with exports and reexports deducted) to the United Kingdom in 1850 as 19,965,000 cwt = 1,014,222 tons. However, the sum of principal imports in the same source (Mitchell 1962:100) amounts to no more than 6,849,000 cwt = 347,929 tons, which leads me to suspect that the former figure in fact applies to thousands of quarters (19,965,000 quarters = 253,555 tons). Schlote (1952:61) gives the annual average wheat imports of the United Kingdom in 1849–1854 as 861,790 tons. In view of the contradictory nature of Mitchell's figures, I have used Schlote's.

13. Farnie (1979:199) estimates output of yarn and cloth, respectively, per hand for the following periods: 1819–1821 = 968 lbs and 322.5 lbs.; 1829–1831 = 1,546 lbs. and 520.7 lbs.; 1849–1851 = 3,079 lbs. and 2,437.8 lbs. I have summed up the total output and divided by the total number of hands employed in yarn and cloth production, yielding the following figures per employed: 1819–1821 = 1,290 lbs.; 1829–1831 = 2,066 lbs. = 0.58 ton; 1849–1851 = 5,516 lbs. = 2.5 tons. I have estimated the number of annual working-hours per employed at 3,000, based on six ten-hour days per week and fifty weeks per year. This would give the following number of hours per ton of cotton manufactures produced: 1819–1821 = 5,172; 1829–1831 = 3,225; 1849–1851 = 1,200.

Table 13.1. *(Continued)*

14. Mitchell (1962:199) gives the number of employed in the wool industry in the United Kingdom in 1850 as 154,000. Assuming fifty 60-hour weeks, the total number of annual working-hours can be approximated as 462,000,000. When this figure is divided by the number of tons of woolen manufactures produced (66,303), the hours of labor required for production of one ton of woolen manufactures can be calculated as 6,968.

15. Clark (1993:228) estimates the output of wheat per worker in Britain in 1851 as 272 bushels = 7,616 kg. Assuming 3,000 hours of work per year, this means 394 hours per ton.

16. According to Blaug (1961:377), quantity of cotton yarn produced can be derived by deducting loss of weight in spinning from consumption of raw cotton, reckoned in the years 1828–1861 at 11 percent. 1 ton x 89 percent = 890 kg.

17. Deane (1957:211) quotes an assessment from 1741 that roughly one-fourth of the weight of raw wool is lost in washing and processing.

18. Schlote (1952:61) estimates the annual average wheat harvest in Great Britain in 1849–1854 at 3,620,000 tons.

19. I have used the figure for tons of raw cotton imported (254,921 tons) reduced by 11 percent (cf. Blaug 1961:377) to estimate yarn production at 226,879 tons.

20. According to Farnie (1979:7), the average annual volume of exports of cotton yarn and cloth in 1839–1841 was 254,100,000 lbs. = 115,213 tons. The mean annual rate of increase in exports 1840–1872 is given as 3.9 percent (Farnie 1979:7), which in 1850 would mean around 168,910 tons.

21. For 1741, Deane (1957:211) gives 262,175 packs of 240 lbs. or 62,922,000 lbs. = 28,541 tons. For 1799 and 1805, I have calculated 75 percent of raw wool consumed in England and Wales, including imports. Deane (1957:220) gives the following figures for wool consumed (including imports): 1799 = 98,000,000 lbs. = 44,452 tons x 75 percent = 33,399 tons; 1805 = 102,000,000 lbs. = 46,267 tons x 75 percent = 34,700 tons. For 1850, I have added raw wool produced (61,235 tons) and imported (27,170 tons) and multiplied the total (88,405) by 75 percent, yielding 66,303 tons.

22. Thompson (1968:75) gives the average annual imports of guano to Britain in 1851–1853 as 165,350 tons.

23. Mitchell (1962:291) gives the value of raw cotton imported to Great Britain in 1850 as £21,532,000. Divided by the number of tons imported the same year (254,921), this would mean a price of £84.46 per ton. Schlote (1952:21) gives the price of raw cotton in 1854 as £50.94 per ton.

24. Mitchell (1962:291) gives the value of imported wool in 1850 as £1,953,000. Divided by the number of tons imported in the same year (27,170), this would mean £71.88 per ton. Schlote (1952:21) gives the price of imported wool in 1854 as £137.18 per ton and (Schlote 1952:116) the average price of wool in 1854–1860 as £7 per 100 lb.s = £154 per ton.

25. Thompson (1968:76) gives the average annual value of imported guano in 1851–1853 as £2,628,000. Divided by the number of tons imported (165,350), this gives an exchange value of £15.89 per ton.

26. Drawing on Farnie's (1979:10) figures for average annual value of exports of cotton manufactures (£18,733,000 in 1814–1816) and mean annual rate of increase (2.9 percent between 1819–1821 and 1859–1861), I have calculated the total value of cotton exports in 1840 as £37,202,000 and in 1850 as £49,513,000. By dividing these figures with the number of tons of cotton manufactures exported (115,213 tons in 1840 and 168,910 tons in 1850), I have estimated the exchange value of one ton of cotton manufactures exported at £322 in 1840 and £293 in 1850.

27. For 1805, Deane (1957:219) estimates a total of £18,500,000 for the final sales value of woolen manufactures n England and Wales. Divided by the number of tons produced (34,699), this gives an exchange value of £533 per ton. Deane (1957:218–219) suggests an overall mu tiplier of 2.5 to estimate the value added to raw wool in the woolen and worsted industries of the early nineteenth century. Applied to Schlote's (1952:21) estimate of the price of imported wool in 1854 (£137 per ton), it would give the figure £342 per ton of woolen manufactures. Using his figure for the price of domestic wool (£0.154/kg) in 1854–1860 (Schlote 1952:116), however, we get £385 per ton.

28. Schlote (1952:61) estimates the average home price of wheat in the United Kingdom in 1849–1854 as 48.2 shillings per quarter. Converting 1 quarter = 12.7 kg, this would mean £222 per ton.

Table 13.2.   Estimates of the purchasing power of £1,000 around 1850 in terms of quantities of some key commodities and their embodied inputs of labor and land

Commodity	Volume for £1,000	Embodied labor	Embodied land
Raw cotton	11.84 tons	32,619 h	58.6 ha
Cotton manufactures	3.41 tons	4,092 domestic h [14,613 h total][1]	1.0 domestic ha [18.9 ha total][2]
Raw wool	13.91 tons	13,743 h	385.3 ha
Woolen manufactures	2.92 tons	24,183 h[3]	107.5 ha[4]
Wheat (domestic)	4.5 tons	1,773 h	5.1 ha
Wheat (imported)	4.5 tons[5]	5,148 h	15.4 ha
Guano	62.93 tons		

Notes:
1. (3.41 × 1,200) + (3.41 × 2,755 × 1.12). I have multiplied the hours embodied in raw cotton by 1.12 in order to reckon with 11 percent loss of weight in processing. If only domestic expenditures of time are reckoned with, the figure is 4,092 hours.
2. 3.41 × 4.95 × 1.12. If only domestic use of space is reckoned with, the figure should probably be less than one hectare.
3. (2.92 × 6,968) + (2.92 × 988 × 1.33). I have multiplied the hours embodied in raw wool by 1.33 in order to reckon with 25 percent loss of weight in processing.
4. 2.92 × 27.7 × 1.33.
5. I am assuming that prices of domestic and imported wheat are similar.

woolen manufactures in the same year (66,303 tons) reflects a total of over 549 million hours of British labor[4] and the productivity of 2.44 million British hectares of pasture and hay.[5] In order to be able to examine relative exchange rates of embodied labor and land in exports and imports, I have calculated the purchasing power of £1,000 around 1850 in terms of raw cotton, cotton manufactures, raw wool, woolen manufactures, domestic wheat, imported wheat, and guano (table 13.2).

These figures would permit a great number of observations on the asymmetric exchanges of embodied labor and land that contributed to the accumulation of industrial capital in nineteenth-century Britain. Let us suggest a couple of examples:

First, in exchanging, on the world market in 1850, £1,000 worth of cotton manufactures for £1,000 worth of raw cotton, Britain at first glance may seem to have gained 123 percent in terms of embodied labor and 210 percent in terms of embodied land. If only domestic use of time and space are considered, however, the gain in hours is almost 800 percent and in hectares about sixty times the space utilized. These gains, representing technological superiority (i.e. capital) accumulated over several decades, further increased as profits were invested in continued technological development. (The efficiency of labor thirty years earlier had been 5,172 hours per produced ton of cotton manufactures, which means a 331 percent increase in real output per hour between 1820 and 1850.)[6]

Second, in exchanging £1,000 worth of woolen manufactures for £1,000 worth of imported raw wool, Britain in 1850 lost 76 percent in terms of embodied labor but gained 258 percent in terms of embodied land.

3. Let us also exemplify how these figures can be used to illuminate the role of industrial export production as a means of environmental load displacement:

First, to export £1,000 worth of cotton manufactures from Britain implied much less of a drain on domestic resources than to export £1,000 worth of woolens—only 17 percent of the embodied labor and virtually none of the embodied land. To import the raw cotton to generate £1,000 of income from textile production rather than rely on domestic wool meant saving 20,091 British work-hours[7] at the expense of 10,521 work-hours in America and saving 107.5 British hectares at the expense of 18.9 hectares in America.[8]

Second, to import £1,000 worth of wheat from Russia and Prussia rather than growing it at home meant saving 1,773 British work-hours at the expense of 5,148 foreign work-hours and 5.1 British hectares at the expense of 15.4 hectares in Russia and Prussia. This does not take into account, however, the time-space demands of the domestic export industry whose profits paid for wheat imports. In terms of the ratio of embodied land and labor to exchange value, neither cotton nor woolen manufactures could compete with wheat, but here we see how the exigencies of demography inevitably constrain economic rationality. The growing population of Britain had first and foremost to be fed, and British wheat production around 1850 (3,620,000 tons × 1.14 hectares) demanded 4,126,800 hectares of the best agricultural land in the country. To spend £94 (1.12 × £84.46) on raw material and 4,092 work-hours in the cotton industry in order to be able to import 4.5 tons of wheat (the equivalent of only 1,773 work-hours but crucially also of 5.1 hectares of prime farmland in Britain)—or 63 tons of guano—is economically rational under conditions of land scarcity, as was very obviously the case in early-nineteenth-century Britain. In exchanging cotton manufactures for foreign wheat, rather than grow the wheat at home, Britain lost over 56 percent in hours of labor but gained almost the entire land area used to cultivate it.

Third, most centrally, from the perspective sketched at the outset in this chapter, the displacement of demands on land represented by the appropriation of the productivity of 1.1 million hectares of cotton fields in North America, which in terms of revenue ultimately generated £66,475,547, meant the liberation of the over 6 million hectares[9] in Britain that would have been required to generate the equivalent amount of revenue from woolen manufactures. This land area exceeds by almost 50 percent the total area of British wheat cultivation (4,126,800 hectares) in 1850. If we add to this the imports of wool from overseas, an additional 0.75 million British hectares were set free, for example, to fuel the labor force.

Finally, this kind of analysis certainly deserves to be expanded to cover the other major commodities that provided the global framework for British industrialization. This applies, for instance, to those periods when Britain relied on imports of iron from Scandinavia, the production of which required huge volumes of Scandinavian labor and charcoal. Other important commodities embodying significant amounts of labor and land in the periphery in the mid-nineteenth century include timber, sugar, tea, coffee, wine, silk, flax, vegetable oils, dyes, hemp, and tobacco.

Conclusion

In conclusion, I would like to refer back to the "zero-sum game" perspective on industrial capitalism that I briefly presented at the outset. It is obvious that only a few of Britain's imports in the mid-nineteenth century actually in themselves contributed exergy or negative entropy to its emerging industrial infrastructure. In terms of energetics, as Britain was then self-sufficient in (and a net exporter of) fossil fuels, the prime candidates were wheat and sugar, which provided food energy for a significant proportion of the labor force (Pomeranz 2000:313–314). In terms of materials, the prime candidates were iron and timber. The thermodynamic perspective that I have advocated, however, has little regard for national boundaries, as long as imports of exergy and exports of entropy have not developed into national interests, as in the current struggles over oil (Klare 2001) or deliberations about emission permits (Martinez-Alier 2002). Unequal exchange can be a very local affair. As the world's first industrial districts were emerging in eighteenth-century Yorkshire and Lancashire, the most significant extractive periphery may have been no farther off than the nearest coalfields, where the severity of working conditions and environmental degradation may well have equaled that of the Alabama cotton plantations (Hobsbawm 1968:252–256, 281, diagram 5b). During the course of the nineteenth century, this periphery expanded to truly global proportions, but the logic remains the same to this day. Although deeply submerged beneath statistics catering to the concerns of neoclassical economics, this logic remains founded on the imperative—for all kinds of complex systems or structures—to maintain a net input of negative entropy. This can be achieved through a variety of social strategies complementing and succeeding each other over the course of history. From this perspective, we have seen how the import of raw materials for the textile industry, although not in itself representing an energy source, served to make room for the energy provisioning of the British labor force. Factory workers and coal miners alike ran on wheat.

The British textile industry for two centuries played a central role in generating revenue to maintain an expanding technological infrastructure, originally as a means of coping with a severe shortage of land (Wilkinson 1973). As this expansion continued and spread to continental neighbors and former colonies, mainstream discourse has conspired to ignore the unequal exchange of (labor) time and (natural) space on which technological development has been founded from the start. The complex webs of the modern world economy no doubt make analyses such as these extremely difficult, but we can remain quite certain that capital, however much it tries, will never be able to delink itself from labor and land. The rationale of machine technology is to (locally) save or liberate time and space, but crucially at the expense of time and space consumed elsewhere in the social system. The general hypothesis offered here is that to save time and space by the application of increasingly "efficient" technologies may often tend to imply that someone else in the world-system is *losing* time or space in the process. The process of globalization that was in full swing in the early days of industrial capitalism then as now relied on what Harvey (e.g. 1996) has called "time-space compression." The point that I wanted to make in this chapter is that such analyses of the very essence of technological development need to be founded on a concrete, empirical understanding of what I would call "time-space *appropriation*."

Notes

This chapter is a slightly revised version of an article published in the journal *Ecological Economics* in 2006. I am grateful to Elsevier Press for permission to reprint it in the present volume.

1. In material terms, land, labor and capital are *not* mutually convertible into one another. Land can nourish labor, and land and labor can yield capital, but capital can create neither land nor labor.

2. The genealogy of the notion of "ecological footprints" goes back to Borgström's (1965) concept of "ghost acreages" (cf. also Catton 1980). Pomeranz's (2000:313–315) calculation of the ghost acreages of some British imports (sugar, timber, cotton) in the late eighteenth and early nineteenth century was brought to my attention after this text had been written, but rests on the same general interpretation of British history (cf. Wilkinson 1973).

3. It is of course important to remember that hectares of land vary enormously in terms of embodied labor as well as natural productivity. I thank John McNeill for prompting me to add this note.

4. I have added the number of working-hours required for production of one ton of woolen manufactures (6,968) and the number of hours required for production of 1.33 tons of raw wool (1,314), in order to reckon with 25 percent loss of weight in processing.

5. I have estimated the number of hectares required for production of 1.33 tons of raw wool (36.8), in order to reckon with 25 percent loss of weight in processing.

6. The reason why no attempt is made here to include capital in these calculations is that capital is itself understood as embodied labor and land, that is, the product of past relations of unequal exchange of time and space. As such, any attempt to justify the rates of exchange discussed here by reference to British capital would merely serve to mystify the unequal process of accumulation that the calculations are intended to reveal.

7. 24,183 − (3.41 × 1,200).

8. It should also be noted that agricultural production of fibers such as cotton, flax, and hemp is more demanding on the soil, and on labor, than most other crops (Pomeranz 2000:218–219), which made this environmental load displacement particularly advantageous from the British perspective.

9. To generate an additional £66,475,547 from sales of woolen manufactures in 1850 would have required an additional output of 194,372 tons (× £342), representing 217,696 tons of raw wool demanding 6,030,196 hectares of land.

References

Blaug, M. 1961. The productivity of capital in the Lancashire cotton industry during the nineteenth century. *The Economic History Review* 13:358–381.

Borgström, G. 1965. *The hungry planet*. New York: Macmillan.

Bunker, S. G. 1985. *Underdeveloping the Amazon: Extraction, unequal exchange and the failure of the modern state*. Chicago: University of Chicago Press.

Catton, W. R., Jr. 1980. *Overshoot: The ecological basis of revolutionary change*. Urbana and Chicago: University of Illinois Press.

Clark, G. 1993. Agriculture and the industrial revolution, 1700–1850. In *The British industrial revolution*, ed. J. Mokyr, 227–266. Boulder, Colo.: Westview.

Clark, R. P. 1997. *The global imperative: An interpretive history of the spread of humankind*. Boulder, Colo.: Westview.

Collins, E. J. T. 1969. Harvest technology and labour supply in Britain, 1790–1870. *The Economic History Review* 22:453–473.

Deane, P. 1957. The output of the British woolen industry in the eighteenth century. *The Journal of Economic History* 17:207–223.

Farnie, D. A. 1979. *The English cotton industry and the world market 1815–1896*. Oxford, U.K.: Clarendon.

Fischer-Kowalski, M. 1998. Society's metabolism: The intellectual history of material flow analysis. *Journal of Industrial Ecology* 2 (1): 61–78.

Frank, A. G. 1966. The development of underdevelopment. *Monthly Review* 18:17–31.

Georgescu-Roegen, N. 1971. *The entropy law and the economic process*. Cambridge, Mass.: Harvard University Press.

Harvey, D. 1996. *Justice, nature and the geography of difference*. Malden, Mass.: Blackwell.

Hobsbawm, E. J. 1968. *Industry and empire: An economic history of Britain since 1750*. New York: Penguin.

Hornborg, A. 1992. Machine fetishism, value, and the image of unlimited good: Toward a thermodynamics of imperialism. *Man*, n.s., 27:1–18.

————. 1998. Towards an ecological theory of unequal exchange: Articulating world system theory and ecological economics. *Ecological Economics* 25 (1): 127–136.

————. 2001. *The power of the machine: Global inequalities of economy, technology, and environment*. Lanham, Md.: AltaMira/Rowman & Littlefield.

Klare, M. T. 2001. *Resource wars: The new landscape of global conflict*. New York: Owl Books/Henry Holt.

Martinez-Alier, J. 2002. *The environmentalism of the poor: A study of ecological conflicts and valuation*. Cheltenham and Northampton: Edward Elgar.

McDonald, F., and G. McWhiney. 1980. The south from self-sufficiency to peonage: An interpretation. *The American Historical Review* 85 (5): 1095–1118.

Mitchell, B. R. 1962. *Abstract of British historical statistics*. Cambridge, U.K.: Cambridge University Press.

Muradian, R., and J. Martinez-Alier. 2001. South-north materials flow: History and environmental repercussions. *Innovation* 14 (2): 171–187.

Pomeranz, K. 2000. *The great divergence: China, Europe, and the making of the modern world economy*. Princeton, N.J.: Princeton University Press.

Schlote, W. 1952. *British overseas trade from 1700 to the 1930s*. Oxford, U.K.: Blackwell.

Schrödinger, E. 1944. *What is life? Mind and matter*. Cambridge, U.K.: Cambridge University Press.

Schumpeter, E. B. 1960. *English overseas trade statistics 1697–1808*. Oxford, U.K.: Clarendon.

Sjödin, E. 1974. *Får*. Stockholm: LT:s förlag.

Thompson, F. M. L. 1968. The second agricultural revolution, 1815–1880. *The Economic History Review* 21:62–77.

Wackernagel, M., and W. E. Rees. 1996. *Our ecological footprint: Reducing human impact on the Earth*. Gabriola Island, B.C.: New Society Publishers.

Wallerstein, I. M. 1974–1989. *The modern world system I-III*. San Diego, Calif.: Academic Press.

Wilkinson, R. G. 1973. *Poverty and progress: An ecological model of economic development*. London: Methuen.

Uneven Ecological Exchange and Consumption-Based Environmental Impacts: A Cross-National Investigation   **14**

ANDREW K. JORGENSON AND JAMES RICE

N ATURAL RESOURCE CONSUMPTION AND RESULTING environmental degradation are among the most pressing issues confronting
us today. Paradoxically, nations with larger ecological footprints
generally experience lower domestic levels of particular forms of environmental degradation within their borders, including deforestation and organic water pollution intensity (e.g. Jorgenson 2003, 2004a, 2005). Moreover, these forms of degradation negatively impact the quality of life and
general well-being of domestic human populations. For example, organic
water pollution resulting from monoagricultural export-oriented production in less developed countries increases infant mortality rates, net of
health expenditures, forms of human capital, and other social factors (e.g.
Burns, Kentor, and Jorgenson 2003; Jorgenson 2004b; Jorgenson and Burns
2004).

The ecological footprint/environmental degradation paradox is not necessarily the consequence of increased problem-solving capacity due to
greater affluence and development. Rather, many social scientists posit
that these relationships are illustrative of structural conditions and asymmetrical processes in which more developed countries externalize their
consumption-based environmental impacts through the tapping of natural
resources and produced commodities of less developed countries, reducing material consumption for the latter while increasing particular types of
environmental destruction within their borders. The general argument concerns the structure of international trade, particularly the flows of exports
from less developed countries to more developed countries. However, these
assertions lack appropriate empirical evaluation.

This chapter begins to resolve the issues discussed above. Specifically, we test the following hypothesis: less developed countries with greater levels of exports sent to higher-consuming, more developed countries exhibit lower domestic levels of per capita consumption, measured as ecological footprints. This hypothesis is sensitive to the potential uneven ecological exchange dynamics promoting disproportionate utilization of natural resources by developed countries at the expense of less developed countries. The ecological footprint demand exhibited by less developed countries, therefore, is not simply the consequence of domestic driving forces, including relative affluence and population pressures, but also the structural relations forged through international trade.

To test this hypothesis, we create an index of weighted export flows that quantifies the relative extent to which exports of countries are sent to receiving nations with higher levels of economic development. This index allows for a more explicit examination of potential asymmetrical processes of international trade between countries. Using ordinary least squares regression, we incorporate the new weighted index into a series of quantitative cross-national analyses of the structural causes of per capita ecological footprints of less developed countries, 2000. We include controls identified by previous studies to be robust predictors of footprints, including level of economic development, urbanization, domestic income inequality, and human capital. We also consider the effects of other export-related factors and the extent to which domestic economies are service-based. Results of this study provide robust support for the tested hypothesis, and underscore the importance of addressing the structural dynamics of international trade when analyzing material consumption and other environmental outcomes, particularly the relative flow of exports and relevant attributes of receiving countries. Prior to the analyses, we review relevant studies and theorization, and describe the steps taken in calculating the index of weighted export flows.

Review of Previous Approaches

Consumption and its environmental impacts focuses on the ecological footprints of nations (e.g. Jorgenson 2003, 2004a, 2005, forthcoming; Jorgenson and Burns 2004; Jorgenson and Rice 2005; Jorgenson, Rice, and Crowe 2005; Rosa, York, and Dietz 2004; York, Rosa, and Dietz 2003). The ecological footprint measures the amount of biologically productive land required to support the consumption of renewable natural resources and assimilation of carbon dioxide waste products of a given population (e.g. Chambers, Simmons, and Wackernagel 2002). More specifically, national footprints consist of the area of cropland required to produce the crops consumed, the area of grazing land required to produce the animal products, the area of forest required to produce the wood and paper, the area of sea required to produce the marine fish and seafood, the area of land required to accommodate housing and infrastructure, and the area of forest required to absorb the carbon dioxide emissions resulting from energy consumption (Wackernagel et al. 2002).

Footprints are measured in area units where one footprint equals one hectare. This natural capital accounting framework captures indirect effects of consumption that are difficult to measure, and the approach does not require knowing specifically what each consumed resource is used for. However, footprints do not identify the locations where the consumed resources originate.

Jorgenson (2003, 2004a, 2005) analyzes the structural causes of per capita ecological footprints, and finds that a country's level of per capita consumption is largely a function of its relative position in the international stratification system, level of urbanization, domestic income inequality, and human capital. Through the unpacking of relative international power into its relevant geopolitical-economic components, Jorgenson (2005) empirically illustrates that economic power in the form of capital intensity, military technological power, and overall export dependence are the structural driving forces of per capita resource consumption.

Social scientists pay considerable theoretical and empirical attention to the environmental impacts of economic development (e.g. Burns, Kick, and Davis 2003; Burns, Kentor, and Jorgenson 2003; Chase-Dunn and Jorgenson 2003; Foster 2002; Jorgenson 2006; Jorgenson and Kick 2003; Moore 2003; O'Connor 1998; Schnaiberg and Gould 1994; Wallerstein 1999). Relative economic power generally takes the form of capital intensity (i.e. GDP, or gross domestic product, per capita), which often refers to the ability of a country to be more competitive in the global marketplace (Kentor 2000). Countries with higher capital intensity generally contain articulated consumer markets that consume greater levels of material resources (Jorgenson 2003, 2004a).

To maintain profits, producers must constantly expand production, which requires additional ecological material inputs (O'Connor 1998). Schnaiberg and Gould (1994) characterize these processes as the heart of the treadmill of production. Producers are usually headquartered in developed countries, and outsource production and resource extraction to export-dependent countries. The expansion of production and consumption usually takes the form of global commodity chains in which resources are added or modified at every chain (Gereffi and Korzeniewicz 1994; Princen, Maniates, and Conca 2002). Produced commodities are usually transported to and consumed by developed countries with high capital intensity, and the majority of profits derived from these goods further increase the economic development of market economies that house the headquarters of producers (e.g. Bornschier and Chase-Dunn 1985).

Many researchers argue that less developed countries generally have lower domestic levels of material consumption and ecological footprints because they tend to export produced commodities and raw materials to higher-consuming, more developed countries (e.g. Clapp 2002; Conca 2002; Jorgenson 2003; Jorgenson, Rice and Crowe 2005; Princen 2002). The latter contain productive economies and articulated markets, while less developed countries generally consist of more extractive-oriented economies and disarticulated markets (Bunker 1985). Moreover, less developed countries with extractive economies are often highly dependent on a small number of primary exports, most notably agricultural products and other natural resources (e.g. Burns, Kentor, and Jorgenson 2003; Jorgenson 2004b). Dependence on agricultural exports lessens the well-being of human populations in many less developed countries (e.g. Jorgenson and Burns 2004). Less developed countries with higher levels of domestic income inequality exhibit relatively lower ecological footprints (Jorgenson 2004a). This type of outcome is often explained by two interrelated factors. First, the majority of the population has substantially lower income levels, and second, the domestic market focuses on the exportation of raw materials and commodities produced by means of dependent industrialization (e.g. Beer and Boswell 2002; Jorgenson 2003).

Overall, countries with higher levels of urbanization consume greater amounts of material resources (Jorgenson 2003; York, Rosa, and Dietz 2003). These areas require more resources to maintain the overall built infrastructure, and urbanized regions contain intensified articulated consumer markets relative to more agrarian areas. However, urban processes in less developed countries differ substantially from more developed nations. Many urbanized regions in less developed countries are characterized by outdated manufacturing sectors that are exported from more developed countries coupled with a shift toward export-oriented development (Grimes and Kentor 2003; Portes, Dore-Cabral, and Landolt 1997). Furthermore, many less developed countries have experienced increased roles as nodes in the exportation of natural resources from regional extractive economies (Bunker 1985).

Thus, the complicated processes of underdevelopment, emerging dependent industrialization, and economic stagnation limit the domestic levels of natural resource consumption in less developed countries. Moreover, this is further exacerbated by their classically dependent, extractive-oriented domestic characteristics and export-oriented production of goods for articulated consumer markets in higher-consuming, more developed countries (e.g. Bunker 1985; Hornborg 2001; Jorgenson 2003, 2004a, 2004b).

Neoclassical economic perspectives suggest that the overall structure of domestic economies greatly determines their overall environmental impacts. More specifically, it is assumed that nations with more service-based economies consume less material resources and emit less waste into regional ecological systems and the biosphere (e.g. Grossman and Krueger 1995; OECD 1998). However, York, Rosa, and Dietz (2003) find no evidence indicating that nations with relatively greater service-based economies consume fewer resources, and likewise, Jorgenson (2006) and Burns and Jorgenson (2004) find no evidence suggesting that less developed nations with relatively more service-based economies experience lower rates of deforestation and methane emissions intensity, net of other factors.

Some social scientists argue that more affluent nations reduce their impacts on the environment within their own borders through the importation of resources and the exportation of wastes, a process commonly referred to as the "Netherlands Fallacy" (e.g. Ehrlich and Ehrlich 1990; Ehrlich and Holdren 1971; Frey 1998; Jorgenson 2003). Developed countries possess the international political-economic power and institutional infrastructure to achieve improvements in domestic environmental conditions while continuing to impose negative externalities globally (e.g. Andersson and Lindroth 2001; Chase-Dunn 1998; Chew 2001).

The Netherlands Fallacy suggests that domestic environmental conditions are not necessarily an accurate reflection of the aggregate environmental burdens engendered by domestic standards of living and rates of material consumption. It is argued that any particular country's environmental impact, positive or negative, is not simply the consequence of domestic factors but also its structured relations with other countries. To more fully conceptualize the complexity of consumption-related dynamics in a globalizing world, it is increasingly important to examine zero-sum relations among countries and the socioeconomic and environmental costs that are differentially incurred as a result (Hornborg 2001, 2003; Jorgenson 2005).

The broadening and deepening of international trade provides a means by which patterns of production and consumption become domestically disassociated, particularly in regards to concomitant environmental impacts

(Andersson and Lindroth 2001; Chew 2001; Jorgenson forthcoming; Rothman 1998:185). Most social-scientific studies of different forms of environmental degradation analyze the effects of overall levels of exports (e.g. Burns et al. 1994; Jorgenson 2005; Kick et al. 1996; Rudel 1998), while other studies address the possible environmental and economic impacts of dependence on exports to a limited number of trading partners (e.g. Galtung 1971; Kentor 2000; Kentor and Boswell 2003). However, the structural processes and outcomes theorized by political-economic scholars and environmental sociologists focus on the environmental impacts of the structure of exports, particularly the flow of raw materials and produced commodities from less developed countries to higher-consuming, more developed countries.

Construction of Weighted Export Flows

We have created a comprehensive index weighted by attributes of receiving countries: export flows weighted by per capita GDP (see also Jorgenson and Rice 2005). The index is calculated for 1990, and quantifies the relative extent to which exports are sent to more developed countries. Data required for the construction of the weighted index include relational measures in the form of export flows and attributional data that quantify characteristics of receiving countries. Export flows data are taken from the International Monetary Fund's 2003 *Direction of Trade Statistics* CD-ROM database. All figures are reported in current U.S. dollars. Attributional data required for the construction of the indices include GDP per capita, which quantifies a country's level of economic development. These data are taken from Maddison (2001), and are in constant 1995 international dollars.

The weighted index is calculated as:

$$D_i = \sum_{j=1}^{N} p_{ij} a_j$$

Where:

D_i = weighted export flows for country i
p_{ij} = proportion of country i's total exports sent to receiving country j
a_j = attribute of receiving country j [i.e. GDP per capita]

The first step is to convert the flows of exports to receiving countries into proportional scores. More specifically, exports to each receiving country are transformed into the proportion of the sending country's total exports. The second step involves multiplying each proportion by the corresponding receiving country's attribute of interest (per capita GDP). The third step is to sum the products of the calculations in step two. The sums of these products quantify the relative level of exports sent to more developed countries that generally exhibit larger ecological footprints.

Hypothesis and Methods

Our primary goal is to test a hypothesis derived from fundamental arguments of environmental sociologists and political-economic scholars concerning uneven ecological exchange between nations. Specifically, we test the following hypothesis: less developed countries with higher levels of exports sent to more developed (i.e. higher-consuming) countries exhibit lower domestic levels of resource consumption, measured as per capita ecological footprints. To test the hypothesis, we incorporate the new index of weighted export flows into a series of cross-national analyses of per capita ecological footprints for less developed countries.

Like other studies that restrict their analyses to less developed countries, we argue that the domestic social infrastructure and relative position of less developed countries in the world economy create conditions in which the social and environmental impacts of political-economic characteristics vary substantially between developed and less developed countries. For example, a developed country might send a high proportion of exports to other developed countries, but its relatively powerful position in the world economy enables the developed country to import natural resources and produced commodities from less developed countries. Moreover, developed countries generally possess domestic infrastructures and technologies that enable them to reduce some forms of environmental degradation within their borders (Burns, Kick, and Davis 2003; Kick et al. 1996).

We employ Ordinary Least Squares (OLS) regression and listwise deletion in all reported analyses. For comparison, the models we use here are similar to those tested in other recent studies of national-level footprints. They include measures of economic development, urbanization, domestic inequality, human capital, domestic economy structure, and other export-related characteristics.

DEPENDENT VARIABLE

- *Combined ecological footprint per capita, 2000*, is the comprehensive measure of the total area required to produce the commodities consumed and assimilate the wastes generated for a given nation. These data are taken from Venetoulis, Chazan, and Gaudet (2004).

INDEPENDENT VARIABLES

- *Weighted Export Flows, 1990 (natural log).* These data quantify the relative extent to which a nation's exports are sent to more economically developed countries. We log this variable to correct for skewness.

- *Gross Domestic Product per capita (natural log), 1990* is included in nearly all cross-national studies of ecological footprints, and measures a country's level of economic development. These data are obtained from Maddison (2001), and are measured in 1990 international dollars. Consistent with most studies, we log these data to correct for skewness.

- *Gross Domestic Product per capita change, 1980–1990* controls for the extent of a country's average annual rate of economic development. We calculate average annual percent change scores using Maddison's (2001) data.

- *Urban population, 1990* (residualized) controls for the percentage of a country's population residing in urban areas. These data are taken from the World Bank (2000). To correct for its high collinearity with GDP per capita, we regress this variable on per capita GDP and use the residuals as measures of urbanization, which allows for analyses of its effects, independent of level of economic development.

- *Exports of goods and services as percentage of total GDP, 1990* (natural log) measures overall levels of exports and controls for the extent of a country's integration into the world economy. These data are obtained from the World Bank (2000). We log this variable to correct for skewness.

- *Domestic income inequality*, measured as gini coefficients, controls for the distribution of income within countries. The years of measurement for gini coefficients vary slightly across countries, but range in the early 1990s. These data are taken from the World Bank (2001).

- *Secondary school enrollment, 1990* (residualized) is an indicator of human capital, and is defined as the ratio of total secondary school enrollment, regardless of age, to the population of the age group corresponding to this level of education. These data are obtained from the World Bank (2000). Like urban population, we residualize these data to correct for its high collinearity with GDP per capita.

- *Services as percentage of total GDP, 1990* controls for the extent to which a domestic economy is services based. These data are taken from the World Bank (2000).

- *Export partner concentration, 1990* quantifies the percentage or proportion of total exports to the single largest importing country. These data are obtained from the World Bank (1996).

Table 14.1.   Descriptive statistics and correlations for all variables included in the analyses

		N	Mean	SD
1	Ecological Footprint per capita, 2000	69	1.586	.799
2	Weighted Export Flows, 1990	69	9.548	.261
3	Gross Domestic Product per capita, 1990 (log)	69	7.640	.800
4	Gross Domestic Product per capita change, 1980–1990	69	.231	2.197
5	Urban Population, 1990 (residualized)	69	.000	12.754
6	Exports/GDP, 1990 (log)	69	3.089	.581
7	Domestic Inequality	69	43.614	9.982
8	Secondary Education, 1990 (residualized)	69	.000	14.771
9	Services/GDP, 1990	69	46.251	9.485
10	Export Partner Concentration, 1990	69	31.577	18.127

	1	2	3	4	5	6	7	8	9
1									
2	.020								
3	.762	.201							
4	−.034	.041	.107						
5	.237	.016	.000	−.620					
6	.369	.302	.420	.047	−.016				
7	−.002	.183	.003	−.280	.370	.168			
8	.034	−.096	.000	−.006	.041	−.046	−.361		
9	.229	.315	.399	−.048	.117	.226	.257	−.210	
10	−.145	.526	−.027	−.154	−.043	.001	.216	−.431	.218

Countries Included in the Analyses

We focus the analyses on less developed countries categorized by the World Bank (2000). Specifically, we include countries not categorized as high-income by the World Bank's income quartile classification. To maximize the use of available data, we allow sample sizes to vary among tested models. Saudi Arabia and South Korea were found to be outliers and excluded from the reported analyses. Table 14.1 provides descriptive statistics and correlations for all variables included in the analyses.

Results and Discussion

Results of the multivariate regression analyses are provided in table 14.2. Our most noteworthy finding is that weighted export flows have a significant negative effect on per capita ecological footprints of less developed countries. The effect is almost identical in magnitude and statistically significant across all models, which provides strong support for the tested hypothesis. This finding, coupled with the often identified paradoxical relationships between the footprints of nations and levels of domestic environmental degradation, provides evidence of the externalization of consumption-based environmental costs by more-affluent nations (Frey

Table 14.2.   Standardized coefficients for analyses of ecological footprints per capita, 2000, in LDCs

	Model 1	Model 2	Model 3	Model 4	Model 5
Weighted Export Flows, 1990	−.171* (−2.314) [1.111]	−.176* (−2.150) [1.167]	−.177* (−2.100) [1.149]	−.182* (−2.147) [1.203]	−.214* (−2.131) [1.400]
Gross Domestic Product per capita, 1990 (log)	.739*** (9.447) [1.243]	.751*** (8.482) [1.358]	.761*** (8.153) [1.410]	.883*** (8.955) [1.621]	.889*** (8.538) [1.507]
Gross Domestic Product per capita change, 1980−1990	.099 (1.092) [1.657]	−.060 (−.615) [1.644]	−.074 (−.708) [1.782]	−.178 (−1.689) [1.861]	−.218 (−1.741) [2.179]
Urban Population, 1990 (residualized)	.338*** (3.764) [1.639]	.254* (2.547) [1.728]	.237* (2.136) [1.994]	.086 (.743) [2.231]	.039 (.292) [2.437]
Exports/GDP, 1990 (log)	.110 (1.381) [1.293]	.138 (1.583) [1.322]	.133 (1.471) [1.316]	.082 (.898) [1.376]	.093 (.946) [1.332]
Domestic Inequality		−.106 (−1.265) [1.226]	−.108 (−1.139) [1.466]	.020 (.201) [1.662]	.097 (.870) [1.721]
Secondary Education, 1990 (residualized)			−.027 (−.312) [1.192]	.002 (.024) [1.262]	−.011 (−.110) [1.479]
Services/GDP, 1990				−.163 (−1.777) [1.403]	−.127 (−1.313) [1.296]
Export Partner Concentration, 1990					−.045 (−.401) [1.720]
Constant	.475 (.225)	.635 (.292)	.787 (.338)	.100 (.047)	1.614 (.564)
Sample Size	69	57	54	52	44
Adjusted R^2	.665	.677	.672	.694	.690

Note: T-Ratios are in parentheses; VIFs appear in brackets; ***p < .001; **p < .01; *p < .05.

1998; Hornborg 2001; Jorgenson 2003; Jorgenson and Burns 2004; Princen, Maniates, and Conca 2002).

Turning to the other predictor variables, we find that level of economic development positively affects per capita footprints, while the effect of rate of development is nonsignificant across all tested models. The former finding is consistent with recent cross-national studies of footprints (e.g. Jorgenson 2003, 2004a, 2005; York, Rosa, and Dietz 2003). Level of urbanization positively affects per capita footprints in models 1 through 3, but becomes nonsignificant and close to null when including services and export partner concentration as additional controls. We speculate that the nonsignificant effect in the two most fully controlled models is partly an artifact of the reduced sample size and the use of traditional linear regression techniques, rather than indirect effects models that treat urbanization as a mediating variable, partly a function of economic development and other social factors (e.g. Jorgenson 2003; Kentor 2001). However, the effect of urbanization is not the central focus of the current study.

Domestic income inequality proves to be a nonsignificant predictor of footprints of less developed countries when controlling for the structure of export flows, which contradicts the findings of other recent studies (e.g. Jorgenson 2003, 2004a). Like York, Rosa, and Dietz (2003), we find no evidence indicating that nations with more service-based economies consume lower levels of material resources. The effect of level of exports is nonsignificant across all tested models, and export partner concentration also proves to be a nonsignificant predictor of ecological footprints. Thus, the cumulative structure of export flows and the attributes of receiving countries are of more relevance than the overall level of exports or diversity of trading partners.

Conclusion

This study provides a new approach to the analysis of international trade, material consumption, and concomitant environmental degradation. Foremost, we created an index that measures the relative extent to which exports of less developed countries are sent to higher-consuming, more developed countries. Using this new index, we tested and confirmed the hypothesis that less developed countries with higher levels of exports sent to more developed countries exhibit lower domestic levels of resource consumption, measured as per capita ecological footprints. This finding is illustrative of the theorized structural conditions in which higher-consuming countries externalize their consumption-based environmental costs through the tapping of raw materials and produced commodities from less developed countries, which tempers material consumption levels, thereby restricting the ecological footprints of the latter countries (e.g. Jorgenson 2005).

Consistent with other recent studies of national footprints, level of economic development and urbanization positively affect per capita footprints of less developed countries while the effect of size of service sector is nonsignificant (e.g. Jorgenson 2003, 2004a; York, Rosa, and Dietz 2003). The latter finding critically challenges neoclassical economic arguments concerning the environmental impacts of domestic economic conditions (e.g. Grossman and Krueger 1995). The overall level of exports and relative diversity in trading partners prove to be nonsignificant predictors of per capita footprints. Coupled with our most noteworthy finding concerning the effect of weighted export flows, these results suggest that the overall structure of exports is of more relevance to understanding variation in the ecological footprints of nations and perhaps the attendant forms of environmental degradation. More specifically, export flows and the attributes of receiving countries are central considerations when analyzing the variety of consumption-based environmental impacts of international trade.

Proponents of comparative advantage theory and other neoliberal perspectives (e.g. Magee 1980; Ricardo 1951 [1821]) might argue that the findings of this study, particularly the negative effect of weighted export flows on the per capita footprints of less developed countries, illustrate the overall environmental "benefits" of trade (i.e. "trade specialization"). However, cross-national studies provide evidence that nations with lower footprints experience higher domestic levels of particular forms of environmental degradation and serious health problems, including elevated infant mortality rates (e.g. Jorgenson 2003; Jorgenson and Burns 2004). Undoubtedly, the health and well-being of populations are largely a function of access to adequate shelter and consumption of minimal levels of food (Jenkins and Scanlan 2001; Jorgenson 2005), both of which are included in the composite footprints analyzed in the present study.

Thus, the per capita footprints of nations could be treated as a partial indicator of human quality of life (see Prescott-Allen 2001). Moreover, a large proportion of the less developed countries included in the current study exhibit footprints below their biocapacity per capita (Venetoulis, Chazan, and Gaudet 2004; Wackernagel et al. 2002). Indeed, their relatively low levels of globally sustainable consumption and high levels of domestic environmental degradation are characteristics of underdevelopment stemming from asymmetrical exchanges between developed and less-developed countries (e.g. Chase-Dunn 1998; Emmanuel 1972; Hornborg 2001; Jorgenson 2005; McMichael 2004).

For less developed countries to share in the development outcomes exhibited by richer, more powerful countries they first must secure access to greater levels of material consumption within the confines of the biologically productive limits of the global environment. Asymmetrical processes of ecological exchange, however, highlight the challenges in doing so when the structure of export flows increases the material consumption opportunities of more economically developed trading partners at the expense of less developed countries. Arguably, such uneven consumption dynamics are not only complicit in promoting increasing global environmental demand but are also linked to the diminishing opportunities of less developed countries to achieve socioeconomic stability and domestic ecological protection.

References

Andersson, J. O., and M. Lindroth. 2001. Ecologically unsustainable trade. *Ecological Economics* 37:113–122.

Beer, L., and T. Boswell. 2002. The resilience of dependency effects in explaining income inequality in the global economy: A cross-national analysis, 1975–1995. *Journal of World-Systems Research* 8:30–59.

Bornschier, V., and C. Chase-Dunn. 1985. *Transnational corporations and underdevelopment.* New York: Praeger.

Bunker, S. G. 1985. *Underdeveloping the Amazon: Extraction, unequal exchange, and the failure of the modern state.* Urbana: University of Illinois Press.

Burns, T. J., and A. K. Jorgenson. 2004. Effects of rural and urban population dynamics and national development on deforestation rates, 1990–2000. Paper presented at the mini-conference of the International Sociological Association sections on the environment and community, San Francisco, Calif., August 2004.

Burns, T. J., J. Kentor, and A. K. Jorgenson. 2003. Trade dependence, pollution, and infant mortality in less developed countries. In *Crises and resistance in the 21st century world-system*, ed. W. A. Dunaway, 14–28. Westport, Conn.: Praeger.

Burns, T. J., E. Kick, and B. Davis. 2003. Theorizing and rethinking linkages between the natural environment and the modern world-system: Deforestation in the late 20th century. *Journal of World-Systems Research* 9:357–392.

Burns, T. J., E. L. Kick, D. A. Murray, and D. A. Murray. 1994. Demography, development, and deforestation in a world-system perspective. *International Journal of Comparative Sociology* 35:221–239.

Chambers, N., C. Simmons, and M. Wackernagel. 2002. *Sharing nature's interest: Ecological footprints as an indicator of sustainability.* Sterling, Va.: Earthscan Publications.

Chase-Dunn, C. 1975. The effects of international economic dependence on development and inequality: A cross-national study. *American Sociological Review* 40:720–738.

————. 1998. *Global formation: Structures of the world-economy*. Lanham, Md.: Rowman and Littlefield.

Chase-Dunn, C., and A. K. Jorgenson. 2003. Regions and interaction networks: An institutional-materialist approach. *International Journal of Comparative Sociology* 44:433–450.

Chew, S. C. 2001. *World ecological degradation: Accumulation, urbanization, and deforestation 3000 B.C.–A.D. 2000*. Walnut Creek, Calif.: AltaMira.

Clapp, J. 2002. The distancing of waste: Overconsumption in a global economy. In *Confronting consumption*, ed. T. Princen, M. Maniates, and K. Conca, 155–176. Cambridge, Mass.: MIT Press.

Conca, K. 2002. Consumption and environment in a global economy. In *Confronting consumption*, ed. T. Princen, M. Maniates, and K. Conca, 133–154. Cambridge, Mass.: MIT Press.

Ehrlich, P., and A. Ehrlich. 1990. *The population explosion*. New York: Simon and Schuster.

Ehrlich, P., and J. Holdren. 1971. Impacts of population growth. *Science* 171:1212–1217.

Emmanuel, A. 1972. *Unequal exchange: A study of the imperialism of trade*. New York: Monthly Review Press.

Foster, J. B. 2002. *Ecology against capitalism*. New York: Monthly Review Press.

Frey, R. S. 1998. The export of hazardous industries to the peripheral zones of the world-system. *Journal of Developing Societies* 14:66–81.

Galtung, J. 1971. A structural theory of imperialism. *Journal of Peace Research* 8:81–117.

Gereffi, G., and M. Korzeniewicz, eds. 1994. *Commodity chains and global capitalism*. Westport, Conn.: Praeger.

Grimes, P., and J. Kentor. 2003. Exporting the greenhouse: Foreign capital penetration and CO_2 emissions 1980–1996. *Journal of World-Systems Research* 9:261–275.

Grossman, G., and A. Krueger. 1995. Economic growth and the environment. *Quarterly Journal of Economics* 110:353–377.

Hornborg, A. 2001. *The power of the machine: Global inequalities of economy, technology, and environment*. Walnut Creek, Calif.: AltaMira.

————. 2003. Cornucopia or zero-sum game? The epistemology of sustainability. *Journal of World-Systems Research* 9:205–218.

International Monetary Fund. 2003. *Direction of trade statistics*. Washington, D.C.: International Monetary Fund Publications Services.

Jenkins, C., and S. Scanlan. 2001. Food security in less-developed countries, 1970–1990. *American Sociological Review* 66:714–744.

Jorgenson, A. K. 2003. Consumption and environmental degradation: A cross-national analysis of the ecological footprint. *Social Problems* 50:374–394.

————. 2004a. Uneven processes and environmental degradation in the world-economy. *Human Ecology Review* 11:103–113.

————. 2004b. Global inequality, water pollution, and infant mortality. *Social Science Journal* 41:279–288.

————. 2005. Unpacking international power and the ecological footprints of nations: A quantitative cross-national study. *Sociological Perspectives* 48:383–402.

————. 2006. Global warming and the neglected greenhouse gas: A cross-national study of the social causes of methane emissions intensity, 1995. *Social Forces* 84:1777–1796.

————. Forthcoming. Global social change, natural resource consumption, and environmental degradation. In *Global social change: A reader*, ed. C. Chase-Dunn and S. Babones. Baltimore: Johns Hopkins University Press.

Jorgenson, A. K., and T. Burns. 2004. Globalization, the environment, and infant mortality: A cross-national study. *Humboldt Journal of Social Relations* 28:7–52.

Jorgenson, A. K., and E. Kick. 2003. Globalization and the environment. *Journal of World-Systems Research* 9:195–204.

Jorgenson, A. K., and J. Rice. 2005. Structural dynamics of international trade and material consumption: A cross-national study of the ecological footprints of less-developed countries. *Journal of World-Systems Research* 11:57–77.

Jorgenson, A. K., J. Rice, and J. Crowe. 2005. Unpacking the ecological footprints of nations. *International Journal of Comparative Sociology* 46:241–260.

Kentor, J. 2000. *Capital and coercion: The economic and military processes that have shaped the world economy 1800–1990*. New York: Garland.

————. 2001. The long-term effects of globalization on population growth, inequality, and economic development. *Social Problems* 48:435–455.

Kentor, J., and T. Boswell. 2003. Foreign capital dependence and development: A new direction. *American Sociological Review* 68:301–313.

Kick, E. L., T. J. Burns, B. Davis, D. A. Murray, and D. A. Murray. 1996. Impacts of domestic population dynamics and foreign wood trade on deforestation: A world-system perspective. *Journal of Developing Societies* 12:68–87.

Maddison, A. 2001. *The world economy: A millennial perspective*. Paris: Organization of Economic Cooperation and Development.

Magee, S. 1980. *International trade*. Reading, Mass.: Addison Wesley.

McMichael, P. 2004. *Development and social change: A global perspective*. Thousand Oaks, Calif.: Pine Forge.

Moore, J. 2003. The modern world-system as environmental history? Ecology and the rise of capitalism. *Theory and Society* 32:307–377.

O'Connor, J. 1998. *Natural causes:Essays in ecological marxism*. New York: Guilford.

Organization for Economic Cooperation and Development (OECD). 1998. *Globalization and the environment: Perspectives from OECD and dynamic non-member economies*. New York: OECD.

Portes, A., C. Dore-Cabral, and P. Landolt, eds. 1997. *The urban Caribbean: Transition to the new global economy*. Baltimore: Johns Hopkins University Press.

Prescott-Allen, R. 2001. *The well-being of nations*. Washington, D.C.: Island.

Princen, T. 2002. Consumption and externalities: Where economy meets ecology. In *Confronting consumption*, ed. T. Princen, M. Maniates, and K. Conca, 23–42. Cambridge, Mass.: MIT Press.

Princen, T., M. Maniates, and K. Conca. 2002. Confronting consumption. In *Confronting consumption*, ed. T. Princen, M. Maniates, and K. Conca, 1–20. Cambridge, Mass.: MIT Press.

Ricardo, D. 1951 (1821). *On the principles of political economy and taxation*. 3rd ed. In *The works and correspondence of David Ricardo*, vol. 1, ed. P. Sraffe and M. M. Dobb. Repr., Cambridge, U.K.: Cambridge University Press.

Rosa, E., R. York, and T. Dietz. 2004. Tracking the anthropogenic drivers of ecological impacts. *Ambio* 33:509–512.

Rothman, D. 1998. Environmental kuznets curves—real progress or passing the buck? *Ecological Economics* 25:177–194.

Rudel, T. K. 1998. Is there a forest transition? Deforestation, reforestation, and development. *Rural Sociology* 65:533–552.

Schnaiberg, A., and K. Gould. 1994. *Environment and society: The enduring conflict*. New York: St. Martin's.

Venetoulis, J., D. Chazan, and C. Gaudet. 2004. *Ecological footprint of nations 2004*. Oakland, Calif.: Redefining Progress.

Wackernagel, M., N. B. Schulz, D. Deumling, A. Callejas Linares, M. Jenkins, V. Kapos, C. Monfreda, J. Loh, N. Meyers, R. Norgaard, and J. Randers. 2002. Tracking the ecological overshoot of the human economy. *Proceedings of the National Academy of Sciences* 99:9266–9271.

Wallerstein, I. 1999. Ecology and capitalist costs of production: No exit. In *Ecology and the world-system*, ed. W. Goldfrank, D. Goodman, and A. Szasz, 3–12. Westport, Conn.: Greenwood.

World Bank. 1996. *World tables*. Washington, D.C.: World Bank.

———. 2000. *World development indicators*. Washington, D.C.: World Bank.

———. 2001. *World development indicators*. Washington, D.C.: World Bank.

York, R., E. Rosa, and T. Dietz. 2003. Footprints on the earth: The environmental consequences of modernity. *American Sociological Review* 68:279–300.

Combining Social Metabolism and   **15**
Input–Output Analyses to Account for
Ecologically Unequal Trade

HELGA WEISZ

ORLD-SYSTEMS THEORY regards the expansion of the industrial capitalist system as intrinsically connected to a spatial separation, on a global scale, between the early and the later stages of the industrial production process, and between production and consumption in general. The first production stages are characterized by the extraction of relatively large amounts of matter and energy from nature, whereas in the later stages comparatively small amounts of material and energy serve as a direct input to produce the final goods. As a consequence, this on-going process of increasing international division of labor could lead to a globally uneven distribution of the costs (in terms of environmental pressure) and the benefits (in terms of material standard of living) of the use of material and energy. Regarding carbon dioxide (CO_2) emissions, such an uneven distribution of environmental pressures has been termed "carbon leakage." More generally it is referred to as "ecologically unequal trade" or "ecological terms of trade." The question I address in this chapter is how ecologically unequal trade can be defined and measured empirically. I argue that an integration of social metabolism and input-output analyses provides a conceptually sound approach to account for ecologically unequal trade between national economies or world regions and demonstrate the feasibility of this approach by presenting a case study for Denmark. The concept of social metabolism in combination with input-output economics holds great promises for an integration of world-system analysis and eco-logical economics. Essentially the idea is that these two traditions together could serve to integrate environmental concerns with concerns regarding social inequality. In particular this chapter addresses the question of how the distinction between extractive and productive economies and the hypotheses of ecologically unequal exchange between different economies of the world-system can be analyzed empirically.

World-Systems Analysis and Ecologically Unequal Exchange

The notion of unequal exchange is central to the world-systems perspective founded by Immanuel Wallerstein (1974, 1980, 1989). This perspective pioneered the study of world economies and has sought to understand uneven development among different world regions. It should be seen as a direct criticism of "modernization" theories and in particular of their essential assertion that the developing countries are merely lagging behind on their path toward modernity, and that their problems are attributable to their traditionalism and their "historical backwardness" (Shannon 1996). World-systems approaches owe a lot to dependency theory (Frank 1966, 1978), a body of work that was also inspired by a rejection of modernization theories. To dependency theorists, the "underdevelopment" in the nonindustrial periphery is due to its exchange relations with the affluent core economies, which keep the periphery in a state of dependency and exploitation to the benefit of the latter (Frank 1966; Bunker 1985). Essentially, a world-systems perspective conceives of the world economy as an interstate capitalist system. Following Marx, the driving force of the capitalist system is considered to be the accumulation of capital by those who control the means of production (Shannon 1996).

Environmental issues only recently gained recognition within world-systems analysis, with the notable exception of Bunker's (1985) pioneering studies on the Brazilian Amazon. World-systems approaches regard the expansion of the industrial capitalist system as being intrinsically connected to a growing spatial separation between the early stages of the industrial production process (characterized by a relatively large throughput of matter and energy) and the later stages (characterized by a comparatively small material and energy throughput). This leads to an increasing international division of labor that, according to world-systems analysis, in turn leads to different internal dynamics in extractive and productive economies and thus to uneven development (see Bunker in this volume). In this view, such a development tends to be accompanied by an unequal distribution of the burden of raw materials extraction, and emissions and wastes generated to the disadvantage of extractive economies, with productive economies enjoying the benefit of a high material standard of living.

Such a "green" perspective on unequal exchange calls, as Hornborg (2001) has suggested, for Marx's labor-focused concept of exploitation to be supplemented by a biophysical one (i.e. focused on material and energy flows). At this point, world-systems perspectives and ecological economics converge. In particular, the concept of social metabolism combined with input-output economics holds great promise for offering the requisite tools for an empirical investigation of unequal exchange in terms of materials and energy.

Social Metabolism and Ecologically Unequal Trade

So far, only a few studies have been published that attempt to investigate empirically unequal exchange between different world regions in terms of materials, energy, or land use. In this section I will discuss this empirical evidence, starting with a brief introduction to the concept of material flow analysis as one approach to operationalize social metabolism (the others being energy flow analysis and human appropriation of net primary production, together denoted as MEFA; see Haberl et al. 2004; Krausmann et al. 2004). The application of the biological concept of metabolism (*Stoffwechsel*) to social systems can be traced back to Marx who, influenced by Liebig and Moleschott, talks about the "metabolism between man and nature as mediated by the labor process" (Marx 1990). Such a biophysical approach to economics arguably did not gain major influence in the decades to come, despite the fact that the relevance of metabolism for Marxist theory as a whole is still a matter of debate (Schmidt 1971; Martinez-Alier 1987; Foster 2000; Sieferle 2001).

Social metabolism, along with increasingly sophisticated and standardized methods to account for its material aspects (denoted as material flow analysis), started to form an integrated school of thought only recently (Baccini and Brunner 1991; Fischer-Kowalski and Haberl 1993; Ayres and Simonis 1994). The analogy with the biological concept of metabolism derives from the observation that biological systems (organisms, but also higher level systems such as ecosystems) and socioeconomic systems (human societies, economies, companies, etc.) decisively depend on a continuous throughput of energy and materials in order to maintain their internal structure. Contrary to the biological notion, the social concept links material and energy flows to social organization, recognizing that the quantity of economic resource use, the material composition, and the sources and sinks of the material flows are historically variable as a function of the socioeconomic production system (Sieferle 1997; Weisz et al. 2001; Haberl and Krausmann 2001; Schandl and Schulz 2002).

Material flow analysis (MFA) relies on a specific physical accounting approach aiming at the quantification of social metabolism. Although applicable to various scales, the most elaborate applications refer to the level of the nation state and above. National (or economy-wide) MFAs are consistent compilations of the annual overall material throughput of national economies, expressing all flows in metric tonnes per year (Eurostat 2001). After the seminal work of Robert Ayres and Allen Kneese (Ayres and Kneese 1969; Ayres 1978), MFA was "reinvented" in the 1990s as a consequence of the growing importance of the notion of sustainable development. In recent years, methods for economy-wide material flow accounting have been harmonized (Eurostat 2001) and a growing number of material flow studies for both industrial and developing countries have been published. As a result, for the first time, aggregated data concerning physical trade volumes of countries in different world regions have become available.

The Physical Trade Balance Approach

One social metabolism approach that was chosen to analyze unequal trade in terms of materials is called the "physical trade balance" (PTB) approach (Eurostat 2001). Foreign trade statistics in almost all countries of the world report annual trade (i.e. import and export) quantities in both monetary (national currency units) and physical terms (e.g. mass units, volume units, or pieces) and distinguish between hundreds or thousands of types of goods. With some precautions (e.g. unit conversions and cross-checks) these data can be aggregated into total physical import and export quantities in metric tonnes. The physical trade balance is defined as physical imports minus physical exports, thus a positive PTB indicates a trade surplus or net imports and a negative PTB indicates a physical trade deficit or net exports.[1]

The first physical trade balances were published for the United Kingdom (Schandl and Schulz 2002) in a long time-series. These data show that net imports into the UK amounted to 150 million metric tonnes (60 percent of which were fossil fuels) in the early 1970s. Starting with the exploitation of the North Sea gas and oil fields by the United Kingdom in 1974, net imports dropped to a level of 11 million metric tonnes in 2000 (mostly biomass and ores). The United Kingdom has thus generally been a net exporter of fossil fuels since 1981, except for a few years in the 1980s, when an oil platform accident occurred, which diminished U.K. oil extraction for some years. If we take the physical trade balance as an indicator allowing us to distinguish between "extractive" and "productive" economies in Bunker's (1985) sense, the United Kingdom should be viewed as a thoroughly productive economy in 1970, when net biomass imports amounted to 37 million metric tonnes, net imports of ores to 18 million metric tonnes, and net imports of fossil fuels to 100 million metric tonnes. By 2000, however, the UK could be viewed as an extractive economy in terms of fossil fuels (net exports amounted to 20 million metric tonnes), although it had remained a productive economy in terms of biomass (PTB 28 million metric tonnes) and ores (PTB 16 million metric tonnes).

Physical trade balances for the European Union as a whole and for each of the EU member states have been compiled for the European Statistical Office, which implemented these accounts as part of its environmental accounting activities (Eurostat 2002; Weisz et al. forthcoming a). These studies show that the EU-15 in 2000 was a net importer of 1 billion metric tonnes of materials, 70 percent of this total being fossil fuels and 20 percent industrial minerals and ores. Overall, the EU-15 imported almost four times as many metric tonnes as it exported. Moreover, the domestic extraction of raw materials in the European Union has increased only slightly since 1970 (15 percent total increase from 1970 to 2000), whereas the amount of imported materials grew by 43 percent in the same time period. This is an indication that the EU-15 economies rely increasingly on imported materials.

All Latin American economies studied so far (Brazil, Chile, Colombia, and Venezuela) show a physical trade deficit, that is, they are net exporters of materials (see Eisenmenger 2002; Pérez-Rincón 2006). Muradian and Martinez-Alier (2001) investigated South-North trade of nineteen materials for the period between 1968 and 1996 and found significant increases in imports to the North, in particular for aluminum (factor seven), pig iron, iron and steel templates, nickel, and petroleum products (factor three to four). Fischer-Kowalski and Amann (2001) compared four affluent economies (Germany, The Netherlands, Japan, and the United Kingdom) with two developing economies (Brazil and Venezuela) and found that all affluent economies are net importers and all developing economies are net exporters of materials.

Is this sufficient empirical evidence to support the hypotheses of ecological unequal trade between developing and industrial economies? I am hesitant to say so for two reasons. The first reason is that there also exists empirical evidence against the hypothesis that the affluent economies exploit the natural resources of the developing countries to their own benefit. For example, a recently finished study of social metabolism for Southeast

Asia revealed that all investigated countries (Laos, Vietnam, the Philippines, and Thailand) were net importers of materials (Weisz et al. forthcoming b; unpublished data from SeaTrans EU-FP5 INCO-DEV Project "Southeast Asia in Transition"). These economies seemingly do not exploit their raw materials for the world market.

Even for the EU-15 the empirical evidence is not unambiguous: Although it is true that in the EU-15 physical imports exceed exports by a factor of four, we also have to consider that imports grew by only 43 percent from 1970 to 2000, whereas exports have increased by 120 percent, and the quantities of physical trade between the EU member states (so called intra-EU trade) grew by 150 percent over this period (Weisz et al. forthcoming a).

A final example: Norway, one of the most affluent countries in the world in terms of per capita GDP, depends heavily on the extraction of huge amounts of fossil fuels, which are exploited to be exported to the world market. Norway's domestic extraction of raw materials amounts to over 50 metric tonnes per capita and year (80 percent of which are fossil fuels), which is four times as much as the EU average of 13 metric tonnes per capita of domestic raw material extraction (Moll, Bringezu, and Schütz 2003; Weisz et al. forthcoming a). Norway can thus safely be considered an extractive economy, despite the fact that it is the most affluent country in the world.

The second problem with the existing empirical evidence is a methodological one, leading us to the central argument of this chapter. Considering that physical trade balances measure imports and exports with their weight as they cross the border, which means that the traded goods are in different stages of processing, we face a bias when simply comparing imports and exports in metric tonnes.

In the majority of cases, the extraction-production-consumption-disposal process starts with large amounts of materials that are gradually reduced; at each stage of the production chain, useful materials are separated out from useless materials, which are disposed of as wastes or emissions (notably there are exceptions, where the products gain in weight during processing, e.g. beer brewery). The differences between the mass of the primary raw materials and that of the final products are particularly high for ores and animal products. In the case of metal mining, the raw ores have to be surfaced and the pure ore has to be isolated. Depending on the grade of the ores, the difference between the raw and purified ore may be enormous (see Ayres and Ayres 1998; Giljum 2004). The total amount of materials extraction (which comprises not only the gross ores but also energy carriers, chemicals, etc.) that has been required to isolate the purified metal ore may exceed the amount of the traded metal commodity by orders of magnitude. The discharge of this primary material turnover represents environmental loads in the country of extraction without showing up in the weight of the traded products. Such environmental distribution effects occur relatively independently of the economic benefits of the transaction. Thus, they are not represented in monetary statistics on international trade. The same holds true for the physical trade volumes. How much something weighs at the point of crossing international borders is represented in the physical trade balances, but this tells us little about the overall amount of raw materials required in the country of origin and in part "left behind" there as wastes and emissions.[2] An analysis of ecologically unequal trade should balance the upstream environmental burdens of both imports and exports. In order to calculate such an "ecological trade balance" we need three things: First, an indicator that measures the environmental burden (for example: energy demand, raw material demand, land requirements, or emissions). Second, an indicator for the production system of a given economy. Third, a procedure to attribute these quantities of upstream requirements to either domestic uses or exports. The same should be done for imports. While the first and second types of information are provided by social metabolism studies, the third type of information can most powerfully be generated by the use of input–output economics.

The Input–Output Approach

More than fifty years ago, Wassily Leontief, the creator of input–output economics, asked himself a question that is formally equivalent to the question that I asked above, and developed a method to investigate it empirically.[3] Since the days of Ricardo, economists generally assume that there cannot be such a thing as unequal trade, because trade would be for the benefit of all trading partners. In its neoclassical version this assumption is known as the Heckscher-Ohlin theory, which predicts that each country exports the commodity that intensively uses its most abundant factor of production. For instance, the U.S. economy was considered to be the most capital-intensive in the world (in terms of capital per worker) in 1947, the year for which Leontief made his first empirical test. The Heckscher-Ohlin theory consequently predicted that U.S. exports would require more capital per worker than U.S. imports. Using the 1947 input-output table, Leontief aggregated factor inputs into two categories, labor and capital, and computed the capital and labor requirements to produce imports and exports. He found that, contrary to the Heckscher–Ohlin theory, the U.S. imports were 30 percent more capital-intensive than U.S. exports (Leontief 1956). This empirical result came to be known as the "Leontief Paradox," and it inspired a number of studies aiming at confirming or disproving the paradox, a discussion that continues today (cf. Wolff 2004).

The details of this debate need not concern us here. What is important is to see the analogy to our question above. Neoclassical economists, measuring everything in monetary units, rarely consider factor inputs other than capital and labor. From a biophysical point of view, however, it is clear that raw materials, energy, or land use are also important factors for the production system. Moreover, the economic process is inevitably connected to the generation of wastes and emissions. Using input–output tables, which are now compiled and published periodically for many countries in the world, and Leontief's famous formula,[4] we are able to calculate any factor input intensities of traded goods, for example raw material intensities, CO_2 intensities, energy intensities, waste intensities, and so on. By multiplying these intensities with the total import and export quantities, we arrive at a corresponding set of ecological trade balances or, as Martinez-Alier (this volume) puts it, "ecological terms of trade," for example CO_2, raw material, energy, or waste terms of trade. In actual fact, this kind of analysis is not new but has been carried out since the 1960s for many countries, using predominantly energy and pollution indicators.[5]

The basis of an input–output model is an input–output table. Such a table is shown in table 15.1, which represents a highly aggregated version

Table 15.1. Schema of an aggregated physical input-output table (example of Denmark 1990, million metric tonnes)

Million Metric Tonnes	Production Sectors			Final Demand		
	Agriculture and Mining	Industries	Services	Domestic	Exports	*Total Output*
Agriculture and Mining	6.1	52.7	0.4	0.7	9.9	**69.9**
Industries	5.1	26.1	3.3	63.6	13.1	**111.1**
Services	0.0	0.0	0.0	0.7	0.2	**1.0**
Domestic Raw Materials	84.3	26.2	0.0			
Imports	4.2	28.4	2.0			
Wastes and Emissions	−29.9	−22.3	−4.8			
Total Input	**69.9**	**111.1**	**1.0**			

Note: Data from Pedersen (1999) aggregated and modified according to Weisz et al. (forthcoming a) by the author.

of the Danish physical input-output table for 1990 (Pedersen 1999). Generally, input-output tables consist of three quadrants, the first of which (the interindustry quadrant) is a symmetrical industry-times-industry matrix, which shows the flows of goods between the producing sectors, that is agriculture and mining, industries, and services. The second is the output quadrant showing the supply of goods from each of the producing sectors to final demand. Finally, the third quadrant (the input quadrant) shows those inputs to each of the producing sectors that are not supplied by the production system but are received from external sources.

Table 15.1 represents a physical input-output table, which means that all flows are measured in units of mass.[6] The overall consistency of the table is therefore guaranteed by the mass balance principle and total inputs (overall and per sector) must equal total outputs. To increase clarity, table 15.1 distinguishes between only a few sectors in each of the quadrants. These are agriculture and mining, industries, and services in the first quadrant; domestic final demand and exports in the second quadrant; and domestic raw materials, imports, and losses in the form of wastes and emissions in the third quadrant.

Using table 15.1 as an example, we shall now consider the difference between direct and indirect requirements. In table 15.1 outputs are shown along the rows from left to right, and inputs along the columns from bottom to top. For example, the agriculture and mining sector in Denmark in 1990 *directly* extracted 84 million metric tonnes of raw materials from the domestic territory, and received 4 million metric tonnes of materials (a mixture of raw materials and manufactured goods) from imports. In the same year, the agriculture and mining sectors generated 30 million metric tonnes of wastes and emissions (which are shown as factor inputs with negative signs in the third quadrant). In addition, the agriculture and mining sector received 5 million metric tonnes of commodities from the industrial sectors (e.g. fertilizers and energy) and 6 million metric tonnes as intrasectoral deliveries (from companies within the same sector, e.g. animal fodder). Not surprisingly, the *direct* outputs of the primary sector predominantly went to the industrial production sectors, which used them as materials inputs to produce the bulk of consumer goods for either domestic final demand (64 million metric tonnes) or exports (13 million metric tonnes). In other words, what can directly be derived from such a table is the well-known fact that the first stages of the economic process are characterized by the extraction and purification of huge amounts of raw materials, with the corresponding generation of huge amounts of wastes and emissions. The outcome of this process predominantly serves as input to other stages of the economic process, in particular industrial production, and does not go directly to final demand.

If we want to know the amount of material factor inputs (be it raw material input, imports, or waste generation) associated with the production of exported commodities, neither the weight of the imports and exports, nor the direct flows as defined above give us sufficient information. If we want to know, for example, the materials required to produce the 0.2 million metric tonnes of exports from the service sector, we not only have to consider the share of the direct inputs to the service sectors (e.g. the share of the 3.3 million metric tonnes received from the industrial sector). We also want to know the amount of material inputs that were needed for the industrial sector to produce the share of the 3.3 million metric tonnes for the service sector. Suppose that we have calculated, for instance, the share of the 53 million metric tonnes, which the industrial sector received from the agricultural and mining sector, that was needed to produce the share of the 3.3 million metric tonnes for the service sector that in turn were needed to produce the 0.2 million metric tonnes of exports for the service sector; we would still not be finished. As we are interested in material factor inputs, we need to consider the amount of materials that the agriculture and mining sector extracted or imported in order to produce its output to the industrial sector in the first place. Also, we have to consider all other inputs to the service sector (e.g. 0.4 million metric tonnes from agriculture and mining or 2 million metric tonnes from imports) and their respective material requirements.

This is a type of problem that seems to continue indefinitely, and actually does.[7] It can be solved mathematically, however, with sufficient accuracy. A quick and practical solution, using matrix calculation, was proposed by Wassily Leontief, and is now at the heart of input-output analysis. Using this model, we can calculate the indirect physical factor inputs needed to produce one unit of exports for each of the sectors. By multiplying these intensities with import or export volume, we arrive at the "ecological terms of trade."

Ecological Trade Balances for Denmark

Denmark is one of the richest countries in the European Union in terms of GDP per capita. In 1990, the base year for our calculation, Denmark hardly produced any industrial minerals, ores, or fossil fuels domestically. These raw materials were mostly imported. The bulk of the materials extracted domestically were construction minerals (such as sand and gravel, which predominantly serve to increase the built infrastructure and are hardly traded)

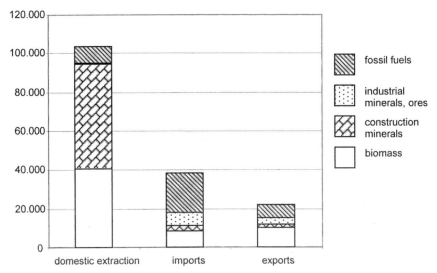

Figure 15.1.   Material flows for Denmark 1990 (in 1,000 metric tonnes). *Source:* Weisz et al. (forthcoming a)

and biomass (see figure 15.1). Denmark was a net importer of 16 million metric tonnes of materials in 1990, with fossil fuels accounting for more than half of this amount.

Adding the amount of materials extracted from the domestic territory with the amount of imports in metric tonnes gives a total of roughly 150 million metric tonnes of material inputs to the Danish economy in 1990. The left-hand column in figure 15.2 divides this amount of material inputs among the producing sectors that directly extract or import these materials (direct material inputs into production sectors). The highest material inputs are found in primary sectors like agriculture and mining. In addition, the construction sector also uses huge amounts of materials extracted directly from the domestic national territory.

The right-hand column in figure 15.2 illustrates the results of the physical input–output analysis proposed above. This analysis divides the same amount of material factor inputs according to *indirect* inputs of the same sectors, that is via deliveries from other production sectors (indirect material requirements of final demand). If we take, for example, the mining sector, we see that its huge direct material inputs are predominantly delivered to other producing sectors. The actual material requirements of the mining sector itself, that is to produce its own final commodities, are much lower.

The reverse is true for the industrial sector and also for services. These sectors *indirectly* use much more material factor inputs than they *directly*

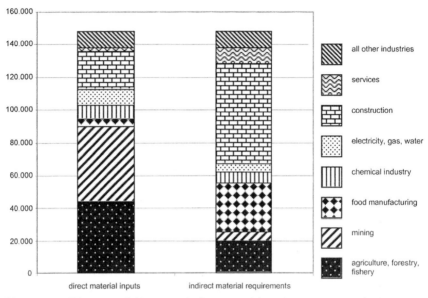

Figure 15.2.   Direct material inputs vs. indirect material requirements per production sector, Denmark, 1990 (1,000 metric tonnes). *Source:* Calculations based on data from Pedersen (1999) and Weisz et al. (forthcoming a)

receive as raw materials and imports to produce their final demand commodities.

Having illustrated the difference between direct and indirect material factor requirements, we can now proceed with our calculation of the ecological terms of trade. To this end, we need to separate domestic final demand from exports. This is shown in figure 15.3. The sum of the indirect material requirements of domestic final demand and exports, of course, must add up to the 150 million metric tonnes of material factor inputs. Although the material requirements for domestic final demand are roughly twice as high as for exports, it can clearly be seen that most of it is related to construction activities. Similarly, electricity and services produce predominantly for the domestic market. Resource-demanding and polluting sectors such as agriculture, food manufacturing, and chemical industry, on the other hand, predominantly produce for the world market. In terms of mass, indirect material requirements for exports amount to more than twice as much as the exported goods themselves.

Finally, we compare the weight of Denmark's imports and exports to the indirect material requirements of exports and imports to arrive at an ecological trade balance (see figure 15.4). Clearly, the physical trade balance

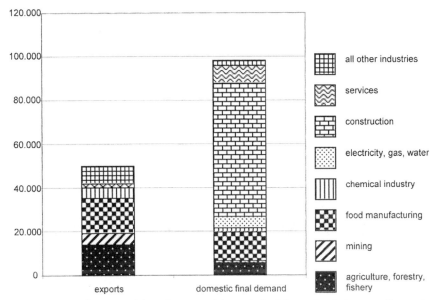

Figure 15.3.   Indirect material requirements of domestic final demand and of exports, Denmark, 1990 (1,000 metric tonnes). *Source:* Calculations based on data from Pedersen (1999) and Weisz et al. (forthcoming a)

approach (shown in the two right-hand columns in figure 15.4) significantly underestimates the degree to which domestic consumption in Denmark relies on foreign material resources. The indirect material requirements for imports far exceed those of the exports. Instead of 16 million metric tonnes of net imports, which were calculated as the direct physical trade balance, the balance of indirect material requirements shows more than 100 million metric tonnes of net imports. Most of these net imports pertain to the electricity and gas sector, showing the great reliance of Denmark's economy on imported fossil fuels in 1990.[8]

Conclusions

In this chapter I have looked at the notion of ecologically unequal trade from the perspective of empirical evidence. I started with the assumption of a world-systems perspective that the expansion of the industrial capitalist system is intrinsically connected to a spatial separation, on a global scale, between the early and the later stages of the industrial production process. The notion of ecologically unequal trade assumes that a globally uneven distribution of the costs (in terms of environmental pressure) and the benefits (in terms of material standard of living) of the use of material and energy, is

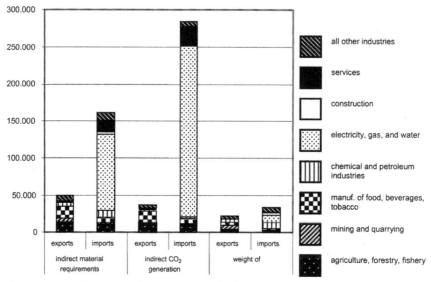

Figure 15.4.   Indirect material requirements and indirect CO_2 emissions of imports and exports, Denmark, 1990 (1,000 metric tonnes). *Source:* Calculations based on data from Pedersen (1999) and Weisz et al. (forthcoming a)

a consequence of this ongoing international division of labor. A review of social metabolism studies that analyze direct trade flows or direct emissions from exporting sectors shows that the results obtained so far do not unambiguously support the hypotheses of ecologically unequal trade between rich and poor countries, nor are they methodologically robust.

In combining social metabolism and input-output analysis, I showed how the problem of measuring ecologically unequal trade can be reframed in terms of balancing the indirect material factor requirements of imports and exports. This requires that we supplement the neoclassical definition of factor inputs, which comprises labor and capital only, with a biophysical concept, including material flows, energy flows, and land use. The type of analysis I have presented here has the obvious advantage of recognizing the complex interrelations between the different sectors of the economic system, an aspect which is often neglected in empirical studies of ecologically unequal trade.

Applied to the case of Denmark, the input-output approach revealed that the reliance of the Danish economy on imported raw materials to satisfy its domestic final consumption in 1990 was more than twice as high as suggested by the physical trade balance approach. The conclusions I can draw at this point are that it is indeed essential to consider the complex interrelations of the economic sectors producing the traded commodities, and that input-output economics in combination with material and energy flow analysis offer the appropriate tools. Regarding the hypothesis of ecologically unequal trade, a definite conclusion would have to rely on a much broader empirical base. More economies would have to be analyzed, and more ecological indicators included.

There are limitations as well. They pertain to the assumptions of input-output economics and are currently being discussed intensively. Nevertheless, if this kind of biophysical input-output analysis will be more widely applied to the question of ecologically unequal trade, methodological improvements can be expected. For a biophysical analysis of the current global distribution patterns of environmental loads, on one hand, and standards of living, on the other, the use of an input-output model of the world economy in combination with biophysical analysis (Duchin, forthcoming) may ultimately turn out to be the most promising strategy of empirical investigation.

Notes

I am grateful to Faye Duchin and Peter Fleissner for their support and help in input-output analysis. Thanks also to Fridolin Krausmann, Klaus Hubacek, and Sangwon Suh, with whom I discussed these issues intensively. This work was supported by a grant from the *Jubiläumsfonds* of the Austrian National Bank (OeNB), project number 10430.

1. This definition of the physical trade balance as being the reverse of the definition of the monetary trade balance (exports minus imports) recognizes that in economies, money and goods move in opposite directions.

2. Schmidt-Bleek (1994) coined the term "ecological rucksacks" to denote such upstream material requirements of commodities.

3. I thank Faye Duchin for making me aware of the formal equivalence between the problem of ecological unequal trade and Leontief's discussion of the Heckscher-Ohlin theory.

4. The basic formula $[(I-A)^{-1}*y = x]$ of the static input-output quantity model, which allows us to compute the factor requirements to satisfy a given bill of final deliveries, be it for domestic or foreign uses.

5. Cf. Cumberland (1966); Ayres and Kneese (1969); Leontief (1970); Bullard and Herendeen (1975); Griffin (1976); Proops (1977); Proops, Faber, and Wagenhals (1993); Duchin et al. (1994); Fleissner et al. (1993).

6. Most studies use input-output tables in monetary units extended by a vector of biophysical inputs. For a recent discussion about the differences of input-output models based on physical vs. monetary tables, see Weisz and Duchin (forthcoming).

7. The problem can formally be represented by a power series, that is, an infinite sum.

8. Please note that if material requirements of imports are calculated using the same tables as for exports, as is commonly done, the interpretation is somewhat different. Such calculations do not show the actual requirements that were needed to produce the imported goods, but rather a biophysical analogy to opportunity costs.

References

Ayres, R. U. 1978. *Resources, environment and economics: Applications of the materials/energy balance principle.* New York: Wiley.

Ayres, R. U., and L. W. Ayres. 1998. *Accounting for resources.* Vol. 1, *Economy-wide applications of mass-balance principles to materials and waste.* Cheltenham, U.K., and Lyme, N.H.: Elgar.

Ayres, R. U., and A. V. Kneese. 1969. Production, consumption and externalities. In *American Economic Review* 59 (3): 282–297.

Ayres, R. U., and U. E. Simonis. 1994. *Industrial metabolism: Restructuring for sustainable development.* Tokyo, New York, and Paris: United Nations University Press.

Baccini, P., and P. H. Brunner. 1991. *The metabolism of the anthroposphere.* Berlin: Springer.

Bullard, C., and R. A. Herendeen. 1975. The energy costs of goods and services. In *Energy Policy* 3 (4): 268–278.

Bunker, S. G. 1985. *Underdeveloping the Amazon: Extraction, unequal exchange, and the failure of the modern state.* Chicago: Chicago University Press.

Cumberland, J. 1966. A regional interindustry model for analysis of development objectives. In *Papers of the Regional Science Association* 17:65–94.

Duchin, F. Forthcoming. Input-output economics and material flows. In *A handbook on input-output analysis in industrial ecology,* ed. S. Suh. Dordrecht: Springer.

Duchin, F., G. M. Lange, K. Thonstadt, and A. Idenburg. 1994. *The future of the environment: Ecological economics and technological change.* New York and Oxford: Oxford University Press.

Eisenmenger, N. 2002. Internationaler Handel und globale Umweltveränderungen: Kann eine Verbindung der Welt-System Theorie mit dem Konzept des gesellschaftlichen Metabolismus zu einem besseren Verständnis beitragen? *Kurswechsel* 4:87–99.

Eurostat. 2001. *Economy-wide material flow accounts and derived indicators: A methodological guide.* Luxembourg: Eurostat, European Commission, Office for Official Publications of the European Communities.

———. 2002. *Material use in the European Union 1980–2000: Indicators and analysis.* Prepared by H. Weisz, M. Fischer-Kowalski, C. Amann, N. Eisenmenger, K. Hubacek, and F. Krausmann. Luxembourg: Eurostat, Office for Official Publications of the European Communities.

Fischer-Kowalski, M., and C. Amann. 2001. Beyond IPAT and Kuznets curves: Globalization as a vital factor in analysing the environmental impact of socio-economic metabolism. *Population and Environment* 23 (1): 7–47.

Fischer-Kowalski, M., and H. Haberl. 1993. Metabolism and colonization: Modes of production and the physical exchange between societies and nature. *Innovation: The European Journal of Social Sciences* 6 (4): 415–442.

Fleissner, P., W. Böhme, H. U. Brautzsch, J. Höhne, J. Siassi, and K. Stark. 1993. *Input-output-analyse: Eine Einführung in Theorie und Anwendungen.* Vienna and New York: Springer.

Foster, J. B. 2000. *Marx's ecology: Materialism and nature.* New York: Monthly Review Press.

Frank, A. G. 1966. The development of underdevelopment. *Monthly Review* 18 (7): 17–31.

———. 1978. *World accumulation, 1492–1789.* London and Basingstoke, U.K.: Macmillan.

Giljum, S. 2004. Trade, materials flows, and economic development in the south: The example of Chile. *Journal of Industrial Ecology* 8 (1–2): 241–261.

Griffin, J. 1976. *Energy input-output modeling.* Palo Alto, Calif.: Electric Power Research Institute.

Haberl, H., M. Fischer-Kowalski, F. Krausmann, H. Weisz, and V. Winiwarter. 2004. Progress towards sustainability? What the conceptual framework of material and energy flow accounting (MEFA) can offer. *Land Use Policy* 21 (3): 199–213.

Haberl, H., and F. Krausmann. 2001. Changes in population, affluence and environmental pressures during industrialization: The case of Austria 1830–1995. *Population and Environment* 23 (1): 49–69.

Hornborg, A. 2001. *The power of the machine: Global inequalities of economy, technology, and environment.* Walnut Creek, Calif.: AltaMira.

Krausmann, F., H. Haberl, K. H. Erb, and M. Wackernagel. 2004. Resource flows and land use in Austria 1950–2000: Using the MEFA framework to monitor society-nature interaction for sustainability. *Land Use Policy* 21 (3): 215–230.

Leontief, W. 1956. Factor proportions and the structure of American trade: Further theoretical and empircal analysis. *Review of Economics and Statistics* 38:386–407.

———. 1970. Environmental repercussions and the economic structure: An input-output-approach. *Review of Economics and Statistics* 52 (3): 262–271.

Martinez-Alier, J. 1987. *Ecological economics: Energy, environment and society.* Oxford: Blackwell.

Marx, K. 1990. *Capital.* Vol. 1. Harmondsworth, Middlesex, U.K.: Penguin.

Moll, S., S. Bringezu, and H. Schütz. 2003. *Zero study: Resource use in European countries; An estimate of materials and waste streams in the community, including imports and exports using the instrument of material flow analysis.* Copenhagen: ETC-WMF.

Muradian, R., and J. Martinez-Alier. 2001. Trade and the environment: From a "Southern" perspective. *Ecological Economics* 36 (2): 281–297.

Pedersen, O. G. 1999. *Physical input-output tables for Denmark: Products and materials 1990; Air emissions 1990–1992*. Copenhagen: Statistics Denmark.

Pérez-Rincón, M. A. 2006. Colombian international trade from a physical perspective: Towards an ecological "Prebisch thesis." *Ecological Economics* in press.

Proops, J. L. R. 1977. Input-output analysis and energy intensities: A comparison of some methodologies. *Applied Mathematical Modelling* 1 (March): 181–186.

Proops, J. L. R., M. Faber, and G. Wagenhals. 1993. *Reducing CO_2 emissions: A comparative input-output study for Germany and the UK*. Berlin: Springer Verlag.

Schandl, H., and N. B. Schulz. 2002. Changes in United Kingdom's natural relations in terms of society's metabolism and land use from 1850 to the present day. *Ecological Economics* 41 (2): 203–221.

Schmidt, A. 1971. *Der begriff der natur in der lehre von Marx*. Frankfurt: Europäische Verlagsanstalt.

Schmidt-Bleek, F. 1994. *Wieviel Umwelt braucht der Mensch? MIPS—das Maß für ökologisches Wirtschaften*. Berlin, Basel, and Boston: Birkhäuser.

Shannon, T. R. 1996. *An introduction to the world-system perspective*. Boulder, Colo., and Oxford, U.K.: Westview.

Sieferle, R. P. 1997. *Rückblick auf die Natur: Eine Geschichte des Menschen und seiner Umwelt*. Munich: Luchterhand.

———. 2001. Introduction. In *Marx's Ecology: Materialism and nature*, by J. B. Foster, 1–5. New York: Monthly Review Press.

Wallerstein, I. 1974. *The modern world system*. Vol. 1, *Capitalist agriculture and the origins of the European world-economy in the sixteenth century*. New York: Academic.

———. 1980. *The modern world system*. Vol. 2, *Mercantilism and the consolidation of the European world-economy, 1600–1750*. New York: Academic.

———. 1989. *The modern world system*. Vol. 2, *The second era of great expansion for the capitalist world-economy, 1730–1780*. New York: Academic.

Weisz, H., and F. Duchin. Forthcoming. Physical and monetary input-output analysis: What makes the difference? *Ecological Economics*.

Weisz, H., M. Fischer-Kowalski, C. M. Grünbühel, H. Haberl, F. Krausmann, and V. Winiwarter. 2001. Global environmental change and historical transitions. *Innovation: The European Journal of Social Sciences* 14 (2): 117–142.

Weisz, H., F. Krausmann, N. Eisenmenger, C. Amann, and K. Hubacek. Forthcoming a. *Development of material use in the EU-15: 1970–2001; Material composition, cross-country comparisons and material flow indicators*. Luxembourg: Eurostat, Office for Official Publications of the European Communities.

Weisz, H., F. Krausmann, and S. Sangkaman. Forthcoming b. *Resource use in a transition economy: Material- and energy-flow analysis for Thailand 1970/1980–2000*. Laguna: SEARCA.

Wolff, E. N. 2004. What happened to the Leontief Paradox? In *Wassily Leontief and Input-Output Economics*, ed. E. Dietzenbacher and M. L. Lahr, 166–187. Cambridge, U.K.: Cambridge University Press.

Physical Trade Flows of **16** Pollution-Intensive Products: Historical Trends in Europe and the World

ROLDAN MURADIAN AND STEFAN GILJUM

I N THE DEBATE ON INTERNATIONAL TRADE, the environment, and sustainable development, a growing number of empirical studies are devoted to the assessment of the international distribution of environmental pressures induced by the production of goods requiring intensive use of natural resources. This chapter contributes to this discussion by analyzing trends in imports and exports of pollution-intensive products in different regions throughout the world. Our results suggest that exports of pollution-intensive products (quantified in units of weight) are increasing across time in nearly all of the regions considered. However, from 1978 to 1996, the share of pollution-intensive exports to total exports (measured in monetary units) decreased in the European Union, United States, and Japan, increased in South America and Africa, and remained constant in Southeast Asia. We also found that the European Union was a net importer of products from polluting sectors during the whole period of analysis. Despite the limitations of the analysis in terms of reliability and completeness of data, the current chapter contributes to the assessment of the worldwide distribution of exports from polluting sectors and, indirectly, to the debate on the "pollution haven" hypothesis.

Pollution Havens and Physical Trade Flows

During the 1990s, considerable research was devoted to empirically testing the "pollution haven" (PH) hypothesis. The debate on this issue has been extensive but inconclusive, in part because this elusive phenomenon is tackled using different methods and concepts. The most common definition of the PH hypothesis is that polluting industries tend to migrate toward poorer countries, looking for weaker or weakly enforced environmental standards. Hence, according to the PH hypothesis, disparities of national environmental standards should lead to an unequal distribution of environmental burdens among different world regions, concentrating the most resource- or environment-intensive activities in developing countries. The PH hypothesis is thus closely related to the discussion about the international distribution of environmental burdens and risks arising from the current process of globalization. Literature on the PH hypothesis is extensive, and it is not within the scope of the present chapter to review it (for thorough reviews see, for example, Neumayer 2001a; Taylor 2004). Although some analyses agree with—or reach ambiguous conclusions on—the above-stated hypothesis (Low and Yeats 1992; Xing and Kolstad 2002; Cole 2004), most empirical studies do not support the proposition that varying environmental standards condition the international location of polluting industries (for a review of the evidence and arguments against the PH hypothesis see Mani and Wheeler 1998; Wheeler 2001, 2002).

To empirically test the relationship between standard-setting and production patterns is a great challenge in relation to methods and data availability. Research on this issue has thus instead dealt with testing "proxy propositions," which should hold if the PH hypothesis were right. According to Neumayer (2001b), there are three main proxy propositions: (a) differences in environmental standards affect international investment flows; (b) production in, and exports from, developing countries become increasingly pollution-intensive; and (c) pollution-intensive industries tend to flee industrialized countries. We could add one more proposition: (d) transnational corporations have a worse environmental performance in host countries with low environmental standards than in their countries of origin (Eskeland and Harrison 2003). Irrespective of the methods or definitions used, most of the empirical analyses testing these propositions (particularly "b" and "c") have adopted monetary variables for characterizing trade flows or production patterns. Hence, the international relocation of polluting sectors has generally been assessed using as dependent variables trade or production data in monetary units. Although the present research does not provide direct evidence either for or against the PH hypothesis—as no direct link with environmental standards, migration of industries, or actual distribution of pollution is demonstrated—it deals with the above-mentioned proxy proposition "b." The analysis we have undertaken specifically tackles the issue of the physical scale of exports. Although unable to reach conclusions about the actual distribution of environmental burdens or the relative specialization of production, our results contribute to the discussion on the international distribution of environment-intensive exports associated with the process of economic globalization. This baseline information on physical flows provides useful inputs for future, more elaborated and comprehensive, empirical research. The main contribution of the present work is the assessment of trends in the trade of goods from polluting sectors, using both monetary and physical metrics. Using trade data in units of weight may shed new light on the subject, for several reasons:

First, it is less difficult to envisage the relationship between physical flows (i.e. compared with monetary flows) and environmental burdens or risks. The environmental implications of both monetary and physical flows depend on a variety of factors that are certainly complex to estimate, such as the technology applied and the characteristics of the natural systems that serve as recipients of waste and emissions. Since the price and the value added of production vary across time and among countries, to establish the relationship between monetary flows and environmental burdens implies adopting additional assumptions, particularly on price and productivity trends. Instead, assessing the relationship between physical flows and environmental impacts or risks is facilitated by thermodynamic considerations (e.g. mass and energy conservation in all production activities). For example, the relationship between emissions and throughput (physical flows) is mediated by a technological factor, whereas several additional factors have to be taken into account in the relationship between monetary flows and actual emissions.

Second, physical flows give a clearer picture of the overall scale of the economic activity. Environmental standards normally refer to environmental performance at the (micro-) level of the production plant. However, the actual environmental implications of an economic activity in a given geographical context also depend on the overall scale of economic activities at the macro-level. Since physical inputs (resources) must correspond to physical outputs (products and wastes), physical flows are a better proxy than monetary flows for estimating the environmental transformations associated with the scale of the economic activity. Such scale effects have usually been neglected in the PH debate.

Third, real prices for most primary commodities (such as metal ores, minerals, and agricultural products) have been steadily declining during the last three decades of the past century (World Bank 2003).[1] Particularly in the case of extractive economies, studies focusing on monetary trade flows might thus yield misleading results, as declining prices may lessen export flows in monetary terms, while physical exports actually increase. This point is crucial when drawing conclusions about the environmental implications of trade patterns.[2]

Fourth, in most cases, environmental burdens are greater in the early stages of the commodity chain. Further along the processing chain, the material intensity of produced goods tends to decrease, whereas the economic added value tends to increase (Fischer-Kowalski and Amann 2001). A focus on purely monetary descriptions would result in a distorted picture of the distribution of environmental burdens along the commodity chain.

Analyses of international trade flows of pollution-intensive products are nevertheless unable to reveal information about the actual distribution of environmental burdens or international migration of industries. Such limitations hold for value-based assessments as well as for the approach adopted in this chapter.

Furthermore, it is worth noting that a general trend toward increasingly environment-intensive exports in developing countries (accompanied by decreasing physical exports from these sectors in industrialized countries) would only weakly support the proposition that developing countries have comparative advantages in environment-intensive sectors. A comprehensive analysis would need to take into account domestic production and consumption patterns. The same holds for trade balances in polluting sectors. Imports larger than exports would mean that a given region relies on imports for meeting its own levels of consumption. However, no statement can be made about the actual distribution of environmental burdens between the importing and exporting region, if figures on domestic production and emissions are not provided. Imports larger than exports would nevertheless suggest that imports should be understood as an important factor when we assess the environmental implications of domestic consumption patterns in a global perspective.

The present chapter has two main objectives: (1) to describe export trends of polluting sectors in different regions of the world, and (2) to describe European trends in the trade of polluting sectors with industrialized versus developing regions. The following section describes data sources and analysis, followed by a section presenting the results. Finally, the last section discusses these results, with particular attention to the environmental and socioeconomic implications for industrialized and developing regions.

Data Sources and Analysis

Trends in Exports of Polluting Sectors in Different Regions of the World

The aim of the analysis presented in this section is to describe trends in the aggregated exports of products from polluting sectors in different regions of the world from 1973 to 1996. Data were derived from the International Trade Statistics Yearbook, a U.N. periodical publication. To our knowledge, this database provides the most comprehensive trade statistics available, which presents data in both monetary and physical units (current dollars and metric tons), following the Standard International Trade Classification (SITC) system. However, it does not specify destination or origin of traded products.

In accordance with the World Bank classification (1998), based on emissions per unit of output and abatement costs, the following were considered as the most polluting sectors: iron and steel; nonferrous metals; industrial chemicals; petroleum refineries; nonmetallic minerals; and pulp and paper products.[3] In assessing aggregated trade trends, we considered seven world regions, defined as follows: 1) Europe: Ireland, Portugal, Greece, Austria, Finland, Belgium, Luxembourg, Denmark, Germany, Netherlands, Spain, France, United Kingdom, Italy, Sweden; 2) Japan; 3) United States; 4) Canada and Australia; 5) South America: Argentina, Brazil, Chile, Colombia, Ecuador, Peru, Venezuela; 6) Africa: Algeria, Central African Republic, Congo, Egypt, Ethiopia, Gabon, Kenya, Madagascar, Morocco, Senegal, Sudan, Tunisia, Zimbabwe;[4] 7) Southeast Asia: Indonesia, South Korea, Malaysia, Philippines, Thailand. Data in current dollars were converted to 1995 dollars using a U.S. GDP (gross domestic product) deflator taken from the World Bank's development indicators (1998).

Trade Patterns of Polluting Sectors in the European Union

The analysis presented in this section aims at describing trade patterns of polluting sectors in the European Union from 1976 to 2000. Data were assembled from EUROSTAT statistics on EU trade, published in electronic form. In this publication, trade statistics are expressed in both monetary (ECU) and physical (metric tons) units. This data set only includes imports and exports from and to the European Union, but specifies the origin and destination. In "polluting sectors" we included the same industrial activities as in the previous investigation. However, trade categories are not exactly the same, since the classification of traded products used by EUROSTAT follows the HS ("Harmonized Commodity Description and Coding System") nomenclature. The two classification systems (SITC and HS) differ in the way they aggregate trade data. Therefore, trade categories cannot easily be converted from one classification scheme to the other. In addition, EUROSTAT trade statistics have much more disaggregated information than the U.N. International Trade Statistics Yearbook. The countries considered are full members of the EU. It is worth noting that the composition of the EU has changed during the period of analysis, contributing to shifts in the composition of its external trade (see below). Data in ECU units were transformed to current U.S. dollars using an exchange rate for different years published in the electronic OECD Statistics Compendium (2002). Later, current dollars were transformed to 1995 dollars.

Here, the classification of regional trade partners was different from the classification used for describing global trade patterns, because the electronic database allowed more comprehensive definitions of regional categories, due to the ease and speed of data processing. In analyzing the EUROSTAT data set, we defined the regions as follows: Africa: all African countries; Southeast Asia: Thailand, Vietnam, Indonesia, Malaysia, Singapore, Philippines, South Korea, Taiwan, Hong Kong; Industrialized countries: United States, Canada, Japan, Australia, New Zealand; Latin America: all Spanish- and Portuguese-speaking countries comprising Latin America.[5]

Results

Trends in Exports of Polluting Sectors in Different Regions of the World

Figure 16.1 shows the development of aggregated exports of pollution-intensive products, in units of weight, in different regions of the world. It reveals that there is a general trend toward increasing physical exports from polluting sectors across time, in almost all regions of the world. It also shows that the physical scale of EU exports of these products is relatively high in relation to other world regions, mainly due to large exports of industrial chemicals, petroleum products, and nonferrous metals.

Figure 16.2 shows changes of the value density (value per unit of weight) of exports of pollution-intensive products over time. It reveals that for Japan this variable shows a clearly increasing trend. In South America, Canada, and Australia, the tendency is the opposite (decreasing across time), while in the rest of the world regions considered it seems that the value density of these kinds of exports is rather stable (Africa) or does not follow a clear-cut trend across time (European Union, United States, Southeast Asia).

Figure 16.3 shows that the European Union, Canada, and Australia have a common trend toward decreasing share of pollution-intensive products to total exports, in monetary terms. In the case of Japan, the United States, and Africa, this variable follows a "U"-shaped curve, while it is stable across time in Southeast Asia. No clear-cut tendency can be observed for South America.

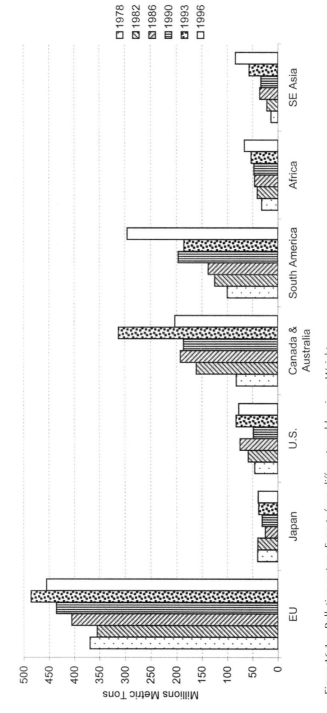

Figure 16.1. Polluting sectors. Exports from different world regions. Weight

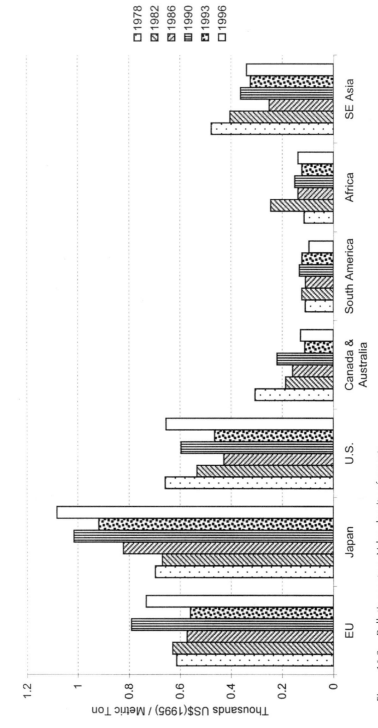

Figure 16.2. Polluting sectors. Value density of exports

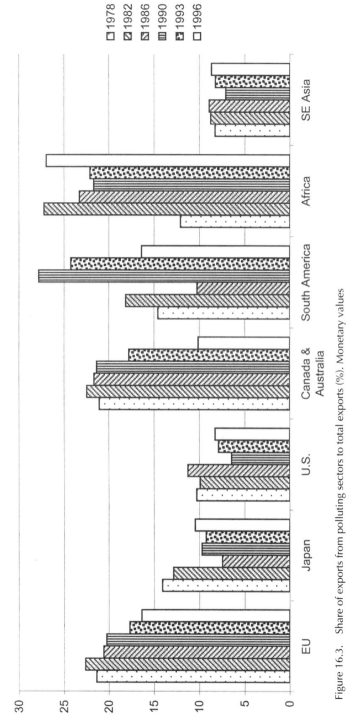

Figure 16.3. Share of exports from polluting sectors to total exports (%). Monetary values

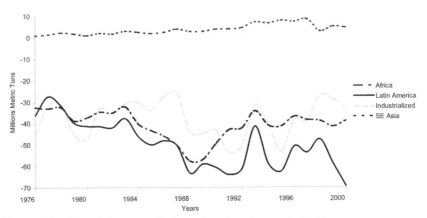

Figure 16.4.   EU trade balance polluting sectors. Exports-imports. Weight

Trade Patterns of Polluting Sectors in the European Union

Figure 16.4 illustrates changes over time of the physical trade balance in polluting sectors, between the European Union and other regions of the world. It reveals that the European Union has had greater imports than exports in polluting sectors with industrialized countries, Latin America, and Africa, during the whole period of analysis. In contrast, EU exports and imports in these sectors have remained fairly balanced with Southeast Asia. Figure 16.4 also reveals that European imports (in units of weight) of pollution–intensive products from Latin America have increased substantially more than European exports of the same kind of products to this region.

Figure 16.5 shows changes across time of the EU Index of Terms of Trade with different regions of the world (for the same sectors as above).

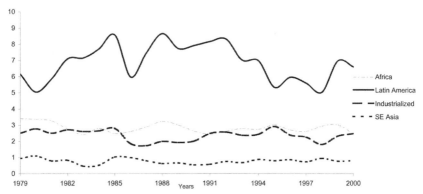

Figure 16.5.   Polluting sectors. EU index of terms of trade. Value density (exports)/value density (imports)

This index is defined as the value density of European exports to a given region divided by the value density of European imports from the same region. The figure reveals that, during the whole period of analysis, the European Union has had a positive Index of Terms of Trade with the other regions considered in the present study. In comparison with other regions, the index is remarkably high for EU exchange with Latin America. Put in a simple way, this means that Latin American exports of pollution-intensive products to the European Union are considerably more weight-intensive (less value-dense) than European exports of the same kind of products to Latin America.

Figure 16.6 shows the evolution of the composition of aggregated EU imports of pollution-intensive products from the developing regions considered above (Latin America, Africa, and Southeast Asia). It reveals that minerals have constituted the bulk of European pollution-intensive imports from developing regions during the whole period of analysis. It also shows that the share of oil refinery products, paper, and industrial chemicals in relation to total imports of pollution-intensive products has increased during the last decades. However, they still comprise less than 20 percent of European imports (in units of weight) in these sectors from the above-mentioned regions.

Figure 16.7 shows that, in contrast, oil refinery products, pulp and paper, and industrial chemicals exports from the European Union to the developing regions have significantly increased their share since the late 1980s, and currently constitute the bulk of EU exports from polluting sectors to these regions.

Discussion

The results presented in figure 16.1 contradict the proposition that the physical scale of environment-intensive exports follows a different trend in industrialized and developing countries. Instead, it seems that there is a general trend toward increasing physical exports of pollution-intensive products in almost all regions considered in the analysis. In comparison with all other regions, moreover, the European Union shows a relatively large physical scale of exports in these sectors during the whole period of analysis. However, when also taking imports into account, the European Union has had consistently larger imports than exports in these sectors across time (see figure 16.4). Therefore, a likely interpretation is that the European Union is importing most of the pollution-intensive products from other world regions (including other industrialized countries), processing them in order

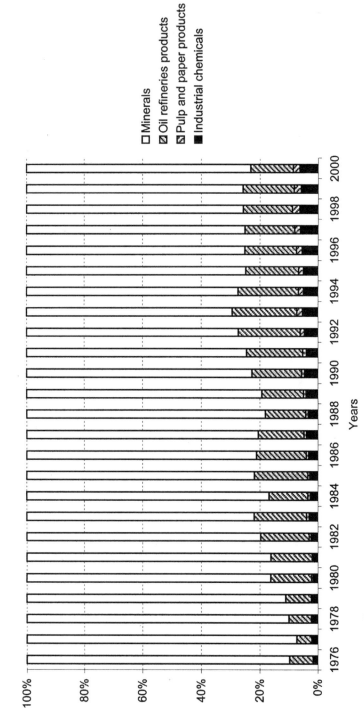

Figure 16.6. Polluting sectors. Composition of EU imports from Latin America, Africa, and Southeast Asia. Weight

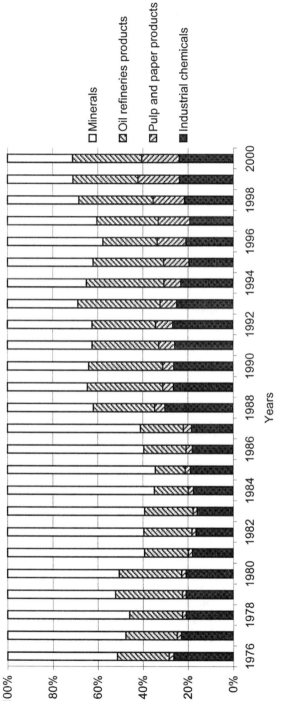

Figure 16.7. Polluting sectors. EU exports to Latin America, Africa, and Southeast Asia. Weight

to add value, and then reexporting them (see also Schütz, Bringezu, and Moll 2004). In order to empirically test this potential explanation, it would be necessary to link physical import and export data with data on total physical production.

Value density is a measure of the weight intensity of exports. Although this measure does not deal with the value added to exports—which would be the most pertinent variable to look at—it may help to identify general trends and to propose working hypotheses on the relationship between the economic value and the physical content of exports. This relationship is important to study in order to investigate whether countries specializing in pollution-intensive and less economically dynamic sectors might be caught in a kind of specialization trap, structurally generated by downward pressures on prices, involving both inability to upgrade (add value to) production and increasing environmental burdens related to a growing (physical) scale. A combined trend toward decreasing value density, increasing scale (in physical units) of exports from polluting sectors, and a mounting share of exports from polluting sectors in relation to total exports (in monetary terms) would suggest that the region is specializing in polluting sectors and reaping less and less income per exported unit of weight (as stated before, however, the final proof of this would require estimations of value added in exports). If an increase in the physical intensity of exports from polluting sectors is not accompanied by substantial technological improvements, an increase in environmental pressure per exported unit of value is very likely. The combination of an inability to upgrade exports and growing environmental pressure may have a considerable impact on future development prospects, as regions facing these trends can be caught in a low-income/high-environment degradation trap. Africa seems to exemplify the unfavorable combination of an increasing share of exports from polluting sectors in relation to total exports (in monetary terms), increasing physical scale, and stagnating value density of pollution-intensive exports. In contrast, Japan illustrates the opposite trend, characterized by a decreasing share of pollution-intensive sectors and a declining physical scale and rising value density of exports from polluting sectors (see figures 16.2 and 16.3).

Our results reveal that, during the past decades, Europe has maintained imports larger than exports in polluting sectors with all the regions considered, except Southeast Asia (see figure 16.4). Moreover, as can be seen in figure 16.5, European imports from polluting sectors have generally been more weight-intensive than European exports from the same sectors. The former result seems to contradict the general proposition that industrialized countries are net exporters of pollution-intensive products (World Bank 1998).

The latter result shows that there has been a continuous physical imbalance in the European trade of environment-intensive products with other regions of the world. Another study dealing with the external trade of the European Union also revealed considerable price differences within the same product groups, for example iron and steel products (Schütz et al. 2004). However, the implications of this trend for the actual distribution of environmental burdens generated by European consumption patterns cannot be addressed in the present analysis. This has been tackled elsewhere (see for example Muradian, O'Connor, and Martinez-Alier 2002).

It is worth noting that the physical trade balance between Europe and Latin America in polluting sectors has become increasingly skewed during the period of study. From a European perspective, it has changed from about minus 35 million tons (exports less imports) in 1976 to approximately minus 70 million tons in 2000 (see figure 16.4). Moreover, during the whole period of analysis, the Index of Terms of Trade has remained larger for Latin America than for other regions (see figure 16.5), indicating that the physical intensity of Latin American exports of pollution-intensive products to the European Union has increased considerably more than the physical intensity of Latin American imports of the same kind of products from the European Union. Although Latin America's most important trade partner is not Europe, but the United States, this trend may have significant development implications, particularly if the relative economic importance of environment-intensive exports compared to total exports increases over time. However, our data show no clear trend toward relative trade specialization in polluting sectors in Latin America (see figure 16.3).

From a strictly economic point of view, specialization in polluting sectors due to comparative advantages jeopardizes people's welfare only if environmental standards are not set at socially efficient levels. In the words of economists, if environmental standards are inefficiently low, then there is excessive environmental degradation relative to people's preferences (Neumayer 2001b). However, besides the difficulties in empirically estimating people's preferences, these efficiency considerations leave aside distributional issues, value contests, and environmental conflicts. The Kaldor-Hicks principle for social efficiency does not contemplate actual (but only possible) compensation between winners and losers due to a given economic activity.[6] If compensation does not occur, conflicts are prone to arise. In a context of weak institutions, as is the case in many developing countries, environmental externalities are likely to occur, because no compensation mechanism is put in place (Murshed 2002). This often leads to environmental protests and conflicts between different economic agents. In such cases, mere efficiency considerations are unable to describe, understand, or resolve social problems related to the distribution of environmental burdens (Clapp 2002; Strohm 2002).

The difference in composition between European exports and imports of polluting sectors to/from developing countries is remarkable. Figures 16.6 and 16.7 show that the share of oil refinery products, pulp and paper, and industrial chemical products is increasing in relation to total pollution-intensive exports from the European Union to developing countries, whereas minerals constitute the bulk of EU pollution-intensive imports from these countries. Due to the large physical flows involved in the trade of minerals, this kind of exchange explains in part the fact that the EU's pollution-intensive imports are larger than its exports. Mineral extraction and processing are among the economic sectors most often associated with social conflicts over alternative land uses or the effects of pollution on local populations (Martinez-Alier 2002). Generally, these conflicts encompass considerable transaction costs for mining enterprises. Besides considerations of resource abundance and labor costs, the costs arising from environmental conflicts may influence decisions over the location of mining and mineral processing activities at the global level (Hall 2002). Such costs may be lower in developing countries due to the disempowerment of local populations and less expensive compensation to affected communities because of lower income and weaker institutions. Moreover, until the beginning of the twenty-first century, the mining sector has faced serious difficulties due to declining prices, which probably has encouraged the migration of mining to places with lower production costs, which often means developing countries.

The results of this study and their interpretation depend on the quality and reliability of the used data sets. We want to emphasize that we have considerable doubts about the reliability of the data source we have used for the first of our two calculations. The U.N. International Trade Statistics Yearbook is a very aggregated database, the extensiveness of which has been achieved at the expense of accuracy. Many developing countries, in particular, have not comprehensively reported data on physical exports. For many export categories, only monetary data are given. In some cases, we thus had to exclude some product categories from our analysis, since the transformation of monetary units into physical units would have required country-specific information on prices per physical unit. For industrialized countries, however, reporting seemed to be more complete. This fact biases results and causes a structural underrepresentation of exports from polluting sectors in developing countries. Nevertheless, due to the scarcity of comprehensive trade statistics in physical units, the International Trade Statistics Yearbook is one of the few world databases currently available that can be used for comparative studies at the global level. Due to the previously mentioned caveats, we consider our results presented here as a first approximation, which should be revised and complemented in the future using more reliable data sources (for instance, statistics from national statistical agencies).

As stated before, there are difficulties in establishing relationships between physical flows and actual environmental impacts or risks. This is especially true when dealing with aggregated data, as the present work does. Nevertheless, assessing changes over time in physical exports of pollution-intensive sectors might shed new insights—different from those arising from monetary approaches—for building hypotheses on the international distribution of environmental burdens arising from global economic integration.[7] In using physical flows for analyzing the international distribution of environment-intensive exports, the current chapter indirectly contributes to assessing some proxy propositions of the pollution haven hypothesis. However, results are far from conclusive and considerable work needs to be devoted to developing this approach further. First, significant improvement of data quality is needed, in particular for imports and exports in physical units of countries in Asia, Latin America, and Africa. Second, the first of our two analyses needs to be extended by including physical imports. Third, taking domestic production into consideration would allow assessing to what extent exports from polluting sectors in industrialized countries are based on domestic production or rely on imports from other world regions. Fourth, for estimating the concrete environmental impacts of specialization in pollution-intensive exports in different regions of the world, it would be necessary to present data in a more disaggregated way, focusing on particular economic sectors, product groups, or commodity chains.

Notes

1. Since 2003, however, a reverse of these trends can be observed, mainly due to the rapidly growing demand for raw materials and energy resources in industrializing countries in the global South, in particular China and India.

2. For example, the World Bank (1998) has published data analysis on trade balances, in monetary terms, for the most polluting sectors. The study has concluded that developing countries tend to have export-import ratios less than one (exports lower than imports), whereas the opposite holds for industrialized countries, which are net exporters in the most polluting sectors. However, if a similar analysis is performed using physical units, the opposite results are obtained (Muradian and Martinez-Alier 2001).

3. In order to obtain comparable results, we have only included product groups listed in the World Bank classification. Therefore, with regard to oil products, our analysis only considers the product groups of "petroleum oils and oils from bituminous minerals" and "residual petroleum products" (SITC Rev. 3 categories 334 and 335), product groups embodying more emissions than crude oil. The inclusion of crude oil, the largest physical trade flow worldwide, would have significantly altered our results, increasing the amounts of physical imports of industrialized and industrializing world regions and the physical exports of oil producing countries.

4. We unfortunately could not include South Africa and Nigeria, ranking first and fourth among African countries in terms of absolute GDP, as these countries did not report data for the whole period of analysis.

5. Please note that the country group of "South America" in the global trade analysis only includes selected countries, whereas the country group of "Latin America" in the European trade analysis comprises all countries in Central and South America.

6. According to this normative principle of neoclassical economics, an act (or a rule) would be said to be efficient if the gains to those who consented to it are sufficient to permit the payment of compensation to those who suffered losses.

7. See Giljum and Eisenmenger (2004) for a review of the discussion and empirical evidence on the use of biophysical indicators for addressing the relationship between trade and the environment.

References

Clapp, J. 2002. What the pollution havens debate overlooks. *Global Environmental Politics* 2 (2): 11–19.

Cole, M. 2004. Trade, the pollution haven hypothesis and the environmental Kuznets curve: Examining the linkages. *Ecological Economics* 48:71–81.

Eskeland, G., and A. Harrison. 2003. Moving to greener pastures? Multinationals and the pollution haven hypothesis. *Journal of Development Economics* 70:1–23.

Fischer-Kowalski, M., and C. Amann. 2001. Beyond IPAT and Kuznets curves: Globalization as a vital factor in analysing the environmental impact of socioeconomic metabolism. *Population and Environment* 23 (1): 7–47.

Giljum, S., and N. Eisenmenger. 2004. North-South trade and the distribution of environmental goods and burdens: A biophysical perspective. *Journal of Environment and Development* 13 (1): 73–100.

Hall, D. 2002. Environmental change, protests, and havens of environmental degradation: Evidence from Asia. *Global Environmental Politics* 2 (2): 20–28.

Low, P., and A. Yeats. 1992. Do dirty industries migrate? In *International trade and the environment*, ed. P. Low, 89–104. World Bank discussion paper 159. Washington, D.C.: World Bank.

Mani, M. S., and D. Wheeler. 1998. In search of pollution havens? Dirty industry in the world economy, 1960–1995. *Journal of Environment and Development* 7 (3): 215–247.

Martinez-Alier, J. 2002. *The environmentalism of the poor: A study of ecological conflicts and valuation.* Cheltenham, U.K.: Elgar.

Muradian, R., and J. Martinez-Alier. 2001. Trade and environment from a southern perspective. *Ecological Economics* 36:281–297.

Muradian, R., M. O'Connor, and J. Martinez-Alier. 2002. Embodied pollution in trade: Estimating the environmental load displacement of industrialized countries. *Ecological Economics* 41:51–67.

Murshed, M. 2002. *On natural resource abundance and underdevelopment.* Background paper for the World Development Report 2003. The Hague: Institute of Social Studies.

Neumayer, E. 2001a. *Greening trade and investment: Environmental protection without protectionism.* London: Earthscan.

———. 2001b. Pollution havens: An analysis of policy options for dealing with an elusive phenomenon. *Journal of Environment and Development* 10 (2): 147–177.

OECD. 2002. OECD Statistical Compendium on CD-ROM. Paris: OECD.

Schütz, H., S. Bringezu, and S. Moll. 2004. *Globalisation and the shifting environmental burden: Material trade flows of the European Union.* Wuppertal: Wuppertal Institute.

Strohm, L. 2002. Pollution havens and the transfer of environmental risk. *Global Environmental Politics* 2 (2): 29–36.

Taylor, S. 2004. Unbundling the pollution haven hypothesis. *Advances in Economic Analysis and Policy* 4 (2): 1408–1434.

Wheeler, D. 2001. Racing to the bottom? Foreign investment and air pollution in developing countries. *Journal of Environment and Development* 10 (3): 225–245.

———. 2002. Beyond pollution havens. *Global Environmental Politics* 2 (2): 1–10.

World Bank. 1998. *World development indicators.* Washington, D.C.: World Bank.

———. 2003. *Global economic prospects and developing countries 2003.* Washington, D.C.: World Bank.

Xing, Y., and C. Kolstad. 2002. Do lax environmental regulations attract foreign investment? *Environmental and Resource Economics* 21:1–22.

Environmental Issues at the U.S.-Mexico Border and the Unequal Territorialization of Value

17

JOSIAH HEYMAN

Borders in a World-System Perspective

World-systems thinking draws attention to unequal relationships of exchange across space, and production and consumption involved in such relations. The main focus is on endpoints, such as consumption and waste in the core or degradation in a raw material–producing periphery. In this chapter, I draw attention to places of transformation in between such endpoints where unequal exchange is enacted, often involving immediate, significant steps up or down in value of labor, materials, and energy (Heyman 1994; Kearney 2004). Such transaction and transformation places have sustained significant populations and political and economic power in the historical and archeological record (e.g. mediating the exchange of luxury goods). Today, they can be found in global air and sea ports, as well as land borders between unequal polities. Such places are crucial to the symbolic processes of giving value to people and goods, or redefining their value; and they are thus characterized by intensive value arbitrage, including brokering of goods and services among delineated territories of the world-system, as well as hosting major manufacturing zones that take advantage of spaces with poorly compensated labor to make goods for spaces with higher purchasing power. These locations have two sets of environmental impacts: playing roles in the environmental dynamics of the world-system as a whole, in particular being key sites for the symbolic abstraction and orchestration of material and energy flows identified as crucial in Alf Hornborg's seminal work (2001); and the immediate impact of concentrated people and activities in these key sites.

It is on the latter topic that I focus in this chapter. My case study is the U.S.-Mexico border, home of one of the larger manufacturing complexes in the contemporary world economy (the maquiladoras, final assembly plants in Mexico for exports, mainly to the United States). This region likewise hosts intense commercial transportation and goods brokerage within the framework of the North American Free Trade Agreement (NAFTA). The immense concentration of unequal exchange in this place draws on and impacts regional biophysical systems. At this seam between the territories of two nation-states, a peculiar phenomenon occurs: monetary valuations of people and goods undergo sudden, stepwise changes as they move across the boundary. Wages, prices, state-bureaucratic action, communal action, and socially constructed meanings strongly differ according to their territorial placement within Mexico or the United States, while corporate, small entrepreneurial, and personal or household activities move across these spaces, taking advantage of the proximity of disparities in money, law, and meaning (see Heyman 2004 on value arbitrage through ports of entry on the U.S.-Mexico border). Unequal territorialized and territory crossing processes thus form my starting point in analyzing the various environmental ills of the U.S.-Mexico border region.

The literature on environmental issues at the U.S.-Mexico border is large and sophisticated (see below), and it would be unfair to dismiss its scholarly and public worth. But to characterize my approach, it is useful to develop contrasts with this literature. The latter tends to view the border as a place where two previously separated societies collide, and that many problems stem from that initial difference. As such, it is not particularly attentive to the border as constituted through relationships across space, or the historical dynamics of those relations. Also, the existing literature tends to see the solution of environmental issues in greater connection and cooperation across the border, in keeping with the two colliding nations assumption. But "connection" has long existed and hopeful attempts at cooperation often founder on the ironically polarizing effects of connectedness; we need to pay attention, rather, to what kinds of connections are forged, their qualities of justice and equality, and their social and environmental outcomes.

A historical world-systems approach clarifies hard questions of political economy and ecology that often confound standard analysis by stressing relational processes beneath surface conflicts and disorders (a useful source on how to think in this mode is Hopkins 1982). My approach here is implicitly historical, referring to the dynamics of the late-nineteenth- and twentieth-century capitalist and state development of the border (see Fernandez 1977; Lorey 1999), though for the sake of space I do not narrate the long and complicated story of the region. Also, for the study of this peculiar and important border the world-systems perspective highlights relationships between apparently opposite "sides"—spaces, classes, cultures, levels of wealth and waste, and so forth. Mexico and the United States are joined in a long-standing unequal relationship that produces, transforms, and reproduces the inequalities and differentiations that are so visible at the border. Thus, we do not have two territories juxtaposed one against the other, but rather a singular process of the territorialization of value into two spaces, "Mexico" and "United States" (on territorialization as a process rather than as a given, see Taylor 1985; Agnew and Corbridge 1995; Paasi 1996). Breaking with the "two nations" perspective helps us understand both polarizing phenomena and ones that cross the territorial boundary, and thus allows for a more complex analysis of economy, culture, politics, and environment on each side.

Environmental Disorders of the U.S.-Mexico Borderlands: A Synopsis

The following summary of the main environmental issues facing the border region is based on Ingram, Laney, and Gillilan (1995), Liverman et al. (1999), and Herzog (2000).

Water Supply

Irrigated farms and large binational urban areas make unsustainable demands on water supplies, including rivers that are overallocated to the point that they cannot sustain riverine habitats downstream, and underground aquifers that are drawn down faster than their recharge rates. At the same time, water is maldistributed, with many households lacking faucet service and receiving only distant hand-carried or truck-delivered supplies that are expensive in price and labor time/effort. Lack of access to piped water is more widespread in Mexican border settlements but occurs in the United States also.

Sewage

Many households lack adequate means to dispose of sewage, again more often in Mexico than the United States but occurring in both nations. Centralized sewage lines do not extend to many settlement areas, while the alternatives, pit latrines and septic systems, are often inadequate or faulty. This is due not just to lack of information, but also limited household and public resources for better systems. Even centralized sewage systems are often inadequate; many but not all U.S. cities use secondary treatment, but most Mexican cities provide only primary treatment, and their systems periodically fail.

Toxic Chemical Wastes

Industrial toxic wastes are sometimes improperly disposed of or spilled accidentally by maquiladoras, and there are also extensive industrial wastes from the metal smelting/refining industry. Such chemicals (1) affect workers directly; (2) dissipate into the air, forming a smog component in some cases; (3) are disposed of in sewer systems, persistently contaminating treated water outputs; (4) are disposed of on the ground, seeping into groundwater aquifers. A related problem is immediately and persistently toxic pesticides from industrial agriculture. There are also nonpoint source consumer chemical runoffs from settlement areas.

Air Quality

Several border metropolitan areas, notably Las Cruces–El Paso–Ciudad Juárez, form air pollution catchment areas subject to smog inversions. Contributors include internal combustion engines, exacerbated by lines of traffic waiting to be inspected to cross the border, and industrial processes giving off volatile organic compounds, heavy metals, crushed rock powder, and so forth. To diesel particulates are added particulates from dirt streets, most common in Mexico but not unknown in the United States, and soot from low-quality combustion processes such as household fires and small-scale brickyards in Mexico. A recent study by the North American Commission for Environmental Cooperation shows significant excess mortality and morbidity among children younger than five in Ciudad Juárez, Mexico, due to increased truck traffic from growing cross-boundary commerce under the North American Free Trade Agreement (Romieu et al. 2003). Recently, maquiladora-style electricity plants have lined Baja California's northern border, supplying power to California (U.S.), and taking advantage of stepwise differentials in labor and fuel cost, environmental regulation, and regulations on plant siting (Ross 2003).

Habitat/Species Decline and Change

Loss of habitat and decline of some plant and animal species has occurred through direct land disturbance (Bahre 1991) and stream channelization (e.g. urban and agricultural clearing of river bottom land), as well as the water draw down (both surface and subsurface) highlighted above.

The five environmental disorders just listed occur within three main contexts. First, key segments of the border are now heavily urbanized, including several multimillion-person megalopolises. The question, then, is what drives urbanization in border regions? Second, border crossings concentrate huge transportation systems for persons and goods, with bottlenecks at inspection points. Again, we beg a question: what in border settings promotes dense webs of transactions and the movement to enact them? Finally, there are vast productive complexes, both industrial and agricultural, which besides their own outputs are contributors to the urbanization and transaction/transportation phenomena listed above. Not surprisingly, we ask why they disproportionately cluster along the border.

Before we proceed further, it is worth noting that much of the border region is arid to semiarid, but this is not the unique cause of its environmental problems. First, a vastly larger region, most of northern Mexico and the U.S. west, is arid and semiarid, so a general environmental characterization cannot fully explain the border's specifics. Second, water shortage is relative to human demand, so this begs the question why population and industry concentrate in a region with few propitious sites. Thus, in framing our examination, we can reject "natural features of the region" as a privileged starting point, although we must remain attentive to the causal force of biophysical processes in interaction with human activities.

Processes Underlying Environmental Disorders

These environmental issues occur away from the border in both nations, and often in just as bad or worse states. Their causes—water demand in arid regions, traffic, industrial pollution, and so forth—are by no means unique, then, and we should bear in mind that all such cases partake of the same broad causes (e.g. capitalist, large-scale urbanization in regions able to supply water only for short time horizons and in unsustainable ways). I am thus not claiming that the border is uniquely an environmental hellhole, which much superficial writing about the region implies. Rather, I start with widely shared social processes engendering environmental disequilibria, and seek to understand how they emerged at the border in a severe way.

Let us begin with major border labor users, maquiladoras and mechanized irrigation agriculture. Maquiladoras concentrate along the Mexican side of the border, although they have diffused to the Mexican interior and Central America. These factories bring parts and subassemblies from worldwide suppliers, finish and assemble them in a low-wage locale (e.g. border Mexico), and reexport them to places (e.g. the United States) where the selling price and volume is comparatively high, based on much higher incomes. A rule of thumb on the border is that a working-class Mexican American makes in one hour what she or he can make in one day across the boundary in Mexico. In other words, maquiladoras realize value through criss-crossing the territorialized difference in wage levels, going from moderate wage-value parts to low-value final assembly to high-value selling price, realizing the step up from parts to whole. The border also allows U.S. managers and engineers to live in the United States, where they are more culturally and socially comfortable, while still directly accessing the poor standards of living (and thus low wages) of Mexican border residents.

A similar case can be made for the location on the U.S. side of the border of irrigated agriculture and nonferrous metal smelting and refining. The location of these production processes is mainly determined by forces other than the price of labor: for agriculture, alluvial soils in desert river valleys, and access to engineered water supplies; for smelters and refineries, central location in a network of mines and mills, since ore is heavy and costly to transport, centralization that allows constant and high-volume supply for capital-intensive plants. Smelters and refineries also have high demands for surface or groundwater for cooling and electrolytic baths. However, the agricultural districts and smelters/refineries in the United States near the border have an incremental advantage over other sites: access to relatively less expensive Mexican workers, both as migrants (often farmworkers) and as U.S.-resident workers in places with saturated and depressed labor markets. (Such labor-based locational effects do not account for border Mexican smelting and irrigated agriculture, since Mexico's highest pay rates actually occur near the United States, but proximity to U.S. markets and infrastructure does affect location.)

We will explore below the environmental effects of concentration of poorly paid employees. Let us focus here on direct pollution from these production processes. Weak territorialization of collective action in Mexico (both public participation and state-bureaucratic regulation) gives locational advantage to producers shifting dirty processes south across the border rather than expending capital on cleaner processes or shutting down such production altogether. Propaganda critical of the maquiladoras and free trade has seized on this "exporting of pollution" and the lack of enforcement of environmental laws in Mexico to make it seem a massive and uniform feature of border industry. Fortunately, Donovan Corliss (2000) provides a finer-grained empirical study. He found a number of Tijuana maquiladoras that moved from the United States to Mexico partly to avoid environmental regulation and the public "right to know" about toxic releases. For example, furniture plants moved from Los Angeles to Tijuana to avoid restrictions on their use of volatile organic finishes, which contribute significantly to urban smog; likewise, the so-called battery recycling industry (more like battery junkyards/metal smelters) moved to Mexico, where there is little control over their handling of lead and cadmium. On the other hand, many maquiladoras use standard production processes whether in the United States or Mexico. In these cases, presumably located at the border because of wage costs rather than pollution exporting, any additional toxic increment over industry best practices was caused by the company and the plant manager. There was little pressure in Mexico to be careful and up-to-date, so that only specific, conscientious individuals and corporations ran relatively "clean" plants. Part of this, in turn, was rooted in personal attitudes but part in consumer/activist environmental pressure (weaker in Mexico than the United States, for reasons that we will see later).

Now, let us turn from production complexes to urbanization, involving the environmental effects of households, and in particular, the border as a setting for territorial-crossing consumption. There is, first, a highly unequal social wage between the Mexican and the U.S. territory. By social wage, I mean not only the prevailing wages paid directly by employers, but also the resident's claim on the collective, redistributed social surplus, through public health infrastructure, schools, medical services, retirement, and so forth. Both societies are unequal, however, and there are prosperous as well as poor (in purchasing power and claim on collective distributions) households in both nations. Second, in complexly patterned ways, the territory of Mexico and the United States mean different things to different audiences. Among other things, Mexico to U.S. residents tends to mean both poverty and leisure (pleasure and release), and a certain kind of exotic, tropical otherness. The United States to Mexican residents means power, honesty, and efficiency, as well as attractive wealth and modernity, but also a corrosive, immoral, and antifamilial, permissive individualism (no one source addresses the full terrain of meanings, but Vila 2000 provides a start). In both analyses, social wage and differential meanings, the point is not just that the two terrains are divided but that individuals and households actively maneuver through them, seeking particular sets of resources and meanings and causing peculiar dynamics in border urbanism.

For example, U.S.-side border cities attract residents in two ways. On one hand, prosperous residents with secure jobs and social wage claims obtain a yet higher standard of living because they can obtain goods, labor services, and meanings from the low-value Mexican side of the border. El Paso, for example, is noted for cheap domestic services and small-scale construction labor. There is also a large commercial sex industry in Mexican border cities, a profusion of bars and restaurants near some ports of entry (and, more quietly, dealers in cocaine, heroin, and marijuana), pharmacies selling medications/drugs inexpensively and without prescription, and innumerable shops selling mass-produced "crafts" and "art" from Mexico. This in turn supports Mexican-side urbanization, from maids to barkeeps to street vendors.

On the other hand, U.S. border cities also attract a steady flow of inmigration, legal and illegal, from Mexico. This is in spite of U.S.-side border cities having chronically saturated labor markets and high unemployment. However, the U.S. side offers households moving from Mexico a much higher typical wage when there is work, and a better, if still quite poor, social wage, whether in the form of police protection, schools, or access to the county hospital emergency room. The irony is that people leave the most prosperous and economically active region of lower-value Mexico for the most depressed region of the higher-value United States; they go from being well employed but miserably paid to being underemployed and somewhat less miserably paid.

Mexican border cities also are shaped by these cross-border transactions. I have already mentioned U.S. household and small business employment of Mexican laborers and purchases of cheap Mexican goods and services, which combine with maquiladoras to bring about steady migratory increase (and retention of natural growth increase) in urban population. There is a smuggling economy, whose impact is discussed below. There are, typical of any border, commercial/customs brokerage and binational business facilitation sectors (bankers, lawyers, accountants, etc.). There is the transportation infrastructure of the border crossing. Finally, there is the value-transacting role of the U.S. border city in the household economy and social status moves of Mexican-side residents, which merits a bit of elaboration.

U.S. border cities have disproportionately large commercial sectors, including both retailers of cheap goods and expensive malls, boutiques, auto dealerships, and so on. Laredo, Texas, for example, has the highest department store square footage per person of any city in the United States, despite a low-wage local economy, because it attracts a high volume of shoppers from Nuevo Laredo, Coahuila, and in the nearby interior, the huge Mexican city of Monterrey. Not only does this create many low-wage, no-benefits store jobs in the United States, but it also adds to the meaning-value of "proximity to the United States" for Mexicans in border cities. Not only are many goods in the United States better in quality or price because of limitations in Mexico's business structure and domestic production, but also the United States conveys an increment in status in the view of some Mexicans. In turn, constant transacting of jobs, services, goods, and meanings back and forth across the border favors the extreme urbanization of this region.

To demonstrate how border urbanization shapes environmental issues, let us look at *colonias* (in Mexico, *colonias populares*), informally developed residential areas with cheap lots, lacking preprovided infrastructure (water supply, sewage, piped gas, electricity, paved streets, police and fire protection, schools, clinics, etc.), and having self-constructed houses. As Peter Ward (1999) argues, informal settlements in both nations result from rapid expansion of regional employment combined with underfunding of public infrastructure, planning, and housing. For the United States, he identifies flawed private markets in housing and land that do not provide standard subdivisions and mortgages to low-income homebuyers, relegating them to self-built housing on plots provided by land speculators. In Mexico, *colonias populares* lack basic services like water, paved streets, and sewage, thereby impacting the local environment, because of the extreme inequalities in that nation's development, in which (1) market mechanisms, like home mortgages and subdivisions, while present, are underdeveloped because of the limited size of and economic fragility of the middle class and upper working class, and (2) collective redistribution is extremely limited because the middle and upper classes pay few taxes and support few services, opting instead for private household solutions (water storage tanks on roofs, for example, rather than adequate water mains with sufficient pressure and cleanliness; see Ingram, Laney, and Gillilan 1995). However, *colonias populares* are by no means unique to the border, and some of their environmental impacts (e.g. particulates from unpaved streets), derive from a general pattern of rapid urbanization, in which basic infrastructure cannot keep up with demand. In all these issues, unequal territorialization of value is a cause, several steps removed.

In the case of U.S. *colonias*, however, household response to unequal territorialization of value is quite direct. *Colonias* attract a wide variety of settlers, some of them migrants from Mexico, others internal migrants within the United States (from inner city barrio rentals to city fringe homeownership, for example). However, whether directly immigrant or not, *colonia* dwellers use a distinctly Mexican self-provisioning household strategy for creating decent housing in the United States, given lack of market power to enter subdivisions and use mortgage lenders. They are occupied largely by people whose value (in the eyes of the larger society, monetarily and meaningfully) is still that of Mexico, that is, extremely low in U.S. terms: farm laborers, casual construction workers, domestics, small repairmen, truck drivers, and so on. Yet they are making a territorial move into or inside the United States, on the basis of the much greater value to be had even for poor people inside this nation—a logic of border crossing explained above. They are people with little power in either of the grand territories of value, acting on the needs and logics that have always made sense to the powerless, that of opportunistic household provisioning. (By "opportunistic," I am highlighting the literal meaning of seizing opportunities; I am not asserting that they think on a short time line, which would be incorrect in many cases of *colonia* residents who build homes for themselves and their children over long time horizons.) Even if we cast aside the common U.S. stereotypes of "dirty" *colonias* (who in fact probably produce less waste except untreated sewage than prosperous urban households), it is important to link the environmental problems that do plague *colonia* residents, including public health problems and disproportionately high expenses for basic services like water, with the overall pattern of combined and uneven development on the border.

Finally, state and counter-state activities concentrate along borders. Laws, regulations, police, the military, and other enforcement and service agencies are obvious forms of territorialization. Joseph Nevins (2002) and I (Heyman 1998, 1999) have argued that cross-border trade and so-called globalization are accompanied not by weakening of the territorial U.S. state, but its strengthening, both ideologically and practically. The reasons are complex, but relate significantly to the territorialization of value and meaning. For example, U.S. immigration policy (legal admittance of permanent and temporary labor migrants) and U.S. immigration law enforcement (keeping migrants out incompletely) allows some seepage of low-value Mexican workers into the high-value and demand U.S. labor market, while generally maintaining the separation of low- and high-wage territories that might collapse if there were a truly open border with free movement of labor. Elsewhere, I have rejected omniscient, capitalist-functionalist models of border law enforcement (e.g. a valve that permits precisely the correct flow of labor into the U.S.) because this lacks a role for ideology and politics in shaping border policy (see Heyman 1998). But even within a more sophisticated economic-political-ideological model, the U.S. state does enforce the territorialization of value.

Leo Chavez (1997) and Tamar Diana Wilson (2000) draw on the provocative, if excessively neat argument of Michael Burawoy (1976) to propose that U.S. immigration law enforcement attempts to keep the reproduction of households in Mexico, where the social wage is quite low, while allowing the direct laborers to enter the United States, where the wage level is relatively higher and the value of products and services is yet much higher. This does not require an omniscient state, since household reproduction is readily perceived in politics through demands on public hospitals, school systems, bus systems, police services, and so forth. These politics draw on unequal territorial meanings, by which immigrants are welcomed as hard workers but their families are perceived as the embodiment of poverty, dirt, and danger. Further territorializations of meaning include seeing zones outside the nation-state as sources of danger and impurity, and envisioning borders as a crucial place for national security operations. This adds up, as Nevins has insisted, to an increasing territorial concept of the nation-state both in popular consciousness and police-bureaucratic practice.

How does this affect the environment? The indirect effects, in terms of reinforcing territorial value differences in labor and collective redistributions, cannot be neglected. The role of the U.S. state apparatus as symbol and propaganda machine in polarizing meanings between the two countries is also important, and will be addressed in the following section. But here I want to concentrate on the direct environmental effects of concentrated state operations, and also their counterpart in smuggling, the transactions that take advantage of state-enforced differences of value at borders. The U.S.-Mexico border region encloses a huge "cat and mouse" game, with enormous resources deployed on each side. On the U.S. side, a large concentration of well-paid jobs is made up of the military and various police agencies, including the Drug Enforcement Administration (DEA), Federal Bureau of Investigations (FBI), and the various branches of Homeland Security (formerly the Immigration and Naturalization Service and the Customs Bureau). These employees add to the urbanization of the border, of course. Also, the police-military agencies of the state are nearly impervious to environmental scrutiny and restriction (e.g. cutting extensive road systems through slow-recovery arid biomes). After all, so-called national security, a sovereign interest, is involved.

On the other side, state law enforcement provides smugglers a lucrative source of profits in transacting values across unequal terrains. For example, in the early 1990s, U.S. immigration law enforcement changed in such a way that it became much more difficult for undocumented Mexican migrants to cross without the aid of a smuggler. Prices for a trip into the United States rose five- to tenfold (from roughly $300 to $1,500–3,000) and the percentage of trips using a smuggler rose sharply. People avoid mentioning it, but drug- and person-smuggling money is a main prop of the border economy. This again contributes to the rapid urbanization of the border, and in remoter areas to trail cutting with widespread littering of the desert.

Environmental Politics at the Border:
An Unequal-Relational Perspective

So far, we have examined how the territorialization of values, meanings, and state power creates a dynamic, booming, but also environmentally stressful set of urban centers along the borderline. We now turn to how this territorialization of resources, meanings, and collective action shapes the social construction of "environmental" issues and the various political responses in two nations. Pablo Vila and John Peterson (2003) document, for example, how U.S.-side residents focus on poverty, lax regulation, and backwardness as a cause of Mexican pollution, and Mexican-side residents focus on the unfairness of the United States coming to make money in their country but leaving behind social and environmental damage. O. Alberto Pombo (2000), addressing water and sewage, notes that the priorities of poor Tijuana residents (piped water) deviate considerably from the expert goals (high quality toilets/sewage mains). And Ingram, Laney, and Gillilan (1995), though not taking an explicit social-construction perspective, describe a series of cross-border misunderstandings and tensions over water and sewage.

I accept the idea of social construction of environmental issues, rather than the naïve and mechanical assumption of direct rational response to objective reality. The question is whether underlying processes at borders characteristically shape such constructions. One candidate is the interplay between territorialized state capacity and individual/household and corporate perceptions of possible action. More concretely, the two governments at the border have vastly different abilities to put in place public, environmental infrastructure. They also have differing abilities to regulate corporate polluters, but both nations are weak in that regard. In the United States, clean water supplies and decent-quality, secondary sewage treatment are the norm, because of well-capitalized public utilities. Most householders take for granted such services, paying regularly for utilities, and do not see their existence as a matter of making priorities and choices. When such services are not delivered, as in the case of U.S.-side *colonias*, this shows the limits of U.S. state capacity vis-à-vis a very marginalized population and the informal real estate market that serves it.

Meanwhile, on the Mexican side, a less adequately funded state (exacerbated by Mexico's centralized budget system that starves state and local governments of funds) means two things. First, many solutions take place at the household level, and are highly unequal. Rich families, for example, invest in high-capacity clean water storage systems to cope with sporadic water supply. Since solutions are immediate and personal, rather than infrastructural and collective, this detracts from systematic management of problems. Second, the decision to use scarce government resources in one or another infrastructure is always political, being incomplete both geographically (e.g. coverage of a middle-class neighborhood but not a poor one) and by type of service (e.g. piped water before sewer mains). How households and broader social groups arrange infrastructure affects not only the physical systems but also the social meanings of "clean environment" in each nation and among the classes within them.

In turn, differential ways of addressing infrastructure must be viewed in terms of long-term processes of unequal exchange. It is hardly a surprise that the fiscal capacities of Mexican border municipalities and most utility ratepayers in them is lower than in the United States. This makes it more difficult to organize nonpoliticized, expert-managed, routine collective handling of waste (human and industrial) in Mexico. Yet it is not the case that population and industry is much smaller on the Mexican side than the U.S. side, in apparent correspondence with the lower resources (though it is somewhat consistent with lower consumption and waste per person); rather, in this case of unequal exchange–driven development, there are more people and industry on the poorer side than on the richer side. Hence the clashing social constructions of Mexican and U.S. residents are both correct; Mexico does not routinely handle its waste as well as the United States, which often harms Mexicans but sometimes spills over to the U.S. side, while simultaneously the United States does profit from Mexico and is indirectly responsible for many of the environmental problems in this region.

Now, as Vila points out, the social construction of environmental issues on the border often leads to polarization. Let us take a shared environmental problem, such as raw or primary-treated sewage releases from Mexico flowing into the United States (see Ingram, Laney, and Gillilan 1995). This is a genuine problem, which gives rise to a lot of arrogant hue and cry among Americans who take sewage treatment for granted, and who also tend to hold stereotypes that all problems of dirt and poverty come from Mexico. In turn, Mexicans, overwhelmed by needs that surpass their collective fiscal capacities, feel bullied by the United States into taking action on the sewage problem, which may not be the first demand of most households (Pombo 2000) although objectively it harms them. After negotiation between the two nations, the United States funds most of the cost of the new infrastructure while a smaller, perhaps symbolic amount is paid by Mexico. U.S. officials and activists perceive budgets that could be used at home going instead to another nation, that is, perceive Mexico as not doing its share or taking its responsibility, while Mexican officials and publics find themselves bullied into choices they might not otherwise take by a superpower that is profiteering off the region as a whole. The long-term cause of polarization is the unequal distribution of public and household fiscal resources by political territories within one single space of capital accumulation and urban agglomeration.

The characteristic diagnosis of border environmental politics is that boundaries and rigid bureaucratic rules surrounding them get in the way of cross-border popular (or activist) cooperation to address environmental problems (see Ingram, Laney, and Gillilan 1995; Liverman et al. 1999; and Staudt and Coronado 2002). This literature has a certain logic. The border arbitrarily bisects biophysical processes and flows, such as watersheds and aquifers. Optimal solutions demand some form of cooperation or coordination. Likewise, empathetic activists and thoughtful local officials often care deeply about shared health and environmental challenges, and try to work across borders to address them. Indeed, a novel binational agency, the Border Environmental Cooperation Commission, was created under NAFTA to institutionalize such initiatives. Briefly, this organization (with a bilingual and mixed national staff) instigates, advises, and ultimately recommends proposals that ameliorate some environmental problems of border urbanism, such as water supply, water treatment, and solid waste treatment. However, it struggles with unequal funding and different models of political participation and decision-making in the two territories. And it is certainly the case that unimaginative bureaucrats and politicians in each nation, defending budgets and turf, often frustrate environmental reforms.

But such a view implies that border society on both sides would naturally tend to come to agreement if it were not for the bad guys in distant state and national capitals. Yet this is far from the case. Border societies have their own tendencies toward polarization (Vila 2000, Grimson and Vila 2002). One reason for this is that unequal exchange across differentially valued territorial domains results in visible inequalities and disparities in capacities for and modes of collective action (mostly, state capacity) and in households' and social groups' demands on and strategies within such territories. Hence, cross-border empathy and collective social action will not be sustained by isolated problem-solving programs, but rather an enduring answer lies in an effective struggle for greater collective equality within and between the two separated territories (see Staudt and Coronado 2002).

Conclusion

I began by reciting the various environmental disorders characteristic of the U.S.-Mexico border. In looking for their roots, we found them not in some singularity of the border environment, but rather in how a random patchwork of largely arid local environments responded to the extreme industrialization, commercial flux, U.S. state activity, and urbanization brought on by the presence of the border itself. To understand this development, we examined how the border as a line between two value terrains favored unequal, stepwise exchange. We noted furthermore that such value inequality interlocks with differential territorialization of meanings and unequal capacity for collective public action. This accounts not only for the rapid development of the border region and for its peculiarities, such as the side with more people and more economic activity (Mexico) having fewer resources for collective problem-solving, but also for the polarizing social construction of environmental issues.

In all of this, we have unconsciously but significantly departed from standard geographic assumptions of public environmentalism. Such perspectives view the problems of the rich and poor nations as separate, and indeed they tend to view nations (equated with societies) as separate and coherent units laid over a preexisting "natural" terrain. Border problems in such a view are ones of incomplete connection and cooperation, and failed or "bad" development. However, public action using such a frame will almost certainly encounter surprising frustrations and paradoxes, and will tend to bypass important causes. The world-system perspective draws our attention to the processes that combine human and biophysical action in making and remaking spaces, in this case, bounded territories. Likewise, it emphasizes the unity of apparently differentiated people and places, and the causes of environmental disequilibrium in "successful" development. This analytical sharpness does not relieve our need to act publicly and collectively, and in practical ways; rather one hopes it will help in such action, through informing tactics and policies, and teaching (broadly meant) about environmental issues.

References

Agnew, J. A., and S. Corbridge. 1995. *Mastering space: Hegemony, territory and international political economy*. London and New York: Routledge.

Bahre, C. J. 1991. *A legacy of change: Historic human impact on vegetation in the Arizona borderlands*. Tucson: University of Arizona Press.

Burawoy, M. 1976. The functions and reproduction of migrant labor: Comparative material from southern Africa and the United States. *American Journal of Sociology* 81:1050–1087.

Chavez, L. R. 1997. Immigration reform and nativism: The nationalist response to the transnationalist challenge. In *Immigrants out! The new nativism and the anti-immigrant impulse in the United States*, ed. J. F. Perea, 61–77. New York: New York University Press.

Corliss, D. 2000. Regulating the border environment: Toxics, maquiladoras, and the public right to know. In *Shared space: Rethinking the U.S.-Mexico border environment*, ed. L. A. Herzog, 295–312. La Jolla, Calif.: Center for U.S.-Mexican Studies, University of California, San Diego.

Fernandez, R. A. 1977. *The United States-Mexico border: A político-economic profile.* Notre Dame, Ind.: University of Notre Dame Press.

Grimson, A., and P. Vila. 2002. Forgotten border actors: The border reinforcers: A comparison between the U.S.–Mexico border and South American borders. *Journal of Political Ecology* 9:69–88. www.library.arizona.edu/ej/jpe/volume_9/GrimsonVila2002.pdf.

Herzog, L. A., ed. 2000. *Shared space: Rethinking the U.S.-Mexico border environment.* La Jolla, Calif.: Center for U.S.-Mexican Studies, University of California, San Diego.

Heyman, J. McC. 1994. The Mexico-United States border in anthropology: A critique and reformulation. *Journal of Political Ecology* 1:43–65. www.library.arizona.edu/ej/jpe/volume_1/HEYMAN.PDF.

———. 1998. Immigration law enforcement and the superexploitation of undocumented aliens: The Mexico-United States border case. *Critique of Anthropology* 18:157–180.

———. 1999. Why interdiction? Immigration law enforcement at the United States-Mexico border. *Regional Studies* 33:619–630.

———. 2004. Ports of entry as nodes in the world system. *Identities: Global Studies in Culture and Power* 11:303–327.

Hopkins, T. K. 1982. World-systems analysis: Methodological issues. In *World-systems analysis: Theory and methodology*, ed. T. K. Hopkins and I. Wallerstein, 145–158. Los Angeles: Sage.

Hornborg, A. 2001. *The power of the machine: Global inequalities of economy, technology, and environment.* Walnut Creek, Calif.: AltaMira.

Ingram, H., N. K. Laney, and D. M. Gillilan. 1995. *Divided waters: Bridging the U.S.-Mexico border.* Tucson: University of Arizona Press.

Kearney, M. 2004. The classifying and value-filtering missions of borders. *Anthropological Theory* 4:131–156.

Liverman, D. M., R. G. Varady, O. Chávez, and R. Sánchez. 1999. Environmental issues along the United States-Mexico border: Drivers of change and responses of citizens and institutions. *Annual Review of Energy and Environment* 24:607–643.

Lorey, D. E. 1999. *The U.S.-Mexican border in the twentieth century: A history of economic and social transformation.* Wilmington, Del.: Scholarly Resources.

Nevins, J. 2002. *Operation gatekeeper: The rise of the "illegal alien" and the making of the U.S.-Mexico boundary.* New York and London: Routledge.

Paasi, A. 1996. *Territories, boundaries, and consciousness: The changing geographies of the Finnish-Russian boundary.* Chichester, U.K., and New York: Wiley.

Pombo, O. A. 2000. Water use and sanitation practices in peri-urban areas of Tijuana: A demand-side perspective. In *Shared space: Rethinking the U.S.-Mexico border environment*, ed. L. A. Herzog, 265–292. La Jolla, Calif.: Center for U.S.-Mexican Studies, University of California, San Diego.

Romieu, I., et al. 2003 (November). *Health impacts of air pollution on morbidity and mortality among children of Ciudad Juárez, Chihuahua, Mexico*. Working Paper, Commission for Environmental Cooperation. Montreal.

Ross, J. 2003 (September 12). Tricky Dick's NAFTA for energy. *Texas Observer* 95 (17): 16–17.

Staudt, K., and I. Coronado. 2002. *Fronteras no más: Toward social justice at the U.S.-Mexico border*. New York and Basingstoke, U.K.: Palgrave Macmillan.

Taylor, P. J. 1985. *Political geography: World-economy, nation-state and locality*. London and New York: Longman.

Vila, P. 2000. *Crossing borders, reinforcing borders: Social categories, metaphors, and narrative identities on the U.S.-Mexico frontier*. Austin: University of Texas Press.

Vila, P., and J. A. Peterson. 2003. Environmental problems in Ciudad Juárez–El Paso: A social constructionist approach. In *Ethnography at the border*, ed. P. Vila, 251–278. Minneapolis: University of Minnesota Press.

Ward, P. M. 1999. *Colonias and public policy in Texas and Mexico: Urbanization by stealth*. Austin: University of Texas Press.

Wilson, T. D. 2000. Anti-immigrant sentiment and the problem of reproduction/maintenance in Mexican migration to the United States. *Critique of Anthropology* 20:191–213.

Surrogate Money, Technology, and the Expansion of Savanna Soybeans in Brazil

18

WILLIAM H. FISHER

I F WE WANDER THROUGH THE BRAZILIAN hinterlands today we can still see villages founded by waves of past settlers as they colonized its vast interior. Towns like Rosário do Oeste in the Brazilian state of Mato Grosso huddle in the shade of spreading *Ficus* and mango trees. Ghosts of diamond prospectors and cattle hands seem to peer from the recesses of the one-story buildings of nicked and fading pastels resting siesta-quiet in the heat of midday. But just a short distance from this old frontier town the rural landscape changes radically as we leave the emerald humidity of the basin to crest a plateau where limpid emptiness appears to descend in all directions. There is no sign announcing that we have entered Brazil's latest incarnation of order and progress, but clearly a boundary has been breached. What appeared empty now comes into focus as striking uniformity—treeless fields in every direction. Dust devils swirl merrily alongside our bus for a short spell before veering off their own way. Further along on the flat-topped *chapada*, spanking new grain elevators loom. Clean attractive company logos boldly painted on their sides proclaim their affiliation with familiar transnational firms Cargill, Bunge, and Archer-Daniels-Midland. The weighing and storage facilities of Brazil's Maggi group intersperse with these. The family-owned firm's elder son, Blairo, the largest soybean planter in the world, has ascended to Mato Grosso state governorship.

Open fields stretch right to the edge of the road, while in the distance dark screens of trees nudge upward into the line of the horizon. The unwary treading on the road's soft shoulders find themselves up to their ankles in a soft powder, residue of particles flicked loose from exposed red soil. For some stretches it looked as though snow has fallen along the roadside, but a closer look reveals the plush long fibers of cotton bolls jarred free by the bumpy ride on the deteriorated road surface. Here the earth and its bounty, soil and crops knocked loose by machine-powered cultivation and transport, suffer rough handling that goes with the speed and volume of the new economic miracle.

Brazil's great north includes the Amazon and has long been a consumer and producer of global commodities. Rubber, spices, furs, vegetable and animal oils, Brazil nuts, and gold have each created fortunes—sometimes great fortunes. Immigrants have run great risks to grab a part of the action. Indigenous peoples have been either shunted aside or put to work while their overlords claimed the wealth extracted. More recently gargantuan mineral complexes have extracted iron, aluminum, and bauxite for shipment overseas. And also recently the great rivers of Brazil's northern region have either been dammed (some of the biggest in the world when first built) or targeted for hydroelectric projects. The energy generated in giant turbines flows out to large industrial enterprises along the coast or great population centers to the south. Although export-oriented economic activity spurring immigration to the region is not new to the Amazon, the expansion of industrialized agriculture is vaster in scale than any previous intrusion. The growing agricultural sector is also more of a linchpin for Brazil's economic orientation of "export or die," enunciated by President Fernando Henrique Cardoso and accepted by his successor, Luís Inácio Lula da Silva.

Careful not to allow his attention to deviate from the obstacle course created by holes in the uneven pavement, our bus driver passes trucks and more trucks. Their long beds are covered with neatly stretched tarps hiding the material to feed the burgeoning appetite of the treeless fields for lime, fertilizer, seeds, and machinery. Other trucks carry the unimaginably vast output of cotton, soybeans, and cattle on the beginning of a voyage that might take them around the world to Rotterdam, Russia, or Japan. At predictable intervals of 60 kilometers we pass towns—Nova Mutum, São Lucas do Rio Verde, Sorriso—that have sprung up since the early 1980s. Their centers are laid out along broad boulevards named for local politicians or prominent pioneers. Streets are lined with single-family houses, commonly surrounded by electric fences. Everything here is large scale—big and new. Even as unrelenting sunlight cascades over us as we amble out at a rest stop, we are inside what Hornborg (2001) calls "the Machine" (map 18.1).

The machine image points to the critical role that tools have always had in shaping the way humans relate to their environment and to one another. But it enlarges the scope of this image by putting human ecology within a

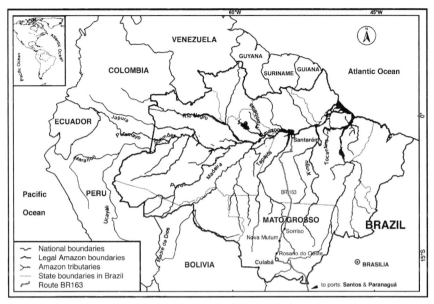

Map 18.1.

larger frame of interactions between societies. The operation of the machine rests on far-flung connections and calls attention to interrelations between global trade, environmental degradation, and technology as part of a single systemic flow of materials and meanings. The fields, the trucks, the grain silos, the leaning millet cover crop, the eroded soils by the roadside, the humans of different social classes unself-consciously segregating into small groups to pass the time, and, yes, even the bright sunlight itself are linked into a vast cyclical process. The structure of exchanges that perpetuate the global inequalities continues, in part, because operations of machinery and know-how are narrowly understood to rely on the cause-and-effect laws pertaining to physical systems. But Hornborg argues that we must broaden our understanding to account for the insight that social relations of inequality comprise a necessary matrix for the operation of the global relations spawned by the "machine" whose functioning will continue to perpetuate these very same unequal relations. Different classes of people and regions will be punished or rewarded both ecologically and economically by global trade based on profit-making.

Unveiling the sociocultural dimensions of the machine requires that we conceptualize world trade as an economic and ecological system circulating flows of values, materials, and energy. The net effect for the periphery is fewer valued resources and less buying power to purchase resources. Insofar as there have been other analyses of the ecological effects of the world-system, Hornborg's analysis complements others (e.g. Biel 2000; Moore 2003; Chew 2001). However, his insistence that this kind of system rests on a certain structure of exchanges makes it necessary to describe human meanings. The power of capital to lay claim to resources and move humans into action rests on the prior existence of resources and of suitable demography and social organization (cf. Wolf 1990). Symbols of value and price must be mapped onto a circulation of materials and energy so that processes of natural production and extraction may be harnessed to circuits of capital accumulation. Once the process begins, ecological and economic crises, either singly or in concert, may be at the root of the collapse of human ecological systems. But to point to a collapse in a structure shows us that certain relations resulting in capital accumulation do not exist at all times and all places: they must be brought into being and may also disappear. Historical analysis is, therefore, essential and comprises the necessary backdrop to understand how appropriate meanings and motivations can be harnessed to specific regimes of production and ownership. The number of failures in which heavy investment has not resulted in successful development in the Brazilian hinterlands and Amazonian regions underline the point that capital on an agricultural frontier can only fulfill its potential as self-increasing value if it can foster relations whereby it is able to "harvest" or appropriate values resulting from the growth of organisms.

This chapter helps to illuminate this point by describing the particular structure of exchange relations that sustain the expansive frontier boom in industrial agriculture. The area I describe is located near the geographical center of the Brazilian state of Mato Grosso, whose closed savanna areas (*cerrado*) have seen some of the most explosive development of soybeans over the last twenty years. The municipality of Sorriso, site of ongoing fieldwork, covers 930,354 hectares of slightly undulating lands transected by the Teles Pires River and its tributaries. Based on its newfound clout as an agricultural powerhouse, it achieved independent municipal status in 1986. During the 2003/2004 growing season an astonishing total of 590,000 ha (or 63 percent) of the area of the municipality was cultivated in soy (EMPAER 2004). Additional area was devoted to cattle and other agricultural activities. Consideration of the full impact of mechanized agriculture in the municipality would also have to factor in the effects of transport, storage, urbanization, and the constructions of roads. Sorriso accounts for about 2 percent of national soybean production and is the largest single municipal producer in Brazil. However, it is but a single municipality among dozens largely oriented toward the production of soybeans, most of which would like to emulate Sorriso's success.

In many respects Sorriso mirrors a wave of colonization of Brazil's interior over the past two decades. The rise of soybean cultivation in Brazil and the increasing dominance of the tropical savannas as areas of cultivation is astounding: "In this century, in a similar [two decade] time period, no other internationally traded commodity of any country has had output expansion equal to that of Brazilian soybeans" (Warnken 1999:9). In a very short time Brazil has become a major player on the global level. "Between 1970 and 1989, world soybean production rose from 42 to 107 million metric tonnes, a 65% increase, while Brazil's output increased from 1.5 to 24 million metric tonnes, an increase of 2,100%" (Warnken 1999:9). By 2003 output had shot up yet further to 52 million metric tonnes, although it dropped back to 49.8 million metric tonnes in 2004 when Asian Soybean Rust destroyed millions of metric tonnes (Benson 2005). In 2005 the soy complex made up about 8 percent of total exports, accounting for US$ 9.5 billion of the US$ 118 billion total (Maia and Oliveira 2006).

Since 1980 the area of soybeans harvested in the savannas has increased by about 10 percent annually (Warnken 1999). In 1990s the savanna (*cerrado* in Portuguese) produced 25.4 percent of Brazil's total soybean crop (Cunha 1994:64). Today over half of Brazil's production is in savanna or tropical forest regions and Mato Grosso generates about 29 percent of Brazil's soybeans. Average yields in the state are well above Brazil's national average, and Brazil surpassed U.S. average yields in 1999 (USDA 2004). The U.S. Department of Agriculture estimates that, while the United States will have difficulty finding new places to plant soybeans, Brazil can expand planting onto both flat uncultivated cerrado (approximately 137 million acres) and pastureland (185 million acres) (Schnepf, Dohlman, and Bolling 2001:6).

Soybean cultivation in Brazil's southern, nonsavanna regions has largely been a result of substitution for other crops such as wheat or coffee (Warnken 1999). To a more limited extent some substitution has occurred on the savannas as well (Veiga Filho 2001). However, the notable feature of planting in the savanna is precisely that much uncultivated *cerrado* (savanna) land, supporting many native noncommercial plants, was replaced by soybean fields (Sousa and Busch 1998:357). The ecological changes have already transformed millions of hectares of native vegetation. Legislation signed in 1995 sets limits on how much native vegetation cover may be cleared. Uncleared land area on a property should be equivalent to 35 percent in Amazonian *cerrados* and 80 percent in the Amazon forest, but these limits have largely been ignored in Mato Grosso.

The environmental effect of clearing millions of hectares of native vegetation represents a significant threat to savanna ecology. The threat is compounded by the speed and extent to which preexisting ecosystems have been modified. The industrial system that has taken hold over the past two decades eliminates existing land-cover, levels the soil surface, and imports all essential nutrients, chemical treatments of soils, herbicides, and pesticides from long distances. At the end of the harvest, the entire crop will be shipped out of the municipality to other parts of Brazil, often for overseas destinations. The simplification of the municipal ecology through removal of native vegetation and grading of soils makes crop growth and sale entirely dependent on movement of material into and out of the area. Under these conditions transportation has become a central focus through which contending interests wrestle for a share of the wealth produced in the region. Complex negotiations are currently underway to develop a comprehensive plan for Amazonian development that will address the infrastructural needs of business. Formidable construction projects for transport arteries have been launched along three big water routes: Itacoatiara, Paranaguá–Paraná, and Araguaia–Tocantins. In addition, there are railway facilities either completed or underway in the Brazilian states of Goiás, Tocantins, and Maranhão. In Mato Grosso, the paving of highway 163 between Cuiabá and the Amazon port of Santarém has become the focus of negotiations. Most soybeans today wind their way to the coastal port of Paranaguá, some 2,100 kilometers distant. Historically, such transport costs ate up a significant portion of farm profits.

The surge in soy exports from Sorriso must be set in the context of Brazil's recent rural development and, as importantly, farming on the savanna must be distinguished from nonsavanna areas. National policies regarding trade, research, and agricultural credits have all had their effect, but soy expansion on the closed savannas also has attracted attention for its contribution to deforestation. Environmentalists have identified industrialized agriculture and cattle ranching as the major culprits behind land-cover change (Fearnside 2000; Brown 2005). The expansion of soybeans into *cerrado* and, increasingly, tropical forest regions has largely been seen through one of two optics. On one hand, conservationists are greatly troubled by continued destruction of wild habitats, including the *cerrado*. On the other, corporate media have largely applauded the dynamism of the agricultural export sector. "The Civilization of the Croplands" is a typical article lauding the "revolution of Brazilian agribusiness" (Salgado 2004). Overall, little attention has been paid to the new kinds of communities spawned by the recent boom, nor on the legacy that their wake will leave on the Brazilian interior.

Sorriso's communities are not unlike others that have anchored the agricultural expansion in Mato Grosso's interior. Within each municipality, hundreds of large farmers, often owning several properties, some of which are held in the name of family members, control hundreds of thousands of acres. Precise figures of land ownership and control are notoriously difficult to come by. Farmers with large areas actually outnumber those owning up to a few acres. They also outnumber the colonizers settled in projects of the National Agrarian Reform Institute (INCRA). Foremen on large farms and some other on-farm posts are held by southern Brazilians, while the heavy labor and land-clearing is provided by northeasterners, primarily from the state of Maranhão. While logging is still of some importance, especially while land remained to be cleared, its prominence is declining, as are cattle ranches. None of these industries is labor intensive, and greater mechanization tends to make them even less so. Population for the municipality totals 35,397 inhabitants, according to the 2000 census. Like statistics of true land ownership, however, population figures are not very reliable. Unofficial estimates, including those of local officials, put the number much higher, between sixty and seventy thousand. While officials have a vested interest in inflating population in their jurisdiction, it is indisputable that every week sees an influx of buses from Maranhão filled with young men hungry for work. The BR 163 highway neatly divides the commercial center and well-to-do residential neighborhoods from the homes of laborers, maids, and clerks. Early mornings witness an invasion of bicycles crossing the highway, as poorer *Sorrisense* make their way to work.

Economic planning by Brazil's military regime was encapsulated in its "National Development Plan" that elaborated goals for different sectors of the economy. In the case of agriculture, planners consciously sought to contribute to the internationalization of Brazilian agriculture. It is doubtful that they could have realized the extent to which their vision has come to pass today! The proliferation of state enterprises, many initiated under the aegis of the military regime, served to link the Brazilian economy with global commodity chains by responding to and even attempting to anticipate the interests of multinational capital (Aguiar 1986). In the case of soybeans, the relationship between researchers at federal universities, research institutes, agribusiness, and even the U.S. government, including funds channeled through the Alliance for Progress, were essential (cf. Fundação Cargill 1982). Research was of a very practical and applied kind, the underlying aim being to develop detailed protocols for scientific farming based on the knowledge produced by agronomists working with machinery employed on a large-scale farm enterprise. The Cargill Foundation was already sponsoring research for soybeans by 1972, well in advance of the migratory wave of Brazilian southerners northward to the savannas. Sousa and Busch (1998) have documented the requirements for moving the temperate soybean plant to the tropical drought-prone climate and acidic, aluminum-laden soils of the savanna.

The federal government targeted immigrants from Brazil's south because their previous technical and administrative experience would allow them to transform financial resources into "physical capital" of the kind desired by planners. Above all, this consisted of machinery and infrastructure combined with knowledge enabling the growth of products demanded by transnational grain traders. The new class of proprietors is almost exclusively male and white. From the very beginning indebtedness was an issue, particularly for the younger immigrants who did not have holdings to sell in order to acquire land. Some solved this issue by joining together and pooling resources and labor, others managed to rent forested areas in exchange for preparing them for cultivation. Government financing was contingent on a commitment to engage in a specific industrial agricultural enterprise. Farmers who managed to get established with land became a class closely attuned to the priorities set by the federal government and its agricultural research and extension services. Their local privileges transformed them into a nascent elite with an interest in defending policies that favored their continued access to the advantages of government support.

The founders of Sorriso did not envision a settlement dedicated to soybean production. Over a half-decade passed before the new town began to fulfill its promise as an agricultural area. This transpired as large landholders of similar southern background were provided credit, suitable crop varieties, and the equipment necessary to cultivate them according to specific technical recipes (cf. Dias and Bortoncello 2003). The background of rural agriculture imported from Brazil's southern states had an important impact but not in terms of the practice of farming itself. Far more essential was the southern farmer identity, which carried a commitment to the canons of success and respectability within an agricultural community. Initially, investors sought to acquire real estate and had notions of establishing a large cattle farm for which there was plenty of recent precedent in Amazonian states. They had no assurance that agriculture was viable or which crops might grow. Agronomists from the Mato Grosso Department of Rural Research, Assistance, and Extension (EMPAER—and its predecessor, EMATER) struggled to come up with suitable crops. Through its POLOCENTRO Project, the federal government assisted colonization efforts. Most efforts directly benefited large proprietors, as properties over

1,000 hectares absorbed 60 percent of project funds (Cunha 1994:57). The government also purchased an initial unpalatable rice crop. It was not until the early 1980s that soybeans were introduced in Sorriso.

During the initial period real estate speculators from the south who had acquired land returned to the southern states to resell parcels. Given favorable prices compared to land in the south, many took the risk, joining a long and illustrious parade of immigrants to Brazil's north in search of wealth. The driving motivation of a relatively well-off citizenry from the agricultural south was not great wealth in the abstract, but enrichment with the aim of emulating the solid, successful rural elite with large properties and prominent local recognition. Today one still hears declarations that "southerners have a vocation for farming" repeated proudly in Sorriso. But this is not to be taken to mean farming the "southern" way, and large farmers violently reject the idea that farming wisdom from the south can be transplanted to the savannas.

It is not wealth alone that elicits admiration and emulation in Sorriso but wealth gained through industrial farming. Logging and cattle ranching as well as commerce and building trades are other prominent industries, but farming is the measure by which status can most effectively be displayed. Recognition extended to rural entrepreneurs inevitably underlines the extent of property holdings and area cultivated. For example, the "Agriculturalist of the Year" recognized by the "Commercial and Industrial Association of Sorriso" is described in the local newspaper as "planting around 16,000 hectares of soybeans and 5,000 hectares of corn" (Minosso 2004). No such status indicators are applied to engineers, retailers, or loggers. In conversation, the number of hectares planted in soybeans or the number of sacks held in storage is used to indicate the importance of community members in the local hierarchy. For their part, middle-class professionals and nonfarmers must seek other outlets for local recognition, and the recent founding of the Rotary Club and a range of evangelical churches appear to be satisfying this need.

The practice of large-scale agriculture in Sorriso is at one and the same time a system of ecology, racial politics, corporate control, and community structure. Changes in any one of these areas reverberate throughout. An examination of their interconnections can begin to trace the factors that give the region its current dynamic. Large-scale farming requires adherence to a strict system of planning. Farmers' plans vary slightly, but various institutions, ranging from banks to accounting firms and multinational corporations, vet all plans. A budget of expenditures and an outline of proposed operations form an intrinsic part of the process of applying for cash credit or purchasing inputs on credit. The level of detail is quite specific. Application of an herbicide will be specified as to the timing, the quantity, the size of machinery and field, and determining how many passes over the field will be made. Thus the process of financing crop production creates a dependence on information developed by agricultural experiments by federal universities, federally sponsored centers for agricultural research, and private research foundations sponsored by firms such as Monsanto, Pioneer, Cargill, Massey Ferguson, and Maggi. Research is imminently practical and geared toward developing products and protocols for the production of export crops on a large scale using commercially available machinery and chemicals. Target ranges for amounts of inputs and quantity and quality of outputs are specified. Protocols (*cartilhas*) developed by banks, grain traders, and agronomic consultants match amounts of brand name chemicals to areas of cultivation with a schedule for procedures and ultimately product delivery and sale.

The mapping of the flow of material and energy onto present and future is linked to the prices of inputs in the present (which the farmer seeks to buy) and the future price of the crop (when the farmer will be in a position to sell). Most farmers must time their purchases to the growing season and there is an increased use of futures contracts to try and hedge against a disastrous price drop at harvest. There is a chasm between the public exaltation of the farmer as a daring swashbuckling entrepreneur and the frustrated contract farmer who has received fertilizer from Cargill on the promise that he will deliver a certain quantity of crop by a deadline or suffer default. The truth is that, except for the very largest farm producers, these are but different portraits of the same person. And yet, the structure of community social standing is largely built on the first image. It is unlikely that immigrants would engage in the risks and uncertainties without the community standing that comes with their position.

Almost all large farmers also contract agronomists as "technical assistance" to give them an opinion free of corporate influence, and whom they can contact when things appear to be going poorly. Corporate influence is hard to eliminate, however, and the number of consulting firms that also sell farm manufactures by multinationals has skyrocketed since 1999–2000, when the crisis in exchange rates hit farmers and cattle ranchers. Large farmers, the so-called rural entrepreneurs, receive a great deal more instruction and extension services than less well-off farmers. "They all receive personal attention," sniffed the secretary of agriculture in Sorriso with some evident irony. Obtaining technical assistance for hundreds of small farmers rests largely on the shoulders of the three-person staff of the family farm–oriented state extension service, who are run to the point of despair trying to serve their truly needy clients.

The way industrial farming is actually done in Sorriso involves a number of actors, products, machinery, and relationships between them. Bank protocols for approved agronomic practice are one facet of the nexus between agronomic knowledge, technology, and markets that farmers must incorporate into their own calculus. What the USDA matter-of-factly refers to as the "federal, university and industry-coordinated framework" within the United States also operates in Brazil to powerfully shape the flow of materials and credit, but farmers must contend with growing conditions in their own fields and rely on local contacts to make the deals for credit, land leases, sharing of machinery, and other transactions that can spell the difference between success and failure.

Specific people, institutions, seed varieties, transportation, and geographical and environmental specificities endow the Sorriso region with a distinct caste. Within the region political struggles over land, zoning, and government expenditures prevent the emergence of alternatives to large farming. Each region has its distinct cost structure for farming, preference for seed varieties, a network of creditors and debtors, and patron–client ties. One way to understand the extent to which the localized structure must be distinguished from the more general national expansion of agriculture is to trace the kind of information-gathering that different actors and institutions engage in. Large farmers insist on the need to talk with others in the municipality about agronomic issues, products, and prices. While the very biggest extend their contacts to state-wide and even national farm associations, most talk with their neighbors, often during events sponsored in the municipal center by agricultural companies putting on product demonstrations. Crop trial demonstrations, called "field days," also draw farmers eager for information and socializing. The town's main social club, "Recordando os Pagos" ("Remembering the Pagos"—Pagos being located in the southern state of Rio Grande do Sul), occupies a choice bit of real estate within the municipal center. Within the club, the paramount social status of large farmers is acknowledged in many ways, including the reference in the name to southern farming communities. Agribusiness corporations sponsor lavish dinners and entertainment that become a focus of town social life. It is not unusual that commercial claims of the sponsors made during a prefestivity presentation are reported in news sections of newspapers while the style choices of prominent families and their table companions are reported on the society page.

Some information is collected outside of festive sales occasions. Companies constantly call farmers' cell phones to enquire on recent purchases or to gauge intentions for future ones. Salesmen for multinationals such as Bayer assiduously ply sales routes in order to meet sales quotas, and farmers complain about the number of commercial representatives they must receive. Canons of hospitality as well as anticipation of unforeseen future eventualities, when specific farm products or credit might be needed, tend to ensure that salespeople are extended at least cursory entrance. Seed companies that wish to sell varieties on the Sorriso market establish local experimental facilities (e.g. *South American Business Information* 2003). There is also intensive monitoring of the price of soybeans on the Chicago commodities market as well as the exchange rate between the Brazilian real and the U.S. dollar. The constant flow of communication creates a sense of connectedness—even the most abject shoeshine boy is likely to know the price of a bushel of soybeans on the Chicago board of trade. It also creates a great distance from other kinds of industry; news and politics (even among local opposition parties) are largely limited to elaborations of the theme of how to manage the progress and wealth brought by industrial agriculture.

While the export crops grown in Sorriso form part of a global commodity chain, a local structure of production and exchange undergirds farmers' practice. Locally, farmers are constrained by the complex of chemicals and machines they are forced to acquire and the farm products they are forced to produce as a condition of acquisition. These include a battery of pesticides, fungicides, herbicides, lime, fertilizer, seeds, and machinery. Once they are integrated into the system, further resources for farming depend on criteria determined by financial institutions and multinational companies. For example, the Bank of Brazil classifies farmers into categories "a," "b," and "c," requiring that the amount of production, productivity per area, area planted, types of machinery, year of purchase, and state of conservation, along with storage and trucks for hauling are quantified into formulas to calculate the amount of credit to which they are entitled. Farms of smaller size with fewer machines and lower productivity are eligible for less credit.

While the technical requirements for farming change from year to year, new knowledge and material is disseminated quickly. A comparison of variable and fixed costs of soybean cultivation in Sorriso in 2003 and 2005 (Richetti, Staut, and Gomez 2005) shows an increase of $151.65 (from US$444.75 to US$596.40 per hectare), about $129 of which can be attributable to rising costs of inputs. The expected increase in production was a mere two 60 kg sacks. As of this writing in January 2006, a sack of soybeans fetched around $12.60 and the price of soybeans was down substantially from the previous year. The decline of the dollar vis-à-vis Brazilian currency has also hit farmers hard, since their exports become worth less while they pay more for imported farm inputs. Hence the squeezing of farm profits make farmers more vulnerable to default. As of December 2005, only about three-quarters of Bank of Brazil credits targeted for rural production in Mato Grosso from the previous growing season had been repaid. Farmers await the outcome of negotiations to extend repayments and establish terms for loans made during the last two years (Anonymous 2006).

Given the unstable price of money in terms of exchange rates, the fluctuating costs of transport and imported products, and the transaction costs of acquiring money credit, soybeans have themselves become a medium of exchange. Farmers attempt to buffer themselves from fluctuating prices while contributing to the preservation of the regional structure of exchange that underwrites the farm enterprise. At their discretion, grain traders will use purchase contracts, whereby they advance inputs such as fertilizer in return for delivery of a specified number of soybean sacks at harvest time, thus also avoiding money in their transaction with farmers. Vouchers for soy stored in commercial silos may be tendered by car and farm machinery dealerships or consulting firms. However much large soy farmers are lauded as pioneers and entrepreneurs, it is clear that the reliance on contract farming severely constrains their independent decision-making regarding on-farm operations. A handful of the largest farmers have escaped from this box. They are large enough so that they may diversify their activities and holdings. They may speculate with currency, make greater use of future markets to cushion themselves from risk of market volatility, and they become suppliers of farm inputs and buyers of production from smaller farmers. They represent sources of fresh credit for strapped farmers, who, of course, also worry about foreclosure and being gobbled up by bigger landowners. Municipal governments and trade associations present this select group as the public face of the agricultural boom, and their names appear in national and international news stories, projecting a distinctly optimistic coloring to the image of farming.

From the air, satellite photos show soybean cultivation as a juggernaut advancing inexorably across the savannas into increasingly dense tropical forest. However, for many a "smaller" farmer within the juggernaut, some of whose holdings number hundreds of hectares, the fear of being smothered and cast aside is never far from mind. His very social standing as a "producer" celebrated within the community may well be his downfall because producers cannot set the conditions for their own production.

Conclusion

Soybeans, cattle, and cotton for sale around the world have replaced millions of hectares of savanna vegetation in Brazil's hinterlands. The savannas have been utterly and relentlessly transformed and the new patterns of production, ecology, and settlement have laid a template for future development. Transfixed by the bottom line in its current account, the Brazilian federal government seems largely oblivious to the social and ecological consequences that will, in turn, condition possible future development. Despite President Lula's one-time lip service to the slogan "another world is possible," Brazil's current government has failed to realize how the system of production and ecology implanted today undercuts any shift toward greater equality of land distribution, more democratic local institutions, and more diversified use of rural areas to attend to multiple uses of the local population, including better nutrition and the development of various forms of employment.

Today, the explosive growth of soybean cultivation on the frontier rests on a "technological package" of chemicals, mechanized agriculture, accounting procedures, massive inequality of land holdings, and an oligopoly of large grain and oilseed traders. The intensification of their interdependence is an important part of the dynamic of regional trends. The current structure of exchange operates as a goad to expansion precisely because farming is so volatile. Farmers face a rising treadmill of investment and production costs necessary to achieve continually higher levels of productivity. Expansion of cultivated areas, even beyond legal limits, comprises a hedge against lower profit margins, and it is also one of the few ways that on-farm profits can be reinvested. Alternative farming practices or industries are not allowed to compete with the tyranny of industrial soybeans and cotton. Farmers attempt to protect themselves against fluctuating prices and currencies by drawing local merchants into using soybean currency. To maintain an export orientation, regional power brokers must solidify a coherent structure of production that brooks no alternatives and yet remains viable ecologically. They must navigate between the Scylla of economic marginalization and the Charybdis of ecological breakdown. The accumulation of profits by large agribusiness commodity traders and chemical and seed purveyors rests on the current spur to expansion based on farmers' constraint of choice. The existing structure of exchange channels choices via the inertia of the debt not yet paid, the crop not yet harvested, and the growing need for new inputs just to break even. Maintenance of the coherence of the structure of production devoted to soybeans hinges on the ability of the government and exporters to shape farmers' behavior. Not many farmers are involved, but it is the size of properties rather than the number of farmers that ultimately counts. Brazil's agricultural miracle rests on a handful of large farmers. The math is inexorable: in Sorriso five hundred or so farmers churn out 2 percent of Brazil's soybean production, and although average farm sizes are smaller in southern states, there are millions of poor rural folk who are either forced from the countryside or languish with little hope. Even those farmers able to play the game are under the gun, for the community holds no place for a failed farmer, and the hometown heroes must continue to indebt themselves to pump out soybeans destined for overseas, or lose what community standing they currently enjoy.

Note

Thanks to Antônio João Castrillon, Loise Nunes Velasco, George Kamides, João dal Poz, José dos Reis, Ana Tibaldi Reis, Odila Bortoncello, Renaldo Loffi, José Augusto Ascoli, and GERA (Grupo de Estudos e Pesquisas do Pantanal, Amazônia e Cerrado) of the Federal University of Mato Grosso for making fieldwork in Sorriso possible. Thanks also to Donald Sawyer for helpful comments during fieldwork as well as to the ever insightful Marcio Silva.

References

Aguiar, R. C. 1986. *Abrindo o pacote tecnológico: Estado e pesquisa agropecuária no Brasil.* São Paulo: Polis.

Anonymous 2006. BB oficializa regras para renegociação das dívidas rurais nesta 3a feira. www.sindruralsorriso.com.br/index/noticia.php?codigo=4972 (accessed February 14, 2006).

Bartlett, P. 1987. Industrial agriculture in evolutionary perspective. *Cultural Anthropology* 2 (1): 137–154.

Benson, T. 2005. A harvest at peril. *New York Times*, January 6, 2005.

Biel, R. 2000. *The new imperialism: Crisis and contradiction in north/south relations.* London: Zed.

Brown, L. R. 2005. *Outgrowing the earth: The food security challenge in an age of falling water tables and rising temperatures.* New York: Norton.

Chew, S. C. 2001. *World ecological degradation: Accumulation, urbanization, and deforestation 3000 B.C.–A.D. 2000.* Walnut Creek, Calif.: AltaMira.

Colitt, R. 2005. Golden days are over on Brazil's soyabean frontier. *Financial Times*, February 10, 2005.

Cunha, A. S. 1994. *Uma avaliação da sustentabilidade da agricultura nos cerrados.* Estudos de Política Agrícola 11. Brasília: Instituto de Pesquisa Econômica Aplica (IPAEA).

Dias, E. A., and O. Bortoncello. 2003. *Resgate histórico do município de Sorriso, portal da agricultura no cerrado Mato-Grossense.* Self-published by authors. Cuiába, MT, Brazil.

Economist, The. 1999. Brazil: Growth in prairies. April 10 (U.S. edition).

EMPAER. 2004. *Evolução da área cultivada no município de Sorriso-MT/1976–2004.* Sorriso, MT, Brazil: Empresa Mato-Grossense de Pesquisa, Assistência e Extensão Rural. Mimeo, 3 pages.

Fearnside, P. M. 2000. Soybean cultivation as a threat to the environment in Brazil. *Environmental Conservation* 7:23–38.

Fundação Cargill. 1982. A soja no Brasil central. 2nd revised and expanded edition. [Privately printed, no place of publication indicated, consulted in the stacks of the main library of University of Brasilia, Brazil.]

Hornborg, A. 2001. *The power of the machine: Global inequalities of economy, technology, and environment*. Walnut Creek, Calif.: AltaMira.

Maia, M., and P. de Oliveira. 2006. *Balança commercial encerra 2005 com resultados históricos*. Ministry of Development, Industry and Foreign Trade. www .desenvolvimento.gov.br/sitio/ascom/noticias/noticia.php?cd_noticia=6828 (accessed January 10, 2006).

Minosso, P. 2004. ACIS elege empresário, e agricultor do ano. *Correio Mato-Grossense*, July 16, 2004.

Moore, J. W. 2003. The modern world-system as environmental history? Ecology and the rise of capitalism. *Theory and Society* 32:307–377.

Richetti, A., L. A. Staut, and S. A. Gomez. 2005. Estimativa do custo de produção de soja. Safra 2005/06 Mato Grosso do Sul e Mato Grosso. Comunicado Técnico 108, September 2005. Dourados, MS, Brazil: EMBRAPA.

Salgado, E. 2004. A civilização do Campo. *Veja* 39 (September 29): 88–96.

Schnepf, R. D., E. Dohlman, and C. Bolling. 2001. Agriculture in Brazil and Argentina: Development and prospects for major field crops. Agriculture and Trade Report WRS013. Washington, D.C.: United States Department of Agriculture, Economic Research Service.

Sousa, I. S. F. de, and L. Busch. 1998. Networks and agricultural development: The case of soybean production and consumption in Brazil. *Rural Sociology* 63 (3): 349–371.

South American Business Information. 2003 (February 20). Monsanto dedicates genetics improvement station at Sorriso.

Últimas notícias: Frete para escoar a soja de Mato Grosso tem forte alta. Sunday, 29 January 2006. opennews.plugar.com.br/cgi-bin/plugarautoriza/plugarautoriza .exe?codigo= 20060129133001870&edt=eb-rural (accessed January 28, 2006).

USDA. 2004. Soybean expansion expected to continue in 2004/2005. United States Department of Agriculture. Foreign Agricultural Service, Production Estimate and Crop Assessment Division. www.fas.usda.gov/pecad2/highlights/ 2004/08/Brazil_soy_files (accessed August 16, 2004).

Veiga Filho, L. 2001. Produtor troca milho pela soja em Goiás. *Gazeta Mercantil*. August 17, 2001, p. 3.

Warnken, P. F. 1999. *The development and growth of the soybean industry in Brazil*. Ames: Iowa State University Press.

Wolf, E. 1990. Facing power: Old insights, new questions. *American Anthropologist* 92:586–596.

Scale and Dependency in World-Systems: Local Societies in Convergent Evolution

19

JOSEPH A. TAINTER

F EW MATTERS SEEM MORE urgent today than sustainability and re-siliency in social and biophysical systems. One factor in addressing these issues is the change in scale that occurs when local people become embedded in larger systems at the national and international levels. Today we call this process "globalization," but that term merely denotes the most recent phase of the world-system development of the past five centuries. World-system development and globalization have social and environmental repercussions that may last centuries. They produce consequences so far dispersed that the connection of cause and effect may be difficult to perceive.

There is a disjuncture in world-systems between the flow of materials and the flow of information. While a periphery incorporated into a larger economy will experience a change in the scale of its economic and political relations, the information pool remains substantially local. This disjuncture of scale undermines the sustainability of local populations. Not only do such people lose autonomy, they may not know that they have done so. As local autonomy disappears, dependency and environmental deterioration follow.

The consequences of this disjuncture became apparent when I read Sander van der Leeuw's (1998; van der Leeuw et al. 2000) and Sarah Green's (Green et al. 1998) descriptions of historical changes in Epirus in the northwest of Greece. In both structure and process, and even in several details, they could have been describing changes with which I was familiar in my home state of New Mexico (Tainter 1999). How could such distant places have experienced changes so similar that their descriptions are almost interchangeable? The answer lies in the disjuncture in scaling of economic, political, and informational relations in world-systems. This disjuncture has implications for how the relationship between global and local processes may be addressed in the future.

Studies in Transformation and Dependency

Epirus

Epirus is one of the most remote parts of Europe (map 19.1). Epirote villages were formerly isolated and closed, most corporate activities were consensual, and knowledge was homogeneous. There were few social, economic, or technical differences among people. As one informant described communities, "Everyone knows everything about everybody else" (Green 1995:271). Relations between villages, and between clusters of villages, were based on proximity, kinship, intermarriage, participation in festivals, and trade (Green

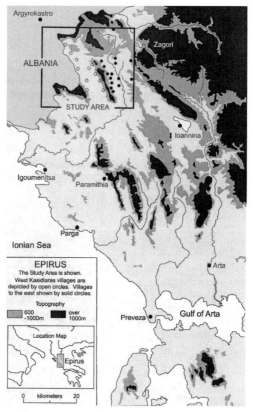

Map 19.1.   Epirus, northwest Greece (after Green 1995:176)

1995:309). The system of land use had long been in operation. People knew the area intimately, and their subsistence practices were suitable to the environment and apparently sustainable (van der Leeuw 1998:57; van der Leeuw et al. 2000:375).

The introduction of roads after World War II initiated many changes (van der Leeuw 1998:57–58; van der Leeuw et al. 2000:375–376). The information pool began to differentiate. Villages acquired headmen, who now served as intermediaries with the outside world. Wage-earning brought social and economic differentiation. Cash became increasingly important, and people were stimulated to acquire material goods. There were now conflicts between personal and social interests. No longer did everyone know everything about everybody else.

In the aftermath of the civil war of 1946–1949, upland cereal cultivation was abandoned. Most vineyards were also abandoned, while those remaining succumbed to blight. When local gardens were abandoned, the fields were turned to pasture, and animal husbandry became dominant (Green 1997b:38; Green et al. 1999:134). Workers emigrated from the region during the 1960s, moving to industrial locations. From the late 1960s through the late 1970s many projects were implemented to develop Epirus. These included drainage, land redistribution to facilitate mechanized farming, electricity, paved roads, and irrigation (Green et al. 1999:30).

Greece became a full member of the European Union (EU) in 1981, and thereafter the European Union's Common Agricultural Policy affected the region. Development and improvement programs aimed at economically depressed regions brought some people to the plains, while the mountains and other marginal areas continued to lose population. Today most people live in towns or villages in the agricultural plains, or along major roads (Green 1997b:36–39; Green et al. 1998:341–343; Green et al. 1999:30, 50–53).

The transhumant pastoralist economy had maintained mountain vegetation as a combination of woodlands and open meadows. Use of wood for fuel and building, continual cropping by herbivores, and intentional burning kept trees from invading areas dominated by grass. With the decline in pastoralism and prohibition of burning (see below), the mountain vegetation changed rapidly. Many areas have become overgrown with a scrub vegetation consisting of oak, bramble, and small trees. The locations of small hill fields are becoming harder to discern. Areas once used for firewood are beginning to recover. In former pastures there has been rapid growth of dense, woody vegetation. The higher elevations are, as a result, now largely closed off to herbivores. Epirotes consider this a degradation of their landscape

(Green et al. 1999:59; van der Leeuw 1998:57–58; van der Leeuw et al. 2000:375–376).

Today, many young Epirotes emigrate to urban areas for work. Villages and towns in mountainous regions now have small, aging populations. The older people live substantially on government pensions (Green et al. 1999:30, 37). Still, these villages are considered home to the dispersed population. Many who work elsewhere maintain a house in such villages, to which they go during festivals and holidays, or for retirement. Some of these returnees cultivate vegetable gardens, using the land in a manner that Green characterizes as "suburban" (Green et al. 1999:60).

Greece's economic status made it a candidate for EU development projects. One EU program concerns the preservation and development of "marginal" areas (Green 1997b:104). The EU approach has been to "focus on protecting, conserving or preserving what was increasingly seen as a 'natural wilderness' containing 'traditional' village settlements" (Green et al. 1999:49). The European Union has sought to develop the cultural heritage of the more remote, mountainous areas by emphasizing ecotourism, attracting visitors to an area of "unspoiled" natural beauty.

The EU program influenced the Greek national administration. There is now greater concern to protect the environments of remote areas. Several national parks have been established in northern Greece, including one in the Zagori region of Epirus. Villages within the park have been affected by new regulations. One can no longer graze animals within the national park, nor can one dig, drill, or build outside village limits. There are further bans on camping or lighting fires within the forests, on swimming in the rivers, and on clearing areas for cultivation. Houses must be built of "traditional" materials, which are no longer freely available. Those who can afford to build in such materials are former residents who return seasonally to the villages with savings from urban employment (Green et al. 1998:353, 1999:111, 124).

These new restrictions generate predictable land-use conflicts between local people and the administrators who implement national policies. Individuals and groups who apply for grants for ecotourism exacerbate these disputes, particularly because of current restrictions on using what were previously common grazing or forest lands, and restrictions on building and other activities. EU development projects have become enmeshed in village factionalism, with some residents favoring conservation and others preferring the development of better facilities and services for residents (Green et al. 1999:49, 60).

Older Epirotes were unaware that the area possessed natural beauty until told by outsiders that it does. They also did not see the landscape as an external, objective entity, but as the place in which they live, and of which they are a part. Now Epirus is being dialectically construed as the converse of the urban environment. New concepts are being imposed on Epirus by those whose experiences can be represented as urban and modern, and thus authoritative. The EU development projects aim to maintain a place such as Epirus in a timeless state. The environment is to have its architecture and cultural practices frozen in an "original" traditional form, while the landscape is to be kept, or even made, "natural" by removing the same people and their traditional activities (Green 1997b:62). The people and the landscape are marketed to those who travel to experience "authentic," indigenous places.

The European Union naturally requires that its projects be efficient and cost-effective, and achieve the intended results. Yet on the local level, EU projects are not about heritage tourism or protecting the environment. Epirotes may know from the outset that a project will fail in its EU objectives, or even be a farce. Projects typically go over budget. A successful project from the Epirote perspective is one that involves many people who benefit economically. Embedding projects in social and economic relations always appears to a bureaucracy such as Brussels as corruption (Green 1997b:81–82, 89–90).

Headmen intermediate between Epirus and the European Union, and are sometimes considered to have suspicious motives. Appointments of personnel bring conflict between "progressive" and "conservative" factions. In the urban conception, culture happens in villages and during festivals, while nature is the wilderness outside villages. To the local opponents of EU projects, the "wilderness" that is to be preserved is seen as grazing lands, sources of wood, and fields, even if disused and overgrown. The removal of human activity from the landscape, in turn, diminishes cultural heritage (Green 1997b:83–84, 91–92; Green et al. 1999:104). Urbanized former Epirotes now consciously express an Epirote identity, but it is an identity that arises from the influence of larger economic and political spheres.

As local self-sufficiency declined, the region has become dependent on the commercial economy and the government. Becoming embedded in larger systems has meant a transformation from autonomy and self-sufficiency to dependency and environmental deterioration.

New Mexico

Sixteenth-century Spanish explorers of New Mexico found Indians living in settled villages. These were soon joined by Hispano farmers. The last to arrive is the group known locally as Anglo-Americans. This discussion emphasizes the Hispanic settlers of New Mexico, and the consequences of their absorption into the United States.

New Mexico is an arid land of great diversity. It is characterized by high mountains, narrow river valleys, plateaus, and deserts. Precipitation is variable and unreliable. The growing season is short, and also highly variable. Colonial New Mexico was one of the most distant outposts of the Spanish empire. Supplies came by wagon train, but metal was so scarce that plows were tipped in wood. Archaeological sites show that some colonists experimented in making stone tools, at which they were not adept (Chapman et al. 1977). Houses contained no furniture except that produced locally. Books and schooling were rare. There was little money and few firearms. Priests were in short supply, and visitors commented adversely on the way that ceremonies were performed. As early as 1776, a visiting priest found the language full of archaisms and hard to understand (deBuys 1985:122). During the period of Mexican independence, from 1821 to 1846, New Mexico was referred to as Mexico's Siberia (deBuys 1985:306).

The economic basis of colonial New Mexico was provided by a system of granting lands to both Pueblos and Hispanos (map 19.2). Within these grants, individual households and fields were privately owned. If the grant contained a suitable river valley, each settler would have a strip of land extending linearly from the river to the *acequia madre*, which would be located at the juncture between the bottomland and the adjoining hills. These lands were divided among a farmer's sons, so that in time Hispano fields became renowned for their narrowness (map 19.3). Beyond the cultivated lands lay the *ejido*, or commons, used for grazing or timber cutting. Depending on terrain, there might be high mountains beyond the common lands, which would be used as needed. Grant boundaries were often vague, but before the American period this was rarely a problem.

Two institutions united rural New Mexico: the church and the irrigation system. Since colonial New Mexico lacked governing institutions at the local level, ditch associations are still often the only local government. Villages were organized by kinship and cultural uniformity. Many villages are isolated, gaining paved ingress only in the 1960s, and telephones and television in the 1970s. The main mode of communication was, and is, face-to-face contact through visits. Everyone in a community had personal knowledge of everybody else (Harper, Cordova, and Oberg 1943; Horvath 1979; Kutsche and Van Ness 1981; Rivera 1998).

With independence, Mexico opened its borders, and American traders descended on Santa Fe. They brought manufactured goods, the availability

of which soon began to transform New Mexico. To obtain such goods took
surplus production and cash. American traders brought knowledge of the
area back to the United States. When war broke out in 1846 between the
United States and Mexico, New Mexico quickly became part of the United
States.

Hispanic villages' isolation and poverty shielded them initially from the
full force of the American economy. Without village schools, English pen-
etrated the countryside slowly. Hispanic lands, however, were vulnerable.
Land grants had to be confirmed in American courts, which could only
be accessed through expensive lawyers. At first villagers were unaware that
their lands might be in jeopardy. Soon lands started to be lost for failure to
pay taxes that the villagers did not know they owed. Sometimes Hispanos

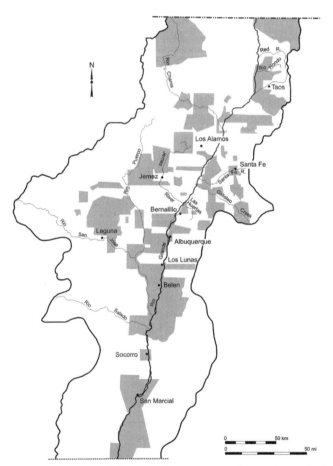

Map 19.2.   Land grants of the middle and northern Rio Grande basin (after Scurlock 1998:111)

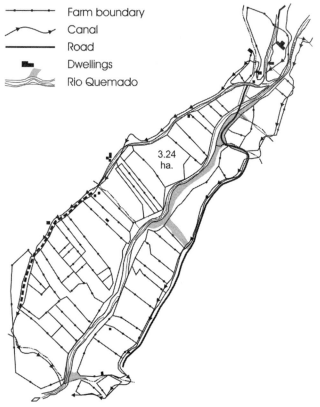

Map 19.3.   Farmlands near Cordova, New Mexico, in 1943 (after Harper, Cordova, and Oberg 1943:71)

continued to occupy these places, unaware that they had lost ownership years before. Lawyers who were retained to establish the claim to a grant could only be paid with part of the same land. Lands beyond the grants that had been available for anyone's use became public domain, and subject to claim by anyone who would settle and farm them (deBuys 1985:121, 177; Rothman 1989:197–198).

As the land base shrank, Hispanos lost the ability to produce sufficient food. They were pushed off large tracts of pasture. Each year pushed the villagers toward dependency on markets for much of their food and other necessities. Cash-crop farming increased. Men left villages for work on the railroads or in Colorado mines. Many became dependent on contractual sheep-raising (Harper, Cordova, and Oberg 1943:78–79; deBuys 1985:209; Rothman 1989:201, 205).

A timber industry soon grew up, cutting either the upland forests that were now in the public domain, or former *ejido* lands. Loggers cut the timber from thousands of hectares, with no thought for regeneration. The largest timber-cutting operation in the southern Sangre de Cristo Mountains exemplified how quickly New Mexico had become integrated into the world economy. It was undertaken in response to the building of the Panama Canal, which began operating in 1914. Shipping through the canal promised to undercut the freight rates charged by the railroad. The railroad tried to remain competitive by laying a second set of tracks. At least 16 million railroad ties were needed, and the operations to produce them logged every suitable stick up to the tree line (deBuys 1985:226–229; Rothman 1989).

Anglo-Americans saw vast grasslands in New Mexico, and did not understand how fragile they were. The ranges were soon overstocked, and when drought came in the late nineteenth century, erosion started that still continues. The alienation of Hispanic lands and the commercial exploitation of this fragile area caused extensive degradation. The Rio Puerco Valley, once known as the breadbasket of New Mexico, had to be largely abandoned when the Rio Puerco itself became deeply entrenched, making irrigation impossible and drying the soil. As vegetation was stripped from soil surfaces, drainages across the Southwest eroded and became entrenched. Topsoil was washed away, and grasses could not grow as quickly as they were grazed. The trees remaining in logged forests produced thousands of seedlings per hectare. As the Forest Service tried to prevent wildfires, these seedlings grew into overly dense secondary forests that lack grass understory and are vulnerable to catastrophic fires. The inability of grasslands to reproduce and the elimination of fire from ecosystems meant that woodlands extended downward in elevation, into what had once been grasslands (deBuys 1985:217–226, 231; Rothman 1989).

The Hispanic and Indian cultures, and the natural beauty of the area, attracted artists and intellectuals. In small, communal villages they believed that they would find the antidote to urban life. The artists and intellectuals understood that Hispanic village culture could not be preserved without an economic basis. By 1930 the average Hispanic farm had but 2.4 hectares under cultivation (map 19.3). The harvest was usually committed to the village store. Few families could subsist or pay taxes without wage labor. The solution was that Hispanos would become artisans and craftsmen. They would produce "traditional" arts and crafts for a burgeoning tourist market. An idealized version of traditional architecture became the norm in Santa Fe and elsewhere. "Traditional" festivals were created for Santa Fe and Taos.

By the mid 1930s, 60 to 70 percent of northern New Mexicans survived on government relief. Within a generation, people had gone from self-sufficiency to dependency. In the Great Depression, only federal programs prevented widespread starvation. The New Deal envisioned returning large sections of the grants to their original owners, and restoring the fertility of eroded lands. Some lands were restored, but farms were so small that it was impossible for a farmer to feed the family and have some to sell. Too little was done to increase the land base, improve irrigation systems, or record titles to ditch systems. World War II ended these efforts (deBuys 1985:210; Forrest 1989:11, 12, 33, 51, 54, 63–180; Rodriguez 1987:346).

Today many Hispanos either depend on government subsidies, commute to jobs in cities, or have emigrated. They may return to the village for weekends and holidays (Kutsche and Van Ness 1981:33). For those who remain in the villages, or maintain close ties to them, there is perpetual struggle. Many keep small cattle herds, which must have a permit to graze on the Forest Service land that Hispanos still consider theirs (deBuys 1985; Raish 2000). The Forest Service regulates access to all resources on its lands, including the timbers needed for traditional construction. The natural beauty and cultural heritage are marketed by urban residents to other urban residents. The region continues to receive funds for development, but projects become part of kin relations and local politics. Contracts are frequently given to relatives, leading to charges of corruption.

There is conflict with a new adversary, environmentalists. This conflict concerns the environmentalist value of using forested lands little or not at all, and the Hispanic tradition of using forest resources as necessary. Environmental interest groups know how to impede agencies such as the Forest Service. The villagers, who still depend on the forests for such vital needs as winter firewood, are reduced to asserting heritage, identity, and traditional rights (Raish 2000).

Summary

Epirus and New Mexico show convergent histories (table 19.1). Formidable terrain and economic marginality kept villages isolated, closed, autonomous, and self-sufficient. The pool of information was homogeneous and, within a village, everyone knew everything about everybody else. Subsistence practices suited local conditions and appear to have been sustainable over the long run. Environments were maintained to support the subsistence system.

New Mexico's isolation ended with the start of American commercial penetration in the mid-nineteenth century, and that of Epirus with the end

Table 19.1.   Aspects of convergent evolution in Epirus and New Mexico

1. Remote areas incorporated into world economy.
2. Villages differentiate socially, economically, and in information pool.
3. Emigration for work.
4. Progressive and conservative factions develop.
5. Traditional subsistence practices decline.
6. Environment loses capacity to support traditional economy due to decline in human maintenance.
7. People depend on government subsidies.
8. Traditional culture becomes difficult to sustain.
9. Upland forests controlled by national governments.
10. Traditional resource use limited or proscribed.
11. Young adults return to villages for holidays.
12. External organizations promote preservation of landscapes and cultural practices.
13. Culture divorced from land use and fossilized as crafts and performances.
14. Natural beauty and cultural heritage marketed by urban residents to other urban residents.
15. Landscapes managed to match urban conception of nature.
16. Development projects socially embedded.
17. Increasing expression of ethnic identity.

of Turkish rule and the building of roads in the twentieth century. In both areas, the influx of manufactured goods caused self-sufficiency to decline, and cash became important.

Life within villages began to differentiate. Men emigrated to find work. People acquired new information about the larger world, and about opportunities and ways of doing things. It was no longer possible to know everything about everybody else. Communities bifurcated into "progressive" and "conservative" factions. Personal and group interests increasingly diverged.

As traditional subsistence practices declined, the biophysical environment lost the capacity to support such practices. Fire stopped being used to control vegetation. In Epirus, grazing was no longer employed to keep pastures free of competing vegetation. In New Mexico, commercial grazing reduced grasses to such a degree that woodlands encroached on former grasslands. In both places there has been an overgrowth of woody plants, and increased erosion.

Many people in both areas survive on government subsidies. Traditional cultural practices have become difficult to maintain in the face of "modernity" and without an adequate economic base. Upland forests are controlled by national governments. There is frequent conflict between villagers and land managers. Traditional resources are now either regulated or proscribed. Traditional architecture is either encouraged or mandated, yet there is no longer free access to the raw materials that it requires and many people cannot afford to buy such materials. In both regions, émigrés return for holidays and other special occasions, and use ancestral villages in a manner that can be labeled "suburban."

Outsiders have become concerned to preserve both the natural beauty and cultural traditions of both regions. Organizations external to the villages now promote projects to integrate economic development with preservation. Typically this means tourism. The natural beauty and cultural heritage of both areas are now marketed by urban residents to other urban residents. The landscapes are to be preserved to match an urban conception of nature. Cultural heritage is preserved and commodified, rather than lived. Divorced from its connection to land use, heritage is to be expressed as craft products and performances. Development projects become socially embedded in each region, which outsiders consider corruption. Both regions are developing explicit manifestations of ethnic identity that mobilize people even as they reinforce stereotypes.

Convergent Evolution: Causes and Consequences

Epirus and New Mexico are separated by history, geography, and tradition. Each was uniquely remote. Yet they display congruence in structure and process, in form and substance, and even in such minute details as the encroachment of woodlands on grasslands and the relationship of traditional architecture to national land management policies.

The parallel transformations in Epirus and New Mexico arose from these regions, becoming enmeshed in commercial systems, and controlled by national governments that are themselves embedded within larger systems. For places like Epirus and New Mexico, the scale of their economic and political contexts has grown from the locality to the national government, and to the international community. The scale of information has not kept pace with these developments. In this regard, Epirotes and New Mexicans are like people everywhere. Their scale of information is local. The information that matters is that which pertains to local affairs: kin, community, politics, economy, infrastructure, government services, weather, sports, and the like.

In this age of globalization, the inclination to value local information conflicts with the scale of events and processes that affect localities. There is, for example, much concern in New Mexico about water. All sources of water are fully allocated, and New Mexico is obliged to deliver to the adjacent state of Texas much of what flows through the Rio Grande and the Pecos River. In 1998 I was invited to address a conference on the future of the Rio Grande Basin. I challenged the audience to consider the basin's future in the context of the distant, unseen factors that affect it (Tainter 1999). What, for example, was the connection between irrigation agriculture in the basin and the East Asian economic crisis that was then underway? The connection is through Intel Corporation's chip manufacturing plant near Albuquerque, which uses great quantities of water. The New Mexico state engineer has required Intel to buy and retire water rights in the basin to offset the amount of water that it uses in manufacturing. Since urban areas need water, this means retiring farmland. To the extent that the East Asian economic crisis might cause Intel to reduce its output of chips, and thus to use less water, it could be possible to perpetuate irrigation agriculture longer, as well as the cultural traditions that are linked to it. Today, in updating this analysis, we would wish to explore the connections among irrigation agriculture, Intel's manufacturing output, and the threat of a pandemic caused by the H5N1 ("bird flu") virus. The lesson is that unless Epirotes, New Mexicans, and other local people become knowledgeable about the full range of factors that affect them, they will continue to be vulnerable to distant processes, and to those who profit from their ignorance.

Addressing the Disjuncture in Scale

A common exhortation of the environmental movement is to think globally but act locally. The problem we encounter is that most people do not think globally. In our history as a species there has never been selective pressure to do so, while there has been relentless pressure to think locally of kin and community. Globalization requires that the scale at which people customarily think must expand. The obvious question is: How do we change a behavior pattern that is so ingrained, and that until now has ensured group survival?

One approach to resolving this impasse would be for world-system theory, either alone or in conjunction with other fields of research, to develop a body of knowledge of such fundamental importance that it would be incorporated into educational curricula alongside other mainstream social sciences. The purpose would be to teach children, starting at a young age and continuing through all levels of education, to think about systems and interconnections at all scales. It would be an attempt to make thinking about the connection of the global to the local so ingrained that, within a generation or two, it becomes normal and unremarkable. People would be trained to consider global processes that affect local viability, whether a new virus, the economy of far-off lands, or distant political upheavals. Students would be taught to think at all scales, to be curious about things that are distant in space and time, and to sense connections that are not obvious. Being taught such thinking early and continuously would, one hopes, produce generations of adults who think more broadly, and more systemically, than those of today. As the populace comes to think in this manner, politicians, business leaders, and managers would learn, and be expected, to do so as well. Journalists, sensing new needs and opportunities, would explore the connections I have discussed.

How would world-system theory (or any other area of social science) comport itself to achieve this goal? I suggest three areas of action.

First, students forced to learn history or geography typically complain that these fields are not pertinent to their lives. To overcome this, world-system theory must demonstrate its relevance to local problems of well-being. Examples of the effects of global processes on local communities, such as those presented here, would be sought and presented. There are many to be found (e.g. Murphy and Steward 1956).

Second, world-system theory would resist the temptation to criticize global political and economic arrangements. It would present itself as the value-neutral science of scale and interconnection in world affairs. World-system theory might become part of hierarchy theory (e.g. Allen and Starr 1982; Ahl and Allen 1996), the field that explicitly addresses scale, interconnection, and context. World-system theory would truly become a theory of world-systems in the broadest sense.

Third, following the development of case studies showing the value of understanding the connection of global to local processes, textbooks and other curriculum materials would need to be developed for all educational levels.

This proposal is, of course, not a panacea. Not all people would be inclined to pursue global analysis, although it is still worthwhile that they be familiar with it. Among those who are so inclined, the understandings they develop will often not be accurate. Yet all that would be required is for enough people to implement their training in global thinking to lead the rest. Intermediaries would emerge who would facilitate the transmission of global information to local communities. Books, magazines, and television broadcasts, showing the connection between global and local, would expand in response to an increased market. As journalists seek information for their stories, positive feedback would reinforce the expanded scale of thinking.

Conclusion

World-systems create a disjuncture in scaling between the flow of materials and the flow of information. Peripheries incorporated into a world-system typically maintain a local scale of information, even as the factors that affect them expand to the national and international arenas. Local communities forfeit autonomy as they lose comprehension of events and processes that affect them. As illustrated in the cases of Epirus and New Mexico, quite different places may be drawn down convergent trajectories in which they lose control of their affairs.

In the age of globalization, this disjuncture in scaling must be remedied. Globalization requires that people become cognizant of the factors that affect them at all scales, from local to international. While this cannot be accomplished easily or immediately, it could perhaps be accomplished in a generation or two through systems of public education. World-system theory, and other fields of social research, could facilitate this revolution by offering a compelling body of cases and theory showing the fundamental connection of local to global processes.

This proposal is utopian and perhaps unrealistic. Yet today's globalization demands that we attempt something like it. The only certainty is that failing to try such a course will condemn many places to follow Epirus and New Mexico down a bewildering slide into poverty, dependency, and environmental deterioration.

Notes

1. I am pleased to thank Sander van der Leeuw and Carol Raish for providing reference materials and reviewing drafts on, respectively, Epirus and New Mexico. I am grateful also to Bonnie Bagley for her comments on an early draft, and Joyce Van De Water for preparing maps 19.1 through 19.3.

References

Ahl, V., and T. F. H. Allen. 1996. *Hierarchy theory: A vision, vocabulary, and epistemology.* New York: Columbia University Press.

Allen, T. F. H., and T. B. Starr. 1982. *Hierarchy: Perspectives for ecological complexity.* Chicago: University of Chicago Press.

Chapman, R. C., J. V. Biella, J. A. Schutt, J. G. Enloe, P. J. Marchiando, A. H. Warren, and J. R. Stein. 1977. Description of twenty-seven sites in the permanent pool of Cochiti Reservoir. In *Archeological investigations in Cochiti Reservoir, New Mexico*, vol. 2, *Excavation and analysis 1975 season*, ed. R. C. Chapman and J. V. Biella, with S. D. Bussey, 119–359. Albuquerque: Office of Contract Archeology, Department of Anthropology, University of New Mexico.

DeBuys, W. 1985. *Enchantment and exploitation: The life and hard times of a New Mexico mountain range.* Albuquerque: University of New Mexico Press.

Forrest, S. 1989. *The preservation of the village: New Mexico's Hispanics and the new deal.* Albuquerque: University of New Mexico Press.

Green, S. 1995. Contemporary change in use and perception of the landscape in Epirus: An ethnographic study. In *Understanding the natural and anthropogenic causes of soil degradation and desertification in the Mediterranean basin*, vol. 1, *Land degradation in Epirus*, ed. S. E. van der Leeuw. Brussels: Draft Report to Directorate General XII of the European Commission.

———. 1997a. Pogoni, Epirus (Greece). In *Environmental perception and policy making: Cultural and natural heritage and the preservation of degradation-sensitive environments in southern Europe*, vol. 1, *Perception, policy, and unforeseen consequences: An interdisciplinary synthesis*, ed. N. Winder and S. E. van der Leeuw, 45–64. Brussels: Draft Report to Directorate General XII of the European Commission.

———. 1997b. *Environmental perception and policy making: Cultural and natural heritage and the preservation of degradation-sensitive environments in southern Europe*, vol. 3, *Notes on the making and nature of margins in Epirus*, ed. N. Winder and S. E. van der Leeuw. Brussels: Draft Report to Directorate General XII of the European Commission.

Green, S. F., G. P. C. King, V. Nitsiakos, and S. E. van der Leeuw. 1998. Landscape perception in Epirus in the late twentieth century. In *The Archaeomedes project: Understanding the natural and anthropogenic causes of land degradation and desertification in the Mediterranean basin*, ed. S. E. van der Leeuw, 329–359. Luxembourg: Office for Official Publications of the European Communities.

Green, S. F., S. Servain-Courant, V. Papapetrou, V. Nitsiakos, and G. P. C. King. 1999. *Policy-relevant models of the natural and anthropogenic dynamics of degradation and desertification and their spatio-temporal manifestations*, vol. 2, *Negotiating perceptions of fragile environments in Epirus, northwestern Greece*. Brussels: Draft final report of the Archaeomedes II Research Project, submitted to Directorate General XII of the European Commission.

Harper, A. G., A. R. Cordova, and K. Oberg. 1943. *Man and resources in the middle Rio Grande valley*. Albuquerque: University of New Mexico Press.

Horvath, S. M., Jr. 1979. *The social and political organization of the Genízaros of Plaza de Nuestra Señora de los Delores de Belén, New Mexico, 1740–1812*. PhD diss., Department of Anthropology, Brown University.

Kutsche, P., and J. R. Van Ness. 1981. *Cañones: Values, crisis, and survival in a northern New Mexican village*. Salem, Wis.: Sheffield.

Murphy, R. F., and J. H. Steward. 1956. Tappers and trappers: Parallel process in acculturation. *Economic Development and Cultural Change* 4:335–355.

Raish, C. 2000. Environmentalism, the forest service, and the Hispano communities of northern New Mexico. *Society and Natural Resources* 13:489–508.

Rivera, J. A. 1998. *Acequia culture: Water, land, and community in the southwest*. Albuquerque: University of New Mexico Press.

Rodriguez, S. 1987. Land, water, and ethnic identity in Taos. In *Land, water, and culture: New perspectives on Hispanic land grants*, ed. C. L. Biggs and J. R. Van Ness, 313–403. Albuquerque: University of New Mexico Press.

Rothman, H. 1989. Cultural and environmental change on the Pajarito Plateau. *New Mexico Historical Review* 64:185–211.

Scurlock, D. 1998. From the rio to the sierra: An environmental history of the middle Rio Grande Basin. Rocky Mountain Research Station General Technical Report, *RMRS-GTR-5*. Fort Collins, Colo.: U.S. Department of Agriculture, Forest Service.

Tainter, J. A. 1999. Rio Grande Basin and the modern world: Understanding scale and context. In *Rio Grande ecosystems: Linking land, water, and people*, comp. D. M. Finch, J. C. Whitney, J. F. Kelly, and S. R. Loftin, 7–11. Rocky Mountain Research Station Proceedings, *RMRS-P-7*. Fort Collins, Colo.: U. S. Department of Agriculture, Forest Service.

Van der Leeuw, S. E. 1998. Main building blocks of our approach. In *The Archaeomedes project: Understanding the natural and anthropogenic causes of land degradation and desertification in the Mediterranean basin*, ed. S. E. van der Leeuw, 43–112. Luxembourg: Office for Official Publications of the European Communities.

Van der Leeuw, S. E., and the Archaeomedes Research Team. 2000. Land degradation as a socio-natural process. In *The way the wind blows: Climate, history, and human action*, ed. R. J. McIntosh, J. A. Tainter, and S. K. McIntosh, 357–383. New York: Columbia University Press.

The Ecology and the Economy: What Is Rational?

20

IMMANUEL WALLERSTEIN

RATIONALITY IS, MORE THAN we admit, in the eye of the beholder. It has something to do with the optimal means to achieve a goal, any goal, what Weber called "formal rationality." And it has something to do with the relative wisdom of the goal that is given priority, what Weber called "substantive rationality" (*Rationalität materiell*). I think it would be useful to approach the issue in terms of what I see as the three mental operations in which scholars/scientists necessarily engage when dealing with any topic. There is the intellectual task of attempting to discern what the phenomenon is, what were its origins, what are its links with other phenomena, what has been its trajectory, and what we may anticipate its future trajectory to be. In the modern world, this intellectual task has been the domain in which scholars/scientists are considered to be the specialists. It is they who regularly study the phenomena, develop their explanations, verify them to the extent that they can, and report their results to the wider community of scholars/scientists, and sometimes to the general public.

But assuming this is well done, or reasonably well done, we are not through with our mental operations. We have the necessary task of moral evaluation. Have the results of the past trajectory of the phenomenon enabled us to realize ends that we consider to be moral ends? Has the phenomenon been morally progressive, regressive, or neutral? What alternatives existed in the past that might have resulted in more substantively rational objectives? (And if they exist, why weren't they taken, which is an intellectual question?) Most important of all, given the existing reality, in which direction ought we to be heading? Proponents of value-neutral objectivity have always insisted that this moral evaluation was outside the defined role of the scholar/scientist. But not all of us have agreed. Gunnar Myrdal (1958) laid great emphasis in his writings on what he called "value in social theory" and refused to segregate this moral task from that of intellectual analysis.[1]

Finally, even if we have accomplished as much as we feel we can do in the intellectual and moral evaluation of a phenomenon, there remains, quite clearly, the political question. In the light of our intellectual analysis, how would it be possible in the present to move toward the achievement of our designated moral objectives? What historical choices do we have? What kind of long-run strategy and short-run tactics will lead us most probably in the direction we think the world ought to move? Scholars/scientists are constantly adjured to leave these political judgments to others—politicians, specialists, citizens. But of course we are all citizens, and we are all in fact specialists in something (usually something relevant). Leaving these judgments to others means endorsing de facto what these others do, even if we think in fact that it is in error.

The rich literature about global environmental change moves uneasily and a bit fuzzily among these three mental operations, without always formulating clearly the distinctions. For, while it is true that no scholarly or scientific activity can ever segregate the intellectual, moral, and political tasks into different spheres for different persons, it is not true that the three conjoined tasks are identical. And it is true that, if we are unsure on which ground we are standing, which mental operation we are pursuing at any given moment, then we are more prone to error in judgment. So, I would like to review what I think have been and ought to be the issues before us in these three mental operations, when the phenomenon in which we are interested is global environmental change.

When we confront the intellectual issues, there is little debate that global environmental change is a constant of the Earth's history, indeed one that precedes by far the existence of human beings on the planet. We also agree that humans have constantly affected in serious ways the ecology of the planet.[2] Human actions have no doubt been motivated by efforts to survive and flourish, and one way to read the Earth's history is to see it as the story of the rise to primacy in the animal world of *Homo sapiens*. The problem has been that, in this rise to the top, human actions have had the consequence of undermining the "conditions of production" in ways that may ultimately sap the ability of humans and others to survive on this planet.

While some environmental historians analyze this symbiotic (and in many ways) hostile relationship of humans and the natural environment (especially the soil, what grows on it, what is located under it) as a continuous historical reality, others see a dramatic worsening of this constant with the advent of capitalism as the defining system of the modern world, what Marx discussed as the "metabolic rift," a theme taken up in some detail in recent years by John Bellamy Foster (2000),[3] and discussed as the "second contradiction of capitalism" by James O'Connor.[4]

The basic difference between a capitalist system and other kinds of historical systems is the minimization of effective constraints on the endless accumulation of capital, which is the defining feature of a capitalist system. This is why capitalism may be said to have created "a new, historically unprecedented relationship . . . between the economic process and nature" (Deléage 1994:38). Under capitalism, the search for profits necessarily presses producers to reduce their costs at the two key bioeconomic moments, that of the extraction of raw materials and that of the elimination of the waste of the productive process.[5] The behavior that maximizes the profits of any given producer is to pay absolutely nothing for the renewal of natural resources and next to nothing for waste disposal. This so-called externalization of costs puts the financial burden on everyone else, which has historically meant that, for the most part, no one has paid. This therefore has meant, as J. R. McNeill (2002:11) has put it, that the "most serious overexploitation" of nature has been at precisely these two points: "sinks for wastes" and "renewable, biological resources."

After five hundred years of such serious abuse in our modern world-system, we live today with an enormous "burden of the past" (Ponting 2002). And the question that is regularly discussed is whether or not we can somehow surmount this burden of the past. The usual concept with which we discuss this analytical question is that of "sustainable development," defined by the Brundtland Commission as development that "meets the needs of the present without compromising the ability of future generations to meet their own needs" (World Commission on Environment and Development 1987:2). There is in the first place the question of whether this is still ecologically possible. I suppose it probably is, although J. R. McNeill (2000:357) does throw some doubt on this when he cites Machiavelli, to open his chapter entitled "Epilogue: So What?," in which Machiavelli talks about ailments that in the beginning are "easy to cure and difficult to understand" and which later are "easy to understand and difficult to cure."

The real question however is not an ecological question but a political one. Is sustainable development possible within the framework of a capitalist system? I have already once expounded my view that, at the present time, there is "no exit" within our existing historical system (Wallerstein 1999). On the other hand, I do not believe that our historical system is going to last that much longer, for I consider it to be in a terminal structural crisis, a chaotic transition to some other system (or systems), a transition that will last at most another twenty-five to fifty years. I therefore believe that it could be possible to overcome the self-destructive patterns of global environmental change into which the world has fallen and establish alternative patterns. I emphasize however my firm assessment that the outcome of this transition is inherently uncertain and unpredictable.[6]

Since I believe that the world-system is in a process of crisis and transition, the moral question of the direction in which we wish to go is inescapable on our agenda. And I observe that most persons engaged in studying global environmental change feel as well that this is true. But what are the moral questions? First of all, there is the question of reparations. As we know, environmental damage may have affected all people, but it has not affected all people equally. There are important class differentials. Even if damage is diffuse, one can escape some of its effects with money. Even more important, there are significant geographic differentials, which correlate highly with the core-periphery axial division of labor. This is why Martinez-Alier (2002:ch. 10) can speak of an "ecological debt" resulting from both the uncompensated negative externalities of raw materials–exporting countries and the use by wealthy states of the space of poorer countries for such things as carbon dioxide sinks.

This is of course not some terrible accident. It was built into the structure of the capitalist system from the beginning. Moore (2003:309) states this well:

> The "local" environmental transformations precipitated by these [expand-ing] frontiers [of Europe] were not simply consequences of European expan-sion; they were in equal measure constitutive of such expansion, condition as well as consequence. Degradation and relative exhaustion in one region after another were followed by recurrent waves of global expansion aimed at securing fresh supplies of land and labor, and thence to renewed and extended cycles of unsustainable development on a world-scale.

Ramachandra Guha (2002) discusses this same issue when he asks the question, "How Much Should a Person Consume?" The implication in the question is that some consume too much, which results in others consuming too little. Guha bemoans that the issue of imbalanced consumption is too little discussed. And asking why, he cites Carl Sauer, who attributes it to Occidental culture, which has the "recklessness of optimism" and fails to understand "the difference between yield and loot" (Guha 2002:50). But it is not a question of Occidental culture but rather of capitalist culture. And the difference between yield and loot is the difference between middle-range profits and short-range profits. Moralizing does not help us to respond to the moral questions.

Nor is Garrett Hardin's "lifeboat ethics" (1998) as a response to the critical situation either analytically possible or morally ethical. First of all, it mistakes the fundamental issue. Were we somehow to reduce world population miraculously by half overnight, this would not eliminate the crisis, merely postpone the moment of systemic collapse. Furthermore, it is clearly politically impractical. It would require massive warfare, and quite probably wreak as much havoc on those who wished to stay in the lifeboat as those they were trying to expel or exclude from it. As for its morality, it is but a variant of what R. H. Tawney called "the Tadpole Philosophy" (1952:109). Tawney is speaking of the ability of some to achieve much within a capitalist system, as though it were some consolation for social evils that "exceptional individuals can succeed in evading them," and that the noblest use of their talents "were to scramble to shore, undeterred by the thought of drowning companions."

Judgement about the past, however, is the least of our moral issues, and probably the least useful to which to devote our energies. The real question is the construction of a more morally acceptable mode of global environmental change. I assume that change is unavoidable, but that there exist some ways of channeling it, limiting it, making its outcome more palatable. Here we come to the other question Martinez-Alier (1994:23) has outlined so clearly:

> The ecological critique of mainstream economics is based on the question of unknown future agents' preferences and their inability to come to today's market, and therefore the arbitrariness of the values given at present to exhaustible resources or to future social and environmental costs. . . . In sum, the ecological critique points out that because of the temporal dimension in material life, the economy involves allocations of waste and diminished resources to future generations.

Here we are not discussing the relationship between the rich and the poor, the core and the periphery, but the living and their future descendants.

The relationship of the generations, however, is larger than the issue of the living and their descendants. Grosso modo, there are four generational claimants to the distribution of resources at any given time: the young, the adults, the elderly, and the unborn. Much of modern politics, not only the politics of the environment, is concerned with this distributive question. Take, for example, the question of health. On the assumption that there exists a given quantum of resources to devote to health needs, what percentage should be allocated (by whatever mode of allocation we use) to children, adults, and the elderly? The unborn enter the picture as well when we decide how much resources we should devote to long-term and long-shot investments in medical research whose benefits may only be seen twenty-five to fifty years from now, if then. Similar questions can be raised about educational allocations. And obviously, they are central when we discuss the bioeconomic allocations involved in ecological decisions.

There is no simple or self-evident mode of deciding the proper allocation among the four generational claimants. In a capitalist system, the allocations are made primarily by the adults in their own favor, which are in fact "lifeboat ethics." It is when we try to find an alternative moral mode of allocation that we see the difficulties involved in substantive rationality. It is here too that we see the wisdom in the long philosophical debates in which premodern historical systems regularly immersed themselves, in a sense to decide precisely such generational allocations and their morality. I have no ready-made formula to offer. But I do think we are called on to discuss such questions publicly, openly, often, and politically, and to search collectively for optimal allocations, while leaving open the possibility of regular rediscussion and redivision of resources. We at present have no collective mode of doing this.

So that brings us to the political question. Can we arrive at such a collective mode of debating and deciding generational allocations? And if so, what might this mode look like? Note that I have said generational allocations. I might have said class, race, gender allocations, but I didn't, for one reason that seems obvious to me. As long as class, race, and gender generate sharp inequalities in social life, there is no hope of sensible generational allocations. So a prerequisite to generational rationality is a major reduction in class, race, and gender inequalities, such that the inequalities that remain are at a structurally minimal point.

This will never happen as long as we are located within a capitalist world-system. Happily, I don't think we shall be too much longer. I cannot make this argument here but I have done so elsewhere (Wallerstein 1998). We are, as I have said, in the middle of a transition, but also a transition whose outcome is inherently uncertain. That is to say, it is quite possible that in 2050, when capitalism is no more, we shall be living in a system that is equally or more hierarchical and inegalitarian than the present one. But it is also possible that we shall be living in a relatively democratic, relatively egalitarian historical system. The outcome will be decided by the political activity of everyone now and in the next twenty-five to fifty years. To be a political victor will almost surely require a good analytical understanding of the historical alternatives, as well as a sharp moral commitment to an alternative vision.

The politics of the world today are triple: There is the conflict among the major loci of capital accumulation (the United States, Western Europe, and Japan/East Asia) for primacy in the next fifty years. This struggle for hegemony is a constant of our present system, and it is now open once again with the clear decline of the United States. Secondly, there is the struggle between the North and the South. This is also inherent in the ever more polarizing reality of the capitalist world-economy. And finally there is the struggle between what I shall call metaphorically the camp of Davos and the camp of Porto Alegre (Wallerstein 2003). While the first two struggles are no doubt terribly important and dominate the concerns of most people who are politically active and continue a long-existing pattern of political division, it is the third struggle that is new. It is a product of the fact that the world-system is in structural crisis. The two camps are fighting not over the realities of the present system but over what will replace it. Make no mistake. The camp of Davos, even though they don't say it and perhaps many or even most of its members don't realize it, is not fighting to preserve capitalism but to replace it with something different, in which they will maintain their privileges and authority.

The World Social Forum (WSF), whose initial meetings were in Porto Alegre, thinks of itself as a "movement of movements." Its governing slogan is "another world is possible." This is not mere sloganeering. Porto Alegre represents a new turn in the history of antisystemic movements. They are not seeking power within the modern world-system. They are laboring to make sure that, in the bifurcation through which we are going, the outcome will be that of a more democratic and egalitarian world.

The very structure of the WSF represents a rejection of the basic strategy of the historic antisystemic movements, the so-called Old Left. The Old Left was oriented to obtaining state power, state by state. And it believed that its organizations had to be unified, centralized, and more or less tightly structured. The WSF brings together movements without any central structure, and certainly no discipline. They are movements of different scope—local, national, regional, worldwide—and of different primary concerns—gender, race, environment, the work place, land reform, and so forth. These movements are adjured to listen to each other, learn from each other, and cooperate without denouncing each other for their failures. Furthermore, the WSF cuts seriously across the North-South divide.

The WSF has been marvelously successful in the first few years of its existence. It has placed itself in the center of the world stage, and it has forced the powerful to recognize that it is a force with which to be reckoned. It has energized movements across the globe, with some new optimism and creative impulse. However, it is now in danger. The problem that the WSF faces is that thus far it has been a movement sticking its finger in the dike, stopping egregious proposals put forth within the framework of the World Trade Organization (WTO), opposing the arrogant impositions of the International Monetary Fund (IMF), encouraging local movements in their immediate struggles against local tyrannies. These are tasks that have to be done. But they are negative tasks. They stop still worse from happening.

A world movement, especially a movement of movements, cannot survive for too long on this negative diet. They need to see alternatives in action—short-run and middle-run, which therefore may portend a long-term construction of a different historical system. This will not be easy. For one thing, the very structure of the WSF limits the ability to engage in collective decision-making of a positive program. It is as though it had to evolve slowly from the base. And, while not organizationally impossible, it is certainly not the most rapid path.

We have been talking about rationality. The WSF is not formally rational in its structure. But its structure reflects the kind of substantive rationality it hopes to promote. Global environmental change? It will go on, of course. Substantively rational decisions about global environmental change? This is a political question. And environmental movements will get essentially nowhere in the next twenty-five to fifty years if they cannot find a symbiotic relationship with all the other kinds of antisystemic movements. It is not a question of merging into one big pot, but of creating a family of movements whose underlying affectionate ties will balance out the inevitable differences of emphases and priorities. It is not a question of saying that everyone is right in promoting their "local" priorities. It is a question of earnest discussion about the pluses and minuses of these priorities.

Finally, a word should be said about the camp of Davos. It is not at all a unified, homogeneous camp. It is divided between the intelligent minority who have normally controlled things and the larger groups of persons with narrower vision and more aggressive tactics. The latter want to smash the camp of Porto Alegre. The former wish to edulcorate it, coopt it, and adapt its objectives to their needs. They come to seduce the camp of Porto Alegre. But in the end, the world they wish to construct will still be deeply inegalitarian and undemocratic.

The intelligent minority of the powerful can be awfully persuasive, combining sensible argument with apparently large concessions, and a new rhetoric. They also of course have money and guns. The camp of Porto Alegre can work with them to stem the radical right from their most immediate and most destructive impulses. But the camp of Porto Alegre cannot really work with what I am calling the intelligent minority of the powerful in constructing a new system, not if they want this system to be substantively rational.

So we have to tread a difficult political line. This requires not only moral commitment but intellectual acuity. The recent history of environmental movements illustrates all the political pitfalls that we face.

Notes

1. See my discussion of Myrdal's views (Wallerstein 2001).

2. See the brief, but clear, discussion of historically early ecological transformations in J. R. McNeill and W. H. McNeill (2003:ch. 1–2).

3. Foster (2000:156) cites Marx (*Capital*, vol. 1, 637–638):

> All progress in capitalist agriculture is a progress in the art, not only of robbing the worker, but of robbing the soil. . . . Capitalist production, therefore, only develops the technique and degree of combination of the social process of production by simultaneously undermining the original sources of all wealth—the soil and the worker.

> 4. The basic cause of the second contradiction is capitalism's economically self-destructive appropriation and use of labor power, urban infrastructure and space, and external nature or environment—"self-destructive" because the costs of health and education, urban transport, and home and commercial rents, as well as the costs of extracting the elements of capital from nature, will rise when private costs are turned into "social costs." (O'Connor 1988:177)

5. It is not that there are zero constraints. Richard Grove (1995) makes the case that colonial governments often enacted environmentalist regulations. (Indeed, he credits them with being the originators of the environmental movement.) He is no

doubt right about their role, but this does not necessarily negate what I am arguing. States have frequently represented the middle-range interest of capital accumulation against the typically short-range view of most individual entrepreneurs.

6. I have expounded all this elsewhere (Wallerstein 1998). See also Prigogine (1996).

References

Deléage, J. 1994. Eco-Marxist critique of political economy. In *Is capitalism sustainable?* ed. M. O'Connor, 37–52. New York: Guilford.

Foster, J. B. 2000. *Marx's ecology: Materialism and nature.* New York: Monthly Review Press.

Grove, R. H. 1995. *Green imperialism: Colonial expansion, tropical island edens and the origins of environmentalism, 1600–1860.* Cambridge, U.K.: Cambridge University Press.

Guha, R. 2002. How much should a person consume? *Global Dialogue* 4 (1): 49–62.

Hardin, G. 1998. Lifeboat ethics. In *The environmental ethics and policy book*, ed. C. Vandeveer and C. Pierce, 393–399. Belmont, Calif.: Wadsworth.

Martinez-Alier, J. 1994. Ecological economics and ecosocialism. In *Is capitalism sustainable?* ed. M. O'Connor, 23–36. New York: Guilford, 1994.

———. 2002. *The environmentalism of the poor: A study of ecological conflicts and valuation.* Cheltenham, U.K.: Edward Elgar.

McNeill, J. R. 2000. *Something new under the sun: An environmental history of the twentieth-century world.* New York: Norton.

———. 2002. Earth, wind, water and fire: Resource exploitation in the twentieth century. *Global Dialogue* 4 (1): 11–19.

McNeill, J. R., and W. H. McNeill. 2003. *The human web: A bird's-eye view of world history.* New York: Norton.

Moore, J. W. 2003. The modern world-system as environmental history? Ecology and the rise of capitalism. *Theory and Society* 32 (3): 307–377.

Myrdal, G. 1958. *Value in social theory.* New York: Harper.

O'Connor, J. 1988. The second contradiction of capitalism. In *Natural causes: Essays in ecological marxism*, 158–177. New York: Guilford. (First published in *Capitalism, Nature, and Socialism*, no. 1 (Fall 1988), and reprinted with four commentaries in *The greening of marxism*, ed. T. Benton, 197–221, New York: Guilford, 1996.)

Ponting, C. 2002. The burden of the past. *Global Dialogue* 4 (1): 1–10.

Prigogine, I. 1996. *La fin des certitudes.* Paris: Odile Jacob.

Tawney, R. H. 1952. *Equality.* 4th ed. London: Allen and Unwin.

Wallerstein, I. 1998. *Utopistics; or, Historical choices of the twenty-first century.* New York: New Press.

———. 1999. Ecology and capitalist costs of production: No exit. In *The end of the world as we know it: Social science for the twenty-first century*, 76–86. Minneapolis: University of Minnesota Press.

————. 2001. The Myrdal legacy: Racism and underdevelopment as dilemmas. In *Unthinking social science*, 2d ed., 80–103. Philadelphia: Temple University Press.

————. 2003. Entering global anarchy. *New Left Review*, n.s., 22 (July–August): 27–35.

World Commission on Environment and Development. 1987. *Our common future*. Oxford: Oxford University Press.

Index

accumulative strategies: disarticulated, 136–37; and ecological conflicts, 234; and global expansion, 102, 123, 124, 129, 137; and landesque capital, 13, 67–68, 72; livestock-based, 147, 149, 150, 155–57, 160. *See also* capitalism

Achagua tribe, 167

Adams, Henry, 230

Aedes aegypti, 18, 200, 203–4, 205, 208, 209

Africa, landesque capital in, 65, 67, 69, 70, 73n2

African coastal trade: before 1850, 144–46; and Kamba peoples, 146–51; and Mijikenda peoples, 151–55; political transformation of, 155–59; socioenvironmental effects of, 16

agribusiness, Brazilian: and agronomists, 354–55; corporate control of, 353–54; and economic planning, 351–53; and land ownership, 11, 351; landscape changes caused by, 345–46; and machine image, 346–48; and regional politics, 355–57; and soybean cultivation, 11, 348–50

agricultural chemistry, 5, 222–23

agricultural surpluses: Kamba trade in, 149; in Venezuelan *Llanos,* 165, 173

agronomists, 354–55

air pollution: from European mining, 15, 125; in Imperial Rome, 37–38; at U.S.-Mexico border, 330, 333

Alliance for Progress, 351

aluminum, 293

Amazonia, landesque capital in, 65, 73n5

American Revolution, 208

anchovies, 190–91

Andes: landesque capital in, 65; mining in, 130–35

aniline dyes, 181

anthropogenic soils: in Amazonia, 71; as landesque capital, 63, 64, 65

Argentina, 197n2

arsenic exposure, 37

Asia, landesque capital in, 65, 73n2

asymmetric exchange. *See* unequal exchange

Auerbach, Felix, 228

Augustus Caesar, 12, 27, 29, 32, 33

Austrian Succession, War of, 208

Ayres, Robert, 292

Aztec Empire, *107*

About the Contributors

Stephen G. Bunker (1944–2005) was professor of sociology at the University of Wisconsin, Madison.

William H. Fisher is associate professor of anthropology at the College of William and Mary, Williamsburg.

Rafael A. Gassón is an archaeologist and coordinator of the postgraduate anthropology program at the Instituto Venezolano de Investigaciones Científicas, Caracas.

Stefan Giljum is an ecological economist and researcher at the Sustainable Europe Research Institute, Vienna.

N. Thomas Håkansson is an anthropologist and associate professor of human ecology at Lund University.

Josiah Heyman is professor of anthropology and chair of the Department of Sociology and Anthropology at the University of Texas, El Paso.

Alf Hornborg is an anthropologist and professor of human ecology at Lund University.

J. Donald Hughes is John Evans Distinguished Professor of History at the University of Denver.

Andrew K. Jorgenson is assistant professor of sociology at Washington State University, Pullman.

Robert B. Marks is Richard and Billie Deihl Professor of History at Whittier College.

Joan Martinez-Alier is an ecological economist and professor of economic history at the Universitat Autonoma de Barcelona.

J. R. McNeill is professor of history at Georgetown University, Washington, D.C.

Jason W. Moore is a PhD candidate in the Department of Geography, University of California, Berkeley.

Roldan Muradian is an ecological economist and research fellow at the Development Research Institute, Tilburg University.

Janken Myrdal is professor of agricultural history at the Swedish University of Agricultural Sciences, Uppsala.

James Rice is assistant professor of sociology at New Mexico State University, Las Cruces.

Joseph A. Tainter is an anthropologist and research professor at the Global Institute of Sustainability, Arizona State University, Tempe.

Immanuel Wallerstein is a sociologist and senior research scholar at Yale University, New Haven.

Helga Weisz is a biologist and associate professor at the Institute for Social Ecology, Klagenfurt University, Vienna.

Mats Widgren is professor of geography at Stockholm University.

Richard Wilk is professor of anthropology and gender studies, Indiana University, Bloomington.

Michael Williams recently retired as professor of geography in the School of Geography and the Environment, University of Oxford.